DISRUPT, DISCREDIT, AND DIVIDE

ALSO BY MIKE GERMAN

Thinking Like a Terrorist: Insights of a Former FBI Undercover Agent

DISRUPT, DISCREDIT, AND DIVIDE

HOW THE NEW FBI DAMAGES DEMOCRACY

Mike German

NEW YORK
LONDON

The opinions expressed in this book are those of the author and not the Federal Bureau of Investigation.

Published in the United States by The New Press, New York, 2019
Distributed by Two Rivers Distribution

ISBN 978-1-62097-380-6 (ebook)

LIBRARY OF CONGRESS CATALOGING-IN-PUBLICATION DATA
Names: German, Mike, 1963– author.
Title: Disrupt, discredit, and divide : how the new FBI damages democracy / Mike German.
Description: New York : New Press, [2019] | Includes bibliographical references.
Identifiers: LCCN 2018054262 | ISBN 9781620973790 (hbk : alk. paper)
Subjects: LCSH: United States. Federal Bureau of Investigation—History. | Political culture—United States—History. | Democracy—United States—History. | Terrorism—United States—History.
Classification: LCC HV8144.F43 G47 2019 | DDC 363.250973—dc23
LC record available at https://lccn.loc.gov/2018054262

The New Press publishes books that promote and enrich public discussion and understanding of the issues vital to our democracy and to a more equitable world. These books are made possible by the enthusiasm of our readers; the support of a committed group of donors, large and small; the collaboration of our many partners in the independent media and the not-for-profit sector; booksellers, who often hand-sell New Press books; librarians; and above all by our authors.

www.thenewpress.com

Composition by Westchester Publishing Services
This book was set in Minion Pro Regular

Printed in the United States of America

10 9 8 7 6 5 4 3 2 1

CONTENTS

INTRODUCTION: A LAWLESS LAW ENFORCER

In 1992, when a fellow agent at the Federal Bureau of Investigation asked me to go undercover to investigate neo-Nazi skinheads in Los Angeles, I would never have imagined that twenty-four years later the FBI and white supremacists would both play influential roles in the 2016 presidential election. But by the middle of 2004, when I resigned from the FBI, I could see it coming.

A vengeful, jingoistic, "with us or against us" rhetoric animated the "war on terror," scapegoating Muslims and immigrants, vilifying political opponents as enemy sympathizers, and dividing American communities against one another by fomenting mutual suspicion and bigotry. Meanwhile, the law enforcement, defense, and intelligence agencies that failed to protect us from the September 11, 2001, terror attacks won broad new powers and a thicker cloak of secrecy to shield themselves from accountability. You didn't need to have spent time with Nazis to worry that this might not end well.

The FBI contributed to this divisive national security discourse. Its leaders, fighting to ensure the bureau's survival amid a post-9/11 restructuring of homeland security assets, publicly denied having any forewarning of the al Qaeda attacks. They blamed legal restraints designed to protect Americans' constitutional rights for their failure, suppressing reports from FBI whistleblowers whose pre-9/11 efforts to stop the attacks were stymied not by the law but by bureaucratic ineptitude at FBI headquarters.

Justice Department and bureau leadership used these false pretenses to wring new domestic spying authorities from Congress. They embraced a new mandate to transform the FBI from a law enforcement organization into a full-fledged domestic intelligence agency, with little discussion of what exactly that meant in a constitutional democracy. Predictably, expanding the FBI's powers without reforming its management problems only ensured a new era of abuse would unfold, and made additional intelligence failures inevitable.

To anchor its new terrorism-prevention mission, the FBI resurrected a discredited theory of terrorist radicalization that it had used to suppress civil rights, labor, and peace activists during earlier eras of social disquiet. It legitimized a network of anti-Muslim activists by hiring them as counterterrorism instructors and expert witnesses. By 2008, the FBI had initiated a national program of racial and ethnic mapping, a crude form of neighborhood profiling that authorized agents to identify "ethnic businesses" and track "ethnic behaviors."[1] In 2014, the FBI quietly stopped identifying "law enforcement" as its primary function, replacing it with the more nebulous "national security."[2]

For many Americans, the profound changes taking place at the FBI went unnoticed until July 5, 2016, when then FBI director James Comey finally dispensed with the illusion that the bureau was an impartial and apolitical law enforcement agency. The FBI had spent the previous year investigating whether Democratic presidential candidate Hillary Clinton mishandled classified information by using a private email server in her Chappaqua, New York, home while serving as U.S. secretary of state. Leaks from the investigation dogged her throughout the 2016 presidential campaign. When Comey announced the FBI would not recommend charges at his July 5 press conference, he nevertheless accused Clinton of being "extremely careless" with classified information, defying Justice Department protocols that prohibited disclosing derogatory information from an investigation not resulting in an indictment.[3] He continued dishing details in congressional testimony that July and September, further violating Justice Department rules restricting public statements or actions that might influence elections.[4] Finally, his October 28, 2016, letter notifying sixteen members of Congress that he had reopened the Clinton investigation leaked to the press, as he expected it would, eleven days before one of the most heavily contested elections in history.[5] It may have altered the outcome.[6]

The beneficiary of Comey's contravention of these long-standing Justice Department policies was Donald Trump, the Republican candidate for president who had run an openly Islamophobic, racist, misogynistic, and xenophobic campaign. Trump won an energetic following among a new brand of white nationalists calling themselves the "alt-right." Long-forgotten former Klansmen became regular commenters on mainstream election news coverage, along with Twitter trolls, unhinged conspiracy theorists, and well-dressed neo-fascist propagandists.

Comey's aggressiveness during the Clinton investigation contrasted with his agency's lethargic response to Russian government attacks on the 2016 election. FBI agents determined in September 2015 that Russian hackers compromised Democratic National Committee (DNC) computers, but they did little beyond calling the DNC help desk.[7] In late 2015, allied intelligence agencies began warning the FBI that Russian intelligence operatives were engaging in suspicious interactions with Trump's campaign team.[8] Yet Comey refused to join an October 7, 2016, public statement by the secretary of homeland security and the director of national intelligence blaming the Russian government for the DNC hacks.[9] The ultimate success of the Russian effort to help elect a compromised U.S. president to office may be regarded as the most significant intelligence failure in history, made worse only by the FBI director's direct contribution to that result.

In a sign of the hyperpartisan times, once Trump took office and Comey finally acknowledged the FBI was investigating his campaign's contacts with Russian operatives, many Democrats who had called for Comey's head for sandbagging Clinton became his staunchest defenders. Likewise, many Republicans who had championed the FBI's transformation into a domestic intelligence agency now attacked it as part of a mutinous "deep state," seemingly shocked that the expanded surveillance powers they handed the bureau after 9/11 could be turned against them. Trump fired Comey in May 2017, later admitting on national television that it was because of the FBI's investigation into his campaign's "collusion" with Russians.[10]

This increasingly hostile political tumult wasn't just happening on Capitol Hill. Throughout the 2016 campaign and the first two years of Trump's presidency, far-right extremists held public rallies from coast to coast, brawling with antifascist counterprotesters in the streets as law enforcement stood and watched. Hate crimes in the United States jumped 20 percent in 2016, then another 12 percent in 2017.[11] Meanwhile, anti-Trump protesters, Black Lives Matter activists, and Standing Rock water protectors were met with militarized riot police, tear gas, rubber bullets, water cannon, and mass arrests.

This book examines how we got here and how the FBI affected, and was affected by, these social and political disruptions. Since its creation in 1908 by President Theodore Roosevelt, a onetime New York City police commissioner, and his no-nonsense attorney general Charles Bonaparte, the bureau has had an outsized influence on American life. Roosevelt and Bonaparte were Progressive Era reformers who envisioned the bureau as a bulwark to protect the public from predations by the wealthy and powerful. They used the Justice Department's law enforcement powers to fight government corruption, bust corporate trusts, prosecute peonage, ensure consumer protection, and preserve public lands. As Roosevelt explained in 1909, his goal for the Justice Department's investigative service was to "secure the conviction of the wealthiest and most formidable criminals," particularly those otherwise protected by "wide political and social influence."[12]

Today's FBI far exceeds anything Roosevelt and Bonaparte could have imagined when they hired three dozen detectives to assist Justice Department investigations. Few federal crimes were then on the books, such as frauds against the government, antitrust violations, crimes occurring on government reservations, and those crossing state boundaries. Congress gradually expanded the FBI's jurisdiction as it professionalized its workforce and pioneered the use of scientific methods for gathering and cataloging evidence. The FBI soon became the preeminent law enforcement agency in the country, and arguably the world.

FBI agents are now charged with enforcing thousands of federal laws, protecting the nation from terrorists and spies, and gathering foreign intelligence inside the United States. They assist other federal, state, local, and tribal law enforcement agencies and foreign governments with investigations, behavioral assessments, criminal identification and crime lab services, and training in the latest law enforcement techniques. They operate in war zones and cyberspace as routinely as they do in the American heartland. Yet the FBI remains a relatively tiny agency of about 35,000 employees (smaller than the New York City Police Department), with fewer than 13,000 badge-and-gun-carrying agents spread across 56

U.S. field offices and 63 American embassies around the world. It's a big job that attracts an incredibly talented workforce.

Of course, many times throughout its history the FBI has betrayed its original mission and used its investigative powers to protect the powerful at the expense of individual rights and the public interest. For decades, Director J. Edgar Hoover ruled like a tyrant, directing his agents to work outside the law to "disrupt, misdirect, discredit, or otherwise neutralize" those opposing government policies or social norms he favored.[13] The Senate's 1975–76 Church Committee investigation into Hoover's abuses found that the FBI employed counterintelligence powers designed for use against hostile foreign threats to suppress labor organizers, civil rights activists, war protesters, and other nonviolent political dissidents. Code-named "COINTELPRO," these covert programs warped the concept of national security into a license to break the law in furtherance of the FBI's version of "public order."[14]

The Church Committee's findings led to reforms that placed constitutional checks on the FBI's national security and intelligence operations and required reasonable criminal predicates to launch investigations. Later Congresses and attorneys general modified these oversight mechanisms incrementally as new threats emerged and additional abuses were discovered. After 9/11, however, they all but dismantled them. Combined with rapid technological advances, these legal and policy changes ensured that today's FBI is operating at the zenith of its powers. Yet Americans know little about how it uses them, who it targets, or why.

WHO DO YOU SERVE, WHO DO YOU PROTECT?

Comey, like all FBI directors before and since, was a registered Republican. President George W. Bush appointed him as the U.S. attorney for the Southern District of New York in 2002, and then deputy attorney general in 2003. But he became widely respected by Democrats for his 2004 refusal to reauthorize a Bush-ordered warrantless internet data collection program that the National Security Agency (NSA) started after the 9/11 attacks. While the laudatory retellings of this episode often overstate the reforms Comey's resistance accomplished, the incident cemented the perception that he was a public servant of unflinching integrity and independence. When fellow Bush appointee Robert Mueller retired as FBI director in 2013, two years after a bipartisan vote in Congress expanded his statutory ten-year term, President Barack Obama saw in Comey his perfect replacement.[15]

Obama had another reason to like Comey. The self-described "six-foot eight-inch, skinny white guy" had been unusually outspoken on racial justice issues throughout his law enforcement career. During his 2003 nomination hearing to become deputy attorney general, Comey described racial profiling as "morally offensive." He argued it was a "dumb" policing tactic because "you not only abuse innocent folks, you miss the bad guys."[16] Noting that "feds" often serve as role models to state and local police, Comey praised Attorney General John Ashcroft for issuing restrictions on racial and ethnic profiling. Though Ashcroft promoted it as a "ban," his racial profiling guidance included broad loopholes that allowed profiling in national security and border integrity investigations. Regardless, Comey pledged to strictly enforce these new rules and dedicated himself to "eradicating" racial profiling in the United States.

Early in his tenure as FBI director, Comey established a policy requiring new agents to visit the Martin Luther King Jr. Memorial. He said he hoped the experience would highlight "the need for fidelity to the rule of law and the dangers in becoming untethered to oversight and accountability."[17] He kept on his desk the original order authorizing J. Edgar Hoover to wiretap Dr. King as a daily reminder of the Justice Department's darkest chapter.

In 2015, Director Comey won accolades for a remarkable speech at Georgetown University titled "Hard Truths: Law Enforcement and Race."[18] In the midst of nationwide protests over police killings of unarmed black people, Comey confronted the widening chasm between law enforcement and communities of color. The first "hard truth" he acknowledged was the unfortunate history of police using their powers to enforce "a status quo that was often brutally unfair to disfavored groups." He cited indignities his Irish immigrant ancestors suffered a century ago, but made clear African American communities bore the brunt of these abuses.

Comey's second hard truth drew the most attention: his clear and candid admission that law enforcement officials today regularly treat white people and black people differently. He argued this inequity is the product of unconscious biases all humans carry, combined with racially tinged cynicism that many officers develop while policing the country's meanest streets. For social scientists who study implicit bias in law enforcement, Comey's hard truths are well-established and measurable facts.[19] Still, it was important that the country's top law enforcer acknowledged the history of state-sanctioned discrimination and affirmed that police bias remained a problem. Comey deserved credit for so forthrightly conceding these truths in a public forum.

What Comey failed to mention in his Georgetown speech, which was unusual given his position as FBI director, was the bureau's responsibility to investigate police brutality and civil rights violations. The FBI's emphasis on counterterrorism and national security since 9/11 has often obscured its role in enforcing civil rights laws, but this obligation is more closely aligned with the original intent of its creators. The idea of using the law to protect the most vulnerable in society is what drew me to the FBI.

AN EDUCATION IN EXTREMISM

I joined the FBI in 1988, a generation after the Hoover-era lawlessness had been exposed and addressed in policy and practice. I knew about the FBI's earlier injustices, but I believed its leaders had internalized the lesson that such misdirected efforts were not just a betrayal of their constitutional obligations but an impediment to effective national security and law enforcement. I saw an FBI that, when operating at its best, protects Americans from the worst kinds of criminals and hostile foreign threats. But its most important function in my view has always been upholding the integrity of our government, our financial systems, and the rule of law by rooting out political corruption, corporate fraud, and police misconduct. I was proud to serve with agents who put themselves in harm's way to protect others and, in the vast majority of cases, performed their duties with exceptional integrity and fidelity to the law.

But I wasn't naïve. I grew up an Army brat during the Vietnam War, so I had no illusion that the government always did the right thing, or did it well. I learned early that hubris, poor leadership, and bureaucratic unaccountability could have disastrous consequences for the nation by undermining faith in the institutions of government. I recognized that any powerful and secretive law enforcement agency could pose a threat to individual liberties and the rule of law if not properly focused and controlled. While the legal guidelines and oversight mechanisms established in the wake of the Church Committee's report were necessary to check abuse, I also knew the FBI needed capable and conscientious people working within its ranks to ensure it operated effectively and in strict compliance with the law in practice. Three years of law school only strengthened my conviction that I could best serve the cause of justice by working where my ideals met on-the-street realities: as a special agent of the FBI.

The political climate when I began my FBI career was remarkably similar to today's. The savings and loan (S&L) crisis that began in the mid-1980s threatened the economy and shook public confidence in our financial markets and the integrity of officials overseeing them. Violent crime rates were high and trust in the police was low, especially in communities of color, where much of the violence and the most aggressive policing took place. Nowhere was this more true than in my first office: Los Angeles, California.[20]

My initial assignment was on a task force investigating the failure of the Lincoln Savings and Loan Association in Orange County, California. The FBI launched hundreds of investigations during the S&L crisis, resulting in more than a thousand prosecutions by 1992.[21] The Lincoln Savings case was one of the FBI's most prominent, partly because it was one of the most costly S&L failures and partly because Lincoln's owner, Charles Keating Jr., was a corporate villain straight out of central casting. Keating was a sanctimonious moralizer who lavished his family, employees, and accommodating politicians with plundered treasure while his mom-and-pop investors—mocked as "weak, meek, and ignorant" in company documents—lost their life savings.[22] Keating's political connections made it difficult for federal regulators to prevent the fraud, but their labors helped the FBI and its law enforcement partners hold him accountable. I was proud to play a small role in a case that punished the wealthy and powerful for crimes against the powerless.

My career at the FBI took a radical turn in 1992, when a Simi Valley jury acquitted four Los Angeles Police Department officers involved in the videotaped beating of motorist Rodney King and LA exploded in violence. The relationship between law enforcement and the communities they served had been tense long before the King beating. LAPD's combative chief Daryl Gates had for years sanctioned indiscriminate "anti-gang" sweeps through black and Latino neighborhoods with little regard for the innocent citizens who lived there. He reveled in controversy, dismissing critics as "cop haters." When community groups raised concerns about the high number of young black men dying in police choke holds, Gates blamed the victims, claiming African Americans' veins didn't reopen as quickly as those of "normal people."[23] The 1992 acquittals were the catalyst for the riots, which cost more than sixty lives, but not the cause of them.[24]

When asked, I eagerly volunteered to go undercover into a network of neo-Nazi skinhead groups planning attacks they hoped would transform the disturbance into a full-blown race war. I spent the next fourteen months embedded in the violent fringe of the white supremacist movement. Together with my Los Angeles Joint Terrorism Task Force (LA JTTF) colleagues, we solved several bombings and secured multiple convictions for manufacturing illegal firearms and explosives and conspiring to commit acts of violence. The operation seized an arsenal of weapons and interrupted plots to attack the First African Methodist Episcopal Church in Los Angeles with pipe bombs and machine guns and to assassinate Rodney King and other prominent figures in the African American and Jewish communities. Together with a successful federal civil rights prosecution of the LAPD officers involved in the King beating, the LA JTTF operation helped demonstrate that the law could be used to protect all communities from all types of violence.

I continued working undercover over the next twelve years, including an eight-month stint infiltrating anti-government militia groups in Washington State that expanded my understanding of the ideologies and tactics of a broader array of far-right extremist groups. The militia movement was influenced by many of the same philosophies and theologies as white supremacists, but often attempted to mask their racism. They avoided swastikas and Nazi salutes in favor of patriotic symbols like the American flag and the Constitution, or at least their peculiar interpretation of it.

The idea behind this adaptation, as explained by an elder white supremacist at a skinhead rally in the early 1990s, was to grow the movement by appealing to a wider audience of people disaffected by a government they viewed as too liberal and too accommodating of minority rights. It didn't matter whether their anger was rooted in opposition to abortion, taxes, gun control, immigration, multiculturalism, or perceived encroachments on traditional family values. These separate affinity groups were encouraged to come together under a unified "patriotic" or "constitutionalist" umbrella that would find wider acceptance than a Nazi banner. Once the more extremist elements within these communities were identified, the neo-Nazi strategist suggested, it would be easy to indoctrinate them to white nationalism as a unifying philosophy. He likely never could have imagined the alt-right's internet troll culture, which appears to have successfully implemented this concept, but I'm sure he would be pleased to see its influence on the national stage.

My time inside these militant groups coincided with significant law enforcement operations that drew national media attention to the far-right movement and the FBI's response to it. These included multiple-fatality incidents like the 1992 Ruby Ridge, Idaho, confrontation between Randy Weaver and several different federal law enforcement agencies that left his wife, son, and a deputy U.S. marshal dead; the tragic 1993 shootout, siege, and fire at the Branch Davidian compound in Waco, Texas, which killed eighty-four people; and the more successful 1996 FBI operation against Freemen in Montana that ended with no casualties. I shared a valor award with the four Bureau of Alcohol, Tobacco and Firearms agents killed at Waco, and I'd like to believe my debriefings with FBI negotiators and Hostage Rescue Team operators after the 1995 Oklahoma City bombing had some influence over the tactical choices that led to a safer outcome in Montana. I was the only person on both sides of these crises at once, watching how these events were interpreted, explained, and exploited by people in the extremist movements, in law enforcement, and in the news media.

I also learned that white supremacy is much more mainstream than many might realize or want to acknowledge. For hundreds of years, the religious, philosophical, and scientific theories of white racial superiority I was introduced to in the far-right underground were broadly accepted as unquestionable. They served as the moral and intellectual justification for government campaigns of mass violence, including colonization, slavery, genocides of indigenous peoples, racial and ethnic subjugation, segregation, and discrimination. The hard-won battles for equal rights under the law are relatively recent phenomena in this historical context. And though many victories have been realized in policy, true equality in practice remains elusive, partly because these attitudes persist in key sectors of our society.

EXTREMISTS AMONG US

While mainstream politicians since the civil rights movement have mostly avoided overtly racist appeals, pandering to bigotry and xenophobia through carefully coded language and imagery has a long history. My time undercover sensitized me to the "dog whistles" some politicians wove into in their speeches and writings, which subtly mirrored the racist and anti-Semitic invective I heard from white nationalists. Conservative populists like Pat Buchanan, who advised Presidents Richard Nixon, Gerald Ford, and Ronald Reagan before running for president himself, promoted a "culture war" to defend "western civilization" and "Christian" values against "multiculturalism." President Reagan exploited racial tensions by decrying Cadillac-driving "welfare queens," just as George H.W. Bush played on white middle-class fears of black crime with his infamous Willie Horton ad. These politicians clearly calculated that a sufficient number of Americans were receptive to racially tinged nativist messages to justify the risk of associating themselves with such odious beliefs.

As a law enforcement officer, I also had to acknowledge that racism remained a problem in my profession, just as director Comey did in his "Hard Truths" speech. The racial turmoil roiling Los Angeles when I started my career was churning within the FBI as well, as the bureau grappled with the legacy of its longest-serving director. J. Edgar Hoover was an inveterate bigot who did not feel blacks or women were qualified to join his celebrated cadre of special agents. It was an attitude commonly shared among government officials when Hoover became director in 1924, as was his fear of and resistance to the civil rights movement during his forty-eight-year tenure as FBI director. It was a liberal Democrat, Attorney General Robert F. Kennedy, who signed the order to wiretap Dr. King, after all.

The progress made in racial and gender equality during the civil rights and women's rights movements had virtually no effect within the FBI. At the time Hoover died in 1972, less than 1 percent of FBI special agents were black, and several of those were messengers or chauffeurs he'd given badges to in a cynical attempt to forestall meaningful integration.[25] There were no female agents. Future directors would struggle to diversify the FBI, impeded in no small measure by persistent racial and sexist attitudes held by those within the bureau who revered Hoover and hoped to preserve his legacy, or simply resented change to their own privileged status.

The minority and female agents who were fortunate enough to get hired in the post-Hoover era did not receive the overdue welcome they deserved. When I joined the FBI in 1988, black, Latino, and female agents had filed or were preparing to file class action lawsuits alleging discrimination in hiring, assignments, promotions, and disciplinary matters. The data these groups gathered amply documented disparities in their treatment by FBI management.[26] But the lack of sympathy and solidarity expressed by their fellow agents was an additional blow that would continue to hold back progress.

William Sessions, a rangy Texas judge appointed by President Ronald Reagan and the first FBI director I served under, named the diversification of the FBI as one of his top priorities, much to the chagrin of reactionary forces still lurking within the bureau. When Sessions attempted to settle the black agents' lawsuit in 1992, the agent population was 87.4 percent white and 88.7 percent male.[27] The FBI Agents Association, an organization whose mission is to represent agents' collective interests in negotiations with FBI management, sued to block the settlement.[28] The Agents Association's lawyer Stephen N. Shulman made the improbable argument that the FBI's proposal to give black agents a role in policy development "violates the equal employment rights of non-black agents."[29] Many inside and outside the bureau would thereafter refer to the Agents Association as the "white agents association."[30] When President Bill Clinton fired Sessions in 1993 for ethical violations surrounding his misuse of official resources, some believed the animosity directed at him by FBI insiders was a major factor in his ouster.[31]

Sessions's replacement, Louis Freeh, echoed his predecessor's commitment to increasing diversity, saying it was not only "the right and fair thing to do" but necessary for the FBI to reach its "maximum potential."[32] During his tenure, the FBI made slow but steady progress. By 2000, Freeh's last full year in office, the percentage of black FBI special agents had increased to 6.2 percent, up from 4.9 percent in 1992. The number of Latino agents had grown from 5.8 percent to 7.1 percent over that time. Both figures were still well short of the proportion of black and Latino Americans in the general population, 12.3 percent and 12.5 percent, respectively, but heading in the right direction.[33]

Then something strange happened. While the next two directors, Robert Mueller and James Comey, repeated their predecessors' rhetoric regarding diversity, the numbers started trending sharply in the opposite direction. By August 2016, African Americans made up only 4.5 percent of special agents, a smaller proportion than in 1992.[34] At the same time, the number of Latino FBI agents fell to 6.5 percent, the lowest since 1996, remarkable considering the proportion of Latino Americans in the U.S. population increased to 17.6 percent during this period.[35] Though the percentage of Asian agents increased, they remain underrepresented as compared to their share of the general population. Women still accounted for just under 20 percent of FBI agents in 2016, but their representation in senior management had decreased by about 40 percent from 2013.[36] The FBI has not published more recent data.

Unfortunately, Comey's "Hard Truths" speech focused on racial profiling by state and local law enforcement rather than within federal agencies. As a result, he missed the opportunity to confront hard truths about continuing discrimination within his own powerful agency. Explaining the discrepancy between these FBI directors' attitudes on diversity and the damning statistics is difficult, but I don't think it's a coincidence that the agency became less diverse after the 9/11 terrorist attacks.

My time undercover with terrorists taught me to understand terrorism as a tactic, not an ideology. Terrorist leaders know they do not have the strength to deal fatal blows to the governments they attack. Their goal instead is to provoke the victim government into an overreaction that will undermine its legitimacy and divide society. The horrible scale of the 9/11 attacks was designed to fracture preexisting fault lines that have split American society by race, religion, national origin, economic circumstance, and political ideology for generations and turn us against one another.

The shock drove the unconscious biases Comey cited to the surface. Hate crimes against Muslim Americans spiked. The government's counterterrorism response included discriminatory measures that reinforced anti-Muslim public sentiments and sowed fear and discord within Arab, Middle Eastern, Muslim, African, and South Asian communities. President George W. Bush's overt demand for acquiescence to his chosen anti-terrorism policies—"You're either with us or against us"—equated opposition to his tactics to treason. A divisive public discourse justifying intolerance and abuse of Arabs and Muslims spread through policy circles and newsrooms. Al Qaeda exploited the U.S. government's extralegal and discriminatory counterterrorism responses to recruit a new generation of followers and justify further attacks, broadening the conflict into the global war it craved. Unfortunately, the FBI was influenced by and contributed to this cycle of action and reaction in ways that amplified, rather than mitigated, the terror that continues to divide American communities.

Terrorists rely on a deft, innate understanding of human nature in developing this strategy, but there's quite a bit of science backing it up. Research demonstrates that fear—the weapon that terrorists utilize—profoundly affects not only what we think but *how* we think. Terrorist attacks generate psychological insecurity among their victims, which produces "increased feelings of aggressiveness toward threatening outgroups" and preferences for "autocratic leadership."[37] In her book *The Authoritarian Dynamic*, sociologist Karen Stenner argued that threats to the established order can trigger a process that moves people with authoritarian predispositions to "produce manifest expressions of intolerance."[38] Another study showed that hypothetical terrorism-threat warnings—like those regularly provided by our own government—can prompt increased support for authoritarian counterterrorism policies even among nonauthoritarians.[39]

The Trump campaign grasped that fifteen years of political polarization and constant terror warnings had created an appetite for a strongman candidate, which he could whet with messages of fear and anger.[40] Trump's dystopian picture of an America in collapse, culturally polluted by nonwhite immigration and under threat from "radical Islam" and "urban" violence, played into themes that reliably appeal to authoritarians, who make up a majority of Republican voters.[41] Rather than muting the racist, Islamophobic, and nativist rhetoric to dog whistles, Trump amplified it with exaggerated threat warnings. He normalized linking Muslims to terrorism and immigrants and African Americans to violent crime, giving bigoted viewpoints legitimacy in the mainstream political debate. Suddenly, people who would shudder to think of themselves as racist could feel comfortable embracing clearly discriminatory counterterrorism, immigration, and criminal justice policies. Rather than being shamed for these beliefs, they found ready acceptance and reinforcement among a vocal and aggressive alt-right community unbound by "political correctness."

The biggest obstacle to this strategy's success was the relative peace and security Americans currently enjoy as compared to recent decades, so the threats necessary to activate these authoritarian impulses were few and far between. Violent crime rates have dropped significantly since the 1990s. Terrorist attacks in the United States are extremely rare and sharply lower than what we experienced in the 1970s and 1980s.[42] The chances of an American being killed in a terrorist attack in the United States since 9/11 are about 1 in 90 million.[43] Yet polls indicate a large proportion of Americans believe crime is rising.[44] Terrorism was the number one concern among voters in the 2016 election, with 69 percent calling it a "critical issue to them personally."[45] Interestingly, terrorism fears in the United States had gradually decreased since the horror of 9/11, but then reversed and began rising again in 2013. By 2016, Americans' fear of terrorism was higher than at any time since 2001.[46] The FBI's exaggerated terrorism warnings during this period no doubt contributed to heightening the public's concerns.

THE LINK BETWEEN TERROR AND BIGOTRY

Christopher Bail, a Duke University sociologist, was curious how activists from a handful of fringe organizations with distinctly anti-Muslim views became regular commenters and on-air terrorism analysts for national news organizations after 9/11. He collected press releases from a variety of advocacy groups working on issues involving Muslims and Islam, then analyzed news stories to see whose messages media organizations picked up. Bail discovered that most advocacy groups issued releases with positive descriptions of Muslims, but journalists predominately chose to quote negative messages of fear and anger produced by anti-Muslim groups. As anti-Muslim views received more media coverage, the organizations that peddled them grew in influence. Their Islamophobic messages quickly became the mainstream counterterrorism narrative.[47]

This network of anti-Muslim activists also found acceptance among those charged with protecting Americans' civil rights. The FBI embraced their simplistic model of terrorist radicalization that imagined a direct pathway from "extreme" beliefs to terrorist violence, despite decades of empirical studies contradicting it. Disrupting movement down this imaginary path from "radical" ideas to violence became the goal of preventive counterterrorism. FBI training quickly became polluted with factually inaccurate and biased materials denigrating Muslims and Arabs as backward and violent.[48]

Following these concepts, the FBI broadly targeted Arab, Middle Eastern, Muslim, South Asian, and African American communities with surveillance, interrogations, and informant infiltration. The Justice Department selectively prosecuted Muslim religious and community leaders for petty legal violations to discredit, jail, or deport them. The government shuttered Muslim charities based on secret evidence and ostracized Muslim civil rights groups with guilt-by-association smears.

The FBI even began to view its own Muslim or Arab employees with suspicion, subjecting them to unjustified scrutiny, disciplinary proceedings, and dismissal despite long records of accomplishment.

"Terrorism" became a thoroughly politicized and racialized concept. The term is now used almost exclusively to describe violence by Muslims, whether or not the perpetrator is tied to a terrorist organization or expresses any clear political motive. Politically motivated violence directed against Muslims or any other marginalized group is rarely called terrorism or treated with the same urgency. While our media and counterterrorism forces focus on Muslim terrorists, data collected by the U.S. Military Academy at West Point shows that far-right extremists commit far more attacks in the United States and cause more fatalities, killing hundreds since 9/11.[49] The FBI has the responsibility to investigate domestic terrorism, civil rights violations, and federal hate crimes, but it doesn't even bother to collect accurate data regarding these attacks. The FBI's annual hate crimes reports from state and local law enforcement agencies typically document 5,000 to 7,000 hate crimes per year, while Justice Department victim surveys count 250,000 or more.[50]

Once intolerance against one out-group becomes acceptable, increasing discrimination against other out-groups can be expected. When the FBI shifted its primary mission from law enforcement to national security, this risk of discrimination increased. The easy mental shortcuts that Comey identified as the root cause of police bias are even more pronounced when they are used not to spot criminals but to predict future threats. Everyone is potentially dangerous, of course, so who the FBI chooses to focus its disruption methods on is often based on innate prejudices—racial, ethnic, religious, or ideological—that distinguish the "us" that need protecting from the "them" who might pose a threat. Given the FBI's composition, the security concerns of white men—the demographic that most strongly supported Trump's candidacy—dominate.[51] Rather than focusing on racist violence from the far right, the FBI prioritized protecting war and energy industries from protesters, naming "eco-terrorism" the primary domestic threat and infiltrating peace groups, despite not a single U.S. fatality attributable to these movements.[52]

It is of course inevitable that there are some racists in the FBI, and there are likely several Islamophobes, given their training. But suggesting bigotry is the primary factor driving FBI policies and practices would mischaracterize a more complicated situation. It would also unfairly tarnish the vast majority of men and women working there who strive to be fair. In this book, I will introduce you to a number of courageous bureau employees who fought discrimination within the FBI, often at significant personal cost. But Comey erred in his "Hard Truths" speech by casually dismissing the notion that "cops, prosecutors, judges, and juries are racist."[53] When we allow stark racial disparities to persist at every step of the criminal justice process, we have to acknowledge the system is racist even if we are uncomfortable hanging that tag on any individual laboring within it. In fact, Comey protected the FBI's racial and ethnic mapping program when the Justice Department rewrote its racial profiling guidance in 2014.[54]

Comey argued correctly that acknowledging unconscious biases in law enforcement is a necessary first step to designing "systems and processes" to overcome them. What he failed to address is that the systems and processes established to check the FBI abuses the Church Committee uncovered have been systematically dismantled since 9/11. With the encouragement of Congress and both the Bush and Obama administrations, the FBI transformed itself into a domestic intelligence agency of unprecedented power that operates primarily in the dark, all but immune from traditional methods of oversight. This unconstrained and highly secretive FBI predictably turned its sights on those it has always viewed as most dangerous to the established order: minority communities, immigrants, and those agitating for political, economic, and social change.

Suggesting the FBI is "lawless," as this chapter heading does, might seem hyperbolic, but it is literally true in two important respects: First, Congress has never passed a legislative charter establishing and circumscribing the FBI's investigative powers. Second, the FBI has often taken the position that traditional constitutional and legal restraints on its criminal investigations do not apply to the secretive intelligence activities it undertakes for the purposes of national security.[55]

There is no doubt that FBI agents and analysts often do exceptional work here at home and around the world, keeping criminals, terrorists, and hostile foreign spies at bay without violating the law or impinging on constitutional rights. You will read some of those stories here. But the purpose of this book is to highlight systemic problems at the FBI that, left unchecked, make the bureau a threat to the very democracy it is intended to serve. My goal isn't to embarrass or condemn but to expose deep-seated issues that need attention from policymakers and the public in order to drive reforms that will better protect all Americans and make the essential work of FBI agents, analysts, and support employees more effective.

Finally, it is important to clarify that though I am focusing on the FBI and the actions of its leaders, they don't act in a vacuum. The bureau is just one subordinate agency in a larger political and social environment. Its employees are beholden to follow the lawful orders of the attorney general and the president, and dependent upon good relations with Congress to obtain the resources necessary to fulfill their mission. Moreover, the FBI cannot for long engage in activities that substantial portions of the American people don't support. For good and for ill, it has to be responsive to public opinion. Of course, bureau leaders have significant advantages in navigating these relationships, since much of what they do is known only to FBI employees and a handful of people in the Justice Department. Information is power, and the FBI is an agency whose job it is to collect it, often in pursuit of ambiguous national security objectives that routinely place the current government's interests higher than the general public's, and the bureau's above all.

The following chapters describe how the FBI is once again using its enhanced national security powers to silence whistleblowers, suppress minority communities, intimidate dissidents, and undermine democratic controls over its operations. I will introduce you to many victims of FBI overreach who learned, as Hillary Clinton did, that this powerful agency could disrupt their lives without ever charging them with a crime. Today, many Americans worry about how an authoritarian president like Donald Trump could be using an FBI that has claimed such broad and unchecked capabilities. But the point is that no president should have such an unbridled domestic spy agency at his or her disposal, if for no other reason than that no president could ever be safe from it. I will use my experience as an FBI agent, whistleblower, ACLU lobbyist, and educator to explain how things went wrong and what is needed to ensure the FBI returns to its origins as a defender of the rule of law and protector of all the people.

Part One

DISRUPTION

1

A "CULTURE OF ARROGANCE"

The FBI was a mess, and by the summer of 2001 its congressional overseers finally had enough. That June, Senate Judiciary Committee chairman Patrick Leahy, a Vermont Democrat, gaveled in an FBI oversight hearing by lamenting that the agency once considered the "crown jewel" of U.S. law enforcement now appeared "unmanageable, unaccountable and unreliable." "Its much-vaunted independence," the former prosecutor charged, had "transformed for some into an image of insular arrogance."[1]

This harsh diagnosis was bipartisan and unanimous. Republican ranking member Orrin Hatch of Utah agreed that "serious issues concerning the operation of the FBI . . . must be addressed." He joined with Democratic senator Chuck Schumer of New York to introduce legislation establishing a "blue-ribbon commission" to conduct "a strategic, thorough review of the FBI" and make recommendations for reform.[2] Illinois Democrat Dick Durbin and Pennsylvania Republican Arlen Specter proposed a second bill to create an independent inspector general focusing exclusively on the FBI, hoping to overcome long-standing bureaucratic obstacles that often blocked the Justice Department's inspector general from investigating bureau misconduct.

Republican senator Chuck Grassley, considered by many to be the FBI's most ardent critic, chafed against these proposals. He argued that the committee already knew what was wrong with the FBI. The brusque Iowa farmer groused that new oversight structures would fail because bureau officials show contempt toward any outside entity "that dares to question its motives or performance" and retaliate against FBI employees who report internal misconduct. He condemned FBI leadership for placing a "higher value on maintaining image rather than rooting out wrong."

Rather than conducting new evaluations of the FBI, Grassley declared, "the time for reform is now."[3]

FBI director Louis Freeh had just announced his resignation, two years before his ten-year term would expire. Senator Grassley saw this transition as an opportunity to identify a director committed to changing a "culture that suppresses dissent and discourages independent oversight." With newly elected president George W. Bush and his first attorney general, John Ashcroft, just settling into office, an effort to remake the FBI into a more effective and accountable law enforcement agency seemed well timed.

The senators were reacting to a growing list of scandals that tarnished the FBI's reputation for integrity and raised doubts about its competence. In Boston, a federal judge uncovered a deal with the devil that bureau officials had made with Irish mobster turned informant Whitey Bulger. In exchange for scraps of information on his Italian Mafia rivals, the FBI let Bulger and his gang get away with murder—literally—and sat mute as innocent people went to prison for their crimes.[4]

The 2001 discovery that veteran FBI supervisor Robert Hanssen had been working as a Russian mole for more than twenty years shook the bureau. FBI managers had ignored specific warnings about Hanssen's loyalty for more than a decade, even as U.S. intelligence assets in Russia were rounded up, imprisoned, and killed.[5] Hanssen's brother-in-law, an FBI agent in Chicago, reported suspicions regarding Hanssen's unexplained wealth, describing piles of cash stuffed in drawers at his home. Earl Edwin Pitts, another FBI agent caught spying for Russia a few years earlier, had fingered Hanssen as a likely double agent during a 1997 interrogation.[6] Yet the FBI's mole hunt focused on an innocent CIA agent, though far less evidence pointed in his direction.[7] Hanssen continued his deadly betrayal until late 2000, when a former KGB agent handed the FBI irrefutable evidence of his treachery in exchange for a $7 million payday.[8]

The opposite problem hobbled the FBI's Chinese espionage case against Los Alamos nuclear scientist Wen Ho Lee. The Lee investigation was tainted by racial profiling and a rush to judgment based on the flawed notion—taken as intelligence gospel—that Chinese spies "virtually always" target ethnic Chinese Americans for recruitment.[9] The FBI launched its investigation after intelligence reports indicated China may have obtained the design for a U.S. nuclear warhead, the W88. An internal Department of Energy (DOE) investigation identified Lee, a naturalized U.S. citizen born in Taiwan, as a prime suspect, but he passed a DOE polygraph. FBI polygraphers reevaluated the DOE's test results and determined he had failed.[10] Though the FBI found no evidence Lee had given anyone classified information, much less information about the W88, agents interrogating him raised the possibility that he'd be executed like Cold War spies Julius and Ethel Rosenberg in an apparent attempt to extract a confession.

The FBI's investigation showed Lee had mishandled sensitive nuclear weapons data by downloading it to unauthorized storage devices, which led to a fifty-nine-count indictment, but the government never charged him with espionage. Still, sensationalized leaks to the media implied Lee was a nuclear spy. Prosecutors claimed he posed an exceptional risk to national security and demanded he be held in solitary confinement while awaiting trial. Explaining the lack of espionage charges, a former FBI counterintelligence official publicly compared Lee's case to the prosecution of Al Capone, "where they couldn't [lock] him up for his racketeering activities, so they cast about and they found something else that they could get him for."[11] Nine months later, the government dropped all but one minor charge, leading the judge to release Lee with a formal apology. The judge wondered aloud whether the government's "draconian" treatment was intended to coerce a guilty plea to avoid submitting its evidence to examination at trial.[12]

The FBI fared little better in its domestic terrorism investigations. In 1992, U.S. marshals attempted to arrest fugitive white supremacist Randy Weaver at his family's mountaintop home in Ruby Ridge, Idaho, leading to a shootout that took the life of Deputy Marshal William Degan and Weaver's fourteen-year-old son, Sam. Weaver, his wife, Vicki, two daughters, and family friend Kevin Harris barricaded themselves in their plywood cabin and refused to surrender. Bureau officials called out the FBI's elite Hostage Rescue Team (HRT). En route to the scene, the team leader instructed agents that they "could and should shoot all armed adult males" seen outside the cabin.[13] This instruction countermanded U.S. law and long-standing FBI policy that allows agents to use deadly force only when they reasonably believe it's necessary to protect themselves or others from death or serious bodily injury. The following day, an HRT sharpshooter fired two rounds that wounded Weaver and Harris, and killed Vicki.

Who at FBI headquarters authorized the team leader's improper order and whether it influenced the sniper's decision to shoot became the subject of intense inquiry during Weaver and Harris's trial for killing Deputy Marshal Degan. Bureau officials actively resisted discovery of the FBI's internal shooting reviews throughout the trial, hamstringing a prosecution that ended in acquittals for both defendants. A Boundary County, Idaho, prosecutor charged the FBI sniper with involuntary manslaughter, but the Justice Department moved the case to federal court and had it dismissed. The Weaver family's subsequent wrongful death suit cost the U.S. government over $3 million dollars. The only person sentenced to prison over the sordid affair was an FBI section chief convicted of obstructing justice by destroying the FBI's after-action report rather than disclosing it to prosecutors.[14]

The 1993 Waco siege was Ruby Ridge on steroids. The Bureau of Alcohol, Tobacco and Firearms (ATF) raided the Texas ranch of the Branch Davidians, an apocalyptic religious cult that was stockpiling illegal firearms and explosives. An ATF undercover agent inside the group warned his superiors that the Davidians had been tipped and were preparing to repel the raid, to no avail. The ensuing firefight left four ATF agents and six Branch Davidians dead. Once again, the FBI inherited a mess. This time, instead of facing a family of five barricaded in a hilltop cabin, agents were squaring off against roughly seventy-five heavily armed adults, living in a fortified compound with a watchtower, at least one underground bunker—and more than forty children. Over the next fifty-one days, FBI negotiators secured the release of twenty-one children and fourteen adults, but FBI managers lost patience. On April 19, 1993, Attorney General Janet Reno approved their request for an assault using modified tanks to pump tear gas into the buildings. The besieged Branch Davidians set fire to the structure rather than surrender. Twenty-five children perished, several of whom were later determined to have been shot or stabbed to death, along with fifty adults.[15]

Once again, FBI officials compounded the tragedy by withholding evidence during the resulting criminal and civil trials and obstructing Justice Department and congressional investigations into their conduct. FBI executives denied that agents used pyrotechnic tear gas rounds during the final assault, only to acknowledge they did six years later when photographic evidence emerged. A special counsel investigation led by former senator John Danforth confirmed FBI agents lied about having used incendiary devices near the compound hours before the fire started, but he determined they did not cause or contribute to the fire that killed seventy-five people.[16] Years of hiding these facts undermined confidence in the government's version of events, however, and fueled dangerous conspiracy theories.

Disgruntled Army veteran Timothy McVeigh would later argue that the government's actions at Waco justified his 1995 bombing of the Alfred P. Murrah Federal Building in Oklahoma City, which killed 168 people. The Oklahoma City bombing investigation showcased the FBI's expertise as an investigative agency, with its agents conducting over 28,000 interviews and collecting more than three tons of evidence to support the successful prosecution of McVeigh and his co-conspirators.[17] In just one example, an agent found the Ryder truck key McVeigh chucked into a debris-covered alley a block away from where he parked the bomb in front of the Murrah building, which became a critical piece of evidence at trial.[18] But the FBI slept through the tech revolution and its antiquated record-keeping system broke down under the stress of this enormous investigation. A late-discovered truckload of evidence never shown to McVeigh's defense attorneys forced a delay in his execution, and gave the bureau another black eye. Though the materials did not exculpate McVeigh, the episode revealed that the FBI's management problems were deeper than the occasional human error. Entire systems were failing.

A TIME FOR REFORM

The Judiciary Committee senators were careful to direct their criticism of the FBI's performance toward its leaders, and reiterate their respect for rank-and-file agents. Senator Hatch emphasized that despite the serious problems raised at the hearings, "the FBI solved the Oklahoma City bombing, the [1993] World Trade Center bombing, and the terrorist attacks in East Africa, among the literally hundreds of thousands of others that do not get the same profile in the press."[19]

Most field agents I knew were ambivalent about this kind of praise. We were too busy working our cases to pay much attention to inside-the-beltway political drama and we felt no collective responsibility for the mistakes of others, much less headquarters bureaucrats. While no one liked seeing the FBI or its leaders unfairly criticized in the press or on Capitol Hill, most of us experienced the bureau's maladministration firsthand and recognized it was a persistent problem that undermined our effectiveness. Senator Grassley deplored the FBI's broken management system as "a real disservice to the hard-working agents on the street."[20] We knew that holding FBI leaders to account was a necessary step toward reform.

The senators also admitted their own failures. Senator Leahy noted that Congress had given the bureau billions of dollars over the years but conceded that his committee needed to exercise more effective oversight to ensure its success.[21] Senator Grassley quipped that any time Congress investigates a bureau scandal, "the FBI ends up with a bigger budget, more program jurisdiction, and the director walks out of this room with a nice pat on the back." He felt Congress asked the FBI to do too much. "I believe that the FBI will become a more efficient and accountable organization," he argued, "through the narrowing of its investigative focus."[22]

People don't usually go to Judiciary Committee hearings looking for fireworks, but if you did, you'd want to keep an eye on Senator Grassley. At the June 2001 hearing, former Justice Department inspector general Michael Bromwich testified that "institutional arrogance" had driven the FBI's refusal to seek outside expertise that could have helped it keep pace with advancements in science and information technology that similar government agencies like the CIA had achieved.[23] Bromwich investigated the FBI's crime lab after Supervisory Special Agent Frederic Whitehurst, a PhD chemist in the explosives unit, raised public complaints. The investigation found lab personnel had submitted inaccurate reports and provided flawed scientific testimony in federal prosecutions for almost a decade. But Bromwich also chided the committee for using hyperbolic and unhelpful rhetoric by labeling the FBI a "cowboy culture."[24]

Senator Grassley, who used that term during the lab investigation hearings, was unamused. The FBI, he snapped, had "attempted to thwart an independent investigation, launched its own sham investigation, and then attempted to discredit and destroy the careers of their own respected scientists who brought these problems to light." He vowed to continue criticizing the FBI whenever it disregarded its fundamental mission to "seek the truth and let the truth convict."[25] Senator Grassley also scolded Bromwich for contributing to the retaliation Whitehurst suffered after bringing the improper lab procedures to light. Grassley, the sponsor of the Whistleblower Protection Act of 1989 (WPA), has championed whistleblowers of all kinds, but particularly those from the FBI and Justice Department.

Back in 1989, the FBI had successfully lobbied for an exemption from the WPA, citing concerns that litigating whistleblower cases could expose classified information. The Justice Department instead promised to write regulations establishing an internal system to adjudicate FBI whistleblower claims. The Whitehurst case revealed, almost a decade later, that the Justice Department had never fulfilled this promise. As a military veteran, Whitehurst had rights other FBI agents did not, which gave him the opportunity to bring a lawsuit in federal court. The FBI paid over $1 million to settle his retaliation claim. Bromwich conceded that his report did not give Whitehurst the credit he deserved for exposing the systemic problems plaguing the FBI lab.[26]

The harsh rhetoric of the Judiciary Committee's June hearing drew quick results. Within weeks, Attorney General John Ashcroft issued an order expanding the Justice Department inspector general's authority to investigate the FBI, and President George W. Bush nominated Robert Mueller III, the U.S. attorney for the Northern District of California, as the FBI's sixth director. Mueller, a square-jawed, combat-decorated Vietnam veteran, had more than two decades of experience at the Justice Department, where he had earned a reputation as a stern but effective administrator. When Mueller took charge of the San Francisco U.S. attorney's office, he forced all supervisors to reapply for their jobs and canceled casual Fridays.[27] Many inside the FBI interpreted his nomination as a Bush administration effort to impose greater Justice Department control over its independent-minded and often wayward bureau. Both the expansion of the inspector general's authority and the Mueller nomination were well received by the committee, but they did not alleviate all the senators' concerns.

On July 18, 2001, the Judiciary Committee held another hearing examining the FBI's institutional resistance to oversight and accountability. Two FBI supervisors who conducted the internal inquiry into the Hostage Rescue Team's Ruby Ridge operation and another who assisted Special Counsel Danforth's Waco investigation talked about the resentment and retaliation they received from FBI superiors for simply doing their jobs. Senator Grassley concluded that the whistleblower protection regulations the Justice Department belatedly implemented after Fred Whitehurst's case were insufficient to protect these FBI witnesses. He took the extraordinary step of citing the federal obstruction of justice statute, 18 U.S.C. § 1505, to publicly warn FBI leadership that further retaliation against these supervisors for testifying before the committee could result in criminal prosecution.[28]

Recognizing the FBI was leaderless and reeling from these scandals, Chairman Leahy quickly scheduled Mueller's nomination hearing for the end of July. Restoring public confidence in the bureau through rigorous oversight remained at the top of the agenda. Mueller vowed to establish a leadership environment that would own its mistakes, welcome constructive criticism, and cooperate with congressional investigations. He pledged to resist political interference in FBI investigations, while still submitting the bureau to the authority of the attorney general. "The Attorney General's the boss," he said, echoing a line Chairman Leahy used earlier in the hearing. Mueller stated in no uncertain terms that as FBI director, he would serve as "a component of the Department of Justice."[29] Everyone seemed to want a restrained and accountable FBI. Mueller's distinguished record and reputation for integrity appeared to convince the senators that he was the man to lead the FBI into the twenty-first century.

Mueller did not have an unblemished record, however. In the early 1990s, conservative *New York Times* columnist William Safire criticized

Mueller for his handling of investigations involving the Bank of Credit and Commerce International (BCCI) while he led the Justice Department's Criminal Division.[30] BCCI was widely known as "the Bank of Crooks and Criminals" for the money-laundering services it provided to drug cartels, arms dealers, corrupt dictators, terrorists, and spies. Senator John Kerry, who investigated BCCI from his perch on the Senate Foreign Relations Committee, agreed that Mueller's Criminal Division was "conspicuously slow" to address the serious allegations against the bank and actively obstructed other independent investigations by improperly denying access to witnesses and documents.[31] CIA officials later admitted they sometimes used BCCI and its affiliated banks to fund covert operations—allegedly helping to arm the Afghan mujahideen, Iran, Nicaraguan Contras, and Saddam Hussein's Iraq—which may have explained the Justice Department's reluctance to investigate BCCI too deeply.[32] When Mueller's name was floated as a potential nominee to lead the FBI a decade later, the *Wall Street Journal* opposed Mueller's appointment, concluding that "it would be a mistake to appoint as FBI head anyone who had any role in the failed BCCI probe."[33]

Looking even further back in Mueller's career, his tenure in leadership positions at the Boston U.S. attorney's office from 1982 to 1988 coincided with key events in the federal government's crooked relationship with Whitey Bulger's Winter Hill Gang. Two FBI agents would later be charged with facilitating three murders and covering up others that Bulger and other bureau informants committed, some of which occurred during the time Mueller served consecutively as chief of the Criminal Division, first assistant, and acting U.S. attorney in Boston.

While the FBI typically holds informant information close to the vest, local law enforcement officials had long questioned how a notorious criminal like Bulger remained free from prosecution for so many years.[34] Some federal prosecutors certainly knew Bulger was an FBI informant. Jeremiah O'Sullivan, a federal prosecutor who led the New England Organized Crime Strike Force before and during the time Mueller worked in Boston, testified that he knew Bulger was a murderer when he investigated him in a 1979 federal horse race fixing case. He testified that FBI agents told him Bulger was an informant and asked him not to charge him. Though a successful prosecution would have sent

Bulger to prison, O'Sullivan said he chose not to indict him as a matter of prosecutorial discretion.[35] O'Sullivan later tried going around the FBI, working with the Massachusetts State Police to get a wiretap up on Bulger and his crew, but it was compromised, allegedly by corrupt agents. O'Sullivan said he didn't challenge the FBI about its informant problem because Bulger's handling agents intimidated him and he feared raising the issue with bureau management would lead to "World War III."[36]

While there is no evidence Mueller was involved in any misconduct regarding the FBI's corrupt relationship with Bulger and his gang of cutthroats, what he knew about the bureau's misuse of informants while he led the Boston U.S. attorney's office deserved scrutiny. Yet no Judiciary Committee senators raised these or any other concerns about Mueller's background during his confirmation hearing. Perhaps the toughest questions came from Democratic senator Dick Durbin of Illinois, who quizzed him regarding racial profiling. Mueller responded, "Racial profiling is abhorrent to the Constitution, it is abhorrent in any way, shape or form." He asserted that the FBI needed "an unblemished record" regarding racial profiling if it wanted to be seen as a law enforcement leader. On a follow-up question about diversity within the FBI, Mueller committed to ensuring "that the FBI, through all its ranks, reflects the diversity in our society."[37]

Eerily presaging future events, Democratic senator Russ Feingold of Wisconsin asked Mueller how he would ensure the FBI's investigative powers targeted criminal activity rather than political dissent, specifically among Arab Americans, who some believed were already being improperly targeted. Mueller replied that he would ensure agents had sufficient evidentiary predicates to justify each investigative step.[38] He said his goal was to establish internal oversight mechanisms to ensure predication is demonstrated before investigations are authorized.

DISRUPTION

The Senate unanimously confirmed Mueller's nomination and he was sworn in as the sixth director of the FBI on September 4, 2001. One week later, terrorists attacked the United States using four hijacked planes as weapons, killing almost three thousand people. The FBI's management-reform agenda went down with the World Trade Center towers.

The FBI was immediately overwhelmed with tens of thousands of tips flooding in from the public, and three massive crime scenes to process, in New York City; Shanksville, Pennsylvania; and Arlington, Virginia.[39] Still, post-incident investigations were what the FBI did best, and it identified the nineteen hijackers as al Qaeda operatives within hours. FBI agents, many of whom had been working al Qaeda–related cases since the first World Trade Center bombing in 1993, began chasing down fresh leads across the globe. Though still handicapped by antiquated computer technology, agents began nailing down details of a plot that had been hidden in the noise of intelligence collection. Even previously distrustful foreign intelligence services opened their books to assist.

Rather than focus their resources on what the FBI and other intelligence agencies knew about al Qaeda, however, Justice Department leaders let fear about what they didn't know drive their responses. The government panicked over the possibility, unsupported by actual evidence, that al Qaeda sleeper cells would launch a second wave of attacks. As in past national security crises, the usual suspects were immigrants, minority communities, and political dissidents.

Attorney General Ashcroft and Director Mueller, who had condemned racial profiling as abhorrent and unconstitutional just weeks earlier, authorized sweeping programs targeting Muslims and Arabs. The FBI formally prioritized the capture of "all fugitives of Arab descent."[40] It launched a program to conduct five thousand "voluntary" interviews of foreign visitors and immigrants from countries where al Qaeda had a presence, creating a climate of fear and suspicion among Muslims across the United States, who were suddenly getting knocks on their doors and unannounced visits to their workplaces.[41] FBI agents surreptitiously scanned mosques with radiation-detection equipment and infiltrated informants and agents provocateurs into Muslim American communities.[42]

The threats to this new suspect class were not subtle. Attorney General Ashcroft announced a new anti-terrorism policy, offering a warning to "the terrorists among us": "If you overstay your visa—even by one day—we will arrest you. If you violate a local law, you will be put in jail and kept in custody as long as possible. We will use every available statute. We will seek every prosecutorial advantage. We will use all our weapons within the law and under the Constitution to protect life and enhance security for America."[43]

In the weeks after 9/11, more than twelve hundred Muslim, Arab, North African, and South Asian men were arrested and detained, often for minor immigration violations that the Immigration and Naturalization Service (INS) acknowledged "generally had not been enforced in the past."[44] The FBI assessed that 762 of these detainees were "of interest" due to possible connections to 9/11 or to terrorism in general. The Justice Department ordered INS not to release or deport any of these detainees until the FBI Counterterrorism Division cleared them of suspicion. Many were held incommunicado, under harsh conditions, and without access to lawyers or notice to family members. Assumed to have participated in the deadliest terrorist attack on U.S. soil, many were abused by guards or other detainees.[45]

The justification for labeling an immigration detainee "of interest," triggering the "hold until cleared" policy, could be as trivial as taking a photo of the World Trade Center, or being in the same location as a subject of a tip.[46] Justice Department official Michael Chertoff reportedly defended the policy using an argument Donald Trump would later make to justify his Muslim travel ban: "We have to hold these people until we find out what is going on."[47] It took an average of eighty days for the FBI to clear a detainee. More than 25 percent of the cases took three months or more, and the longest took 244 days. Most detainees were not charged with criminal offences, only civil immigration violations.[48] None appear to have been charged with terrorism offenses, and certainly nothing directly related to 9/11.

In addition to immigration arrests, the FBI exploited an existing law that allows for the apprehension and detention of material witnesses who might otherwise flee rather than testify. The FBI jailed seventy people under the material witness statute, including U.S. citizens. In many cases, there was no legal proceeding for which the imprisoned witness's testimony was required, which suggested the Justice Department was abusing the statute to hold people while they were being investigated as potential terrorists.[49] All but one were Muslim.[50]

The FBI and Justice Department considered these and other sweeping actions part of a larger "disruption strategy" meant to preempt terrorist plots. This strategy presumed the national security emergency triggered by 9/11 sanctioned the FBI to selectively employ coercive measures beyond those established through the normal criminal justice system. FBI counterterrorism official and former Navy SEAL Arthur Cummings told Garrett Graff, author of *The Threat Matrix*, how the FBI's concept worked in practice: "We have nothing on a possible second wave [of attacks], so we had to disrupt everything. Anyone who might be anywhere—get them off the street."[51] The FBI believes that aggressive action targeting broad groups of potential terrorists, or any persons agents believe are at risk of recruitment, can disrupt plotting even if no actual terrorists are ever identified.

In an interview with PBS's *Frontline*, Cummings said that the FBI's new intelligence-driven terrorism-prevention model represented a major change in the way FBI agents approached terrorism investigations: "The old paradigm was, we have no information in our records to show that they're engaged in terrorism. The new paradigm is, we have [no] information to show they're not engaged in terrorism. That is a significant paradigm shift. You basically investigate it and collect against it until you can make a deliberate and informed judgment that they are not involved in terrorism."[52] Of course, proving a negative—that someone was not a terrorist—is all but impossible.

The FBI explicitly designed its disruption strategy to justify government action where no objective evidence demonstrating involvement in terrorism or violent crime exists, in order to prevent plots that that might never form. Because everyone is a potential future terrorist, this paradigm shift justifies prophylactic mass surveillance, as the FBI can't predict what details of any particular person's life it might later find important. The enormous intake then necessitates systemic profiling to narrow the data down to a manageable set of suspects.

The Justice Department codified the concept of disruption in its "Strategic Plan 2001–2006," written shortly after 9/11. Its first objective was to "prevent, disrupt, and defeat terrorist operations before they occur."[53] Bureau leadership emblazoned this slogan across the lobby of FBI headquarters in Washington, D.C., to cement the new mission into the minds of agents and staff.[54] The strategy's operational lynchpin was the development of "a comprehensive intelligence program that can identify emerging threats and patterns, find relationships among individuals and groups, and provide useful information to investigators in a timely manner."

In order to identify patterns and relationships, the FBI needed data, and lots of it. That meant increased intelligence collection, which required support from Congress and the American people. Anyone who had been paying attention to the Senate Judiciary Committee hearings that summer could have guessed that FBI mismanagement played some role in the failure to detect a plot as complex and multifaceted as 9/11. Admitting as much might undermine support for giving the bureau more power, however. Here, another kind of disruption took place. Bush administration officials adopted a unified stance, vigorously denying press reports that the intelligence agencies had preattack warnings, while blaming the legal limits on executive power for their failure to uncover the plot.

Mere hours after the attacks, James Baker, former White House chief of staff and close adviser to both Bush presidents, went on ABC News to blame the intelligence reforms established as a result of the Senate's 1975–76 Church Committee investigation for "unilaterally disarm[ing] . . . our intelligence capabilities."[55] Vice President Dick Cheney and Defense Secretary Donald Rumsfeld had resisted the Church Committee's investigation of U.S. intelligence activities from its inception, when they served as staffers to President Gerald Ford.[56] They feared robust congressional oversight would threaten national security by creating a risk-averse culture within the intelligence agencies. They opposed legislative limits on intelligence powers as a usurpation of constitutionally granted executive authorities. But the truth was, these legal limits had not prevented intelligence agencies from gathering critical evidence portending the 9/11 attacks.

Most of us working in the FBI learned within days that our fellow agents had collected significant pieces of the puzzle, only to be stymied by bureaucratic incompetence at headquarters and other intelligence agencies' refusal to share what they knew. But Director Mueller, Attorney General Ashcroft, and other Bush administration officials all described the attacks as a bolt out of the blue, perpetrated by a new enemy that operated with such stealth and cunning that they tripped no alarms. At a September 17, 2001, press conference, a surprisingly well-informed reporter asked whether the FBI had missed any warning signs that might have prevented the attacks. The questioner referenced rumors that the CIA had failed to inform the FBI that a foreign terror suspect had entered the country, and that bureau agents may have squandered potential leads in San Diego and Minneapolis. Despite the suspicious particularity of the question, Mueller was unequivocal: "There were no warning signs that I'm aware of that would indicate this type of operation in the country."[57]

Framing al Qaeda as a relentless enemy capable of slipping unseen into the country and lurking among us while plotting our destruction served several purposes. First, it absolved the FBI and other intelligence agencies of failing to prevent the attack. No one could fault the intelligence establishment for failing to predict a black swan event for which there was no precedent and no warning. Second, it justified unleashing the agencies from traditional legal and moral restraints in order to prevent, rather than simply respond to, the follow-up attacks they predicted. Third, it amplified public fear in a way that generated support for more aggressive security measures.

The strategy worked. Just weeks after 9/11, all but one of the Senate Judiciary Committee members, who months earlier were preparing new controls over the FBI, voted to vastly expand the bureau's secret surveillance and data collection powers. The USA Patriot Act was a wish list of broadened authorities the FBI had long coveted. It loosened restrictions found in statutes like the Foreign Intelligence Surveillance Act, the Electronic Communications Privacy Act, and the Bank Secrecy Act, among others, to give the government greater access to data about Americans' travel, communications, and financial activities without probable cause warrants. The Senate passed the Patriot Act with just a single "no" vote, never examining whether these authorities were necessary to correct any legitimate intelligence deficiency.[58]

A few months later, Attorney General Ashcroft further liberated the FBI by loosening its investigative guidelines. Attorney General Edward

Levi had promulgated the first investigative guidelines to govern the FBI in 1976, after the Church Committee uncovered COINTELPRO, J. Edgar Hoover's counterintelligence programs designed to suppress dissent and punish his political enemies. The Levi guidelines aimed to prevent future COINTELPROs by limiting the FBI's power to act without a reasonable indication of criminal wrongdoing. Subsequent attorneys general could modify these guidelines because Congress never codified them in statute. The Ashcroft guidelines authorized the FBI to use more aggressive investigative techniques by weakening evidentiary predicates for investigations and lengthening the time limits governing their use. These were the same predicates Mueller said were essential to preventing abuse during his nomination hearing. The new rules allowed agents to go anywhere the public could, such as political meetings and religious services, to conduct surveillance even where they had no reasonable suspicion of wrongdoing.[59]

Just as Senator Grassley predicted, failure at the bureau once again led to expanded authorities, more resources, and a pat on the back.

UNLEASHED

For an agency already burdened with a dysfunctional information-management system, the massive influx of data resulting from these loosened restrictions only created more problems. Bigger haystacks make finding needles harder. To make matters worse, thousands of FBI agents, analysts, and supervisors with no terrorism experience were now tasked with assessing the flood of information coming in over the transom. Fear of failing to act on some scrap of information that might later be found relevant to an attack led agents and managers to pass even the most spurious threat information up the chain of command. Arthur Cummings explained the FBI's new mind-set: "A lead may seem to be 99 percent absolute garbage. But we have no tolerance for the one-tenth of one percent. That could get somebody killed."[60]

Mueller simplified matters for FBI managers by instituting a "no lead goes uncovered" policy, removing discretion in determining whether a tip merited attention. This directive might have been fine as a public messaging strategy highlighting the bureau's resolve, but it was a terrible counterterrorism policy. Chasing thousands of specious "ghost" leads wasted investigative resources and conditioned agents to expect nothing would come of them. The law prohibits triggering false fire alarms because they dull response times. Yet the bureau promoted "see something, say something" campaigns to encourage aggressive public reporting, inundating agents with false alarms that FBI policy required them to cover. Jack Cloonan, a New York agent with more than a decade of experience in international terrorism investigations before 9/11, said that this daily threat stream left agents "running around with their hair on fire" just because "no one had the guts to stand up and say, 'That's bullshit.'"[61]

The FBI's oft-repeated contention that al Qaeda sleeper cells were lurking among us increased public suspicion not just of immigrants and foreigners but of fellow Americans. Arab, Middle Eastern, Muslim, South Asian, Somali, and Sikh Americans would become a new suspect class, just as Japanese Americans, civil rights activists, communists, anti-war protesters, and labor organizers had in earlier national security crises. A loud cadre of Islamophobic activists and policymakers promoting themselves as terrorism experts demonized these groups and the civil society organizations that defended them as a fifth column that put the nation's security at risk.

To his credit, Mueller condemned the spike in anti-Muslim violence in one of his first post-9/11 press conferences, on September 17, 2001. Though it took place less than a week after 9/11, the director noted that the FBI had already opened forty new hate crimes investigations. But Mueller also dismissed concerns expressed by Arab and Muslim Americans that the FBI was targeting their communities based on ethnicity. Mueller stated, falsely as it would turn out, that all FBI interview requests were predicated on evidence related to the 9/11 attacks. Given that thousands of such interviews were taking place across the country, the public could be forgiven for assuming that other participants in the 9/11 conspiracy might still be at large and preparing to attack.[62] It shouldn't have been surprising that "see something, say something" leads from the public tended to identify innocuous behavior by American Arabs and Muslims as suspicious, or that the growing new terrorist watch lists were overwhelmingly populated with Arab and Muslim names.[63]

In June 2003, John Ashcroft's Justice Department issued what it called a "ban" on racial profiling in federal law enforcement.[64] While the *Guidance Regarding the Use of Race by Federal Law Enforcement Agencies* prohibited any reliance on race or ethnicity in making routine or spontaneous decisions in "traditional law enforcement activities," it established broad loopholes for national security and border integrity investigations. The purported racial profiling ban effectively authorized the FBI to racially profile in terrorism investigations.

I have no doubt that Mueller's first priority was to marshal the FBI's resources in the most effective way possible to identify the perpetrators of the attacks and their co-conspirators, to protect against further atrocities, and to find justice for the victims. But many Bush administration officials had long championed expanding executive power to its zenith, particularly in the realm of national security. They saw the 9/11 attacks as an opportunity to recalibrate the balance of power between the three branches of government.

Vice President Cheney chose NBC's *Meet the Press* as the venue to set the tone for the new Global War on Terror on the first Sunday after the attacks, telling the world we'd be going to the "dark side" and using "any means at our disposal."[65] I was troubled by similar sentiments I heard expressed in the halls of FBI offices. "The rules are off," one agent said almost gleefully. "We can do anything we want now." I asked him if he really thought the Constitution was "off," but he just looked at me quizzically and went along without response. Ali Soufan, an experienced FBI agent who on 9/11 happened to be in Yemen investigating the USS *Cole* bombing, wrote that a colleague from headquarters directed him to identify the attackers "by any means necessary."[66] Mike Rolince, an FBI supervisor and my former boss while I was stationed in Providence, Rhode Island, said the message he heard was "rule-of-law be damned."[67]

As much as I shared the grief and anger at the attacks, I was troubled to hear these sentiments coming from our nation's premier law enforcement officers. By some accounts, Mueller—a lifelong prosecutor—also struggled to adjust to what President Bush called a "war footing," where criminal trials would take a backseat to intelligence collection and covert actions. But it's hard to know how Mueller felt because he is a bit of an ideological enigma. The registered Republican published no legal scholarship that might hint at his views, which was somewhat unusual for a Justice Department lawyer with ambition to climb the ranks. He famously avoids talking to the press except in the most perfunctory manner, and his public speeches rarely stray from traditional law and order bromides. Mueller is often described as apolitical, which has always confused me. That someone could attain high offices in the Justice Department bureaucracy, including positions requiring presidential nominations and Senate confirmations, without being political seems hard to fathom. He is clearly very driven and effective in earning the confidence of his superiors and overseers in Congress.

Garrett Graff is one of the few journalists who spent significant time with Mueller. Graff suggests that Mueller could have asserted a much stronger role in curbing the Bush administration's extralegal policy responses in the aftermath of 9/11. I think he's right. Mueller was the only one involved in these early meetings who had actually fought and bled in a war, and he hadn't been at the FBI long enough to be blamed for the bureau's earlier missteps. President Bush could have made scapegoats of CIA director George Tenet and NSA director Michael Hayden for their agencies' failures, which meant they were unlikely to resist unwarranted executive demands. Even Ashcroft could have been faulted for deprioritizing terrorism and slashing the FBI's requested counterterrorism budget before 9/11. Bush's decision to keep them, and even defend them, ensured they would all be willing to get plenty of chalk on their cleats, a football analogy Hayden often used to describe a person who runs to the very edge of the legal boundary. He was apparently oblivious to the fact that football rules consider any contact with the white lines out-of-bounds.[68]

Mueller may have been too consumed with the global investigation of the 9/11 attacks and ensuring the survival of the FBI to resist the Bush-Cheney agenda. Many in Congress were talking seriously about taking terrorism away from the FBI and creating a new domestic intelligence agency from scratch, modeled on Britain's MI5. This was not an idle threat. The formation of a new Department of Homeland Security (DHS) attested that major organizational overhauls were open for consideration.

As an FBI section chief said when I brought a mismanaged terrorism case to his attention in late 2002, "If we aren't careful, we'll all be carrying DHS badges."

Graff attributes Mueller's acquiescence to his innate modesty, a Marine's deference to the chain of command, and his self-perceived lack of expertise with regard to terrorism. "Coming into it, I wasn't as familiar with al Qaeda and Osama bin Laden," Mueller later admitted.[69] One would think, then, that Mueller would surround himself with experienced FBI agents who knew the most about al Qaeda and how to conduct successful counterterrorism operations and prosecutions. In reality, the opposite was true. Mueller had a vision for how he wanted to remake the FBI in his own image, and little patience for anyone who would raise inconvenient objections, especially from a position of knowledge. The Senate Judiciary Committee's reform agenda was pushed aside as Mueller sought to build a more powerful and secretive FBI.

The bureau was in for a disruption of its own.

2

A LACK OF INTERNAL CONTROLS

In the spring of 2002, Coleen Rowley and her colleagues in the FBI's Minneapolis office were getting worried. They weren't the only ones.

The previous summer, supervisors at FBI headquarters in Washington, D.C., stymied the Minneapolis Joint Terrorism Task Force's (JTTF) request for a warrant to search the personal belongings of Zacarias Moussaoui, a Frenchman they had arrested on August 16, 2001, for overstaying his visa after a flight instructor reported his bizarre behavior. Moussaoui had paid $6,300 in hundred-dollar bills for twelve hours of training in a 747 flight simulator, despite having no job, pilot's license, or aviation experience. Minneapolis JTTF agents found Moussaoui agitated and evasive. He was unable to explain the source of the $32,000 he had brought into the United States, the purpose of his international travels, or why he wanted to learn to fly a jetliner. His roommate told the agents Moussaoui had been training to fight, approved of "martyrs," and believed it was acceptable to kill civilians who harmed Muslims.[1]

The Minneapolis agents suspected Moussaoui was a terrorist planning to hijack an airplane and they wanted to search his laptop and personal effects. At the time, agents could open terrorism cases as either criminal or intelligence investigations. In a criminal investigation, agents work with federal prosecutors and can seek search warrants from local magistrates. In intelligence investigations, agents must apply for warrants though FBI headquarters to a secretive court in Washington, D.C., established by the Foreign Intelligence Surveillance Act (FISA). Though the legal standard—probable cause—is the same, the perception is that FISA orders are easier to obtain. They also allow broader and more secretive searches than warrants authorized by criminal courts.

When Congress enacted FISA in 1978, in response to the Church Committee investigation, lawmakers worried that agents might use this secretive new system to circumvent the rigor and accountability of the criminal courts. To prevent an end run around the Fourth Amendment, Congress required agents seeking FISA warrants to certify that their "primary purpose" was to obtain foreign intelligence, rather than to gather evidence for a criminal prosecution. Under rules in place at the time of Moussaoui's arrest, whenever there was an option between the FISA Court or criminal courts, the prudent course of action was to seek a FISA warrant first.

The Minneapolis agents opened an intelligence investigation and asked FBI headquarters to seek an emergency FISA warrant. The headquarters supervisors refused, however, claiming there was insufficient evidence. They further declined the agents' request to reverse course and seek a criminal search warrant from a local judge. The agents continued pursuing their intelligence investigation to bolster their FISA request.

Inquiries with French intelligence revealed Moussaoui was a known extremist who in the 1990s had recruited people to fight in Chechnya with Ibn al-Khattab, an associate of Usama bin Laden.[2] An exasperated Minneapolis supervisor pled with headquarters, arguing they were "trying to keep someone from taking a plane and crashing into the World Trade Center."[3] But the headquarters supervisors only increased their resistance, refusing to submit the Minneapolis agents' twenty-six-page warrant application to the FISA Court. Out of options, the Minneapolis agents began processing Moussaoui for deportation so French officials could search his effects.[4]

When a hijacked Boeing 767 airliner crashed into the north tower of the World Trade Center on September 11, 2001, Rowley immediately requested headquarters' permission to seek a criminal search warrant to examine Moussaoui's belongings, but the supervisors still balked, telling her it was probably just a "coincidence."[5] Only when a third hijacked plane crashed into the Pentagon did they finally give Minneapolis permission to take their warrant request to a judge. The ensuing search of Moussaoui's notebooks revealed he had received wire transfers from the same al Qaeda paymaster who funded the 9/11 hijackers.[6]

The headquarters supervisors' refusal to approve Minneapolis's requests is even more perplexing given their access to intelligence threat streams that the Minneapolis agents never saw. Some of the headquarters staff who obstructed the Moussaoui case received a July 10, 2001, memo from a Phoenix FBI agent expressing alarm that several subjects of his terrorism investigations were training in aviation. The Phoenix memo urged headquarters to query other FBI field offices to determine if al Qaeda was strategically embedding operatives in the aviation industry to facilitate an attack. The Phoenix agent's memo mentioned both Usama bin Laden and Ibn al-Khattab. Another April 2001 memo sent to all counterterrorism units at FBI headquarters warned that terrorists with links to bin Laden and al-Khattab were engaged in "serious operational planning" for an impending attack against U.S. interests.[7] When questioned after 9/11, no headquarters supervisors responsible for overseeing the Moussaoui case admitted having seen it.[8]

Reports of other missed chances circulated within the FBI in the days and weeks after the attacks.[9] These blunders weren't what was bothering Rowley in the spring of 2002, however. It was the FBI director's failure to acknowledge them.

A PURPOSEFUL SHADING OF THE TRUTH

The FBI reported Moussaoui's August 2001 arrest almost immediately after 9/11, but Bush administration officials, including FBI director Robert Mueller, dismissed the notion that the bureau had information that could have been used to prevent the attacks. During a September 14, 2001, press conference, reporters asked Mueller whether he was surprised that some of the 9/11 pilots trained in the United States. "If we had understood that to be the case, we would have—perhaps one could have averted this," Mueller replied.[10]

When questioned specifically about Moussaoui's arrest at a September 17 news conference, Mueller unequivocally denied the FBI had missed warning signs that al Qaeda might stage "this type of operation."[11] The following day, the *Chicago Tribune* quoted French authorities confirming they had given the FBI information linking Moussaoui to bin Laden before 9/11, but an unnamed FBI official claimed the file contained "very sketchy information" that raised no cause for alarm.[12] Even when the Justice Department finally indicted Moussaoui on December 11, 2001, for conspiring with al Qaeda to commit the 9/11 attacks, Mueller maintained there was no intelligence failure. "All I can tell you is that the agents on the scene attempted to follow up aggressively," he argued, but "attorneys back at FBI [headquarters] determined that there was insufficient probable cause for a FISA, which appears to be an accurate decision."[13]

These statements infuriated Rowley and her colleagues. They knew FBI headquarters' obstruction of their investigation was bound to come out during Moussaoui's trial and worried that these public misstatements could undermine the prosecution. Rowley called the director's office and left a message warning his staff that Mueller's comments about the Moussaoui case weren't accurate.[14] Yet the false denials continued and the headquarters supervisors that had blocked the Moussaoui search warrant before 9/11 remained in their positions. Minneapolis agents started adding extra paragraphs detailing the Moussaoui case to every communication they sent to headquarters, to ensure no one could later claim ignorance. "They were afraid [Moussaoui] wouldn't even get prosecuted it would be covered up so much," Rowley told me. "What are you supposed to think? When you're hearing the highest levels saying there's no way we could have known . . . the natural thing [to ask] is, 'What are they going to do with this case?'"[15]

Rowley's role in the Moussaoui case was admittedly modest. She was the Minneapolis office's chief division counsel (CDC), an in-house FBI attorney. While the CDC position is vital to ensuring field office staff complies with the bureau's many policies and guidelines, the pecking order is such that her counsel regarding intelligence investigations could be overruled by FBI lawyers at headquarters. Likewise, local prosecutors in the Minnesota U.S. attorney's office made the ultimate decisions regarding FBI criminal investigations.

The real value Rowley brought to her position was in the street smarts she developed over more than twenty years as an FBI agent, where she came up through the ranks conducting complex criminal investigations in some of the toughest environments the bureau had to offer, including the elite organized crime squad in New York City. Rowley reviewed the Moussaoui case after his arrest and concluded there had been sufficient evidence to seek either a FISA order or a criminal search warrant. The headquarters supervisors who disagreed and blocked the search later admitted they didn't know the legal standard necessary to obtain a FISA order.[16]

The Bush administration resisted calls for investigations into the failure to uncover the 9/11 plot. But in February 2002, Congress initiated a bipartisan inquiry by the House and Senate Intelligence Committees. They wanted to talk with everyone involved in the Moussaoui case, including Rowley. She scheduled an interview for May 21, 2002, in Washington, D.C.

A few weeks earlier, on May 8, 2002, Mueller appeared before the Senate Judiciary Committee for the first time since his nomination hearing. The Phoenix memo had leaked to the press a week before, angering many committee members who had been told the FBI had had no intelligence presaging the attacks. But Mueller remained adamant there was no intelligence failure, testifying, "While here, the hijackers did all they could to stay below our radar. They contacted no known terrorist sympathizers, they committed no crimes, they blended into the woodwork. In short, the terrorists managed to exploit loopholes and vulnerabilities in our systems to stay out of sight and to not let anyone know what they were up to, beyond . . . a very closed circle."[17]

Mueller acknowledged that the Phoenix memo exposed analytical weaknesses in the bureau's pre-9/11 counterterrorism methods, which he endeavored to fix by reorganizing the FBI. In his testimony, Mueller faulted his agency's pre-9/11 posture as "reactive" and "dispersed," contrasting it with the "proactive" methodologies he was developing, where analysis and decision-making would be centralized at headquarters. Understandably, this proposal confused the senators, since the Phoenix agent's memo exemplified proactive intelligence collection and forward-thinking analysis. It was headquarters that failed to act.

Rowley stewed over Mueller's misrepresentations as she prepped for her interview with the Joint Intelligence Committee staff. She began writing notes to bolster her memory, but the document soon turned into a thirteen-page missive to Director Mueller. Rowley decried a headquarters culture of unaccountability and risk aversion, chastising Mueller for retaining and even promoting the "careerist" supervisors who had sabotaged the Moussaoui investigation. She castigated Mueller's plan to centralize counterterrorism investigations at headquarters, given the negligent responses to the Phoenix memo and the Moussaoui investigation. Though she balked at the term "cover up," she accused Mueller and other FBI officials of shading the truth to minimize institutional embarrassment and "perhaps even for improper political reasons."[18]

Accusing FBI leaders of acting for political purposes is one of the most damning charges an agent can levy. The bureau remains haunted by the five-decade legacy of J. Edgar Hoover, who used his agency's unchecked intelligence authorities to suppress political dissidents, intimidate elected officials, manipulate the media, and exaggerate threats to covertly influence public policy.[19] Agents carry this historical burden in everything they do.

The Church Committee emphasized that the FBI's political abuses were not partisan, rather they were intended to "entrench the Bureau's own position in the political structure, regardless of which party was in power." It acknowledged, however, that the FBI's actions were designed to serve "ideological purposes," namely Hoover's fervent anticommunism, which painted any challenges to the existing social order as threats to national security.[20] The Church Committee warned that the bureau's ability to covertly accumulate and selectively disseminate domestic intelligence information could subvert democratic processes.

The bipartisan reforms that followed the Church Committee investigation were intended to assert constitutional controls over FBI intelligence activities through written investigative guidelines, judicial supervision of intelligence wiretaps, and strengthened congressional oversight. Congress established the FISA Court and imposed a statutory ten-year term for FBI directors to foster independence from electoral politics, while also limiting their ability to entrench themselves in office as Hoover did. Many national security hawks bristled at these restraints, but most rank-and-file FBI agents embraced their role as objective and apolitical fact finders. Rowley's allegations would resonate with many agents frustrated by FBI mismanagement.

Director Mueller's May 8, 2002, testimony before the Senate Judiciary Committee provided the first clue as to why he and other Bush administration officials remained so adamant, in the face of contrary evidence, that the intelligence agencies had no forewarning of the 9/11 attacks. It wasn't just to protect the FBI from criticism. "The patience, skill, and exploitative approach used by the hijackers," Mueller argued in his prepared remarks, "means that our preventive efforts must be massive, globally collaborative, and supported by ample technology and analytical capability."[21]

Pretending the failure was caused by a lack of intelligence, rather than mismanagement, was necessary to justify requests for a radical expansion of executive power and the repeal of post–Church Committee reforms. At Attorney General John Ashcroft's urging, Congress passed the USA Patriot Act within weeks of the attacks, loosening restrictions in FISA and a dozen other surveillance statutes so the FBI could surreptitiously gather information about anyone it deemed "relevant" to a terrorism or espionage investigation, rather than just predicated targets. It removed the FISA "primary purpose" test so agents could more easily use the secret court system to gather evidence for use in criminal trials. It would be years before many in Congress would learn, from the *New York Times*, that President Bush had secretly authorized the National Security Agency to violate the clear statutory requirements of FISA to conduct mass surveillance of Americans' electronic communications without judicial authorization.[22]

FBI agents assigned to chase the voluminous tips this electronic dragnet produced derided them as "Pizza Hut leads" because they routinely led to dead ends at takeout restaurants.[23] They complained both internally and to the NSA but received no relief.

The NSA's warrantless surveillance program wasn't the only new counterterrorism tactic that found resistance among FBI agents. In November 2001, Pakistani intelligence agents arrested Ibn al-Shaykh al-Libi as he tried to escape Afghanistan during the American invasion. Al-Libi ran a terrorist training camp in the late 1990s and was the first high-value al Qaeda associate captured. The Pakistanis turned him over to American forces for a cash reward that December. FBI task force agents from New York's international terrorism squad I-49, the lead unit responsible for al Qaeda investigations like the 2000 attack on the USS *Cole* and the 1998 East African embassy bombings, were assigned to interview al-Libi in Afghanistan.

Jack Cloonan, one of I-49's most experienced agents, recognized that al-Libi could become a key witness in the upcoming trials of Zacarias Moussaoui and attempted shoe bomber Richard Reid, as they both had trained at the Khalden camp al-Libi supervised. Cloonan told the interviewing agents to read al-Libi his rights and handle it "like it was being done right here, in my office in New York."[24] Though miles from home and confined to a U.S. military detention facility, the New York task force agents used the FBI's traditional rapport-building techniques to gain al-Libi's confidence. He began providing valuable intelligence about al Qaeda operations that the FBI shared throughout the intelligence community. But the CIA had different plans. One day a CIA agent showed up in the interrogation room, shackled al-Libi hand and foot, duct-taped his mouth, and bundled him onto a plane bound for Egypt, threatening to find his mother "and fuck her" as they left.[25] Al-Libi would not be the star witness Cloonan and his team imagined, but he would prove useful to other Bush administration policy goals.

President Bush, CIA director George Tenet, and Secretary of State Colin Powell would later use al-Libi's confession to his Egyptian inquisitors that Saddam Hussein's government provided chemical and biological weapons training to al Qaeda terrorists as evidence to justify the 2003 U.S. invasion of Iraq. Once back in CIA custody in 2004, al-Libi recanted, claiming that his statement had been coerced through torture.[26]

When Mueller came to New York for a meet and greet at the FBI office a few weeks after the CIA rendered al-Libi to Egypt, Cloonan confronted him with a question about how agents should respond to inappropriate treatment of terrorism suspects captured in war zones. The *New Yorker*'s Jane Mayer reported that Mueller told the auditorium full of agents that he was "not concerned about due process abroad."[27] Cloonan decided to retire shortly thereafter, but he wasn't the last agent to raise objections over abusive CIA and military interrogation tactics. Like the president's warrantless electronic surveillance programs, however, the "enhanced" interrogation methods and renditions to torture were highly classified, so agents risked prison if they dared to publicize their concerns. Their choice was to conform to the new paradigm or leave, as Cloonan did.

BLOWING THE WHISTLE

Back in Minnesota, Coleen Rowley knew that sending the director a letter documenting management failures in the Moussaoui case would be a dangerous breach of bureau protocol. The FBI followed a paramilitary chain of command that required messages from agents to higher management go through their direct line of supervision. Violating this protocol was an affront to every supervisor in the chain and would almost assuredly result in retaliation. Rowley expected she might be "blackballed" in some fashion, but she knew no supervisor would approve, much less forward, a communication criticizing FBI management.

Rowley decided someone had to speak up. The Minneapolis case agent and supervisors were all relative short-timers compared to her twenty-one years on the job, so they faced a greater risk to their careers. Rowley was well known and respected throughout the FBI and had no messy disciplinary issues that could be dredged up to discredit her. Still, she ended the letter by formally requesting protection under federal whistleblower laws.

After finishing her interview with the Joint Intelligence Committee staff at the FBI's J. Edgar Hoover Building in Washington, D.C., Rowley dropped off copies of her letter at the director's office and the FBI's Office of Professional Responsibility, then jumped in a cab to Capitol Hill. Rowley hand-delivered the letter in sealed envelopes to the offices of Senator Dianne Feinstein (D-CA) and Senator Richard Shelby (R-AL), Intelligence Committee members representing both parties. She caught a taxi to the airport and flew home, wondering whether anyone would even read it. But she felt satisfied that she had done all she could do to make sure Congress knew the truth about the Moussaoui case.

Two days later, Rowley would become the FBI's most famous whistleblower. On May 23, 2002, CNN broke the news that an FBI agent had accused bureau managers of obstructing the Moussaoui investigation in the weeks before 9/11.[28] *Time* magazine put her picture on the cover and dubbed her letter "the bombshell memo."[29] The Senate Judiciary Committee asked Rowley to fly back to Washington to testify at a public hearing on June 6, 2002. Director Mueller immediately requested an inspector general investigation into Rowley's allegations, giving the impression that the issues she raised had been unknown to higher headquarters.

Though Rowley had been careful not to put any classified material in the letter, the FBI reportedly stamped it "secret," raising the potential that Rowley could be accused of mishandling national security information.[30] More upsetting to Rowley, when reporters asked Attorney General John Ashcroft if Rowley would face disciplinary action for releasing the letter to Congress, Ashcroft only allowed that she wouldn't be fired.[31] Senators Leahy and Grassley joined Minnesota senators Paul Wellstone and Mark Dayton in warning Ashcroft and Mueller not to retaliate against Rowley for blowing the whistle on the bureau's missteps surrounding the Moussaoui investigation. "That's what saved me," Rowley told me. "You think, 'Oh my God, you have to have four senators to act within two or three days to say you won't be fired?' That's what it takes?"[32]

In the face of growing criticism over Rowley's revelations, Ashcroft and Mueller responded with a bombshell of their own. On May 30, 2002, Ashcroft publicly issued new Attorney General's Guidelines for FBI criminal and terrorism investigations, significantly expanding the FBI's investigative powers. It was an effective pivot. "It seems when the F.B.I. fails," the ACLU's Laura Murphy told the *New York Times*, "the response by the Bush administration is to give the bureau new powers, as opposed to seriously look at why the intelligence and law enforcement failures occurred."[33]

Mueller invited Rowley to meet with him the evening before the June 6 hearing. He commended her integrity and told her if she ever had concerns again she should bring them directly to him. Rowley described the meeting as cordial but unnerving. She felt Mueller was attempting to win her over, to perhaps soften her criticism. But he did not ask for a copy of her testimony and she didn't offer it.

The following morning, the *Washington Post* published statements Mueller made during a ninety-minute interview that took place just hours before he met with Rowley. The normally press-shy Mueller revealed that the FBI was tracking a "substantial" number of al Qaeda supporters inside the United States who "may have sworn jihad." He warned this round-the-clock surveillance was severely taxing FBI resources. The *Post* described Mueller's comments as "among the strongest government assertions that people with suspected connections to Osama bin Laden's al Qaeda network remain in the United States."[34] This questionably timed fear-mongering was not the administration's only diversionary tactic.

Just as the hearing started, the White House announced President Bush would address the nation that evening to discuss the establishment of the Department of Homeland Security, the largest reorganization of government agencies since World War II. Chairman Leahy wondered aloud whether the announcement was intended to distract attention from the committee's hearing on Rowley's allegations. Mueller refused to say whether the president had consulted him about this announcement or how it would affect the FBI's reorganization.

Mueller testified first. Asked by Senator John Edwards (D-NC) whether a timely response to the Phoenix memo and the Minneapolis agents' request for a FISA warrant could have helped the FBI disrupt the 9/11 plot, Mueller maintained the Bush administration line. "I do not believe it likely that it would have," he replied. Senator Maria Cantwell (D-WA) questioned Mueller's reform proposals and expressed concern that increased information collection under the new Attorney General's Guidelines would only complicate the FBI's information management: "Our fundamental problem before Sept. 11 was that at the end of the funnel of information we were not processing it correctly, and we are now only going to widen that funnel and put more information into it. . . . You had all the information. It was not processed. It was not analyzed. It was not disseminated. . . . Instead you are saying we need to do more eavesdropping."[35]

With so many different issues at play during the hearing, Rowley wasn't called to testify until after three p.m. Though her testimony received front-page coverage in several newspapers, she felt the issues she raised were drowned out by the competing story lines. Still, she felt she'd done her duty to correct the public record regarding the Moussaoui case.

One positive development was that the senators got Mueller to say on record that Rowley would not face reprisals. In fact, Mueller went further, reiterating a vow he made to protect all FBI whistleblowers: "I issued a memorandum on November 7th [2001] reaffirming the protections that are afforded to whistleblowers in which I indicated I will not tolerate reprisals or intimidation by any bureau employee against those who make protected disclosures, nor will I tolerate attempts to prevent employees from making such disclosures."[36]

Mueller was true to his word; Rowley did not suffer direct reprisals. She received unkind letters from some former agents, but the FBI Agents Association backed her, as did most managers and agents in the Minneapolis field office. She did not feel that her position as chief division counsel was in peril. When *Time* later named her Person of the Year alongside corporate whistleblowers Sherron Watkins and Cynthia Cooper, it was a double-edged sword, however.[37] The publicity made retaliation less likely, but it also undermined her support among agents and the inspector general's staff, who now questioned her motives for coming forward.

Mueller and other Bush administration officials continued denying the attacks were preventable as they demanded stronger intelligence powers and used them more aggressively. On June 27, Mueller testified before the Joint Intelligence Committee, and he again maintained the hijackers did nothing to draw law enforcement attention. But the committee staff uncovered an FBI intelligence assessment from November 2001 that said the nineteen hijackers maintained "a web of contacts" inside the United States. The Joint Intelligence Committee ultimately determined the hijackers had associated with at least fourteen individuals who had come to the FBI's attention during counterterrorism or counterintelligence investigations, including four subjects of active FBI investigations.[38]

Despite such evidence, little changed at the FBI. The headquarters supervisors responsible for the pre-9/11 failures remained in their positions, and some were even promoted.

A DOUBLE STANDARD OF DISCIPLINE

In October 2002 testimony, Mueller confirmed that no headquarters personnel were disciplined for pre-9/11 failures.[39] Few bureau employees would have been surprised. Agents had long complained about a double standard whereby bureau executives received little or no punishment for misconduct that would result in severe discipline for agents and support staff. Supervisors were almost never held responsible for management decisions, no matter how damaging and contrary to law and policy. Agent complaints against managers were ignored at best, and more often resulted in open retaliation, both of which suppressed internal dissent.[40]

Mueller spoke carefully when he vowed to protect FBI whistleblowers, promising to prevent reprisals against employees who made "protected disclosures." This term had a specific meaning in the FBI's whistleblower protection regulations, which functioned more as a trap than a shield. Congress exempted the bureau from the Whistleblower Protection Act of 1989 (WPA), caving to FBI concerns over potential exposure of national security secrets during litigation. Instead, the WPA required the Justice Department to issue regulations providing bureau whistleblowers with commensurate protections within an internal system. Justice failed to comply for almost a decade, until FBI lab supervisor Frederic Whitehurst's whistleblowing brought the deficiency to light. The late-produced Justice Department regulations provided far less protection than the WPA. Under the regulations, for an FBI employee's report to be a "protected disclosure," it had to be submitted to certain specific high-ranking bureau officials, or directly to the Justice Department inspector general. The lowest ranking person in FBI field offices who could receive a whistleblower complaint was the special agent in charge (SAC). Reporting through your direct supervisor, as is the customary procedure within the FBI's rigorously maintained chain of command, forfeited all protections.[41]

In 2015, the U.S. Government Accountability Office studied the Justice Department's handling of sixty-two FBI whistleblower claims closed from 2009 to 2013. It found 89 percent of these cases were closed for technical reasons, like reporting to the wrong official. It adjudicated only four cases over that period and awarded corrective action in only three. It took from eight to over ten and a half years to resolve those winning cases, almost half a typical agent's career.[42]

I followed Mueller's remarks closely because I was in the middle of a woefully mismanaged undercover terrorism investigation. In March 2002, a supervisor from the FBI's Tampa field office asked me to work undercover in what sounded like a golden opportunity to infiltrate the U.S. support network of a Muslim terrorist group based overseas. Tampa opened the investigation after a suspected money launderer and self-described supporter of the Muslim terrorist group contacted a local white supremacist group seeking assistance (the FBI asked me not to name the groups). Pairing Muslim terrorists and white supremacists might seem strange, but it made perfect sense to me. Operational elements of a terrorist group tend to be practical and mission-oriented, rather than rigidly ideological. As one subject of the investigation explained, "The enemy of my enemy is my friend."[43]

The white supremacist group had been leafleting, which is a common recruiting technique. The supporter of the Muslim terrorist group saw one of their anti-Semitic flyers and reached out with a proposal for short-term cooperation. A meet and greet between underlings followed, and then a summit with the leaders to cement the agreement. Fortunately, the FBI had an informant placed within the white supremacist group and by sheer luck, the group asked him to attend to provide security. The informant recorded the entire encounter.

At the meeting, the Muslim terrorist group supporter explained that the post-9/11 security environment made it difficult for him to continue providing services to the overseas organization. Citing their shared hatred of Jews, he asked the white supremacist leader if his group could assist, since they would attract less law enforcement attention. On the way back from the meeting, the white supremacist asked the informant if he knew anyone that could provide the requested services. The informant said he did.

From my perspective, this was a perfect opportunity for an undercover operation that could neutralize a foreign terrorist support network inside the United States, gather useful intelligence on the overseas group, and arrest local white supremacists as a bonus. It could also help restore public confidence in FBI counterterrorism efforts. Usually, developing a plan to infiltrate a group takes time. Here, both sides had requested assistance and were just waiting for someone to answer their call. Simple. My initial meeting with the Tampa supervisor went well, and though he referenced some paperwork problems with the case, we started preparing for the operation.

Things started going sour quickly, however. The administrative issues only worsened, and I grew concerned they would imperil any potential prosecution. At headquarters, Mueller's reorganization of the Counterterrorism Division left the management of ongoing cases a bureaucratic mess. Part of the problem was that the case was unusual, involving international terrorism, domestic terrorism, drugs, and money laundering, all of which were typically overseen by different units at FBI headquarters.

Weeks and then months passed as the bureaucrats debated which unit would have operational oversight, with each trying to avoid responsibility. Then, in casual conversation, the informant mentioned to me that he had left the FBI recorder unattended during part of his initial meeting with the subjects. He said he thought they would talk more freely without him in the room. No doubt this was true, but it was a clear violation of the wiretap statute, which requires the FBI to obtain a judicially authorized warrant to record private conversations unless at least one participant consents.[44] As long as the informant had the recorder with him, his consent provided the legal justification for the FBI to monitor the conversations. Leaving the device unattended rendered the FBI's continued recording of the conversation illegal.

The informant's open admission of this error made it clear his handlers had not instructed him properly. Mistakes like this happen from time to time, and inadvertent violations can be addressed without tainting the ongoing investigation. The tape must be immediately segregated from the investigators so a prosecutor not involved in the case can identify and separate any illegally recorded sections from otherwise admissible portions of the tape. But here, months had passed, and the recording had been transcribed and disseminated to the investigators. I knew it was unlikely that a court would find this kind of violation harmless. I called the Tampa supervisor to discuss how to resolve the situation. He told me that we would move forward and simply pretend the illegal recording didn't happen.[45] I was stunned, and unwilling to mischaracterize illegally obtained evidence. I felt it was my duty to report the entire matter to FBI leadership.

Following Mueller's 9/11 testimony, I researched the proper procedures and recognized I should report the misconduct to the Tampa SAC.

I notified my chain of command in Atlanta that I was going to call the Tampa SAC to make a whistleblower disclosure. My managers asked me to send the complaint to them so they could forward it to the Tampa SAC, which I did. The retaliation was swift and unconcealed.

Tampa management removed me from the investigation and falsified records to hide their misconduct. They used Wite-Out to alter the dates on one key document, indicating their lack of concern that an internal investigation would detect their deception. Headquarters officials threatened to prevent me from ever working undercover again and made good on it by refusing to approve my next undercover operation, stalling another terrorism investigation. Following regulations, I reported these reprisals to the FBI's Office of Professional Responsibility (OPR), but they refused to take my statement. The inspector general's office finally did take my statement, but then turned the investigation back over to OPR, which remained uninterested. Finally, I emailed Director Mueller to alert him to the issue, but he didn't respond. The reprisals intensified.

The FBI's Inspection Division got involved, and the inspectors informed me they were pursuing counterallegations the Tampa managers made against me. The charges were bogus and the inspectors quickly concluded I had done nothing wrong, but the message was clear. My future at the FBI would consist of beating back false allegations until something stuck, and neither OPR, the inspector general, nor Director Mueller would act to protect me. After eighteen months working within the system to rectify the situation, without success, I decided to report the whole sordid mess to the FBI's overseers on the Senate Judiciary Committee. Knowing that far greater retaliation would result from taking my concerns outside the bureau, I resigned.

I wasn't the only FBI whistleblower that suffered reprisals during this period.

In October 2002, the same month I submitted my complaint, OPR unit chief John Roberts told CBS News's *60 Minutes* that the FBI maintained a double standard of discipline that treated high-ranking executives more leniently than agents and support staff.[46] After the show aired, Roberts claimed his boss, Assistant Director Robert Jordan, threatened him and humiliated him before his colleagues. The Justice

Department inspector general investigated Roberts's allegations and confirmed troubling inconsistencies in FBI disciplinary procedures and promotions. The inspector general also determined that Assistant Director Jordan showed poor judgment and "left the clear appearance of retaliation against Roberts."[47]

The inspector general's report expressed confidence that bureau leadership was determined to reform the FBI's disciplinary and promotion processes, but a subsequent review in 2009 showed the problem had only worsened.[48]

POLITICIZING INTELLIGENCE

For many who do blow the whistle, management's failure to properly address the reported misconduct is simply another abuse of power. After her June 2002 testimony, Coleen Rowley grew frustrated that FBI counterterrorism policies and practices appeared more designed to drive the Bush administration's agenda than prevent terrorism. She followed up on Mueller's invitation to send concerns directly to him, but he did not respond. Then, in testimony before the Senate Intelligence Committee on February 11, 2003, Mueller claimed that FBI investigations showed "several hundred" extremists "linked to al Qaeda" were inside the United States, potentially preparing attacks. He warned that Iraq's weapons of mass destruction program posed a clear threat to the United States because Saddam Hussein could provide chemical, biological, or radiological weapons to terrorists.[49] Rowley felt she had to issue a public challenge to this march to war in Iraq.

On March 5, 2003, the *New York Times* published her open letter to Director Mueller accusing FBI leadership of politicizing intelligence:

> The FBI is apparently the source for the public statement that there are 5,000 al-Qaeda terrorists already in the U.S. I would ask you to inquire as to whether this figure is based on any hard data. If it is, rather, an estimate based largely on speculation, this can only feed the suspicion, inside the organization and out, that it is largely the product of a desire to gain favor with the administration, to gain support for FBI initiatives and possibly even to gain support for the administration's initiatives.[50]

Rowley reminded Mueller that the FBI's role was to provide "unbiased, objective intelligence and national security advice to the country's leaders" and questioned whether there was any evidence demonstrating a link between al Qaeda and Iraq, as Bush administration officials had claimed. She warned that any attack on Iraq would undermine relationships with European allies and increase terrorism rather than reduce it. Mueller did not respond, and the U.S. military's "shock and awe" invasion of Iraq began on March 20, 2003.

Rowley knew that sending the letter to the *New York Times* would leave her unprotected by FBI whistleblower regulations, so she expected some kind of reprimand. Her supervisor's attempt to reassure her by suggesting the FBI was unlikely to pursue an Espionage Act investigation had the opposite effect, however. As its name suggests, the Espionage Act of 1917 was designed to target spies who provide national defense information to hostile foreign nations, not whistleblowers who provide the public with evidence of government malfeasance. The law, passed during World War I, drew controversy for its broad scope. As a result, prosecutors had rarely used it over the intervening eighty-six years, and almost exclusively against actual spies rather than whistleblowers.

Still, the possibility of being charged with a crime, particularly a crime carrying draconian penalties, was frightening. When her supervisor asked if she was retiring soon, Rowley understood the only possible response was "yes." She was told an OPR investigation would not be completed before she retired, so long as she left as soon as she was eligible. With her family financially dependent on her pension, Rowley concentrated on making it through the next twenty months. She stepped down from her position as CDC and volunteered for every mundane, inconvenient assignment—from night surveillances to holiday shifts—until she quietly retired in December 2004.

When I made my whistleblower complaint, I figured, like Rowley did, that my good record would protect me. I thought my experience working successful undercover operations would make me valuable to an agency that now prioritized terrorism prevention. I had never been involved in misconduct and was well known within the FBI because I often assisted agents around the country in preparing their own operations. What's more, President Bush and Director Mueller had specifically called on agents to report mismanaged terrorism investigations, and the problems with this one were so obvious.

The only thing I couldn't understand was why they would be so brazen in their reprisals and cover-up. Wite-Out? If Director Mueller was serious about reforming the FBI, senior officials who falsified agency records to hide their mistakes should have been the first to go. Yet the bureau promoted them. Mueller's reorganization wasn't reforming FBI management practices; it was entrenching them.

In hindsight, I realized being known and respected throughout the bureau didn't protect me, it made me a better target. Openly retaliating against a popular and successful agent sent a strong message to other employees who might consider reporting misconduct. FBI management was clearly more interested in suppressing internal dissent than ensuring its counterterrorism cases were competently managed.

The *New York Times*'s Eric Lichtblau covered my resignation from the FBI. I think he was sympathetic to my plight because Attorney General John Ashcroft had once yanked his Justice Department press pass after he wrote a series of critical articles, so he had experience with irrational reprisals. The FBI issued a press release calling my allegations "untrue," and claimed its investigation showed no attempted collaboration between domestic and international terrorism supporters. Nevertheless, Senators Grassley and Leahy championed my cause, appearing on NBC News' *Dateline* to support me even though the FBI didn't allow me to show them a single document to verify my story. They put pressure on the inspector general, who finally began an earnest investigation.

A year and a half later, the inspector general issued a report confirming that Tampa agents and supervisors had mismanaged the investigation, then falsified FBI records and retaliated against me to hide their misconduct. But the inspector general accepted the FBI's conclusion that no terrorist activities were discussed during the tape-recorded meeting. Senator Grassley and his chief investigative counsel, Jason Foster, noticed discrepancies in the inspector general's report, and they continued seeking records from the FBI, finally obtaining a redacted version of the transcript. Here's how Senator Grassley described the transcript in a March 2007 FBI oversight hearing: "It is frightening evidence of white supremacists and Islamic militants talking about working together. . . . The Islamic militant says that anyone 'willing to shoot a Jew' is a friend. . . . In other parts of the transcript they talk about their shared admiration for Hitler, arms shipments from Iran, their desire for a civil war in the United States, and their approval of suicide bombings, and, last, assassinating pro-Israeli journalists in the United States. This is all in their very first meeting with each other."[51]

Grassley asked Mueller if he had read the transcript or shared it with other agencies for its intelligence value. Mueller replied he had not, as the inspector general report indicated there was no lost opportunity to conduct a counterterrorism operation. The FBI and inspector general were more interested in maintaining the fiction that the bureau had not mishandled another terrorism investigation than ensuring law enforcement and intelligence agencies had access to relevant terrorism intelligence.

After leaving the FBI, I joined the American Civil Liberties Union's Washington Legislative Office. An old college friend who remembered my fixation with joining the FBI throughout school said he never could have imagined me working at the ACLU. I agreed, but said I never would have imagined the federal government would have a torture policy, either. I hadn't changed so much as the world had changed around me.

At the ACLU, my duties included lobbying Congress for stronger protections for intelligence community whistleblowers, and I was pleased to find broad bipartisan support for reform. In 2007, the House passed the Whistleblower Protection Enhancement Act, which would have expanded full whistleblower rights to the FBI and intelligence agencies, including judicial review in federal courts. But the Senate's version omitted these protections, and the two bills could not be reconciled.

Meanwhile, I heard regularly from FBI employees seeking assistance. Depending on their situation, I would refer them to employment lawyers or whistleblower advocacy groups like the Project on Government Oversight, the National Whistleblower Center, the James Madison Project, ExposeFacts, or the Government Accountability Project. Often, they just wanted to report the information to a responsible member of Congress, and I worked closely with Judiciary and Intelligence Committee staffs to set up meetings or help them pass along information in the appropriate manner. But because the FBI's protections were so weak, I felt it was my obligation to warn them that blowing the whistle could cost them their jobs.

In 2007, Democratic presidential candidate Barack Obama inspired hope among whistleblower advocates when he promised, if elected, to enhance protections for all federal employees, including national security whistleblowers.[52] But the FBI always managed to resist such efforts. When Congress finally passed the Whistleblower Protection Enhancement Act in 2012, increasing protections to federal employees and contractors, it again exempted the FBI and other intelligence agencies. To compensate, President Obama issued Presidential Policy Directive 19, establishing an internal procedure for adjudicating reprisal complaints from other intelligence agencies' whistleblowers, but again the FBI's procedures remained unchanged. PPD-19 required the attorney general to conduct a study evaluating the effectiveness of the FBI whistleblower regulations and propose reforms within 180 days, however. The Justice Department took more than three years to produce its recommendations, which were wholly inadequate and dead on arrival in Congress.

Finally, Senators Grassley and Leahy introduced the FBI Whistleblower Protection Enhancement Act of 2016, which would have significantly improved the administrative process for adjudicating bureau whistleblower claims and provided for federal court review. It would have expanded protections to cover reports made through the chain of command, rather than just the handful of designated officials. The FBI opposed the bill.

As the congressional session came to a close after President Donald Trump's election, one FBI employee's case hung in the balance. Supervisory Contract Specialist Darin Jones had made a complaint about an improperly awarded $40 million contract. He was fired, and because he made his complaint through the chain of command, the Justice Department dismissed his retaliation complaint on procedural grounds. He had one last appeal available, to the deputy attorney general, which had been pending for more than two years. As the term expired, Senators Grassley and Leahy made herculean efforts to pass an abridged version of the bill that would just expand protection to chain-of-command reports like the one Jones had made. Deputy Attorney General Sally Yates denied Jones's appeal the day President Obama signed the bill, terminating his employment mere hours before the law that might have protected him went into effect.[53]

In at least one respect, FBI whistleblowers were more fortunate than other bureau employees, though. They at least had the choice to shut up and conform to the new regime's expectations. Others didn't have that option.

3

FEAR OF FOREIGNNESS

For all that FBI director Louis Freeh did wrong that left his agents ill-prepared for the 9/11 attacks, strengthening the bureau's relationships with foreign countries was one thing he got right. The bureau's Legal Attaché program, which stations FBI supervisors at U.S. embassies to serve as liaisons to foreign law enforcement and intelligence agencies, began during World War II. But Freeh recognized the shrinking globe was making America more vulnerable to international threats. As borders opened when the Cold War ended and new technology allowed Americans to engage in global commerce through cyberspace, criminals no longer had to be in the United States to harm Americans. To deal with these challenges, Freeh strengthened the Office of International Operations and doubled the number of countries where legal attachés, or "legats," as they were known in the bureau, resided.

Special Agent Gamal Abdel-Hafiz personified the kind of recruit that Freeh's more worldly FBI sought to develop. He was the first foreign-born Muslim agent in the FBI, and possibly the first Muslim agent, period. Abdel-Hafiz's career accomplishments include significant roles in some of the FBI's most notable terrorism cases. He was stationed in Saudi Arabia during 9/11 and covered thousands of leads across seven Arabian Peninsula nations. Despite this exemplary counterterrorism record and the unwavering support of those he worked most closely with, the FBI's internal security apparatus repeatedly targeted him after 9/11 based on his religion, ethnicity, and national origin—the very qualities that made him so valuable to the bureau in the first place.

SEEING SECURITY THROUGH DIVERSITY

Abdel-Hafiz was born in Egypt and immigrated to the United States in 1984 after completing a college degree in Arabic-English translation. He went into business and found success managing 7-Eleven stores in Fort Worth, Texas. He married and became a U.S. citizen in 1990. After a violent robbery at one of his stores, Abdel-Hafiz decided to change careers, accepting a translator position at a U.S. company in Saudi Arabia. When the Gulf War broke out in 1991, he felt an obligation to serve his country and applied to the FBI. The New York office hired him as an Arabic linguist in 1994.[1]

His counterterrorism career started a few months later when his boss brought him hundreds of cassette recordings to be transcribed for the upcoming trial of "Blind Sheikh" Omar Abdel-Rahman, the alleged spiritual leader of the terrorist organization al Gama'a al-Islamiyya (Islamic Group). An FBI informant made the recordings during a months-long undercover operation that captured the sheikh and nine followers plotting to bomb New York City tunnels and landmarks.[2] Abdel-Hafiz organized a team of translators to ready thousands of pages of transcripts for trial.

New York agents and supervisors recognized his unique talents and recommended he apply to become an FBI special agent. He passed his entrance tests and polygraph in 1995 and was given a date to start training at Quantico. But his boss came to him with a problem. The other translators balked at testifying in open court against Abdel-Rahman, fearing his supporters would retaliate. He asked Abdel-Hafiz if he'd be willing to stay in New York to testify. Abdel-Hafiz said, "Yes, sir," and put his special agent training on hold.

Abdel-Hafiz testified nineteen different times, impressing the prosecutors with his precise translations and resilience on the witness stand in the face of withering cross-examination. Adding to his stress, the prosecutors received a credible threat against his life during the trial. Undaunted, he pledged to continue testifying. The FBI put Abdel-Hafiz and his wife in temporary housing and provided security, which he appreciated, but they would not reimburse the cost of moving his household goods. Abdel-Hafiz was frustrated that bureaucratic rules took precedence over his safety. The government ultimately won convictions against all ten defendants, and Abdel-Hafiz reported to the FBI Academy in Quantico, Virginia, the following month, just shy of his thirty-seventh birthday.

Director Freeh made a practice of running with new agent classes at the academy. During Abdel-Hafiz's training, Freeh thanked him for his work on the Blind Sheikh case and for signing up as an FBI agent. Abdel-Hafiz recalled with pride that Freeh read a note from the prosecutors that said, "We wouldn't have been able to accomplish the same results without the contributions of Gamal Abdel-Hafiz."[3]

One unsettling part of FBI training is not knowing where you'll be assigned after graduation. The only near certainty is that you won't go back where you came from. Luckily for Abdel-Hafiz, he processed through New York. His prayers were answered when the bureau assigned him back home, to the FBI field office in Dallas, Texas. Dallas management quickly recognized the asset they'd been handed, as Abdel-Hafiz was well known and highly regarded in local Arab and Muslim communities. He became instrumental in helping the Dallas office build bridges to communities that often felt alienated by unwarranted suspicion. But Dallas leadership also realized, to their credit, that Abdel-Hafiz was a national resource they would have to share.

A few months after Abdel-Hafiz arrived in Texas, terrorists detonated a truck bomb in front of Khobar Towers, a housing complex in Saudi Arabia, killing nineteen U.S. service members. The FBI sent Abdel-Hafiz to Saudi Arabia for a thirty-day temporary assignment to assist the bureau's investigation. He stayed for seven and a half months. At one point, the Saudi government refused to give the FBI access to jailed suspects and Freeh ordered his agents to pack up and leave. Amid the turmoil, the FBI team leader asked Abdel-Hafiz to stay as the bureau's sole representative on the Arabian Peninsula. Abdel-Hafiz protested, pointing out that with only six months on the job, he hadn't yet fully grasped the FBI's byzantine paperwork requirements. "Gamal, we don't want you here for that," Abdel-Hafiz recalled the team leader saying, "I recommended you because you know how to deal with the Saudis and how to handle yourself here."[4]

Abdel-Hafiz was finally relieved when the FBI appointed Bassem Youssef to serve as its first legat to Saudi Arabia. Youssef was the FBI's only other Egyptian-born agent, having joined the bureau nine years before Abdel-Hafiz. Youssef's family came to the United States in 1972, when he was a teenager, settled in Southern California, and became U.S. citizens.[5] Like most Arab immigrants during that period, the Youssefs were Christian, part of a Coptic sect that made up the largest religious minority in Egypt. Youssef entered the FBI in 1988, the same year I did. The bureau made effective use of Youssef's Arabic skills by assigning him to international terrorism investigations in Los Angeles. In the early 1990s, Youssef recruited intelligence sources close to the Blind Sheikh and, reportedly, to an obscure terrorism financier named Usama bin Laden.[6] Working undercover, Youssef infiltrated a U.S.-based al Qaeda support network, thwarting a bomb plot against a Masonic lodge in Los Angeles.[7] The CIA awarded Youssef its National Intelligence Distinguished Service Medal, and Freeh promoted him in February 1997 to open the FBI's first legat office in Saudi Arabia.

Another experienced, foreign-born FBI agent, Wilfred Rattigan, was assigned as the assistant legal attaché (ALAT) under Youssef in February 1999. Rattigan was born in Jamaica, came to the United States as a teenager, and graduated from John Jay College and the Howard University School of Law before joining the FBI, also in 1988. He worked in the New York office for eleven years on counterintelligence, organized crime, and drug cases. He conducted undercover operations and investigated crimes aboard aircraft at JFK International Airport before being promoted to ALAT.

Their performance appraisals show the FBI rated Youssef and Rattigan highly. A December 1999 FBI inspection of the Saudi Arabia legat office credited Youssef with setting up the office and expanding its territory to cover seven contiguous Gulf states. The U.S. ambassador praised Youssef as "just the right man" to represent the FBI in Saudi Arabia. The inspection report said Rattigan had "a positive attitude and work ethic" and was "universally commended for his helpfulness and responsiveness." Rattigan was studying Arabic and Islam in his spare time, and the report said he had impressed Saudi officials with "his knowledge of the Arabic culture and language."[8]

Youssef concluded his legat assignment in July 2000 and returned to the United States, where the FBI named him chief of the Executive

Secretariat Office at the National Counterintelligence Center.[9] The FBI promoted Rattigan to the legat position, and in February 2001, Abdel-Hafiz arrived from Dallas to serve as his ALAT. While no one could have been adequately prepared for September 11, 2001, Director Freeh's investment in these three talented agents ensured the bureau had experienced, knowledgeable, and capable personnel to guide its new missions throughout the Middle East.

But the FBI squandered this advantage. Youssef's Counterintelligence Center position was eliminated in a post-9/11 reorganization and he never worked in counterterrorism operations again. Within two years, the FBI would demote Rattigan after he filed a discrimination complaint and fire Abdel-Hafiz on a trumped-up charge. Abdel-Hafiz won his job back on appeal the following year and returned to Dallas as a street agent, but all three of these experienced counterterrorism agents would spend the rest of their careers in litigation against or under investigation by the bureau rather than on the front lines of the fight against al Qaeda. All three believe that unjustified suspicions based on their race, ethnicity, and religion derailed their careers just when their experience could have been most helpful to the FBI.

SEEING DIVERSITY AS A THREAT TO NATIONAL SECURITY

Abdel-Hafiz and Rattigan had both experienced discrimination on the job before 9/11. Abdel-Hafiz was involved in a convoluted dispute in 1999 that centered on his faith and ethnicity. An old friend called Abdel-Hafiz after his employer received a subpoena to testify before a Chicago grand jury. Abdel-Hafiz discovered the subpoena was part of a wide-ranging Chicago FBI investigation, code-named Vulgar Betrayal, that was examining alleged U.S. fund-raising activities to support the Palestinian terrorist group Hamas. Abdel-Hafiz contacted the Chicago case agents and told them his friend would be willing to testify if they sent him a subpoena. Everyone seemed pleased with this lucky break. A few weeks later, the friend called again to say his boss had asked to talk directly to Abdel-Hafiz. The Chicago agents asked Abdel-Hafiz to pursue a meeting, but then they made an unusual request. They asked Abdel-Hafiz to wear a hidden wire to surreptitiously record the interview.

The FBI policy at the time instructed agents not to record interviews and instead take notes and write reports called FD-302s. Recording conversations was standard for undercover operations, however. By asking him to secretly record the conversation, the Chicago agents and prosecutors were essentially asking Abdel-Hafiz to work undercover using his true name and official identity. Abdel-Hafiz was understandably uncomfortable with this proposal. His boss in Dallas suggested he accept the meeting and just write a report afterward as he would in any other interview, or alternatively, record the interview with the subject's knowledge.

The Chicago team refused these suggestions and insisted he record the interview covertly. Abdel-Hafiz later told me it "just didn't make any sense" to believe that the subject was going to meet someone he knew was an FBI agent and confess to being a terrorist. He refused Chicago's proposal, and this is where the conversation should have ended.

Abdel-Hafiz had completed the FBI's undercover training a few years earlier, so he knew that all undercover assignments were entirely voluntary. I often worked as a counselor at undercover schools, and I met Abdel-Hafiz during his training. I know he was taught that undercover agents can refuse a case for any reason, or no reason at all. This rule existed to ensure agents couldn't be coerced into taking dangerous or just plain dumb assignments against their better judgment.

The Chicago agents and prosecutors didn't take no for an answer. They pressed Abdel-Hafiz, who explained that operating in a deceitful manner using his true name would put him and his family at unnecessary risk and undermine his work with Muslim communities. The Chicago team claimed he said "a Muslim does not record another Muslim," which they interpreted as placing his religious obligations above his duty to the FBI.[10] Abdel-Hafiz insists this interpretation distorts his explanation that many in the Muslim community would view this tactic as a betrayal of trust. Regardless, the Chicago agents refused Abdel-Hafiz's offer to memorialize the interview in an FD-302 and threatened to get FBI headquarters to order him to record the meeting. Abdel-Hafiz replied that he would only do it if his boss, Dallas special agent in charge Danny Defenbaugh, ordered it, since Defenbaugh was most knowledgeable about his counterterrorism work and the value of his relationships with local Muslim communities.

Abdel-Hafiz remembers Defenbaugh's response as unequivocal: "Hell no! Even if you said yes, I would tell you not to do it. Gamal, I have to tell you, they are asking you to do it because they don't trust you."[11] This intuition appeared to bear out when a Dallas colleague told Defenbaugh that Chicago agents were spreading rumors that Abdel-Hafiz was a Muslim mole working to defeat FBI counterterrorism efforts. Defenbaugh reportedly stated in a deposition that he heard one of the Chicago agents call Abdel-Hafiz a "camel jockey."[12] With Defenbaugh's encouragement, Abdel-Hafiz filed an Equal Employment Opportunity (EEO) complaint. He wanted to make clear he would not stand for attacks on his integrity.

Abdel-Hafiz never met with his friend's boss and the FBI closed the Vulgar Betrayal investigation in August 2000 without filing criminal indictments.[13] When Abdel-Hafiz won promotion to the ALAT position in Saudi Arabia, he figured this nonsense was behind him. When the EEO board determined that bigoted comments by a co-worker were not actionable, Abdel-Hafiz decided not to appeal and focus instead on his new assignment. He figured he'd made his point.

Rattigan's troubles started when he was in Saudi Arabia. He felt the Saudi legat office was dangerously under-resourced, especially after the 2000 USS *Cole* bombing in Yemen increased its investigative load. The FBI staffed the legat office, which covered seven countries, with two agents and an office assistant crammed into an 870-square-foot converted storage room.[14] Headquarters rebuffed Rattigan's concerns, however. Once he was promoted to legat he came to believe that headquarters managers were setting him up for failure based on racial animus. He felt his instincts were confirmed when he heard the deputy assistant director at the Office of International Affairs (OIO) refer to a Latino colleague as "that gas station attendant."[15] Rattigan complained to Director Freeh, alleging a pattern of racial discrimination. His complaint triggered retaliatory investigations designed to impede his performance and justify his removal from the legat, according to court filings.

Such petty bureaucratic infighting would be detrimental to the FBI's mission at any time. But after 9/11, thousands of critical leads flooded the Saudi Arabia legat office. The Saudis had called Rattigan with condolences, letting him know they employed additional staff to assist with U.S. queries, twenty-four hours a day, seven days a week. This unprecedented Saudi cooperation was welcomed, but the office remained woefully understaffed and the antiquated computer systems made keeping up with the accumulating leads a monumental challenge.

When Rattigan requested more resources, headquarters stalled, sending inexperienced agents on thirty-day temporary duty rotations. This response only increased his administrative burden, however, as the legat's staff needed to arrange travel, housing, and local transportation for each new arrival, while still attending to their own duties. By the time the temps became proficient, they were ready to head back home. The legat office also lacked a cleared translator, so they had to fax documents to FBI headquarters for translation, creating further delays. In the middle of this chaos, headquarters continued sending FBI supervisors to evaluate Rattigan's performance rather than address the mushrooming terrorism leads.[16]

In December 2001, Rattigan formally converted to Islam after four years of study. Though the FBI had perceived Rattigan's interest in Arabic culture as a positive attribute during its 1999 inspection of the legat office, it now viewed his religious conversion as a potential threat.

IDENTIFYING THE THREATENING "OTHER"

The confluence of the Robert Hanssen spy case and 9/11 changed the FBI in two fundamental ways, with severe ramifications for foreign-born employees. First, it launched an aggressive internal security regime empowered to identify and neutralize potential "insider" threats. At the same time, the Bush administration defined the nature and scope of the foreign terrorist enemy in terms that cast a wide net of suspicion.

Laudably, President Bush visited the Islamic Center of Washington, D.C., less than a week after 9/11 to make clear that Islam was not a threat and that the billion-plus Muslims living peacefully throughout the world, including millions of patriotic American Muslims, were not the enemy.

"Islam is peace," the president declared. "These terrorists don't represent peace."[17] But in his first address to Congress, President Bush also made clear that while not all Muslims were terrorists, the targets of the global war on terror were all Muslim. The enemy, he declared, was "a radical network of terrorists" practicing "a fringe form of Islamic extremism" and "every government that supports them."[18] This "extremist" label was diffuse. It could apply to any Muslim or group of Muslims and any country in the Muslim world whose government opposed U.S. foreign policy. "You're either with us or against us in the fight against terror," he later simplified.[19]

The FBI embraced this ambiguous conception of the threat. An FBI official told Congress in 2002 that "the lesson to be drawn" from 9/11 was that the threat did not emanate from any one terrorist organization but from the "globalization of radical Islam." Al Qaeda, he argued, was "but one faction of a larger and very amorphous radical anti-Western network that uses al Qaeda members as well as others who share common hatred or are sympathetic to al Qaeda's ideas."[20] This expansive description of the enemy erased important distinctions of nationality, sect, political ideology, organizational interests, and tactical goals of disparate entities, blending them into one malleable mass. It gave the Bush administration flexibility to target any group of Muslims anywhere by simply deeming them "radical." It also transformed Muslims everywhere—including those inside the United States and even inside the FBI—into presumptive suspects, as they could "radicalize" at any moment.

The FBI established a new Security Division in December 2001, assigning 624 employees to identify and root out potential traitors.[21] Ties to foreign nations became inherently suspect even as the FBI struggled to recruit linguists, analysts, and agents with knowledge and familiarity of Middle Eastern languages, geography, and cultures. The FBI reassigned approximately 4,000 of its then roughly 12,000 agents to the 9/11 investigations, with 1,000 permanently reassigned to counterterrorism duties.[22] Few had worked counterterrorism before, and the FBI lacked certified and experienced instructors. A cadre of self-styled terrorism "experts" filled the breach, many of them funded by conservative foundations and driven by political agendas or religious and ethnic prejudice. In the post-9/11 atmosphere of fear and uncertainty, this "Islamophobia network" found an amenable audience inside the FBI, just as it did in the media.[23] They began training FBI agents and their law enforcement partners to view Arabs and Muslims as monolithic, backward, and inherently violent.[24]

The wars in Iraq and Afghanistan and intensified focus on Muslim terrorism created a more permissive atmosphere for anti-Muslim and anti-Arab animus within the FBI, just as the internal security apparatus began scrutinizing employees with ties to certain foreign nations. These xenophobic impulses infect FBI policies and practices right up to the present day.

According to a lawsuit Rattigan filed in 2005, the FBI investigated his conversion to Islam, interrogating his assistant over whether she felt he could meet his FBI obligations after becoming "one of them."[25] Another analyst confirmed that Rattigan's religion was discussed at FBI headquarters and that rumors circulated regarding Rattigan's "loyalty to the U.S. versus the Saudi Arabian government."[26] A supervisor assigned to evaluate Rattigan alleged he had "gone native" because he had worn traditional Saudi clothing at an embassy function. The Security Division investigated but determined the claim unfounded.[27] Though Rattigan's immediate supervisor rated him as meeting expectations and formally extended his assignment in Saudi Arabia, FBI headquarters recalled him to the United States in June 2003 and demoted him. After Rattigan left, the FBI doubled the staffing at the Saudi Arabia legat office and reduced its territorial responsibilities to cover just two countries. A jury later awarded Rattigan $400,000 in a discrimination lawsuit, but the Justice Department successfully appealed by arguing that the courts lacked jurisdiction over FBI security decisions.[28]

The FBI interviewed Abdel-Hafiz while he was ALAT in Saudi Arabia, seeking dirt on Rattigan, but he supported his boss's discrimination claims. To him, the OIO managers seemed disappointed because they assumed any ambitious ALAT would cooperate in ousting a sitting legat to open an opportunity for promotion. Abdel-Hafiz wasn't willing to support false allegations in any event. His counterterrorism work was still earning accolades, however, especially after he obtained the key confession that cracked the 2002 Lackawanna Six case. It involved six

Yemeni Americans who trained in an al Qaeda camp and then returned home to Lackawanna, New York. The Bush administration touted the arrests as a significant victory that disrupted an active al Qaeda sleeper cell in the United States, and credited Abdel-Hafiz for his work.[29] But Abdel-Hafiz was about to find out how little his well-earned reputation protected him.

In November 2002, the Chicago agents and prosecutor from the Vulgar Betrayal case resurfaced their old allegations that Abdel-Hafiz had refused to record a fellow Muslim, but this time in the media.[30] Abdel-Hafiz was in Saudi Arabia when the *Wall Street Journal* contacted him for comment. Agents are prohibited from speaking with reporters without permission, so he forwarded the request to headquarters, but he did not receive a response in time. Fox News and ABC News picked up the story and embellished it, inaccurately alleging the investigation involved persons with direct links to bin Laden rather than suspected ties to Hamas.[31] The anti-Muslim advocacy network's echo chamber kept the story in the headlines, and Bill O'Reilly publicly called for Abdel-Hafiz's termination.[32] Abdel-Hafiz felt the bureau didn't adequately challenge the allegations or highlight his counterterrorism record.

Part of the reason for the FBI's muted defense was that Abdel-Hafiz's ex-wife had filed a complaint alleging he had made a fraudulent homeowner's insurance claim years earlier. The FBI opened an internal investigation, and Abdel-Hafiz gave them full access to his financial records and storage unit in Texas. He also agreed to take a polygraph, as he had twice in the past. He had taken his latest polygraph the previous summer and it had not gone well. Before the test began, the examiner asked Abdel-Hafiz if he was the Muslim agent who refused to record other Muslims. Abdel-Hafiz took offense, leading to a heated argument. Finally, after three tests, the examiner grudgingly admitted he passed. Six months later, he was called for another polygraph regarding the alleged insurance fraud. This time, the polygrapher said he failed, and there was little Abdel-Hafiz could do but swear the test was wrong. The FBI fired Abdel-Hafiz in May 2003, claiming that not mentioning the insurance issue on his security clearance application constituted a material omission. Though the termination had nothing to do with the allegations swirling in the news, Abdel-Hafiz's lawyer told him it was clear the

FBI rushed its adjudication process in response to the negative media coverage.

Now freed from the FBI media restrictions, Abdel-Hafiz was finally able to tell his side of the story. Coverage in the *Dallas Morning News* and *D Magazine* and on PBS's *Frontline* all highlighted Abdel-Hafiz's counterterrorism successes and portrayed his dismissal as misguided and discriminatory.[33] He appealed his termination and won his job back in January 2004. Hoping to escape further controversy, he asked to work financial crimes rather than international terrorism.

Bassem Youssef's post-9/11 troubles came from asking for a counterterrorism assignment.[34] Youssef felt his Middle Eastern heritage, an asset before 9/11, was now stirring unjustified suspicion. He heard rumors that people thought he was the Muslim agent who refused to record other Muslims. Frustrated that the FBI was not putting his counterterrorism experience to use, he complained to his congressman, Republican Frank Wolf of Virginia, a national security hawk and strong supporter of the FBI. Representative Wolf asked Director Mueller to come to his office so Youssef could make his case directly. Unbeknownst to Youssef, Mueller had already approved his transfer to the International Terrorism Operations Section, but Youssef had yet to be notified. He never got that assignment, nor any other counterterrorism posting. The Justice Department's Office of Professional Responsibility later found reasonable grounds to believe the FBI retaliated against Youssef for confronting Mueller in Representative Wolf's office.[35]

Of course, the FBI has an extremely talented workforce, so it had plenty of experienced counterterrorism agents who could have filled the void left by the post-9/11 sidelining of Youssef, Rattigan, and Abdel-Hafiz. Agents from the New York Joint Terrorism Task Force, as just one example, had been chasing al Qaeda–linked terrorists for the better part of a decade. But the FBI officials that Director Mueller brought in to lead the FBI's new mission lacked operational counterterrorism experience. Several FBI executives, including Mueller, demonstrated scant knowledge of Middle Eastern terrorist groups during depositions in Youssef's discrimination lawsuit. Many of those running the FBI's counterterrorism operations couldn't explain the relationships between different Middle Eastern terrorist groups, or even the relevant differences between the Sunni and Shia sects of Islam.

Executive Assistant Director Gary Bald, who Mueller named deputy assistant director for counterterrorism operations in 2003, admitted having no previous operational experience in counterterrorism prior to his promotion. While he acknowledged that "subject matter expertise could be helpful," he said it was not a prerequisite: "It is certainly not what I look for in selecting someone for a position in the counterterrorism [program]."[36] FBI agents working counterterrorism cases felt this deficiency hampered their effectiveness. In a report examining the FBI's transformation three years after the attacks, the 9/11 Commission staff found that "many field agents felt the supervisory agents in the Counterterrorism Division at headquarters lacked the necessary experience in counterterrorism to guide their work."[37] FBI management's ignorance of Middle Eastern culture didn't just harm the bureau's counterterrorism efforts, it made it easier for xenophobia to spread like a cancer.

It wasn't just Muslim FBI employees who became targets of the newly empowered internal security regime. Old stereotypes about Chinese Americans posing a heightened risk for espionage persisted despite the embarrassment over the Wen Ho Lee case, driving biased counterintelligence investigations inside the FBI and out and blinding agents to real threats.

Half a world away from the turmoil in the Saudi Arabia legat office, Los Angeles FBI special agent Rita Chiang was a stellar performer on the Chinese counterintelligence squad. Born in Taiwan and fluent in Mandarin and Cantonese, Chiang was a unique resource for the FBI, which she joined in 1984. In May 2000, the FBI received information indicating that one of its longest-standing informants in Chinese counterintelligence matters, Chinese American businesswoman Katrina Leung, was a double agent.[38] The bureau determined that someone in its LA office had leaked classified FBI materials to Leung, which she had shared with Chinese intelligence agents.

As part of its investigation, the FBI subjected Chiang to three polygraphs in the summer of 2001.[39] The examiner claimed the first two tests were inconclusive, but the third "indicated deception." Chiang was never allowed to see the polygraph results or any other evidence suggesting she posed a security risk, but the FBI placed her on administrative leave on January 14, 2002. As the *Los Angeles Times* reported, her fellow agents seized her weapon and credentials and "escorted" her out of the building, ordering her to stay home while they investigated her as a spy.[40] She walked in the door that day as an agent entrusted with protecting our nation's deepest secrets, and left a suspected traitor. Her fear, bewilderment, and humiliation could only have been compounded by the realization that her managers placed more faith in a box of wires than the competence and integrity she had demonstrated over eighteen years of honorable service. In hindsight, Chiang believed the polygraph exam was merely a pretext the FBI used to justify focusing its mole hunt on her because of her ethnicity and national origin.

Fourteen months later, FBI agents arrested Chiang's supervisor, J.J. Smith, who had been regarded as the bureau's premier Chinese counterintelligence agent before his retirement in November 2000. Smith had served as Leung's primary handler since recruiting her in 1982, paying her over $1.7 million dollars. A 2006 inspector general report revealed that Smith, a married white male, had engaged in a sexual relationship with Leung for virtually the entire time she served as his informant. Smith admitted sharing counterintelligence information with Leung, who told the FBI she also rifled Smith's briefcase to purloin classified records when he wasn't paying attention.[41] The FBI learned of the affair a month *before* Chiang's suspension. After pleading guilty to making false statements to the FBI, Leung and Smith both were sentenced to probation, an extremely light punishment for the conduct originally alleged.

The FBI reinstated Chiang but limited her security clearance, perversely reasoning that the unjust treatment gave her reason to harbor a grudge against the government, increasing the risk she posed.[42] She sued the FBI for discrimination in 2005.

Director Mueller argued in a court statement that Chiang's suspension was justified by the failed polygraph and her acknowledgement of "personal ties and contacts with an individual who had been closely associated with a foreign government."[43] This vague assertion suggests no actual impropriety, however, and such guilt by association would implicate most agents who had worked foreign counterintelligence for twenty years. Finally, Mueller cited "other specific national security risk and vulnerability factors." He did not explain what these mysterious "vulnerability factors" were, but he denied they involved her sex, age, race, or national origin. Her former LA FBI supervisor submitted a statement plainly contradicting his director: "Chiang was discriminated against because of her ethnicity."[44]

BUILDING AN ARCHITECTURE OF DISTRUST

This heightened suspicion of "foreignness" in the 9/11 aftermath was predictable given the FBI's history and scientific research regarding threat responses.[45] But rather than establishing mechanisms to check these institutional and psychosocial biases, bureau leadership cemented them into official policy by implementing its Post-Adjudication Risk Management (PARM) program in October 2002.

Initially, PARM was intended to a resolve a short-term conflict between competing security needs.[46] As the FBI turned its focus toward foreign terrorist threats and expanded its collection of electronic communications, it needed linguists to translate the growing backlog of intercepted materials. The best linguists, of course, are native speakers who have spent considerable time where the foreign languages are spoken, as they can better interpret regional dialect, idiom, and cultural references essential to fully comprehending a conversation or text. But FBI management remained convinced that naturalized U.S. citizens or anyone with strong ties to foreign countries posed greater security risks.

All FBI employees and contractors, including linguists, must be U.S. citizens and pass rigorous background investigations to obtain required security clearances. The FBI also conducts routine reinvestigations every five years and retains the power to investigate changes in circumstances or allegations of misconduct. But FBI managers determined they needed more scrutiny for linguists born abroad or who were in close contact with family or friends residing in one of twenty-seven undisclosed countries. The PARM program authorized the Security Division, at its discretion, to place linguists under continuous evaluation, monitoring their travel, finances, computer use, and communications and subjecting them to more frequent counterintelligence interviews and polygraphs. Perhaps not surprisingly, *The Guardian* reported in 2017 that fifteen of the PARM countries are in the Middle East.[47]

This unremitting scrutiny took a toll. According to a 2004 inspector general audit of the FBI's language program, twelve of the 193 linguists subjected to PARM failed their polygraphs, a "deception indicated" rate almost three times the 2 percent failure rate across the FBI.[48] Assuming these polygraphs identified real threats ignores the evidence.

In October 2002, the same month the FBI initiated PARM, the National Research Council of the National Academies of Sciences, Engineering, and Medicine published a nineteen-month study regarding the validity and reliability of the polygraph, concluding that "its accuracy . . . is insufficient to justify reliance on its use in employee security screening in federal agencies."[49] The report warned that while polygraphs could theoretically deter security violations and elicit confessions, the high number of false positives would impair morale and discourage skilled individuals from seeking positions in national security agencies.[50] Misguided faith in the polygraph's effectiveness created security risks as well, because trained operatives of hostile intelligence agencies would likely know how to beat the machine. The FBI's own expert, Supervisory Special Agent Drew C. Richardson, told the Senate Judiciary Committee in 1997 that "there is virtually no probability of catching a spy with the use of polygraph screening techniques."[51] He complained the FBI censored his research because the results were critical of the bureau's practices. Finally, no less an authority than Aldrich Ames, the CIA officer who passed two counterintelligence polygraphs during the nine years he spied for the Soviet Union and Russia, mocked polygraphy as "junk science that just won't die."[52]

The PARM program contributed to a growing national security deficiency. Linguists lost to the PARM-related polygraph exams were difficult to replace, which left the FBI unable to meet its translation needs. A 2009 follow-up audit by the inspector general found the FBI took more than nineteen months to process and hire a language program applicant, with background investigations alone taking fourteen months on average. Only one of every eighteen linguists the FBI processed in 2008 was hired.[53] From 2005 to 2008, the number of bureau linguists fell, and the FBI could not meet its needs-based hiring goals. The backlog of unreviewed audio material in priority cases increased significantly. The inspector general documented 47,000 hours of unreviewed counterterrorism intercepts, and over 1.1 million hours of counterintelligence recordings.[54] In short, the FBI risked national security by implementing an unscientific security protocol that deprived it of critical resources when it needed them most.

In 2005, the FBI expanded PARM to include foreign-born agents and analysts in addition to linguists.[55] According to a 2015 report in the *New York Times*, almost 1,000 of the FBI's 36,000 employees were under PARM review by 2009, many of them of Middle Eastern and Asian descent.[56]

When a former supervisor asked Gamal Abdel-Hafiz to return to Dallas's international terrorism squad in 2005, he agreed. When I asked him why he would take the risk after all the bureau put him through, he shook his head and laughed. "This is my home, my kids' home," he said. "If I hesitate to make my home safe, I'm an idiot." His squad mates welcomed him back. In 2007, he transferred to the Dallas Field Intelligence Group, which required even higher security clearances. All was going well, until he received a subpoena to testify in Wilfred Rattigan's discrimination case in 2012. He said an FBI lawyer called to dissuade him from attending, but he took vacation to testify in support of his friend and colleague. Afterward, Abdel-Hafiz filed an EEO complaint against the FBI lawyer. Just before he was deposed in the EEO suit, the FBI's Security Division notified him in writing that it had placed him in PARM. The Security Division did not tell him why, except to reference his Egyptian heritage, but the timing was suspect as he had not been to Egypt for more than five years. He felt it was retaliation for supporting Rattigan's lawsuit and filing the EEO complaint. He scoffed at the senselessness so late in his career: "I worked for you for eighteen years, if you didn't know if I was a threat for all that time, shame on you!"

Being subject to PARM was no joke, though. Because the Supreme Court had determined that an agency's security clearance decisions are virtually unreviewable, as Chiang and Rattigan discovered, the Security Division wields enormous power over all FBI employees who need clearances to keep their jobs.[57] Under constant examination, those on the

PARM program can find themselves subjected to selective punishment for minor rules violations that are otherwise rarely enforced. Rather than restrain the Security Division to ensure its suspicions were based on objective fact rather than biases, the FBI gave it virtually unchecked autonomy.

"What's unfair is they tell you it is not an adverse action and it won't affect you," Abdel-Hafiz recalled, "but they won't tell you how long it will last, nothing." He knew an agent in New York who was on PARM for four or five years. Abdel-Hafiz still had well-connected supporters in FBI management, but when he complained about being in PARM, they told him no one could intervene in Security Division decisions. In August 2014, FBI director James Comey visited the Dallas office and held a question and answer session. Abdel-Hafiz told Comey the FBI was using PARM as an intimidation tactic against Muslim and Arab employees. Comey claimed unfamiliarity with the program and asked one of his staff members to hear Abdel-Hafiz's concerns. The director said he would follow up, but Abdel-Hafiz never received a response. On January 3, 2015, the *New York Times* published a story exposing PARM and its impact on Muslim and Arab FBI employees.[58] Abdel-Hafiz reached out to Comey's office and was told they were still formulating an answer. None came before Abdel-Hafiz retired in October 2015.

The PARM program creates harm beyond the innocent victims it unfairly subjects to intensified scrutiny. More damaging to the FBI as an institution is its official establishment of suspect classes of employees based entirely on ethnicity and national origin, with no evidence that such discrimination actually improves security. The xenophobic bigotry this program reinforced within the bureau was reflected in FBI training materials the ACLU of Northern California, Asian Law Caucus, and *San Francisco Bay Guardian* obtained through a Freedom of Information Act lawsuit in 2011, while I was working at the ACLU.

The FBI counterterrorism training materials we received, which spanned from 2003 to 2011, included inaccurate and bigoted assertions denigrating Arabs and Muslims. "Islam," one slide declared, "transforms [a] country's culture into 7th century Arabian ways."[59] Another document claimed Islam "alleviated some of the weaknesses that inflicted

[sic] the Arab mind in general," though it was "not able to change the cluster Arab mind thinking into a linear one."[60] The FBI's counterterrorism reading lists featured works published by overtly anti-Muslim advocacy groups and self-professed terrorism experts. We sent several of the documents to investigative reporter Spencer Ackerman, who produced an award-winning series in *Wired* magazine showing that anti-Muslim and anti-Arab training materials were prevalent not just in the FBI but in the Departments of Justice and Defense as well.[61]

Counterintelligence training products were just as bad. PowerPoint presentations purporting to educate agents about "the Chinese" were filled with gross orientalist stereotypes, with one slide warning: "Never attempt to shake hands with an Asian."[62] The marginalization of experienced agents like Chiang, Youssef, Rattigan, and Abdel-Hafiz had consequences beyond the loss of their knowledge and talents. The lack of diversity within the FBI allowed prejudice to fester. It would leave a new generation of FBI employees, like FBI intelligence analyst Said Barodi, with the feeling they had targets on their backs.

Barodi was born in Morocco and came to the United States as a teenager in January 2001. After 9/11, he earned his degree in global affairs with a concentration on the Middle East and North Africa from George Mason University. He obtained U.S. citizenship in 2006 and joined the FBI as an Arabic linguist in 2007.

He found the agents at FBI headquarters had little respect for linguists and tended to distrust those born abroad. Barodi was not subjected to PARM, as Morocco was not a country of concern, but the agents' wariness manifested in other ways. When he was assigned to monitor a wiretap, for instance, the case agents wouldn't brief him about the investigation, apparently concerned that he could leak information or intentionally mistranslate the recordings. This made translations more difficult because he didn't understand the context of the conversations. Likewise, agents often didn't allow linguists to minimize the translations. Rather than translating long discussions about some trivial matter, like a child's report card, linguists often simply mark that part of the recording "nonpertinent." Agents demanded that Barodi summarize these nonpertinent sections, apparently afraid he might intentionally fail to translate relevant conversations. Barodi said the agents seemed to think the Arabic linguists were "too close to the enemy" to be considered full members of the team.[63]

It wasn't just the agents who seemed not to trust Arabic linguists. After Barodi and other linguists successfully obtained Top Secret/Sensitive Compartmented Information (TS/SCI) clearances, the Security Division would only grant them Top Secret access. Withholding access to the more highly classified SCI materials limited their opportunities for advancement. Barodi finally decided to force the issue by volunteering for a potentially life-threatening assignment abroad that required the SCI clearance. Even after the FBI selected him and purchased plane tickets, the Security Division failed to provide him SCI credentials. Barodi had to physically go to the Security Division office to demand his proper badge days before he flew overseas.

After a few years, Barodi felt he had more to contribute. He requested training as an intelligence analyst, which required a course at the FBI Academy. It was here that Barodi first saw openly Islamophobic training materials and experienced overt anti-Muslim bias. Petty slights and snarky comments directed toward Middle Eastern analysts were commonplace, and some fellow trainees refused to interact with them. He knew of Arab and Muslim analysts who were pulled out of classrooms in front of their colleagues to address unspoken security concerns, and later, taken off cases because of questions about their loyalty. Barodi filed an EEO complaint regarding the Islamophobic training, but the EEO office dismissed it because he was not in the classroom when the material was presented. After the first *Wired* story was published, EEO recontacted Barodi with renewed interest. Ackerman continued reporting, exposing even more problematic FBI training materials received from other sources. In one, an unnamed agent described draft training materials which warned agents that "you should not trust a Muslim coworker."[64] An FBI supervisor who witnessed this 2011 presentation confirmed that they were told Muslim FBI agents should not be allowed to interview Muslim subjects, as they had a religious obligation to protect Islam. The supervisor said he interrupted the presentation to refute this statement.

After initially downplaying the scandal by blaming one bad instructor, Director Mueller finally ordered a comprehensive review of FBI training materials.[65] According to a March 2012 letter from Senator Dick Durbin, the FBI identified and removed 876 pages and 392 presentations containing offensive or erroneous information and established new training guidelines. Senator Durbin complained that these guidelines lacked the necessary detail to ensure this problem would not recur.[66] He was right.

The *Wall Street Journal* reported that from 2012 to 2016, the FBI paid Sebastian Gorka and his company at least $103,000 to train Joint Terrorism Task Force personnel. Gorka was known for his bombastic anti-Muslim lectures and dubious academic credentials.[67] The FBI reportedly fired him in 2016 after receiving complaints about an August 2016 presentation.[68] Barodi witnessed one of Gorka's presentations in mid-2016, which he called "very Islamophobic." Gorka later became a lightning rod for criticism after President Donald Trump hired him as a White House aide. In addition to his history of anti-Muslim statements, *The Forward* reported his association with a Hungarian nationalist organization that affiliated with the Nazis during World War II and an anti-Semitic militia later banned in Hungary.[69] The FBI never explained how Gorka was hired under its reformed training guidelines, much less how it took four years to fire him.

Barodi moved on to his first assignment at the Washington, D.C., field office, where his supervisors gave him excellent performance ratings. He also won a monetary award and letter of commendation from Director James Comey. Yet the petty humiliations and harassment escalated.

In January 2016, Barodi traveled to see family in Morocco, which included a stop in Paris. He filed a detailed itinerary with the FBI as required, which the bureau approved in August 2015. After visiting Morocco, he returned to Paris to catch his flight home. While waiting at the airport gate, a man dressed in plain clothes and speaking American-accented English approached him with questions about his travels. Barodi was trained to be cautious about speaking with strangers while traveling, and he thought this could be a foreign agent attempting to gather information about bureau business. Barodi ignored the man and walked away. He approached Barodi again, this time more insistently. Within earshot of other passengers, he said he knew Barodi was with the FBI and had been in Morocco.

Barodi found this breach of security protocols disturbing and confusing. The man said he was with the U.S. Department of Homeland Security, but when Barodi asked to see his badge he flashed an airport ID rather than DHS credentials. Barodi accused him of racial profiling and refused to discuss his travels. When the man walked away, Barodi snapped photographs with his cell phone to give to FBI security. As the plane began to board, Barodi approached the man and asked for his name and badge number so he could make a complaint. The man pressed his hand against Barodi's chest but ultimately disengaged and allowed Barodi to board the plane.[70]

Customs officials detained Barodi upon arrival at Dulles International Airport in Virginia. They berated him for photographing the man in Paris, though they wouldn't confirm he was a DHS employee. Like the man in Paris, these officials asked probing questions about Barodi's travels, which he declined to answer because he felt they were motivated by ethnic and religious bias. Barodi tried calling his FBI supervisor but it was a weekend, so all he could do was leave messages. Hours passed in stalemate with the Customs officials. Finally, agents from the FBI's Joint Terrorism Task Force arrived, but rather than defend their colleague in this interagency spat, they treated Barodi as a terrorism suspect. They referenced recent ISIS attacks in Paris and the mass shooting in San Bernardino, prompting a perplexed Barodi to protest that they knew he was not a terrorist. They demanded he delete the photographs of the man who accosted him, and when he did, the Customs officials let him go.

The following Monday, Barodi's supervisor berated him for "embarrassing the bureau." He said OPR was initiating a disciplinary investigation against Barodi for unprofessional conduct. Barodi countered that he was the victim of racial profiling and had a constitutional right to refuse to answer the Customs officials' improper questions, to no avail. A month later, with the investigation ongoing, FBI security officers stripped Barodi of his SCI clearance and transferred him to a squad that handled less-sensitive cases.

Barodi knew other foreign-born FBI employees were suffering similar abuse. In May 2016, a group of minority employees met with Director Comey to discuss discrimination inside the bureau.[71] Barodi was one of nine Arab and Muslim employees who provided written "struggle stories" detailing their mistreatment, which were handed to Comey at the meeting. Comey promised to look into the allegations. Within three months, two of the nine received notice the FBI intended to fire them. Barodi was one of them.

Barodi sent Director Comey an email referencing the May meeting and reiterating his contention that anti-Muslim bias motivated the OPR investigation against him. Barodi wrote that Arab and Muslim agents and analysts were loyal Americans eager to aid the FBI's mission, but they were also willing to fight for a discrimination-free workplace. Comey's reply seemed to justify profiling FBI employees based on their national origin for security purposes. According to *The Guardian*, a portion of Comey's email read: "Let's imagine we have an employee whose family lives in Russia and who travels to Russia to visit them every year. Do you agree it makes sense to have some additional layer of scrutiny in that situation? I suspect you do."[72]

While a relatively small number of naturalized U.S. citizens working in the intelligence agencies have betrayed their adopted country over the years, there are many more native-born Americans, like Robert Hanssen and J.J. Smith, who have done the same.[73] Perhaps Hanssen and Smith escaped scrutiny through decades of misbehavior because the FBI blinded itself with biased and inaccurate threat profiles. There is simply no evidence that singling out foreign-born employees for more stringent scrutiny is an effective method of identifying spies.

The investigation of the Paris airport incident concluded that Barodi acted unprofessionally and lacked "candor" in his interviews with Customs officials, a bureau euphemism for lying.[74] The FBI fired Barodi in January 2016. He fought the dismissal through the FBI's internal appeals process. Remarkably, six months later he won. The appeals board determined his infractions did not merit termination. But there was a catch.

The Security Division had to approve his reinstatement, and they appeared to be in no hurry.

Barodi's case is rare only in that he was willing to talk publicly about the FBI's mistreatment. For several other agents and analysts I've met, the fear that the bureau might revoke their security clearances, the lynchpins to professional viability in their chosen field, inhibits them from making public complaints or filing lawsuits. The FBI refused to reinstate Barodi's clearance and terminated his employment on February 22, 2018.

4

TARGETING THEIR OWN

Unwarranted national security concerns over the loyalty of foreign-born employees don't explain all the irregularities with the FBI's workforce management. Native-born Americans who fall afoul of the bureau's cultural norms can find themselves subjected to Kafkaesque persecutions, too.

The Justice Department inspector general's 2009 audit of the FBI's internal disciplinary process concluded that there was a double standard that provided senior managers with more lenient treatment than the rank and file. But the surveys it conducted show that FBI employees' mistrust of the system wasn't just because it is rigged to protect management. They complained that punishments were inconsistent across the board.[1]

That this capricious treatment persisted after the inspector general first documented the problem in 2002 suggests that FBI managers prefer to maintain a disciplinary system that provides flexibility when determining outcomes. Managers can protect favored employees while weeding out those who don't fit the "good ol' boy" culture. To maintain such a system, bureau managers must employ subjective methods of examination that appear objective but can be manipulated to achieve the desired result.

CONTRADICTIONS AND COUNTERMEASURES

The security screening polygraph is one of the most useful tools for masking discrimination under a cloak of scientific objectivity, just as it has been for the PARM program. After the Robert Hanssen spying scandal, the FBI ramped up its use of polygraph examinations despite their known unreliability. The number of positions requiring periodic security screening polygraphs went from 550 in March 2001 to 18,384 in February 2005, with plans to eventually expand coverage to all FBI employees, task force members, and contractors.[2]

The FBI claimed its actions were in response to the Webster Commission's 2002 examination of how the FBI failed to detect Robert Hanssen's betrayal for over two decades. Chaired by former FBI and CIA director William Webster and charged with analyzing FBI security programs and suggesting improvements, the study recommended that the bureau develop a focused counterespionage polygraph program for bureau employees with the highest Sensitive Compartmentalized Information (SCI) clearances.[3] But, as the inspector general later pointed out, the Webster Commission warned against a broader polygraph program within the FBI, citing the CIA's experience after the Ames case. Hundreds of false positive tests generated by a more aggressive CIA polygraph screening program stalled the careers of trustworthy officers for years and devastated agency morale.[4] The FBI's only apparent nod to the overwhelming evidence against the reliability of polygraph screenings was a policy mandate that no employee could be terminated based "solely" on a bad polygraph result. The policy requires retests and a security investigation, overseen by a senior review panel, to assist in any determinations regarding the employee's assignment and security clearance retention. But this policy is irregularly implemented in practice.

In March 2018, the inspector general reported that bureau employees who failed polygraphs often retained access to highly classified information, sometimes for years, before their cases were fully investigated and adjudicated.[5] Though the inspector general criticized this failure to limit access to sensitive information, this result is entirely proper given the documented unreliability of polygraph screenings in identifying security threats.

The inspector general properly criticized the FBI for inconsistency in how these cases were handled, however, and for failing to properly document polygraph case information. The arbitrary application of the rules and the lack of due process in security determinations leave FBI employees at the mercy of a "priesthood" of polygraph examiners and security officers.

An FBI analyst I'll call Logan (a pseudonym the *Huffington Post* gave him in a 2016 exposé) claims the bureau found a way to make polygraph determinations even more unfair and arbitrary.[6] Logan is a third-generation Chinese American whose father enjoyed a successful thirty-year career in the intelligence community (he wouldn't tell me what agency). Logan grew up in Washington, D.C., but spent summers shuttling between Newark, New Jersey, and New York City working in his grandparents' laundry businesses. Logan's childhood dream was to become an FBI agent, but it was derailed by a visit to the eye doctor when he was just a teenager. The doctor diagnosed him with aniridia, a congenital eye defect that causes increased sensitivity to light. He could see fine, but the condition made it unlikely he'd ever be able to complete the FBI's outdoor firearms qualifications. So Logan went into finance instead, pursuing a career as an investment banker.[7]

Robert Hanssen's betrayal of the FBI really ticked Logan off, though. He learned the FBI was ramping up an intelligence analyst program and figured his banking experience would be valuable for analyzing whether agents' financial conditions portended potential security risks. He could use his training to help the agency he always wanted to work for. He applied in 2002, passed the preemployment polygraph, received training at Quantico, and won assignment as a financial analyst in the counterintelligence division. His dream came true, just not in the way he had expected. A few years later, he took an assignment as an intelligence analyst in the Criminal Investigations Division, hoping to develop work experience in different bureau programs. He was very successful and was promoted quickly, rising in just a few years to be the unit chief in an analyst support program.

Logan didn't experience anything he interpreted as discrimination during his time at the bureau. The only interaction that seemed inappropriate was when a bureau security officer warned him to be careful in choosing friends, then asked whether he dated Asian women. Logan found the question offensive but accepted it as a poorly phrased warning about dating foreign nationals. So Logan was taken aback when a fellow Chinese American analyst confided that he avoided applying for national security assignments because he feared the FBI would suspect him of spying. It was more a casual remark between friends than a complaint, as the analyst seemed happy working criminal matters. But Logan was disturbed that a capable employee would avoid pursuing an assignment out of fear of discrimination. Unlike Logan, the analyst was a native Chinese speaker, so it seemed like wasted talent for the bureau as well. The analyst told Logan no one had ever said or done anything overtly racist toward him, but he sometimes sensed his co-workers mocking his accent behind his back.[8]

When Logan accepted a joint-duty position with another government agency, this analyst warned him that the bureau might become suspicious of an Asian American seeking broader experience within the intelligence community. As a third-generation American who had no close family overseas, had never been to China, and didn't speak Mandarin or Cantonese, Logan didn't think his friend's self-imposed boundaries could possibly apply to him. Logan told me some of his fellow Asians might consider him "whitewashed," but that didn't bother him. "Yeah, I do have those tendencies," he said, "because I grew up in the United States and that's what I am."

Logan took his first on-duty personnel security polygraph in 2008, six years into his career. During the initial exam the polygrapher told him he seemed to be panting, so they'd have to run the test again. The second run was fine and the polygrapher said he passed, but just barely. It was an odd remark, but the polygrapher seemed to be trying to help. Logan said the polygrapher told him, "If you ever have to do this kind of thing again just make sure you don't let anything affect how you breathe."

Logan's next five-year reinvestigation was in 2013, and it required another polygraph. After this one, the polygrapher told him he failed, and that it was the worst result he'd seen from an active employee. He told Logan to go back to work and wait for a phone call. But no call came. Months passed without any interruption in his work. Logan figured he was on some kind of supersecret probation. The Security Division finally called a year later and scheduled an August 2014 retest. The delay had his mind swimming. If the FBI considered him a security risk because he failed the test, why did they give him access to classified information for over a year? What could they be looking at in his background? His emails? What restaurants he went to? The concern that a second failed test might mean losing his job weighed on him. By the time he went to take the polygraph, he was in a near panic.

He arrived on time but was left in an empty waiting room for forty minutes. This polygrapher seemed unfriendly, skipping the chatty banter that helped lighten the mood before previous exams. He told Logan he knew he failed his previous test, which Logan worried might cause him to prejudge the results. After the background interview, the polygrapher remarked that Logan smiled when discussing his father's previous U.S. government service, which Logan acknowledged made him proud. Logan said the polygrapher then said that showing that pride might make "some people" think he was "part of a father-son spy ring." Logan froze. "I think he was trying to get a reaction out of me," he told me. He wanted to jump out of his chair but he knew he couldn't threaten or assault an FBI agent, either. Finally, he said, "I take great offense to that." The polygrapher questioned how he could be so calm in the face of such an accusation. Logan said he was not going to dignify the remark with a response.

Logan said it seemed like a game. After the first test run, the examiner said he couldn't tell if he passed because Logan was using countermeasures, purposely breathing in a way to prevent an accurate reading. Logan denied it, saying he was just nervous and feeling short of breath. The polygrapher told him no innocent person would be short of breath. He demanded Logan write a statement explaining his unusually labored breathing. Logan wrote a few sentences about what he was experiencing physically and explained he was just trying to catch his breath. He said the agent told him the statement was too technical, crumpled it up, and threw it across the room. Logan was shocked by the agent's seeming disregard for the bureau's evidence retention policies.

Logan said the polygraph examiner demanded that he write a simpler statement and suggested specific language acknowledging that his actions were intended to achieve a favorable outcome. Of course, Logan wanted to pass the test, and since he'd been told his breathing was the problem after an earlier exam, he was consciously trying to control it. Logan felt the polygrapher's behavior was just theatrics at this point, but he wanted to show he was being cooperative with the process. He wrote another statement following the polygrapher's directions, saying he deliberately tried to calm himself during the most stressful parts of the exam in the hopes of achieving a "more positive outcome."[9] The statement made clear that he was only trying to demonstrate to the polygrapher's satisfaction that he had committed no security violations. The polygrapher accepted this statement and told Logan to go back to work, where he continued to have access to a wealth of government secrets. Clearly, the FBI didn't think he was a spy, Logan reasoned. As weeks turned into months, Logan thought it might be another year before he was called in to take another retest. Perhaps he'd have to endure this humiliating process every year for the rest of his career, he thought.

But three months after the test, right before Christmas 2014, Logan's assistant director called him into his office. He was ashen-faced and expressed shock and dismay that an employee as diligent as Logan could have trouble with the polygraph. He told Logan the FBI had suspended him. Three months later, the FBI fired him.

The FBI's termination notice accused Logan of using countermeasures to thwart the polygraph and claimed his written statement acknowledging that he was trying to calm his breathing amounted to a confession. Deeming Logan's statement a confession was essential to the FBI's termination decision, because according to research cited by the National Research Council, there's no evidence to support the claim that polygraph examiners can accurately identify countermeasures.[10] Dr. Drew Richardson, by then a former FBI supervisor, wrote a letter supporting Logan's appeal, dismissing the notion that a polygraph examiner could detect a respiratory countermeasure.[11] Richardson wrote that "normal" breathing varied by person and situation and that "anxiety connected with the . . . 'fear of consequences' which is independent of any deception or countermeasure application could readily impact respiration."

Logan believes that the countermeasures accusation is simply a tactic the FBI uses to justify terminating an employee based solely on polygraph results, in contradiction of policy. Almost a year and a half passed between his initial polygraph in 2013 and his termination in 2015. The FBI found no evidence to indicate he posed any kind of security threat. He now believes that ethnic bias was a leading factor in the way he was treated during, and in response to, his 2013 and 2014 polygraph exams.

The National Research Council report discussed the few existing studies of racial bias in polygraphs but found they do not meet academic standards of scientific reliability. It emphasized, however, that there is research that suggests stigmatizing qualities (including race, religion, age, gender, and disability) and examiner expectancies can influence polygraph results.[12] It found that . . . "truthful members of socially stigmatized groups and truthful examinees who are believed to be guilty or believed to have a high likelihood of being guilty may show emotional and physiological responses in polygraph test situations that mimic the responses that are expected of deceptive individuals."[13]

Of course, without available data for researchers to study, no one can conclusively say whether polygraph results are influenced by racial, ethnic, or religious bias. The FBI's polygraph data could inform the debate about racial, ethnic, and gender diversity in the bureau. The FBI conducted over eleven thousand polygraphs in 2005, the last year it published such figures, which was before it broadened its policy to test all employees, task force members, and contractors. Roughly a quarter of the many thousands of bureau applicants fail the polygraph each year and are denied employment. An additional 2 percent of onboard employees fail the test and have their careers sidelined, or ended.[14] There's little doubt the FBI knows whether there are racial, ethic, or gender disparities in its polygraph data, but it has not made that data public so the public can evaluate its impact.

RETALIATORY FITNESS-FOR-DUTY EXAMS

Jane Turner was a remarkably accomplished FBI agent. She was the first female agent to qualify for the Seattle Division's SWAT team, and she was selected to be a behavioral profiler, a highly sought position later made famous by the film *The Silence of the Lambs*. In her varied career she worked drug and organized crime cases in New York City, the FBI's largest and most intimidating office, and then became the first female senior agent at a two-person office in Minot, North Dakota, where she investigated crimes on Indian reservations.

Working in "Indian Country," as the FBI calls it, is one of the most difficult assignments in the bureau. The FBI has jurisdiction over violent crimes occurring on Indian reservations, including homicides, sexual assaults, and crimes against children, along with drugs, gangs, and public corruption. Agents assigned to these remote outposts often work alone, or team with the Bureau of Indian Affairs and tribal law enforcement agencies. They can be hundreds of miles from the nearest FBI office or federal prosecutor, and the crimes they investigate can be horrific. Native Americans are victims of violent crimes at rates doubling that of any other ethnic group, most often at the hands of nontribal members, and are the demographic most likely to be killed by police officers.[15] Child abuse cases are, of course, often the most tragic. Turner once missed her daughter's birthday party because she had to investigate two infanticides.[16]

The Justice Department and the FBI have often been accused of neglecting their responsibilities to address crimes against Native Americans.[17] But Turner volunteered for this work and was good at it, despite the hardships. A former federal prosecutor called her "the best agent I worked with at the time."[18] She became a nationally recognized expert in crimes against children and consistently received high ratings in performance evaluations. That was, until she filed a discrimination complaint with the Equal Employment Opportunity Office (EEO) alleging a male supervisor, whom she had competed against for the position, began taking retaliatory measures against her by not crediting her statistical accomplishments and reducing her mileage reimbursements, creating a hostile work environment.[19]

After EEO investigators interviewed the supervisor, for the first time in her career Turner began receiving unsatisfactory performance ratings. Worse, she said bureau officials attempted to sabotage her child sexual abuse cases, undermine her relationships with local law enforcement, and undercut her accomplishments so they could justify taking disciplinary action against her. They transferred her to Minneapolis, where her supervisors put her under surveillance, questioned colleagues about her sex life, fabricated allegations against her, and ordered her to take a "fit-for-duty" exam by bureau-contracted psychologists.[20]

This last form of reprisal is particularly pernicious. Painting victims of retaliation as mentally ill makes it easier to dismiss their complaints about bureau managers' outrageous behavior as the rantings of a troubled employee. Who would believe the FBI would sabotage its own criminal investigations to punish an employee who just wanted to be recognized for the exceptional work she was doing? In my own case, who would believe FBI officials would crudely falsify bureau records with correction fluid to avoid responsibility for mishandling an investigation?

The bureau sent Turner to FBI-contracted psychologists who subjected her to what she called the most humiliating experience of her career. Though they documented that her psychological tests were within normal limits, she said they found her unfit for duty based on unsubstantiated accusations made by the same FBI managers she had charged with retaliation. Turner said she urged the psychologists to review FBI records that disproved these misrepresentations, but they refused, questioning why bureau managers would lie. The bureau placed Turner on administrative leave based on their psychologists' report, stripping her of her badge and gun. Turner then hired two independent psychologists, who administered a broad battery of tests, reviewed the bureau contractor's report, and documented its deficiencies. They both found her fit for duty and urged her reinstatement. When a second bureau-contracted examination confirmed her fitness to return to work, the FBI was forced to relent.[21]

Turner weathered the abuse and kept working until she was assigned what seemed like a layup of a case. An employee of a federal contractor working at the landfill where FBI agents were sifting for evidence through rubble from the World Trade Center allegedly stole a fire truck door that was damaged in the attack. Turner's investigation found that other company employees also purloined artifacts, and the U.S. attorney planned indictments for the first anniversary of 9/11. The contractor's attorney argued that FBI agents took souvenirs from the site as well, but Turner dismissed this as a clever defense tactic. Weeks later, however, Turner learned that a banged-up Tiffany globe that she noticed on an FBI secretary's desk had come from the World Trade Center. She felt she had no choice but to seize it as evidence and bring it to the Justice Department inspector general.

The inspector general's subsequent investigation found many FBI agents took items as macabre mementos from the World Trade Center, as well as from crime scenes like the Oklahoma City federal building, the Unabomber's cabin in Montana, and the U.S. embassy bomb sites in East Africa.[22] The U.S. attorney declined to prosecute the government contractor in Turner's case, and no FBI employees were charged with the thefts. Turner was told that her performance rating would be lowered to "does not meet expectations," which she knew would likely result in her termination. She retired to avoid being fired, then sued the FBI for retaliating against her for making protected disclosures. Turner felt vindicated when the Tiffany globe was finally returned to the parents of its owner, Gregory Milanowycz, who was killed in the attack.

On February 5, 2007, a jury awarded Turner $565,000 in damages for the FBI's retaliation against her for making the employment discrimination complaint, later reduced to the statutory maximum of $360,000.[23]

The internal process to adjudicate her whistleblower retaliation claims would take several more years to resolve. On January 13, 2013, Deputy Attorney General James M. Cole confirmed the FBI retaliated against Turner for whistleblowing but determined it had not created a hostile working environment and had not constructively discharged her. She would get no back pay.[24] Turner's case, in which Equal Employment Opportunity laws provided access to the federal courts, makes clear that the FBI's interest in keeping bureau whistleblowers locked in an internal adjudication process has nothing to do with national security. Instead, the FBI fights to keep bureau whistleblowers out of court because they lose when juries hear all the evidence.

Turner's experience with gender discrimination at the bureau was, unfortunately, not unusual.

LOSS OF EFFECTIVENESS

It is hard to believe that FBI managers, who lead a highly competent workforce with a critical mission, would intentionally use scarce government resources to harm the careers of effective employees for no good reason, much less that bureau leadership would allow them to get away with it. It is easy to give the benefit of the doubt to those we entrust with so much authority over our security.

This is why an inspector general report issued in February 2016 is a must-read for any skeptic who doubts that senior FBI officials would marshal significant resources to falsify records to damage the careers of agents who fall out of favor with management. It is entitled "Investigation of Alleged Retaliation Against FBI Employee Julia A. Cowley," and you won't find it on the inspector general's website. It was made public instead when it was made part of the official court record in a discrimination lawsuit Cowley and three colleagues brought against the FBI in 2014.[25]

Cowley came to the FBI in 1999 with a master's degree in forensic science from George Washington University and years of experience as a special agent and forensic scientist with the Tennessee Bureau of Investigation.[26] She worked white collar crime, public corruption, and civil rights cases in the Boston Division until January 2010, when she received a promotion to the Behavioral Analysis Unit (BAU) at the National Center for the Analysis of Violent Crime (NCAVC). This unit houses the FBI's criminal profilers, who provide expert assistance to law enforcement officers throughout the country and around the world, analyzing crime scenes, profiling suspects, offering advice on interview tactics, and even supporting undercover operations like my own. The BAU is easily one of the most highly sought assignments in the FBI, and only agents that have particularized education and years of experience conducting complex investigations get these jobs. The BAU does more than just profile serial killers. It has separate units for crimes against children, terrorism, and cybercrimes, among others, since each require different specialized training and experience. Cowley and her colleagues were assigned to the Crimes Against Adults Unit, which then covered crimes such as murders, sexual assaults, and kidnappings, as well as organized crime, white collar crime, and civil rights investigations. The fact that they won these assignments is a pretty good indication they were elite investigators and highly regarded within the FBI.

In 2012, Cowley and two female colleagues reported their unit chief for violating internal BAU policies by insufficiently staffing case consultations and peer reviews, lying in an internal investigation to harm another female agent's career, and discriminating against them in assignments because they were women. After raising their concerns with the unit chief, NCAVC management ordered a reorganization of the BAU. Cowley and her two female colleagues were transferred, leaving the unit responsible for investigating sexual assaults against adults without a female profiler. Cowley and one of the other female agents were assigned to the BAU unit responsible for cybercrimes, an area requiring very specific training and technical knowledge that neither possessed. This transfer diminished the value the BAU could provide to law enforcement agencies seeking assistance and would have required costly and time-consuming retraining for the affected agents to become certified in these fields. Cowley felt the transfer was intended to reduce the women's effectiveness so that further actions could later be brought against them. The inspector general would determine that six of the seven agents negatively affected by the reorganization were women.[27]

A male agent in the BAU reported this retaliation against the three women to the inspector general right before the transfers were announced. Afterward, Cowley also complained to the IG, which referred the matter for investigation by the FBI's Inspection Division. The Inspection Division reviewed the complaints and determined they did not merit investigation, as there was no evidence of misconduct. Cowley then went around the chain of command by sending emails detailing the misconduct to the assistant directors of the Inspection Division and Office of Professional Responsibility, and to Deputy Director Sean Joyce, the second-highest official in the FBI. Deputy Director Joyce instructed the associate deputy director to meet with Cowley and her colleagues and determine a course of action.

The inspector general documented a flurry of emails among the assistant directors and section chiefs complaining about Cowley jumping the chain of command. The emails dismissed the complaints as "false and malicious" and developed a set of talking points arguing that Cowley and her three colleagues (including the male profiler who supported the three women's discrimination claims) were a "disruptive force" who created the toxic environment within NCAVC. Cowley's section chief emailed an acting assistant director and an acting deputy assistant director questioning Cowley's mental and emotional health, and suggested a fitness-for-duty exam.

Deputy Director Joyce ordered the FBI's Inspection Division to conduct a special inspection of the NCAVC. It conducted the inspection over two weeks in April 2013, selectively interviewing sixty-one current and former NCAVC managers and staff but refusing requests from three others who would corroborate Cowley's complaints. The inspectors concluded Cowley and her three colleagues were to blame for the low morale on the unit and recommended "loss of effectiveness" determinations against all four of them. A loss of effectiveness determination compels a supervisor's involuntary transfer to another unit, but because it isn't technically considered a demotion under FBI policy, no due process protections are provided. The absence of due process requirements distinguished loss of effectiveness determinations from regular misconduct adjudications and make them a favored tactic for retaliating against supervisors like Cowley and her colleagues who raise complaints about their superiors.[28]

Luckily for Cowley, a new Justice Department inspector general, Michael Horowitz, was sworn in in April 2012. Horowitz vowed to put a greater emphasis on protecting FBI whistleblowers and established an official FBI whistleblower ombudsman to emphasize his commitment. Horowitz's office took a hard look at the way the FBI treated Cowley's complaint, and its findings are disturbing.

The inspector general found "serious procedural and factual defects in the handling of the NCAVC special inspection and its aftermath that vitiated what appeared on its face to be compelling support for the [loss of effectiveness] determinations."[29] The FBI's inspection relied on "little more than rumors" in building a case against Cowley and never gave her an opportunity to challenge the allegations or explain her actions. The inspector general report detailed one finding from the FBI's inspection that accused Cowley and her colleagues of skipping out on a NCAVC conference in Long Island in order to go sightseeing in New York City. The inspector general found that contemporaneous documents and witnesses proved the profilers did attend the conference, or were in consultations with local law enforcement agencies on specific cases, as approved by their management. The inspector general discovered contemporaneous emails and sign-in sheets confirming these facts, which the FBI inspectors apparently didn't seek. A Facebook photo of two of the supervisors touring NBC Studios, which the FBI inspectors had used as evidence they skipped the conference, was determined to have been taken the day after the conference.

Another example involved a finding that a Richmond Division assistant special agent in charge pled with the BAU unit chief to exclude Cowley from a particular case because she was difficult to work with. The inspector general contacted the Richmond official and found he had not made any negative comments regarding Cowley, and instead had "positive impressions" of her.

The FBI inspectors had also determined Cowley "improperly accessed" a BAU database to query other profilers' work and said Cowley admitted she did this to document cases being assigned to profilers who did not have the proper certifications. In fact, the inspector general found the FBI inspectors had never asked Cowley about the database, and no policy restricted BAU staff from accessing it anyway, so long as it was for official purposes. In short, the inspector general found that the "facts" the FBI inspectors relied on to find Cowley and her colleagues had lost effectiveness were "in dispute, incomplete, and in some cases, inaccurate."[30] Cowley and her colleagues settled their lawsuit against the FBI after the inspector general's report confirmed that the loss of effectiveness determinations were improper retaliation for their complaints.

In the end, however, the mismanagement and discrimination alleged in Cowley's original complaint was never properly investigated. None of the senior FBI officials responsible for conducting the bogus inspection and fabricating evidence to support the retaliatory loss of effectiveness determinations against Cowley and her colleagues were ever disciplined.

After Senator Chuck Grassley made repeated inquiries about the use of this tactic to retaliate against whistleblowers like Cowley, the FBI announced in March 2015 that it would provide supervisors subjected to loss of effectiveness determinations notice and an opportunity to respond.[31] But the larger question about the lack of integrity in internal investigations has not been adequately addressed. If bureau leaders can't be trusted to conduct honest investigations against their own agents, especially effective ones like Julia Cowley and Jane Turner, how can members of the public who fall under FBI suspicion due to racial, religious, nationalistic, or ideological bias ever protect themselves?

The FBI's embrace of its new mission to identify and interdict threats before they materialize meant the FBI would broaden its dragnets to capture not just individuals it suspected of wrongdoing but people it suspected of associating with those individuals, or sharing their beliefs. The profiles the FBI developed for these new suspect classes looked an awful lot like those J. Edgar Hoover's bureau targeted years ago: immigrants, minorities, and political dissidents. Normalizing discrimination and the silencing of dissent allowed biases to harden into policy. Part Two reveals how the FBI developed the architecture necessary to make its modern suppression of these suspect communities appear necessary and justified.

Part Two

DISRUPTING DIVERSITY AND DISSENT

5

THE RADICALIZATION THEORY

In January 2006, Julia Shearson, a Harvard University–educated civil rights advocate, took her four-year-old daughter on a weekend road trip to Canada. A single mother born and raised in Ohio, Shearson found driving vacations were a relaxing and economical way to spend quality time with her daughter away from the normal distractions of daily life. Returning home through the Peace Bridge border checkpoint in Buffalo, New York, her tranquil holiday met a bitter end. She handed her papers over to a U.S. Customs and Border Protection (CBP) officer and the words "ARMED AND DANGEROUS" popped up on the monitor.[1] Her government, she learned, considered her a terrorist.

CBP officers handcuffed Shearson in front of her terrified little girl and perp-walked her past a long line of gawking travelers. The officers refused her request for counsel and began to interrogate her and, remarkably, her daughter. Shearson asked why she was being detained, but the CBP officials didn't seem to know, saying simply, "They haven't told us much." They appeared to be waiting for instruction from some outside authority. As time passed, the CBP officials' attitudes softened. "One guy seemed so distressed by the whole charade," Shearson later told me, "that he said under his breath, 'This is why I hate this job.'"[2] Two and a half hours later they released her with no explanation. Documents would later show the CBP officials contacted the FBI's Joint Terrorism Task Force, but the JTTF case agent declined the opportunity to interview Shearson and told them to just let her go.[3]

As a convert to Islam, Shearson was acutely aware of the antipathy many American Muslims faced after al Qaeda's horrific 9/11 attacks. As executive director of the Cleveland chapter of the Council on American-Islamic Relations (CAIR), she saw firsthand how the government's sometimes misguided counterterrorism tactics tore ordinary families apart and left entire communities bewildered and afraid. But she couldn't fathom how anyone could consider her a threat.[4]

Not one to take her treatment that night at the border lightly, Shearson embarked on a quixotic legal struggle—taking on the most powerful and secretive national security establishment that has ever existed in this country—to get an explanation for what had happened to her. Documents Shearson unearthed through a precedent-setting six-year Freedom of Information Act (FOIA) lawsuit show she was number PPN TSC 384610, T94 in the FBI's Terrorist Screening Center database.[5] Government records also revealed her inclusion in the FBI's Violent Gang and Terrorist Organization File, the Treasury Department's Treasury Enforcement and Communications System, and the National Counterterrorism Center's Terrorist Identities Datamart Environment (TIDE).[6]

Shearson still doesn't know why she was placed on FBI terrorist watch lists, much less how she could be considered "armed and dangerous." She had never been arrested or owned a gun. In fact, she's a pacifist who actively participates in interfaith education and outreach. It would be difficult for anyone to paint her as an extremist, much less an armed and dangerous terrorist. She was never barred from interacting with federal, state, and local law enforcement officials in her work, which makes it fairly clear the government never really thought she posed a threat.

Shearson could have been a victim of false reporting by someone intending to do her harm, or by someone well-intentioned but simply mistaken. In a heightened threat environment where the government urges a frightened public to report all "suspicious" activity, those charged with preventing harm develop a natural tendency to err on the side of caution. Determining that someone isn't a terrorist today is hard enough. Proving that they will not become one in the future is all but impossible. The watch-listing standards nominally require "reasonable suspicion" that someone is "associated" with terrorism or a terrorist group, a low and subjective threshold. But FBI documents obtained by the ACLU show these standards are inconsistently applied and riddled with caveats and exceptions.[7] Subjects of FBI preliminary investigations are automatically watch-listed, for example, even though a preliminary investigation can be opened based on "information or an allegation," a significantly lower standard than reasonable suspicion. The FBI's rules also allow the watch-listing of people who are not under investigation at all.

It may have been a mistake. Justice Department inspector general audits over the last fifteen years have repeatedly criticized the FBI's mismanagement of the terrorist watch lists, the largest of which (TIDE) contained over 400,000 identities in January 2008 and grew to 1.6 million by 2017.[8] Roughly 16,000 of these are U.S. persons (citizens and lawful permanent residents).

In one example, Rahinah Ibrahim, a Malaysian national in the United States on a student visa, learned she was on the no-fly list in January 2005, when she was arrested at San Francisco International Airport while attempting to fly overseas. Ibrahim sued to get taken off the list, but the Justice Department fought for years to block the lawsuit on national security grounds.[9] When the case finally went to trial in December 2013, the FBI agent who put Ibrahim on the no-fly list testified it was an accident. He had misread an FBI form and checked the wrong box by mistake. Nine years after her ordeal began, the Justice Department conceded Ibrahim never posed a threat to national security.[10]

I was fortunate enough to work with Julia Shearson when I was with the ACLU and found her to be a woman of remarkable courage, compassion, and integrity. But I believe her placement on the watch list was no accident. I see it as part of a broader FBI assault on Muslim American civil society that employs the same tactics it has used throughout its history whenever it perceived threats to the established order, only enhanced with modern technology.

Explaining how someone so obviously not a threat could wind up listed as "armed and dangerous" on a government watch list requires an understanding of the FBI's terrorist radicalization model. Radicalization theories assert that terrorists go through a discernable process that transforms them from normal human beings into fanatics bent on committing horrible acts of violence. The process takes its name from the premise that exposure to "radical" ideas initiates this transformation. The FBI considers radicalization models crucial to preventative counterterrorism because they describe pre-terrorist behavioral indicators they can targeted for monitoring, infiltration, intervention, or disruption before an act of terrorism is committed.

For instance, an FBI intelligence assessment published in 2006, "The Radicalization Process: From Conversion to Jihad," suggests that converts to Islam pose a heightened risk of becoming terrorists.[11] Though the government's radicalization models vary somewhat, this report asserts that terrorists follow a four-step progression from a "preradicalized" state to engagement in terrorist activities. Adopting a new ideology is the first step on the path.

"The Radicalization Process" identifies increasing religiosity, demonstrated through frequency of mosque attendance, wearing traditional Muslim attire, or even growing a beard, as indicators that the convert has reached the second stage of radicalization. Involvement in a "pro-Muslim social group or political cause" and "proselytizing" are listed as signs of progression to the third stage. Portraying Muslims' grievances over discrimination and human rights violations as indicators of increased dangerousness is a common feature in radicalization literature, which turns the exercise of First Amendment–protected rights into a justification for scrutiny.[12]

The fourth and final step identified in "The Radicalization Process" involves actually joining a terrorist group and engaging in terrorism. The assessment acknowledges that not all Muslim converts become terrorists, but it suggests they should still be watched because they could be "targeted for radicalization" by terrorist recruiters.[13] Though written in dispassionate tones, xenophobia and anti-Muslim bigotry permeate the document and the concepts it imparts. No FBI agent would write, and no supervisor would approve, a report that suggested converting to Christianity might put someone on the path to joining Christian terrorist groups like the Ku Klux Klan or Irish Republican Army.

"The Radicalization Process" specifically identifies prisons, universities, internet chat rooms, places of employment, and bookstores as venues where "radicalization" can occur, along with mosques and halal meat markets.[14] These "nodes" of radicalization are merely places many Muslim might congregate, which appears to be the point.

The FBI also developed a secret checklist its agents use to assign radicalization scores to the subjects of its investigations, which leaked to *The Intercept* in 2017. Called "Indicators of Mobilization to Violence," the survey includes several obvious questions any reasonable counterterrorism investigator should ask, such as: Has the subject been convicted of a violent felony or previously committed an act of terrorism? But many mirror the indicators described in "The Radicalization Process," such as: "Is the subject a religious convert?"; "Has the subject changed his physical appearance?"; and "Does the subject have a passport?"[15] These behaviors are quite commonplace and obviously do not indicate someone is mobilizing to commit a terrorist attack.

Reading these intelligence materials makes it easier to understand how agents responsible for the watch list may have erroneously concluded that Shearson, a hijab-wearing, mosque-attending Muslim convert, international traveler, and university-trained political activist working for a Muslim civil rights organization, could be dangerous.

Empirical research refutes the simplistic notions advanced in these radicalization theories. Studies of individuals who have committed terrorist acts concluded long ago that there is no profile, no discernable pattern or predictive pathway, that leads to terrorist violence.[16] While the concept that terrorists are "radicals" may seem intuitive, evidence shows the vast majority of people who hold radical beliefs do not engage in or support terrorist violence.[17] Many who *do* commit terrorist acts are not driven by extremist ideologies but by a host of other personal, social, and situational motivations.[18]

Forensic psychiatrist and former CIA case officer Marc Sageman has argued that even government counterterrorism experts, who have access to massive volumes of intelligence and the most sophisticated analytic methodologies, cannot accurately predict who might engage in political violence. He wrote, "No one inside or outside the government has yet devised a 'profile' or model that can, with any accuracy and reliability, predict the likelihood that a given individual will commit an act of terrorism."[19] There is also no evidence to suggest that government efforts to suppress radicals reduce violence. Yet the Justice Department and the FBI still cling to radicalization theory as a method of identifying a pre-terrorist population that must be monitored and potentially disrupted. The FBI promotes this concept in training for its own agents and the wider law enforcement community and allows it to drive counterterrorism policies and practices.

To understand how the FBI uses radicalization theory to define the targets for its disruption strategy, I will explore the bureau's history of treating radicals as national security threats.

A BRIEF HISTORY OF THE FBI'S PURSUIT OF RADICALS

In 1907, Attorney General Charles Bonaparte asked Congress to establish a permanent detective force within the Department of Justice. A bipartisan majority of Congress refused, arguing that "a system of spying on men and prying into . . . their private affairs" was not "in accord with the American ideas of government."[20] One congressman referenced a newspaper report that President Theodore Roosevelt had already compiled "a mass of evidence concerning the peccadilloes and estrayings of Senators and Representatives," which gave legislators even more reason to worry about how he might use an unbound investigative bureau.[21]

Until this point, the Justice Department leased Secret Service agents from the Treasury Department whenever it needed investigators. Roosevelt had used his Justice Department to serve the progressive ideals of his "square deal," by focusing on fraud, peonage, antitrust, and government corruption. But Congress funded and authorized the Secret Service specifically to suppress counterfeiting and protect the president. When the Justice Department used additional appropriations to lease these Secret Service agents to conduct other kinds of investigations, it circumvented the jurisdictional limits Congress had imposed. Congress not only refused to approve Bonaparte's request for his own investigators, it banned the Justice Department's practice of leasing Secret Service agents.[22]

With President Roosevelt's support, Bonaparte waited until Congress adjourned, then created the Justice Department's investigations bureau on his own initiative, hiring thirty-four agents.[23] When Congress returned, the House Appropriations Committee threatened legislation to limit this new bureau's investigative jurisdiction, but the political atmosphere on the issue had shifted.[24] Roosevelt gave a speech arguing that continued resistance to a Justice Department detective force benefited only "the criminal classes." He noted recent convictions of "a Senator and Congressman for land frauds in Oregon" and charged that the congressmen opposing the proposal simply "did not themselves wish to be investigated."[25] After Congress censured Roosevelt for these remarks, he released details of an active Secret Service investigation implicating a key opponent, Senator "Pitchfork" Ben Tillman, in a corruption scandal, rendering continued resistance untenable.[26] Tillman was never charged with a crime.

After extracting pledges that this new investigative force would never be used for political spying, Congress agreed to appropriate funds for the Justice Department's investigators, based on Attorney General Bonaparte's promise to personally develop and oversee a system of internal controls to prevent abuse.[27] To this day, the FBI has no legislative charter defining the scope of its authority. It wouldn't take long for the Justice Department's internal controls against abuse to prove insufficient.

The bureau was created during a time of extreme economic inequality and social upheaval resulting from the rapid technological advances of the industrial revolution. Labor violence was common as unions struggled to secure safe working conditions in factories, fields, and coal mines, and owners resisted with hired detectives and strikebreakers. With Roosevelt out of office the following year, Congress grew more comfortable using the Bureau of Investigation (BOI), as it was then known, as a means of social control.

In 1910, in reaction to sensationalized reporting of "white slavers"—networks of foreigners luring women into sexual bondage—Congress passed the Mann Act, prohibiting the transportation of women across state lines "for prostitution or debauchery, or any other immoral purpose."[28] The panic over white slavery was exaggerated and short-lived, but the bureau would use the broad "immorality" language in the statute aggressively to target people engaged in consensual extramarital or interracial sex, as well as prostitution. The *Encyclopedia of United States National Security* described the Mann Act as "a tool by which the federal government could investigate criminals who evaded state laws but had no other federal violations."[29] Worded differently, the Mann Act allowed the bureau to selectively investigate and prosecute people the government feared or hated but could not otherwise charge with a crime. The FBI used the Mann Act to investigate black heavyweight champion Jack Johnson, whose dalliances with white women had become a matter of public agitation, and much later, Charlie Chaplin, whom J. Edgar Hoover despised for his liberal political views.[30] Chaplin was acquitted at trial and President Trump pardoned Johnson in 2018.

The onset of World War I opened the door for an expansion of the BOI's investigative mandate, and its leaders eagerly leapt through it. Prewar concerns about foreign spies and saboteurs led to an expansion of the BOI's budget in 1916, specifically so it could respond to State Department requests for information about suspected German agents.[31] Congress also bolstered the bureau's powers shortly after the war began in 1917 by passing the Espionage, Selective Service, and Immigration Acts, and later the Sedition Act—broad new legislation that criminalized speaking out against the war, resisting the draft, and associating with anarchist organizations.

While the BOI was still nominally assigned to the specific tasks of uncovering German spies and policing draft dodgers, congressional hearings in 1918 revealed it had also been using these new authorities to investigate Americans' political views. Its agents assembled dossiers on individuals whose writings, opinions, and affiliations demonstrated a potential for disloyalty. Employing guilt by association, the agents molded seemingly dissimilar aspects of the bureau's various investigations into a single broad conspiracy. Under an umbrella category of "pro-Germanism," the bureau linked brewers' associations (often filled with German immigrants) to pacifists (who opposed war against Germany) and socialists (whose labor advocacy threatened war industries). Bureau officials interpreted prewar interactions with German officials, travel to Germany, or academic exchanges as inherently suspect, and criticism of U.S. policies or social conditions as sympathy for America's enemies. When bureau agents saw German government propagandists embracing unrelated causes, such as political agitation "among the Irish, among the Jews, [and] among the Catholics," they assumed these activists were part of a German conspiracy to undermine the United States from within.[32]

A U.S. Senate subcommittee led by North Carolina senator Lee Slater Overman initiated a series of hearings in 1918 to explore these purported links and invited BOI director A. Bruce Bielaski to testify. Bielaski noted that Justice Department rules did not authorize the public release of information gleaned through its investigations except in support of prosecutions, but he indicated he would make an exception given "the importance of the subject matter under investigation."[33] When Bielaski laid the bureau's files open and began naming names during these public hearings, none of those who had resisted the bureau's creation ten years earlier would have been surprised to learn that its secret intelligence operations targeted members of Congress, as well as prominent journalists, peace activists, clergy, academics, and lawyers. The bureau's files smeared dozens of innocent, patriotic Americans as seditious German sympathizers during wartime, destroying reputations and careers.

The disclosure of the files also shed a sanitizing light on the bureau's secret intelligence methods, exposing its flawed analyses, dubious tactics, and eagerness to construe innocuous facts in the most sinister ways. The hearings revealed that agents relied heavily on paid informants, including some with criminal records, and statements coerced from vulnerable witnesses. The bureau's analytical methodology, to the extent there was one, was so sloppy the files included information and conclusions that could quickly be disproven with readily available public information.[34]

Once the files were published, individuals named during the hearings finally had the opportunity to point out the bureau's errors. For instance, the BOI released a letter seized from a suspected German agent that identified Senator Hoke Smith of Georgia and Gilbert Hitchcock of Nebraska as supporters of a German front group called the American Embargo Conference, which supported an arms embargo to Europe during the period before the United States entered the war. Senator Smith testified that he had never heard of the German agent or the organization and had in fact voted to table the arms embargo bill the group favored.[35]

Senator Hitchcock, who had championed the bill through Congress, explained that his support of the arms embargo was well known long before the German agent passed off this supposedly secret intelligence to his spymasters. But he noted that his support for the embargo lasted only during the period of officially declared neutrality on the European war. His position changed once German hostilities against U.S. interests became apparent the following year.[36] Supporting legislation that tracked official U.S. policy could hardly be seen as anti-American, except by those determined to twist the facts to fit predetermined narratives. Others the bureau accused of holding pro-German sentiments defended their innocence before the committee, with one likening the hearings to "being tried for witchcraft."[37]

Still, the bureau and many of the committee members stood by their work. T. Henry Walnut, a former assistant U.S. attorney who worked with the bureau during this period, later defended their methods: "We were concerned at the time not so much with crimes that had been committed as with endeavoring to identify those persons in the community whose thinking, whose talk, and whose associations were such that they might be suspected of being enemy agents or disloyal. When you are concerned with such intangible matters there is no way to measure the relevancy or irrelevancy of any particular bit of information. It must all go in the file."[38]

He also admitted that "it is true we caught no spies." The collateral costs of the bureau's imprecision were significant. Many victims smeared as disloyal in the bureau's files were unable to ever fully clear their reputations.

The war ended shortly after the Overman Committee's hearings began, seemingly nullifying its purpose of exposing enemy propaganda efforts. But rather than disband the inquiry, the chairman deftly shifted its target to include the purported threat from "radicalism." Archibald E. Stevenson, a self-proclaimed expert on the "radical movement" who had volunteered his services as special agent to the BOI the previous year, provided the analytical leap that enabled the committee's expanded agenda.[39] Stevenson had compiled a file of thousands of suspected radicals, and his testimony linked German socialists to a global conspiracy involving Russian "Bolsheviki," American anarchists, trade unionists, and pacifists.[40]

American pacifists, he argued, were not driven by individual conscience but by the influence of German propaganda, which he likened to a "poison gas" that had spread across the nation compelling even unwitting and otherwise loyal Americans to do Germany's bidding.[41] The committee followed Stevenson's logic, widening the scope of its hearings to encompass an appraisal of what he called the American "intelligentcia," which he described as the more serious threat to the American way of life.[42] These dangerous intellectuals included pacifists, labor organizers, university professors, and civil rights lawyers, who he claimed established a support network that allowed radical and alien ideas to fester and grow inside the United States. Stevenson saw American universities as hotbeds for radicalization.[43]

Stevenson denounced the National Civil Liberties Bureau (NCLB), the precursor organization to the ACLU, whose offices Justice Department agents raided before the hearings. The evidence of the NCLB's participation in a seditious conspiracy included its legal defenses of draft resisters and union "radicals" who had been charged with violating the wartime statutes criminalizing anti-war speech and its publication of "pacifist literature" that provided instructions on how to claim conscientious objector status.[44]

Because the bureau identified radical ideas as threats to national security, it became natural for its agents to view institutions dedicated to examining and questioning political and social orthodoxy—academia, the news media, and clergy—as incubators of sedition. Law enforcement suppression of radical ideas was therefore seen as a necessary and appropriate government response. The bureau, which had fewer than three hundred agents during the war, relied heavily on private sector volunteers like Stevenson not just to compile this so-called intelligence but to conduct raids and make arrests.

Stevenson was affiliated the American Protective League (APL), which became the nation's most prominent right-wing vigilante organization after Attorney General Thomas Gregory officially sanctioned it to assist BOI operations in 1917. Boasting more than two hundred fifty thousand members nationwide, the APL functioned as a private army of informers and thugs for hire.[45] These "citizens' defense" organizations were primarily financed by big business, so it was not surprising that they tended to view opposition to their benefactors' financial interests as threats to national security. Strikebreaking and anti-union violence became their forte, which the bureau tacitly supported through intelligence-sharing arrangements. These tactics furthered the bureau's goal of suppressing the radical labor organizations it considered dangerous, particularly the Industrial Workers of the World (IWW), whose members were routinely harassed, arrested, beaten, and even murdered by these "patriotic" organizations.[46]

While it is certainly true that people identifying themselves as anarchists were responsible for a significant amount of terrorism in the early 1900s, solving discrete acts of political violence was not the focus of the bureau's intelligence operations, or the Overman Committee's hearings. Indeed, the politically motivated violence taking place during this era was not exclusively or even predominantly coming from the Left. The bureau all but ignored racist and anti-immigrant violence before, during, and after the war, including by more militant organizations like the Ku Klux Klan, which reconstituted in 1915 and quickly grew to more than one million members. This reactionary violence tended to serve establishment interests in quelling civil rights advocacy and labor organizing in black communities and ensuring black cooperation with the draft.[47]

The racist underpinnings of the concerns regarding the "radical" threat were most clearly on display when Overman Committee members asked Stevenson for his recommendations to address the problem. After one senator noted that literacy tests for new immigrants would not suffice because "some of these fellows that come here can read and write and yet they are anarchists and Socialists," Stevenson agreed with Senator Overman's proposition that blocking all nonwhite immigration would be the more effective strategy "before we dilute Americanism even further."[48] Indeed, though the Overman Committee's mission was nominally to protect "Americanism," it was clear that the power structure of the time viewed only a portion of the U.S. population as true Americans. Three years after the hearings, Senator Overman would lead a filibuster that defeated federal anti-lynching legislation. As the *New York Times* paraphrased his argument, "decent hard working negroes" didn't need such protection, and "the ignorant negroes of the South would interpret the bill as a Federal license to commit the foulest of outrages."[49]

While the Overman Committee hearings were somewhat successful in suppressing legitimate social movements, they were ineffective in identifying actual threats to American security. With the bureau and Congress focused on policing Americans' thoughts and associations, a violent group of anarchists became even more active.

On April 28, 1919, a mail bomb arrived at the home of Seattle mayor Ole Hanson, who had arrested thirty-eight IWW leaders after putting down a peaceful general strike, but it failed to detonate.[50] The following day, a similar device exploded at the home of Georgia senator Thomas W. Hardwick, who had sponsored the Immigration Act of 1918, severely injuring his wife and a member of his staff. A search of the mails discovered more than thirty bombs addressed to other prominent politicians, judges, law enforcement officials, and business leaders across the country. Senator Overman was one of the intended recipients, as was Rayme Finch, the BOI's most famous radical hunter.[51] A month later, nine larger bombs exploded almost simultaneously in seven different cities, including in the front yard of Attorney General A. Mitchell Palmer, who had been unsuccessfully targeted in the earlier letter bomb campaign.[52] That bomb detonated prematurely, killing the man who placed it and giving investigators an early clue as to the identities of the perpetrators. Pamphlets left at all the bomb sites made clear that anarchists were responsible.

Rather than reassess its methods and the direction of its intelligence operations, the Justice Department expanded them, establishing within the bureau a formalized "Radical Division," soon renamed the General Intelligence Division (GID). Attorney General Palmer appointed a promising young Justice Department official, J. Edgar Hoover, as its head, and granted the bureau great leeway to go after the bombers. Using skills he had developed during a clerkship at the Library of Congress combined with information pouring in from official sources and paid informers at a rate of 600 to 900 reports a week,[53] Hoover began assembling a massive catalog of "radicals" that soon swelled, like the watch lists later would, to include 450,000 entries.[54] Hoover's agents produced 60,000 detailed biographies on people showing "any connection with an ultra-radical body or movement," focusing primarily on the authors and publishers of political materials.[55] The usual suspects were again journalists, labor unions, progressive politicians, and civil rights lawyers, such as future Supreme Court justice Felix Frankfurter.[56] Hoover also targeted the African American press and black activists, such as those associated with the National Association for the Advancement of Colored People and Marcus Garvey's Universal Negro Improvement Association.[57]

Hoover was particularly concerned about radicalization in black communities, believing that foreign propagandists were instigating the increasing agitation for civil rights and equal protection. Despite an epidemic of lynching across the United States and a series of riots during the "Red Summer" of 1919, when white mobs attacked and torched black neighborhoods in thirty-eight cities, killing hundreds and leaving thousands homeless,[58] Hoover remained more interested in evaluating African American newspapers for signs of communist influence than protecting black communities from racist violence.[59] In November 1919, the bureau published a report to Congress entitled "Radicalism and Sedition Among the Negroes as Reflected in Their Publications," which claimed the Communist Party of America was "the cause of much of the racial trouble in the United States at the present time."[60] The report argued that "radical" sentiments expressed in the African American press, including essays that advocated for black civil rights, labor solidarity, and opposition to Jim Crow laws and lynching, demonstrated "the identification of the negro with such radical organizations as the I.W.W. and an outspoken advocacy of the Bolsheviki or Soviet doctrines."[61]

The National Association for the Promotion of Labor Unionism Among Negroes rejected the allegation of foreign influence in a letter to the influential Union League Club of New York City. The letter cited the "disenfranchisement of more than 2,000,000 Negroes," the "lynching of more than 270 Negroes since war was declared," and the unfair treatment of blacks under Jim Crow laws in a plea for the club to support policies to alleviate this suffering. The letter argued that unrest in black communities "grows out of the unjust conditions in this alleged land of the free and home of the brave. They are the true bolshevik propaganda. Without the conditions the agitator could not exist."[62]

Hoover quickly put his intelligence about radicals to use as bureau agents engaged in hundreds of warrantless raids against suspected anarchists, arresting more than six thousand people across the country, mostly immigrants who were fast-tracked for deportation under administrative procedures established by the wartime Immigration Act. Government officials boasted of seizing four bombs during a raid of a Communist Party office and showed reporters four iron balls soaking in a pail of water "for safety."[63] But these alleged bombs were never entered into evidence in any legal proceeding, and no mention was made of them in the Justice Department's testimony regarding the raids.[64] All but a handful of the guns seized during the raids turned out to be stage props belonging to an amateur drama club.

When a conscientious Labor Department official responsible for processing the deportations refused to sign the orders without individualized evidence of wrongdoing, the bureau's intelligence information was often found lacking. Fewer than one in ten of those arrested in these "Palmer raids" ended up being deported. That official, Assistant Labor Secretary Louis Post, was quickly hauled before Congress to explain why he should not be impeached for his failure to perform his duties under the Immigration Act. His vigorous defense of the constitutional requirement of due process of law for all those in government custody helped to sway public opinion against the raids. Post later wrote, "At no place in all that nationwide raiding of January, 1920, were any weapons or explosive materials or destructive mechanisms discovered from which an inference of projected crime, private or political, could be reasonably drawn. Even as to criminal thoughts the proof was flimsy—absurdly so in contrast with the severity of the raiding."[65]

A federal judge similarly found that the bureau's conduct appeared designed more to generate press attention than to address security threats posed by the detainees: "Pains were taken to give spectacular publicity to the raid and to make it appear that there was great and imminent public danger, against which these activities of the Department of Justice were directed. The arrested aliens—in most instances perfectly quiet and harmless working people, many of them not long ago Russian peasants—were handcuffed in pairs, and then, for the purposes of transfer on trains and through the streets of Boston, chained together . . . [and] exposed to newspaper photographers."[66]

A lawyer's committee that included such luminaries as Harvard Law School's Roscoe Pound and Zechariah Chafee and future Supreme Court justice Felix Frankfurter published a report in May 1920 documenting the "continual illegal acts" committed by Justice Department agents while carrying out the Palmer raids, which included warrantless searches and arrests, torture, and destruction of private property.[67] The lawyers' committee warned that these tactics were unlikely to make the public safer: "No organizations of radicals acting through propaganda over the last six months could have created as much revolutionary sentiment in America as has been created by the acts of the Department of Justice itself. . . . There is no danger of revolution so great as that created by suppression, by ruthlessness, and by deliberate violation of the simple rules of American law and American decency."[68]

Despite its abandonment of constitutional restraints, the bureau never solved the 1919 bombings.[69]

In September 1920, a horse cart loaded with hundreds of pounds of dynamite and scrap iron was detonated in front of the J.P. Morgan & Co. building on Wall Street, killing thirty-eight and injuring hundreds in what was then the deadliest terrorist attack in U.S. history. Bureau investigations again failed to identify the culprits, and anarchist bombings would continue to haunt the country over the next dozen years.[70]

Despite the ongoing violence, the public rejected the excesses of the Palmer raids, which drove an era of reform designed to refocus the bureau on its original law enforcement mission. In 1924, new attorney general Harlan Fiske Stone asserted that the bureau would from then on concern itself with illegal conduct rather than political opinions and would ensure that "its agents themselves be not above the law or beyond its reach." He argued that "when a police system passes beyond these limits, it is dangerous to the proper administration of justice and to human liberty, which it should be our first concern to cherish."[71] The General Intelligence Division disbanded, but in a fateful turn of events, Attorney General Stone tapped its director, J. Edgar Hoover, to lead the bureau during this period of reformation.

Hoover disavowed his role in the Palmer raids, but he never lost his obsession with radicals or his fondness for using lists to keep track of those he disagreed with.

The reforms only lasted until the next security crisis justified a departure. When war began to engulf Europe in 1939, President Franklin Delano Roosevelt authorized Hoover to reestablish the GID. The bureau, now renamed the Federal Bureau of Investigation, was officially back in the business of policing Americans' political opinions. Congress pitched in by passing the Alien Registration Act of 1940, better known as the Smith Act, which outlawed membership in organizations that advocated sedition and required aliens living inside the United States to register with the government.[72] Once again, the bureau's intelligence methods explicitly authorized the "disruption" of First Amendment activities and the compilation of lists of Americans determined to be disloyal based on their ideology, speech, and associations. Even as the FBI's intelligence operations expanded to counter the threat from Nazi Germany, communism would remain Hoover's principal concern. Though the Soviet Union was an ally during World War II, American communists still made up the largest portion of Hoover's secret list of persons to be rounded up in a national emergency. When the war ended and a second Red Scare engulfed the nation, the bureau's intelligence files again provided grist for unscrupulous congressmen to smear innocent Americans.[73]

Hoover kept the bureau's role in these activities under wraps, beguiling presidents, congressmen, and journalists with small bits of intelligence, scandalous rumors, and outright falsehoods that both titillated their curiosity and stoked their fears about what the FBI might have on them. Meanwhile, Hoover professionalized and polished the law enforcement side of the FBI, both legitimately, by improving training and discipline for FBI agents and advancing the forensic sciences, and less so, by manipulating the press, exaggerating the criminal threat, and aggrandizing the bureau's exploits. The new FBI crime lab proved its value when its handwriting analysis of ransom letters proved key to the 1935 murder prosecution of Bruno Hauptmann for the botched kidnapping of aviator Charles Lindbergh's baby boy.[74] On the other hand, Hoover's staged arrest of fugitive gangster Alvin "Creepy" Karpis demonstrated how this powerful law enforcement agency was also willing to shade the truth to polish its image.[75] After the chairman of the Senate Appropriations Committee impugned Hoover's lawman image by pointing out he never made an arrest, the FBI hatched a plan to include the director personally in a highly publicized arrest. Karpis, whom the bureau had previously dubbed "Public Enemy No. 1," was a dangerous career criminal who had vowed not to be taken alive. Agents located him in Hot Springs, Arkansas, in March 1936, but he eluded them before Hoover could be whisked into town for the arrest, demonstrating a willingness to put bureau publicity before public safety.[76] When Karpis was again located in New Orleans a month later, Hoover arrived in time to participate in his arrest, for which he took personal credit to great media fanfare.

More than thirty years would pass before Hoover's abuses were uncovered. In 1971, activists calling themselves the Citizens' Commission to Investigate the FBI burglarized a small bureau office in Media, Pennsylvania, uncovering evidence that agents had been spying on and harassing anti-war and civil rights protesters. The documents, which the Citizens' Commission sent to news outlets and members of Congress, revealed that the FBI remained focused on universities, particularly black student groups. Initially, only the *Washington Post* published them. One FBI memorandum encouraged agents to aggressively seek interviews of political dissidents in order to sow "paranoia" by creating the impression there was "an FBI agent behind every mailbox."[77]

A note referencing "COINTELPRO" led NBC News to file FOIA requests that uncovered nationwide counterintelligence programs targeting political activists. These and other revelations about intelligence abuses at the CIA and Defense Department led Congress to act. In 1975, the Senate established a bipartisan select committee to study the government's intelligence activities, which became known as the Church Committee, after its chairman, Senator Frank Church.

The Church Committee investigation found that the FBI "was more than simply violating the law or the Constitution. In COINTELPRO the Bureau secretly took the law into its own hands, going beyond the collection of intelligence and beyond its law enforcement function to act outside the legal process altogether and to covertly disrupt, discredit and harass groups and individuals. A law enforcement agency must not secretly usurp the functions of judge and jury, even when the investigation reveals criminal activity. But in COINTELPRO, the Bureau imposed summary punishment, not only on the allegedly violent, but also on the nonviolent advocates of change."[78]

The Church Committee report concluded, "The unexpressed major premise of the programs was that a law enforcement agency has the duty to do whatever is necessary to combat perceived threats to the existing social and political order."[79] At its height, the FBI had opened more than 500,000 domestic intelligence files, including 65,000 in 1972 alone, and it kept a "Security Index" listing 26,000 people in the United States "to be rounded up in the event of a 'national emergency.'"[80]

COINTELPRO was nominally designed to prevent violence by suppressing membership in and "neutralizing" five specified threat groups, which included the Communist Party USA, the Socialist Workers Party, Black Nationalist Hate Groups, and the New Left. But these programs expanded to cover disruption activities aimed against legitimate nonviolent political organizations, like civil rights groups, student groups, and underground newspapers expressing sentiments agents found dangerous. The FBI supervisor responsible for the Black Nationalist COINTELPRO, for instance, admitted it targeted "organizations that you might not today characterize as black nationalist but which were in fact primarily black."[81]

The FBI established its fifth COINTELPRO, targeting "White Hate" groups, in 1964 and put a number of Ku Klux Klan members on the Security Index in response to intense pressure from President Lyndon Johnson after Klansmen killed three civil rights workers in Mississippi.[82] But the Church Committee found the White Hate program was much more limited than the other programs and used fewer techniques that "carried a risk of serious physical, emotional, or economic damage to the targets."[83] It "precisely" focused on specific, named suspects and did not broaden to cover nonviolent right-wing organizations, which may explain why it was considered the most successful of the programs in achieving its aim of reducing violence.

REFORM AND RECIDIVISM

The Church Committee's revelations of FBI intelligence abuses led to an era of reform and a strengthening of constitutional controls. Congress established standing intelligence committees and the Foreign Intelligence

Surveillance Court to oversee national security intelligence operations. Once again, members of Congress proposed a statutory charter to govern the FBI's investigative activities, but the effort failed. Attorney General Edward Levi seized the initiative by developing Justice Department regulations that governed the FBI's authorities, which became known as the Attorney General's Guidelines (AGG).[84]

Levi's guidelines attempted to codify Attorney General Stone's earlier effort to refocus the FBI on criminal law enforcement by requiring "specific and articulable facts giving reason to believe that an individual or group is or may be engaged in activities which involve the use of force or violence" before a full domestic security investigation could be opened.[85] Congress again left the attorney general in charge of defining the scope of the FBI's investigative authorities. This approach made it possible for successive attorneys general to modify the AGG as they saw fit, and many did, loosening the rules over time. The Justice Department promulgated separate sets of guidelines to govern the use of confidential informants, undercover operations, foreign intelligence collection, national security investigations, and terrorism enterprise investigations.

Circumscribing the bureau's authorities was essential to curbing its tendency to view challenges to government policy as threats to security. But rules don't enforce themselves. The most infamous breach of its new guidelines occurred during President Ronald Reagan's first term, when the FBI opened a wide-ranging investigation into the Committee in Solidarity with the People of El Salvador (CISPES). CISPES is a U.S. advocacy organization formed in 1980 to oppose U.S. government support for El Salvador's right-wing military dictatorship in its brutal civil war against leftist guerrilla groups. Millions fled the conflict, but U.S. policy did not recognize them as refugees and instead deported them back to El Salvador. CISPES was part of a religious and political sanctuary movement that sought to protect these refugees through protest and acts of civil disobedience.

The FBI initially opened an investigation into whether CISPES and its leaders were operating in violation of the Foreign Agents Registration Act (FARA), a rarely enforced 1938 law that requires individuals and organizations lobbying for foreign powers to register with the U.S. government. The case was opened in June 1981, shortly after the

FBI's Boston field office forwarded an article from a John Birch Society newsletter, *Review of the News*, written by far-right political operative and journalist John Rees, to FBI headquarters.[86] The article claimed that "key radicals" from President Jimmy Carter's White House and State Department "were consciously striving to turn the whole of Central America over to the Communists." It argued CISPES was central to a foreign plot to support Marxist revolutionaries in El Salvador, which included the Communist Party USA, the U.S. Peace Council, the Catholic Conference, and Maryknoll nuns. It urged the Justice Department to open a FARA investigation.[87] Despite the article's outlandish claims, the bureau started an investigation that quickly broadened.

The FBI recruited an informant, Frank Varelli, who had come to the United States from El Salvador with his family after a failed assassination attempt against his father, a former chief of the national police. Varelli infiltrated CISPES and provided intelligence that helped the Dallas FBI field office open an international terrorism investigation in March 1983. There were a number of bombings targeting U.S. government facilities in the months that followed, including an April 1983 bombing at the National War College in Washington, D.C. An anonymous caller claiming responsibility for the attack on behalf of the "Armed Resistance Movement" said in a phone message, "We are in solidarity with the people of El Salvador." A later written communiqué was a little more ambiguous, claiming the action "was taken in solidarity with the growing liberation movements in El Salvador, Guatemala, and throughout Central America."[88] CISPES representatives had participated in a demonstration in D.C. the day after the bombing, so it is understandable that the FBI may have mistaken these generalized solidarity messages as references to the organization.

The CISPES investigation quickly grew into a nationwide effort, but it didn't focus on solving the bombings. In four years of operation, the CISPES investigation gathered information on 2,375 individuals and 1,330 groups. It involved all 59 FBI field offices and generated 178 "spin-off" investigations, the last of which didn't close until 1988.[89] Varelli also established a back channel for the FBI to informally share information about political activists in the United States with El Salvador's national guard, which was then linked to right-wing death squads.[90]

During the investigation, Varelli authored an intelligence assessment describing a CISPES conspiracy that included the Russian KGB, the Palestinian Liberation Organization, and the Communist Party USA.[91] He later claimed he knew CISPES was nonviolent and that he produced this report at the FBI's direction, following the bureau's "standard line." During testimony before the House Intelligence Committee in 1987, Varelli said the FBI told him "that CISPES was a radical 'terrorist' organization of the type I had encountered in El Salvador." "In retrospect," he said, "I now realize that the purpose of the FBI's attention directed towards the CISPES was political and not criminal."[92] A New Orleans FBI document written when the investigation started confirms Varelli's impression that the investigation had political motives. It argued the FBI had to "formulate some plan of attack against CISPES and specifically against individuals . . . who defiantly display their contempt for the U.S. government by making speeches and propagandizing their cause while asking for political asylum."[93]

But not all FBI and Justice Department officials agreed that CISPES deserved investigation. The FBI headquarters official who approved Varelli's recruitment stressed to his handling agent that "he is not to report on activities of individuals within this organization concerning their exercise of the rights guaranteed by the Constitution of the United States."[94] A few field offices closed or attempted to close their CISPES spin-off cases, citing civil liberties concerns. At one point, a headquarters communication warned thirty-two offices that their CISPES investigations were straying beyond what the Attorney General's Guidelines authorized. Finally, in June 1985, a Justice Department official reviewed a summary of the case and determined it needed to be closed because it violated the guidelines: "It appears that this organization is involved in political activities, involving First Amendment rights, and not international terrorism."[95] No criminal charges were ever lodged.

The Attorney General's Guidelines did not prevent FBI officials from conducting an expansive and abusive investigation into Americans' political activities, but they did give FBI agents in field offices and supervisors in headquarters a standard they could point at to resist improper directives. And the guidelines gave a responsible overseer at the Justice Department the legal authority to finally shut it down.

Varelli ended up going public with his story, claiming his handling agent misappropriated his salary. His most sensational accusations were that FBI agents working on the case engaged in illegal break-ins at CISPES offices, and that his handler directed him to seduce one of the nuns working with CISPES so the FBI could coerce her into becoming an informant. The FBI denied these claims, and no documents were discovered to substantiate them. A Senate Intelligence Committee investigation did find evidence the FBI leaked classified information to the Salvadoran national guard, however, in violation of the law and U.S. policy. The committee also confirmed that Varelli provided the FBI with information about the Salvadoran government's involvement in death squad murders and a secret anti-Communist "hit list," but the FBI did not open an investigation because it could put Varelli in danger.[96] The case was a major embarrassment for the FBI and evidence that, while J. Edgar Hoover was dead and gone, the bureau's tendency to abuse counterterrorism powers for political purposes hadn't gone away.

Indeed, the same pattern would repeat as new threats—real, exaggerated, and wholly imagined—emerged in the future. Legitimate concerns about a terrorist group or hostile nation might justify starting an investigation. But, following the logic of the radicalization theory, the FBI would broaden its scope to examine the activities of law-abiding groups that champion the same cause or community the terrorists claim to represent. This expanding focus creates a conundrum for the FBI, as its law enforcement tools are ineffective against individuals who are not engaging in illegality. It cannot successfully prosecute these individuals, so instead it resorts to intimidation tactics designed to disrupt and dissuade their lawful political mobilization.

It is easy to understand why governments victimized by terrorism embrace the radicalization theory. First, it identifies political opponents as threats to national security, empowering the government to target them in the name of counterterrorism. The First Amendment to the Constitution guarantees five freedoms: speech, belief, association, press, and the right to petition the government with grievances. The radicalization theory turns the exercise of these freedoms into indicators of dangerousness, which then justifies taking measures to suppress them.

Second, by identifying disenfranchised communities as incubators of terrorism, the radicalization theory legitimizes past discrimination and justifies increasing security measures, which can be selectively applied to any population deemed potential enemies.

Finally, it justifies making these increased counterterrorism powers permanent. Since a "radical" ideology can never be entirely eradicated, the radicalization theory creates perpetual suspect classes that remain dangerous even in a preradicalized state. Individuals in these communities continue to be "at risk" of becoming radicalized, or "vulnerable to recruitment," even when they show no evidence of threatening behavior. If the progression to violence is an unseen mental process, continuous monitoring, selective and preemptive prosecutions, and draconian punishments become necessary parts of a permanent counterterrorism regime. Simply put, the radicalization theory justified the counterterrorism approach the government wanted to take. The plan a counterterrorist would draw up to tackle the estimated five thousand militants who trained at al Qaeda camps by 9/11 is very different from one that would be drawn up to stop "radical Islam."[97]

The radicalization theory establishes who the enemy is, and the disruption strategy provides the tools to suppress them. Watch lists are just one method of social control the FBI can impose on suspect communities. Though no actual security benefit was realized by placing Julia Shearson on a terrorist watch list, the FBI could consider her ordeal at the border a successful implementation of its disruption strategy, as her awareness of FBI scrutiny triggered the same "paranoia" about agents lurking behind mailboxes that the bureau imposed on an earlier generation of political activists. Seeing how these tactics were used against Muslim civil society as a whole, and Shearson's organization, the Council on American-Islamic Relations, in particular, makes this case more clearly.

6

DISRUPTING MUSLIM CIVIL SOCIETY

Some might suggest that Julia Shearson's placement on the watch list isn't a result of error or flawed profiling models but instead her involvement with the Council on American-Islamic Relations (CAIR).[1] Founded in 1994, CAIR is the largest Muslim civil liberties organization in the United States. Likely for that reason, the anti-Muslim advocacy organizations and public officials that make up the "Islamophobia network" have long made CAIR a favorite target, repeatedly smearing it as a supporter of terrorism even though the government has never charged it with wrongdoing or frozen its assets.

Like the far-right groups that inspired the CISPES investigation, the anti-Muslim activists that Duke University professor Christopher Bail calls the "foundation of the fringe" found inroads into the FBI long before 9/11.[2] The theories of Muslim radicalization they promoted put dozens of Arab and Muslim religious, charitable, and social organizations in the crosshairs of sweeping FBI investigations, raids, and asset seizures. The al Qaeda attacks operationalized this "intelligence" to justify a broader government assault on Muslim American civil society.

U.S. policymakers first began using the term "radical Islam" to describe Ayatollah Khomeini's regime in Iran, which had overthrown the U.S.-backed shah in 1979 and held fifty-two Americans hostage for 444 days.[3] Pundits stretched the concept to include any group of Muslims opposing U.S. foreign policy, regardless of political ideology, nationality, or religious sect. In a 1984 essay, Harvard-trained historian Daniel Pipes, who often used the terms "radical" and "fundamentalist" interchangeably, presented the idea that "fundamentalist Muslims" stretching "from Morocco to Indonesia" posed a threat to the United States.[4] Obviously, a number of terrorist groups and hostile governments from these regions demanded FBI attention at that time, but conflating them into a single global movement of radical Islamic fundamentalists misrepresented their nature and obscured the threats they posed.

In the mid-1990s, Pipes also warned that a Muslim "fundamentalist infrastructure" existed inside the United States. "With almost no oversight," he wrote, "they collect and launder money here, provide communications links, and spew out propaganda."[5] He urged the government to shut them down. His think tank, the Middle East Forum, and the journal it publishes, the *Middle East Quarterly*, found purchase with the post–Cold War national security establishment looking for a new menace that could justify discarding its Church Committee restraints. Though he is considered more of an activist than a scholar, his controversial writings would be found among the FBI's training materials more than a decade later.[6]

Where Pipes helped provide an intellectual framework for FBI counterterrorism policy, Steven Emerson and his Investigative Project on Terrorism (IPT) provided substance—however distorted. In 1994, Emerson produced an award-winning PBS documentary called *Terrorists Among Us: Jihad in America*. Like Pipes's essays, Emerson's film melded disparate events to make them appear as parts of a unified international "jihad movement" targeting the United States.

In his 2002 book *American Jihad*, Emerson said his interest in investigating terrorism support networks in the United States started when he stumbled upon a Muslim youth convention in Oklahoma City in December 1992. He claimed to have seen speakers preaching "Destroy the West" and hawking children's coloring books entitled "How to Kill the Infidel."[7] Shocked, he reached out to "some contacts at the FBI" only to learn that Church Committee restrictions prohibited bureau agents from tracking this sort of activity.[8] "Investigations could only be done on particular individuals and then only if these individuals appeared to be in the act of committing a crime," he wrote.[9]

Then-recently-retired FBI associate deputy director Oliver "Buck" Revell appeared in *Terrorists Among Us* and at events promoting it. He supported Emerson's conclusion that there was "an infrastructure in the United States that supports Hamas and Hezbollah" and, in a 1995 paper published in Pipes's *Middle East Quarterly*, he claimed there was little the FBI could do to track it.[10] Revell offered several policy recommendations to strengthen the FBI's ability to interdict the "Muslim radicals" who had "infiltrated" the United States and were using it as "a base of operations."[11] His proposal included establishing a central repository of information on terrorist suspects, strengthening laws prohibiting material support of terrorism, and loosening the Attorney General's Guidelines. He complained the guidelines prevented the FBI from monitoring the "open activities" of groups that advocate for violence and terrorism "until the FBI has reason to believe a crime has been or is about to be committed." "To prevent terrorism," he wrote, the FBI "must be able to collect this information."[12]

Like all good conspiracy theories, the narrative Pipes, Emerson, and Revell wove included a lot of compelling evidence. There were indeed Muslim terrorist cells that plotted horrific attacks here in the United States, right under the noses of FBI investigators who appeared ill-equipped to stop them. But buying into their conspiracy required ignoring conflicting facts and taking unsupportable leaps of logic. The most obvious contrary truth, which Revell almost certainly knew if Pipes and Emerson didn't, was that far from being inhibited by its new rules, the FBI was then engaged in several wide-ranging domestic investigations of Arab and Muslim political, social, and religious organizations.

The term "Islamophobia" wasn't popularized in English until the late 1990s, but U.S. immigration policies expressly discriminated against Arabs and Muslims until at least 1944, and less overtly since.[13] Columbia University professor Edward Said's 1978 book *Orientalism* stoked controversy by critiquing the tendency of Western observers to treat Arabs, Muslims, and Asians as homogenous "threatening Others."[14] The FBI had Said, a U.S. citizen, and his fellow Palestinian rights activists under periodic surveillance throughout the 1970s and 1980s.[15] These were nominally national security and counterterrorism investigations, but they consisted predominately of monitoring the political activities of groups opposing U.S. policies in the Middle East rather than gathering evidence of terrorist conspiracies.[16]

In 1993, the FBI initiated an investigation in Tampa, Florida, targeting University of South Florida (USF) professor and Palestinian activist Sami al-Arian, who Emerson featured as an example of a U.S.-based Muslim extremist in his 1994 film. The al-Arian investigation would intercept hundreds of faxes and more than 472,000 telephone calls, totaling 20,000 hours of recordings.[17] In 1995, the FBI raided al-Arian's home and an Islamic research center he ran with his brother-in-law Mazen al-Najjar, seizing at least fifty boxes of documents.[18] In 1997, FBI and INS officials arrested al-Najjar on a visa violation, then held him on secret evidence alleging al-Arian's research center was a front for the Palestinian Islamic Jihad (PIJ). USF placed al-Arian on paid leave while it conducted an internal investigation. Finding no wrongdoing, and receiving no further information from the FBI, USF allowed al-Arian to return to his regular duties in August 1998. A U.S. immigration judge released al-Najjar on bond in 2000, after ruling the government's secret evidence did not show al-Najjar or al-Arian's research center had provided support to the PIJ after its 1997 designation as a "specially designated terrorist" group.[19]

The FBI started a decade-long investigation of the Holy Land Foundation (HLF), the largest U.S. Muslim charity, in 1994. Giving alms to the needy, or *zakat*, is one of the five pillars of Islam, so organizations develop to assist the faithful in meeting this obligation. HLF formed in 1989 as a U.S. nonprofit organization to fund charitable efforts throughout the world, and particularly to bring humanitarian relief to Palestinians living under Israeli occupation in the West Bank and Gaza.[20] The FBI's HLF investigation would collect hundreds of boxes of documents, hundreds of hours of audio- and videotapes, and thousands of pages of financial records.[21]

In July 1996, the Chicago FBI opened another far-reaching investigation, targeting what it described as "the Hamas criminal enterprise within the U.S."[22] It grew to become Operation Vulgar Betrayal, the investigation that later dogged Muslim American FBI agent Gamal Abdel-Hafiz with inappropriate questions about his loyalty. Heavily redacted FBI documents from the Vulgar Betrayal case file obtained by the conservative legal advocacy group Judicial Watch indicate the investigation scrutinized "thousands of individuals and hundreds of organizations and businesses in forty-two [FBI field offices]."[23] The documents list hundreds of Muslim organizations, businesses, and mosques as subjects of the investigation, including HLF and CAIR. Documents from the Vulgar Betrayal file detail a plan to interview five hundred leaders, investors, and donors to major Muslim nonprofit organizations across the United States.[24] The investigation collected so much financial data from the targeted organizations that the FBI had to hire a private forensic accounting firm to analyze them.

The Vulgar Betrayal investigation seems to have tracked the premise of a 1995 article Emerson wrote for the *New Republic*. Emerson's article again quoted former FBI assistant director Revell, who claimed there was "an extensive subterranean network in the United States of radical militants whose activities are not illegal" but needed to be watched.[25] Emerson's description of the Hamas "infrastructure" in the United States, which he said included HLF, CAIR, and zakat committees in the West Bank and Gaza, was based in part on Chicago businessman Muhammad Salah's confession to the Israeli domestic security service Shin Bet. Emerson called Salah the "commander of the military wing of Hamas in the United States."[26]

Salah, a U.S. citizen, was arrested at a Gaza checkpoint in January 1993. In his hotel, Israeli authorities found approximately $97,000. Salah said he was distributing charitable donations raised from the United States to relieve the humanitarian crisis caused by Israel's mass deportation of 415 Palestinians during the first intifada. Shin Bet held Salah incommunicado and interrogated him for fifty-four days, during which he signed elaborate confessions implicating American charities in funding and directing Hamas political and terrorist operations in Israel. Salah disavowed the confession before his military trial, arguing he was physically abused, deprived of sleep, threatened, and psychologically manipulated into signing it (he passed a Shin Bet polygraph exam denying knowledge of terrorist attacks described in the statement, according to his attorney and court documents).[27] But facing a life sentence, he pled guilty in exchange for a five-year sentence in an Israeli prison, with credit for the almost two years he had already served.

The U.S. government was originally skeptical of the Israeli allegations against Salah and the reliability of his confession, but when Hamas began suicide bombings in April 1993, four months after Salah's arrest, attitudes hardened.[28] The U.S. government began expanding its laws to target not just those who conspire to assist terrorist acts but those who support foreign organizations it labeled as terrorists. In January 1995,

President Clinton issued Executive Order 12947, which exercised his economic sanctions power under the International Emergency Economic Powers Act (IEEPA) to designate Hamas as a foreign terrorist organization.[29] The EO conferred broad authority to the secretary of the treasury to freeze the assets of any individual or entity associated with a designated terrorist group.

In contrast to the watch lists, the "specially designated terrorist" (SDT) list is public, principally so people will know what entities they cannot do business with. The Treasury Department's Office of Foreign Assets Control (OFAC) manages the SDT list, along with sanctions programs targeting money launderers, drug dealers, weapons proliferators, and other transnational criminals. Today the OFAC list runs over a thousand pages.[30]

In 1996, Congress passed the Antiterrorism and Effective Death Penalty Act (AEDPA), establishing severe criminal penalties for anyone who provides "material support or resources" to entities the U.S. government designates as foreign terrorist organizations, or to individuals associated with them.[31] The statute's broad definition of "material support" included financial resources and services, training, and personnel. The Supreme Court interpreted the material support prohibition broadly, finding that the government need not show a defendant had the specific intent to support a banned group's terrorist activities to win conviction, only that he or she had known the group was an SDT on the OFAC list. Even a benign effort, such as coordinating with an SDT to safely supply humanitarian aid to civilians caught in a conflict zone the SDT controls, could result in criminal sanction under the Supreme Court's analysis.[32] The law criminalizes everyone associated with an SDT, and anyone providing material support to an SDT can themselves be designated an SDT, in an ever-broadening chain reaction.

In July 1995, Salah became the first American citizen the U.S. government designated an SDT. The Treasury Department froze his assets without charging him with a crime, consulting a judge, or holding a hearing. Israel released Salah from prison six months early and he returned home to Chicago in 1997, where he remained free from confinement but couldn't accept so much as a donated meal without seeking a government license. In a 1998 civil forfeiture proceeding, Vulgar

Betrayal agents seized $1.4 million from Salah's frozen funds and the Quranic Literacy Institute, which had employed him before he went to Israel. This seizure represented the FBI's first use of civil forfeiture laws, which do not require proof beyond a reasonable doubt like criminal trials, in a terrorism investigation.[33] As these cases demonstrate, the post–Church Committee reforms were not nearly the handcuffs Revell and others pretended they were.

FBI leaders like Revell seemed not to understand that requiring reasonable criminal predicates to justify investigations doesn't just protect the rights of the innocent. Strong guidelines also help the FBI avoid wasting resources by focusing their efforts where objective evidence, rather than speculative bias, indicates criminal activity is taking place.

Despite the sweeping scope of these investigations, the FBI did not uncover evidence of terrorist plots, weapons trafficking, or other dangerous activity that justified prosecution, even after the material support prohibition passed in 1996. Sami al-Arian remained a regular—though controversial—professor, activist, and television pundit for several years after the FBI raided his home and office. He campaigned for George W. Bush in 2000 and accepted an invitation to the White House in June 2001, so the FBI could not have believed he was a dangerous man.[34]

By 1999, some FBI and Justice Department officials became concerned about the Vulgar Betrayal case as well, though it is unclear precisely why due to the documents' heavy redactions.[35] The FBI closed the criminal case in 2000 without leveling any indictments. As the CISPES case had demonstrated a decade earlier, though the guidelines weren't sufficient to prevent agents from initiating overbroad investigations, they provided a standard that more judicious FBI and Justice Department personnel could reference to eventually shut them down.

From a security standpoint, one has to wonder whether the duration, scope, and intensity—and ultimately the futility—of these investigations into the supposed Hamas "infrastructure" inside the United States throughout the 1990s distracted the FBI from the growing threat from al Qaeda. Perhaps focusing these investigative resources on actual terrorists—whether from Hamas, al Qaeda, or anywhere else—rather than supposed support networks might have been a more effective strategy for protecting American security.[36]

The importance of maintaining strong investigative guidelines from a civil liberties standpoint is illustrated by what happened with these cases once they were loosened after 9/11.

CHANGED RULES AND CHANGED ATTITUDES

Just weeks after the 9/11 attacks, Congress passed the USA Patriot Act, which expanded the FBI's authority to use secretive foreign intelligence powers to collect volumes of information about Americans that it could more easily use in criminal prosecutions. The Patriot Act also expanded the material support prohibitions to ban the provision of "expert advice and assistance" to designated foreign terrorist groups.[37] A few months later, John Ashcroft amended the Attorney General's Guidelines to give the FBI the authority to conduct more aggressive investigations for longer periods of time with less of an evidentiary predicate. His guidelines specifically authorized FBI agents to conduct "general topical research" and attend public events to gather intelligence, even where they had no reasonable suspicion that anyone was doing anything wrong.[38] Civil libertarians recognized these changes were designed to increase surveillance of political and religious activities, since bank robbers and drug dealers don't typically hold public events.[39]

The Bush administration shuttered eight Muslim American charities in the years following 9/11, utilizing the broad sanctioning authority under IEEPA that allows the government to freeze an organization's assets based on secret allegations.[40] FBI raids and highly publicized investigations stigmatized several other Muslim charities that were never formally charged or designated as terrorism supporters but could no longer attract funding as a result of the negative attention. Since zakat is an obligation in Islam, the disruption of these charities and the fear of criminal penalties for giving to the wrong charity chilled American Muslims' free exercise of their religion. The uncertainty caused by these aggressive anti-terrorism financing measures also inhibited non-Muslim humanitarian and peace-building organizations from working in conflict zones where terrorist groups operated. In the end, the Justice Department convicted only one U.S. Muslim charity, the Holy Land

Foundation, for materially supporting terrorism, in what remains a highly controversial prosecution.[41]

But these new authorities weren't necessary to arm the Bush administration's war on Muslim civil society. For the most part, the post-9/11 prosecutions and asset freezes targeting Muslim charities would rely on evidence the FBI had been gathering since the early 1990s. The amended guidelines did reflect changed attitudes at the top of the Justice Department and FBI, however, as they sought to bolster their anti-terrorism record with raids, arrests, and prosecutions as Congress and the 9/11 Commission exposed their pre-9/11 failings. Obviously, a core group of agents, supervisors, and prosecutors had already bought into the narrative Pipes, Emerson, Revell, and others were selling, and the new rules and attitudes empowered them to go after more peripheral actors. As for why the Bush administration chose to immediately target Muslim charities, Paul Craig Roberts, a former Reagan administration Treasury Department official, told ACLU researchers, "I think . . . it was an easy, soft target."[42]

The government designated the Holy Land Foundation as an SDT and froze its assets in December 2001. Challenging an SDT designation is difficult, as the government needs only a reasonable suspicion to justify its decision and the designated entity has no right to see the evidence against it. Under the Administrative Procedures Act, which governs this type of agency action, a judge would have to find the Treasury Secretary acted in an "arbitrary and capricious" manner to overturn a designation. The Holy Land Foundation's designation challenge failed in March 2004. The following July, the Justice Department filed criminal charges against the Holy Land Foundation and five of its leaders (the HLF-5) for providing material support to Hamas, money laundering, and tax violations.[43]

The Justice Department indicted Sami al-Arian in February 2003 under the 1970 mafia-busting Racketeer Influenced and Corrupt Organization Act (RICO) for providing material support to the PIJ. On August 20, 2004, the FBI in Chicago charged Muhammad Salah in a racketeering conspiracy to finance Hamas terrorist attacks in Israel and with obstruction of justice for making false or incomplete statements during a civil suit brought against him by the family of an American victim of a Hamas shooting in Israel.

Sami al-Arian's six-month trial ended with no convictions in December 2005. A jury acquitted on eight of the most serious charges and deadlocked ten to two for acquittal on nine other charges.[44] On February 2, 2007, a jury acquitted Salah of conspiring to support Hamas. The first HLF-5 trial ended the following October with no convictions after the jury issued acquittals on some charges for two defendants and deadlocked on all the others, resulting in a hung jury. The Justice Department inspector general raised more questions about the efficacy of the Bush administration's terrorism enforcement actions when it published a 2007 audit revealing the FBI and Justice Department had exaggerated terrorism conviction statistics from 2001 to 2005 by claiming immigration, drug, or document fraud convictions were terrorism-related when the records showed no such connection.[45]

These embarrassing disappointments didn't cause the Justice Department to reevaluate its approach to counterterrorism. Instead, agents and prosecutors became more aggressive in their drive to punish these defendants and intensify their surveillance, infiltration, and provocations in Muslim American communities.

Though the jury rejected the terrorism charges against Salah, it convicted him for obstructing justice by submitting false or incomplete statements in the civil lawsuit brought by the family of a victim of an Hamas terror attack. The government requested a ten-year sentence, arguing for terrorism enhancements despite the jury's acquittals on the terrorism charges.[46] The judge sentenced Salah to twenty-two months in prison.[47] On November 5, 2012, the Treasury Department finally removed Salah from the SDT list.[48]

Al-Arian, who spent three years in prison before his trial ended, much of it in solitary confinement, remained in detention pending a retrial on the deadlocked counts. In May 2006, he agreed to a plea deal with the U.S. attorney in Florida to avoid a second trial and put an end to his ordeal. He would admit to assisting the PIJ by helping a colleague associated with the terror group with an immigration matter and by lying to a journalist. He would accept voluntary deportation in exchange for a sentence recommendation that amounted to time served and an agreement not to seek further grand jury testimony.[49] The judge refused to abide by the prosecutor's recommendation and sentenced al-Arian to serve another eleven months in prison. Then, ignoring the agreement with the U.S. attorney in Florida, federal prosecutors in the Eastern District of Virginia subpoenaed al-Arian to appear before a grand jury there and charged him with criminal contempt when he refused.[50] Al-Arian would spend another two years in custody, then six more under house arrest before the government finally dropped the contempt charges and deported him to Turkey in 2015.

RADICALIZING THE FBI

I didn't know anything about these 1990s investigations of Arabs and Muslims when I worked for the FBI. I first became aware of Emerson and Pipes when a truck bomb exploded in front of the Alfred P. Murrah Federal Building in Oklahoma City in 1995. Before investigators identified far-right extremist Timothy McVeigh as the bomber, Emerson and Pipes each made public comments suggesting Middle Eastern terrorists might be to blame.[51] They weren't alone, as many others, including FBI officials, jumped to the same conclusion.[52] But I had just emerged from a year undercover with neo-Nazis, and I surmised early based on the location, target, and timing that the attacker was a far-right extremist. That those calling for extraordinary responses to terrorism committed by Muslims did not widen their approach to examine far-right violence once McVeigh and his crew were identified made it clear to me their interest was politics rather than preventing terrorism.

I was well aware there was a lot of specious terrorism research and analysis being produced inside and outside the government, however. I read as much academic literature on the subject as I could to prepare for my undercover roles, but very little came close to describing what I was experiencing inside white supremacist cells planning acts of terrorism. At that time, in the early 1990s, there were basically two schools of terrorism research. The first saw terrorism as a tactic that rational actors employ strategically as part of a wider political conflict. These scholars suggested that terrorist violence could not be properly understood except in context with the political, social, and economic environment in which it took place.[53] Researchers from this school could not imagine explaining why someone would join a terrorist group like the Irish Republican Army in 1972, for instance, without discussing Bloody Sunday, British capitalist-imperialism, and the partition of Ireland.

The second school of thought argued that terrorism was the product of a defective mind. These researchers looked for psychological disorders or conditions that could explain such aberrant behavior.[54] Terrorism studies from both schools were criticized for promoting theoretical models over data-driven analyses, using weak research methods, and failing to meet standards of scholarly rigor.[55] Just as all terrorism is political by definition, counterterrorism research is often driven by politics as well. Simply choosing which acts of political violence will be analyzed as "terrorism" and which will not is a political decision that fundamentally skews the research.

Those invested in maintaining the existing sociopolitical order preferred the psychological defect approach to the topic because it narrowed the counterterrorism discourse to determining what is wrong with "them"—the terrorists—and how they can be stopped before they do harm. If terrorists are mentally deranged fanatics, no adjustments to the political, economic, or social order need to be debated. Governments threatened by terrorism, which tended to be the primary sponsors of anti-terrorism research, preferred this model as well because it justified increasing and centralizing state power to protect against an unpredictable and irrational enemy. A multitude of empirical studies over the decades found little evidence of psychological abnormality among terrorists, however, and by the mid-1990s a consensus emerged that there was no psychological illness or profile that could be used to identify pre-terrorists.[56]

So, I was troubled after 9/11 when FBI officials began talking about disrupting radicals again. I feared a repeat of the Hoover-era abuses would be justified by the bureau's reliance on this concept. I knew that basing counterterrorism tactics on a defective model was unlikely to be effective. Yet the government began investing millions of dollars in terrorism research that ignored the previous decade of empirical studies and abandoned scholarly methods to relentlessly push the concept of ideological radicalization as the explanation for terrorism. These researchers often characterized the radicalization process in medical terms, calling it the spread of an ideological "virus," "contagion," or "infection."[57] They used vague and subjective terms to describe both the symptoms and the disease. For instance, one model claimed "indicators" of terrorism were "grievances," which combined with a "cognitive opening" might cause "vulnerable" or "alienated" persons to begin a "radicalization" process that could lead to "violent extremism."[58]

Radicalization theory rehabilitated the notion that terrorism was the product of a defective mind, while eluding the scientific rigor of psychiatric diagnosis. The lack of precise definition or objective measurement for these indicators became an advantage, as they could appear reasonably neutral on paper while allowing the government to selectively apply them to any individual or group it chose to target.[59] Everyone has grievances, so the government can adjust its suppressive countermeasures to target whatever population becomes a political threat. In effect, the "indicators" of radicalization are simply proxies for prohibited categories of law enforcement targeting: race, ethnicity, religion, national origin, and political ideology.

Insidiously, the identification of "grievances" as an indicator of radicalization paints anyone who challenges the government's theories or tactics as a potential target of its counterterrorism efforts. This circular reasoning stifles academic debate as researchers using sound social science methods are marginalized from government-funded programs, and it puts a target on the backs of Muslim American activists and civil rights advocates who oppose these counterterrorism policies.

PERSECUTING THE UNINDICTED

The Justice Department retried the HLF-5 case in 2008. The judge was more deferential to the government during the retrial, allowing prosecutors to admit hearsay evidence he excluded in the first trial and show the jury grisly videos of Hamas terrorist attacks that had no relation to Holy Land Foundation funds.[60] The second jury convicted the HLF leaders, and the judge sentenced them to prison terms from fifteen to sixty-five years. They appealed. The Fifth Circuit Court of Appeals found the trial court had erred in admitting certain irrelevant evidence and hearsay testimony from an FBI informant. It also said allowing a Treasury Department witness to opine from the witness stand that it was illegal to provide funds to zakat committees not on the department's list of banned organizations was improper. But the appeals court deemed these errors "harmless" and upheld the convictions and sentences.[61]

Though the HLF prosecution was the Justice Department's biggest "win" in its anti-terrorism financing effort, it was also its most controversial. The HLF indictment acknowledged that Hamas was a complicated organization, with a military wing that engaged in terrorism and a social wing that provided food, medical care, and educational opportunities to Palestinians living in the occupied territories.[62] Government documents reveal its investigators saw HLF take measures to distance itself from Hamas after the U.S. government designated it an SDT, but they interpreted these efforts as a ruse to hide their "true spirit and intent" rather than an attempt to comply with the law.[63]

The most controversial part of the HLF case is that the government never alleged that HLF gave funds directly to either wing of Hamas, or even that HLF funds were diverted to Hamas. The government acknowledged that the $12 million in HLF donations at issue in the trial went to six "zakat committees" in the West Bank, which were organizations set up to distribute charitable aid in the Muslim tradition. The prosecutors did not dispute that HLF's donations to the zakat committees went to the charitable ends they were intended to serve. The government's argument—proffered through two Israeli intelligence officials who the judge let testify in alias in a closed courtroom—was that Hamas controlled the zakat committees and that HLF should have known it.

The Treasury Department had not designated these zakat committees as banned SDTs at the time HLF provided the donations, however, nor before the trial. It still hasn't designated them as such. Trial evidence showed that the U.S. Agency for International Development (USAID), the United Nations, and the Red Crescent had all provided funds to these same zakat committees during and after the time HLF did.[64] A former U.S. consul general to Jerusalem testified that State Department policy prohibited him from meeting with Hamas or its representatives, but he met with zakat committees without rebuke. He said no U.S. official had ever told him the zakat committees in question were associated with

Hamas. The government's theory was that any humanitarian assistance provided to Palestinians in the West Bank and Gaza benefited Hamas by helping it win "hearts and minds" in the community and freeing it to use its resources on militant activities rather than social services.[65]

The HLF case set a terrifying precedent for organizations around the world that provide humanitarian aid in conflict zones, particularly in Muslim-majority nations where many U.S.-designated SDTs operate. Several charities filed an amicus brief in the HLF defendants' appeal, arguing that the government's broad and arbitrary application of the material support prohibition in the HLF case erased confidence that aid organizations could safely provide humanitarian assistance so long as they avoided listed SDTs.[66] The government's aggressive targeting of U.S. Muslim charities chilled American Muslims' religious practices, as they could face criminal liability for donating to or associating with non-designated Muslim organizations that the Treasury Department might later deem too closely associated with an SDT.[67] Under the government's reasoning in the HLF case, anyone who provides material support to an associate of an SDT is itself an SDT. So, anyone who provided support to an individual who provided support to an SDT could be similarly designated and prosecuted in a chain reaction.

To make matters worse, prosecutors in the first HLF trial improperly released a list of 246 Muslim organizations and individuals it called "unindicted co-conspirators and/or joint venturers." The list included some of the largest and most influential Muslim American organizations, including CAIR; the North American Islamic Trust (NAIT), which finances and holds title to mosques and Islamic schools across the country; and the Islamic Society of North America (ISNA), the largest Muslim educational and social services organization in the United States.[68]

Identifying unindicted co-conspirators and joint venturers is a prosecutorial tactic used to ease the admission of hearsay statements at trial under federal rules of evidence. It is a controversial practice even when the list is kept under seal, as it tends to infer criminal culpability without levying a specific charge or providing a forum for the unindicted co-conspirator or joint venturer to defend itself. Indeed, these entities are often "unindicted" because the government recognizes it does not have evidence to prove their guilt. As a result, Justice Department policy strongly advises against public release of unindicted co-conspirator lists. Prosecutors in the HLF-5 case did not seek to introduce hearsay statements from CAIR, NAIT, or ISNA at trial, and later called their failure to seal the unindicted co-conspirator list in the HLF case an "unfortunate oversight."[69] CAIR, NAIT, and ISNA sued the Justice Department and a federal judge determined the government's public release of the unindicted co-conspirator list violated their Fifth Amendment due process rights.[70]

The Islamophobia network seized on the unindicted co-conspirator list to falsely suggest the Justice Department had charged CAIR with participating in a criminal conspiracy to support Hamas. The Justice Department has never levied such allegations, and to the contrary, it issued a letter in 2011 explaining that the Obama administration had reached the same conclusion as the Bush administration: neither the facts nor the law supported a decision to prosecute CAIR.[71] The Dallas U.S. attorney who oversaw the HLF prosecution confirmed that the decision not to prosecute CAIR was based on the evidence, not political pressure.[72] In fact, CAIR has a long record of condemning terrorism throughout its existence.[73]

Unfortunately, rather than correcting the record, the FBI contributes to this slander by publicly ostracizing CAIR from its community outreach events. In April 2009, the FBI wrote to Senator Jon Kyl (R-AZ) declaring it had temporarily suspended liaison activities with CAIR based on its purported association with an organization that may have previously been associated with Hamas. This no-engagement status would remain, the letter said, "until we can resolve whether there continues to be a connection between CAIR or its executives and HAMAS."[74] Two years later, FBI director Robert Mueller indicated in public testimony that CAIR remained officially banished from FBI events. Under questioning from Representative Louie Gohmert (R-TX) in the House Judiciary Committee, Mueller said, "We have no formal relationship with CAIR because of concerns with regard to the national leadership."[75]

This repeated public shaming by the nation's premier law enforcement agency is a direct assault on CAIR's First Amendment rights, and those of the communities it serves. The FBI's comments are clearly designed to harm CAIR's reputation and make it more difficult for the organization to attract members and donors, who could risk criminal liability if the government later designates CAIR an SDT. The FBI has no problem meeting with CAIR representatives when they are assisting with its counterterrorism efforts, however. In December 2009, for instance, CAIR brought the families of five young men who went to Pakistan to join an al Qaeda–affiliated terrorist group to the bureau's attention so they could be arrested before the men engaged in violent acts.[76]

The FBI's public rebuke of CAIR is also peculiar because the government has powerful tools to take action against any entity it reasonably believes provides material support to terrorist organizations. The Treasury Department has frozen the assets of other Muslim organizations without notice or hearings, based entirely on a secret administrative record that never has to be revealed. If the FBI had any credible evidence that CAIR supported terrorism or posed a threat, it could shut the organization down without submitting its evidence to adversarial challenge. The government has certainly acted more aggressively against other organizations.

In February 2006, the FBI raided the Ohio charity KindHearts for Charitable Humanitarian Development, and the Treasury Department froze its assets *pending an investigation* into whether it was providing material support to terrorist organizations.[77] Patriot Act amendments to IEEPA authorized the Treasury Department to freeze an entity's assets while conducting an investigation. For any charity, such a "temporary" asset seizure amounts to an organizational death sentence.

KindHearts was established in 2002 to fill the void created by the government's shuttering of other Muslim American charities, with the specific goal of staying in strict compliance with the law so Muslim Americans could safely satisfy their religious obligations. Neither KindHearts nor its leaders were ever charged with a crime. In May 2007, the Treasury Department notified KindHearts that it had made a "provisional determination" to designate it as an SDT, which is not authorized under the law. In 2011, a federal judge ruled the Treasury Department had violated KindHearts' Fourth and Fifth Amendment rights by failing to secure a probable cause warrant before seizing its property and failing to provide due process.[78] The damage was already done, however.

KindHearts effectively went out of business the day the FBI raided its offices and Treasury froze its assets.

In the volumes of financial records, phone calls, faxes, and emails gathered during these cases, several running more than a decade, there was no evidence presented that any of these defendants committed an actual act of terrorism. None of the thousands of wiretapped conversations caught any of them planning or ordering an attack. The government found no bombs or illegal weapons during its searches of defendants' homes and businesses. The government's theory, which launched intrusive and resource-intensive investigations of hundreds, perhaps thousands, of Americans, was that banning material support would starve terrorist groups of the resources necessary to continue harming innocent people. When the jury announced convictions in the second HLF-5 trial in 2008, the FBI explained its strategy: "Fighting terrorism by choking off its funding source is one of the many techniques we use to proactively disrupt and dismantle terrorist enterprises before they strike."[79]

Reasonable people can differ on whether the types of support the government alleged these defendants provided to Palestinian terrorist groups justified the scope or intensity of these investigations, prosecutions, and ongoing punishments. But there is little question that these tactics did not "disrupt and dismantle" the terrorism enterprises they targeted. In 2006, years after the government seized Muhammad Salah's funds and froze HLF's and other Muslim charities' assets, Hamas won legislative elections in the occupied territories and took control of the Palestinian Legislative Council.[80] In 2007, it fought a battle with its Palestinian rival, the U.S.-backed Fatah Party, emerged victorious, and took over governance of the Gaza Strip. It survived two wars with Israel, the latest in 2014, and according to the *Times of Israel*, by January 2017 Hamas had restored its military capabilities to prewar levels.[81] The PIJ likewise remains a deadly and some say growing threat to Israel.[82] So, these efforts did not achieve the goals the FBI had set for itself. Al Qaeda, despite serious setbacks, has similarly remained a threat and has actually expanded its geographic reach.[83] Terrorist groups the United States is actively fighting around the world, like ISIL, Boko Haram, and al-Shabab, didn't exist when the war on terror began and could arguably be considered products of the West's war on terror.

Clearly, the FBI is not responsible for national policy. Congress passed the material support laws and the FBI is obligated to enforce them. But FBI leadership does have discretion over how and where it devotes its resources, and a responsibility to safeguard the constitutional rights of the guilty and innocent alike as it conducts its work. As an intelligence agency, it also has an obligation to speak truth to power regarding the efficacy and impact of these types of investigations, and to be honest with the American public about the nature of the threats we face without fear-mongering. The FBI's heavy-handed methods and derogatory public statements targeting Muslim American civil society infringed on the religious and political rights of Muslim communities throughout the United States and inhibited the ability of humanitarian organizations to provide aid to victims of war, famine, and natural disasters around the world. If grievances generate terrorism, as the FBI's radicalization theory suggests, employing tactics that inflame them would seem more than counterproductive.

Yet despite their ineffectiveness in reducing terrorism, material support cases remain the bulk of the Justice Department's successes in international terrorism prosecutions after 9/11, rather than the interdiction of actual terrorism plotting. Increasingly, the FBI manufactures both of these types of cases through informant-led sting operations targeting the gullible more than the dangerous and in the process artificially inflate the terrorism threat rather than mitigate it.[84] This methodology requires the identification and development of informants to saturate Muslim American communities seeking to identify troubled individuals who can be lured into sting operations, rather than evidence-based investigations following logical links to actual terrorists. The community itself becomes the target.

7

SCAPEGOATING MUSLIM AMERICAN COMMUNITIES

With its disruption strategy, the FBI sought to cast as wide a net as possible to suppress terrorist support networks through aggressive interventions and surveillance of "at-risk" populations. The harsh and selective enforcement measures taken against Muslim civil society groups discussed in the previous chapter represent one end of the spectrum of activities that might be considered terrorism disruptions under the FBI's new rulebook. As troubling as many of these cases are, there is perhaps greater reason for concern when the FBI employs disruption tactics against people who it never charges with terrorism-related crimes. These targets may not know the source of their troubles and do not have a forum to defend themselves from spurious allegations and continuing harassment. These actions are often less individually dramatic, but they occur at a far higher rate and without accountability, creating a cumulative burden on the targeted communities.

The radicalization theory identifies the target population for these disruptive activities, and the changes to law and policy after 9/11 empower them by lifting the barriers designed to protect the innocent. The tactics of the disruption strategy include a "range of tools" documented in the FBI Counterterrorism Division's 2009 Baseline Collection Plan, which dictates what types of intelligence should be collected in each phase of investigation outlined in the 2008 Attorney General's Guidelines. It lists "arrests, interviews, source-directed operations to effectively disrupt [a] subject's activities" as potential disruption activities and recommends that interviews "specifically address the subject's . . . potential recruitment as a source."[1] Each of these tactics can have a disruptive effect on the broader community as well as the targeted subject.

VOLUNTARY INTERVIEWS

After 9/11, FBI agents conducted interviews of nearly eight thousand Middle Eastern and South Asian immigrants and visitors to the United States.[2] The Justice Department recruited state and local law enforcement officers to assist them, though some, like the Portland (Oregon) Police Bureau, refused to cooperate based on civil rights and privacy concerns.[3] Thousands of people of Iraqi origin received visits from the FBI as it conducted new waves of interviews before and during the 2003 Iraq War.[4] Yemeni communities and Chechens were next, after the Umar Farouk Abdulmutallab underwear bombing attempt and the Boston Marathon attacks, respectively.[5] Many U.S. citizens, permanent residents, and immigrants of Arab, Middle Eastern, Muslim, and South Asian (AMEMSA) communities grew to fear the knock on the door signaling an unannounced evening visit from FBI agents in the years since 9/11.[6]

A friendly request for an interview might not seem particularly intrusive. But these interviews can be unsettling, particularly when the questions suggest the FBI agents think the interviewees might be associated with terrorists or other national security threats.[7] An agent asking probing questions about a mosque or social organization might cause the subject to withdraw from involvement with those entities out of concern that a terrorist threat may be lurking there, or that the FBI may be monitoring them. When FBI agents visit a home or workplace to question people they can cause serious reputational harm by alerting co-workers, bosses, landlords, or neighbors to the bureau's interest in them.

Many people subjected to these "voluntary" interviews have reported FBI agents asked them about their political opinions. An article in a 2008 FBI textbook, *Terrorism and Political Islam*, may explain why. It instructs agents interviewing Muslims to ask "indicator questions" about the interviewee's attitudes regarding the Iraq War, the Palestinian-Israeli conflict, and the 9/11 attacks to gauge where that person falls along an ideological spectrum. The article contends the scale "can range from a person loyal to the United States who desires to be an honest and reliable informant for law enforcement on the one end, or at the other end of the spectrum one who is militant and preparing to carry out jihad."

A subject answering with "a patriotic and pro-Western stance could potentially evolve into a street informant or concerned citizen," it states, while expressing hostility to U.S. policies could reveal a "militant ideology."[8] The assumption is that a person sharing the agent's political views is safe, while someone questioning them is not. Leaving aside the inaccuracy of this analysis, FBI agents asking inappropriate political questions creates a chilling effect, leading Muslim Americans to believe that publicly expressing their political opinions can draw unwanted and unwarranted law enforcement scrutiny.

Concern over FBI voluntary interviews as a tool of political intimidation increased in the weeks before the 2016 presidential election. FBI agents conducted a wave of voluntary interviews targeting Muslims across at least twelve states, asking whether they knew about any al Qaeda threats targeting the election.[9] Coming as they did during a campaign in which Republican candidates expressed open hostility toward Muslims—calling for immigration bans, registries, and police patrols of Muslim neighborhoods—the potential suppressive effect of these interviews on Muslim American voter turnout can hardly be overstated.

The FBI's use of selective prosecutions makes "voluntary" interviews with agents a high-risk activity for those in the suspect community. Federal law prohibits making false statements to government agents through a statute that Supreme Court Justice Ruth Bader Ginsburg said gave prosecutors "extraordinary authority . . . to manufacture crimes."[10] It can be an easy charge to make in terrorism-disruption cases because the FBI has access to a vast quantity of detailed personal information through the electronic surveillance dragnets and its broad investigative powers. Agents can scour government records for inconsistencies or identify associations with someone the subject might not want to reveal in an interview. The more statements and information the FBI can coax out of a person, the more likely they can find a conflict from a previous interview or document filed with a government agency.

Of course, where a person refuses a voluntary interview the government can sometimes compel a statement with a grand jury subpoena. This tactic can create a "perjury trap," which is why Sami al-Arian and Muhammad Salah were trying to avoid testifying in grand juries and civil trials. An example of this dubious tactic involves Sabri Benkahla, a Muslim American who won acquittal in a 2004 FBI terrorism case that charged him with attending a Taliban training camp in 1999. After failing to convict him, prosecutors subpoenaed him to testify in a grand jury that continued investigating his 1999 travels and charged him with perjury and obstruction of justice for denying he attended the terrorist training camp it had failed to prove he attended at the earlier trial.[11] Benkahla was convicted and sentenced to ten years. George Washington University law professor Jonathan Turley expressed the dilemma: "If your client testifies, he is charged with some false statement. If he doesn't testify, they charge him with criminal contempt."[12]

In some cases, FBI agents resisted this tactic of targeting the person first and then finding the crime. In Oxford, Mississippi, in 2003, the U.S. attorney's office reportedly initiated a "convenience store initiative," targeting roughly 150 mostly Arab and Muslim store owners looking for suspicious sales of Sudafed and possible tax violations. The Drug Enforcement Administration and Bureau of Alcohol, Tobacco, Firearms and Explosives led the initiative, but FBI agents in the Oxford resident agency found out about it.[13] When their complaints to the U.S. attorney fell on deaf ears, Senior Supervisory Resident Agent Hal Neilson and four of his agents reported to FBI management that "the only individuals targeted by the [convenience store initiative] were of middle eastern descent and the only apparent nexus for investigation was ethnicity." He sought legal advice from FBI headquarters, "in the interest of insuring the civil rights of U.S. persons."[14] The U.S. attorney's office initiated a retaliatory investigation of Neilson's unrelated business investments and charged him with failing to disclose a financial interest in a government lease and making false statements to cover it up. The FBI fired him. A jury acquitted him at trial, however, and he eventually won reinstatement. He retired from the FBI in 2012.[15]

EXPLOITATION OF IMMIGRATION AND CITIZENSHIP BENEFITS

Other times, the FBI seeks interviews in conditions that are less than voluntary. For example, U.S. Customs and Border Protection (CBP) has vast authorities at border checkpoints and ports of entry, and its agents often question U.S. citizens and legal permanent residents, as well as foreign nationals. Muslim Americans have complained to the Department of Homeland Security (DHS) for more than a decade that CBP officers routinely question them about their religious practices, political beliefs, and charitable donations in violation of their First Amendment rights during these stops.[16]

The FBI has a formal program with U.S. Citizenship and Immigration Services that allows bureau agents to put holds on citizenship and immigration benefits based on national security concerns. Called the Controlled Application Review and Resolution Program (CARRP), it gives the FBI the power to delay or deny benefits that the immigrations services would otherwise provide, with no notice to the immigrant or due process procedures to challenge the alleged national security concerns. As with the no-fly list, many immigrants have reported that FBI agents engage them in multiple interviews and often offer to let their immigration or citizen application proceed if they agree to become an informant.[17]

In 2016, an anonymous intelligence source provided *The Intercept* with classified government documents describing a joint FBI/CBP program to exploit these mandatory interactions to collect intelligence and develop informants. The FBI provides CBP with intelligence requirements, perhaps particular countries or regions they are interested in, and CBP then identifies travelers who fit the request. Another FBI training presentation demonstrates a close working relationship between Joint Terrorism Task Forces and DHS in developing informants in Rochester, New York's Yemeni community. One slide recommends employing an "immigration relief dangle," which means enticing the subject with promises of assistance in obtaining immigration benefits. Somewhat cynically, the materials direct agents to select immigrants "who will ultimately receive their benefits anyhow," suggesting that the targets of these "dangles" are innocent of connections to terrorist groups. Rather, they are simply exploitable because they might believe their cooperation is necessary to receive the benefits they seek.[18]

In April 2018, the Justice Department charged FBI agent Terry Albury with the unauthorized transmission of classified documents to a media outlet, widely believed to be *The Intercept*. Albury, the only black agent in the Minneapolis field office, had leaked the documents in "an act of conscience," according to his lawyer, to raise public concern about FBI profiling of minority communities.[19] On October 18, 2018, Albury was sentenced to four years in prison.[20]

INFORMANT DEVELOPMENT AND DEPLOYMENT

FBI policy requires all agents to participate in its informant development program by recruiting and employing confidential human sources. Informants can be anything from jailhouse snitches to concerned citizens providing information to law enforcement to protect their communities from criminals. Informants often cooperate for some benefit—reduction of charges or sentence, immigration benefits, or financial reward. Many times, FBI agents who come into contact with Muslims through interviews, investigations, watch list hits, immigration proceedings, or community outreach events pitch them to become informants. Asking a criminal to become an informant is straightforward. But asking a noncriminal to spy on their faith community or social group is very different, and it creates a difficult dilemma for individuals who need government assistance but have no relevant threat information to provide.

FBI director Robert Mueller repeatedly denied that the bureau sent informants into mosques on fishing expeditions, but the evidence shows otherwise.[21] One informant, Shahed Hussain, prowled Newburgh, New York, mosques with his fancy cars and expensive wardrobe for almost a year before James Cromitie, a low-level drug dealer, took the bait. Hussain's FBI handler testified that he tasked Hussain to look for anyone expressing "radical Islamic thoughts."[22] Another convicted fraud artist turned informant, Craig Monteilh, alleged that in 2006 the FBI tasked him with pretending to convert to Islam to infiltrate Southern California mosques and gather "as much information on as many people and institutions as possible."[23] Monteilh claimed his handlers told him to target anyone who appeared especially devout, criticized U.S. foreign policy, or played a leadership role at the mosques.[24] His most sensational claim was that the FBI encouraged him to have sex with Muslim women so they could later be pressured into becoming FBI informants, mirroring Frank Varelli's claims from decades past.[25]

Identifying and recruiting informants became much easier in December 2008, when Attorney General Michael Mukasey again loosened the FBI's investigative guidelines. The changes were sweeping, condensing five sets of guidelines into one forty-six-page policy. The Mukasey guidelines created a new category of investigation called an "assessment," which agents could open on their own initiative for thirty days, so long as they claimed their purpose for doing so was to prevent crime, protect national security, or collect foreign intelligence.[26] Assessments require no factual predicate to suggest the subject of the inquiry has done anything wrong and can be renewed for additional thirty-day periods with just a supervisor's approval. There is no limit to the number of renewals. During assessments, agents are authorized to search government and commercial databases, subpoena telephone subscriber information, conduct overt and covert interviews and physical surveillance, and recruit and task informants to gather information. In the first two years agents had this authority, they opened more than 82,000 assessments of people and organizations. Only 3,315 of these assessments found evidence to justify the next level of investigation.[27]

One type of assessment authorizes agents to investigate people simply for the purpose of determining whether they could be a suitable informant. In 2011, the FBI expanded its internal policies to allow agents to rifle through people's discarded garbage during these assessments to find information that could be used to coerce them into becoming informants.[28]

More troubling is evidence that shows the FBI uses the no-fly list as a tool to compel people to submit to interviews.[29] The most egregious of these cases involve U.S. citizens who flew overseas without a problem only to find themselves barred from returning home at the end of their trip. Trapped in a foreign country, perhaps with an expiring visa, depleted vacation funds, and no accommodations, they are forced to turn to the local U.S. embassy for assistance. In several documented cases, embassy officials referred them to FBI agents, giving the watch-listed person little choice but to submit to an interrogation to resolve their predicament. Several of these Americans, including U.S. military veterans, reported that the FBI agents offered to take them off the no-fly list if they agreed to work as informants. Some have had to sue the U.S. government in order to obtain waivers to fly back into their own country.[30]

COMMUNITY OUTREACH AND COUNTERING VIOLENT EXTREMISM

FBI documents obtained through the Freedom of Information Act in 2011 showed the bureau also exploited community outreach and mosque outreach events for intelligence gathering and informant recruitment.[31] The FBI documents included details from conversations agents had with community members at these events which were entered into bureau intelligence files and disseminated to other unnamed agencies.[32]

During the Obama administration, FBI, Justice Department, and Department of Homeland Security community outreach efforts directed to Muslim American communities were subsumed into "countering violent extremism" (CVE) programs. CVE was a counter-radicalization program, built on the notion that suppressing extreme ideas would stop the progression to terrorism. The program involved law enforcement outreach to mosques, Muslim community groups, schools, social services organizations, and mental health professionals to teach them radicalization indicators to look for and report. Focusing CVE on Muslim communities was stigmatizing and reinforced Islamophobic themes that Muslims were prone to violence, uncooperative with law enforcement, and needed to be monitored. Some FBI CVE efforts focused on K-12 schools, with a "Don't Be a Puppet" interactive website for children and a handbook for teachers and administrators.[33] It also introduced a "shared responsibility committee" pilot program, formalizing what had been an ad hoc effort by some field offices to recruit community volunteers to sit on secret boards that would evaluate and monitor individuals of concern to the FBI.[34] The Justice Department shut the pilot program down in the face of public criticism, but there have been indications ad hoc efforts continue.[35]

MANUFACTURING TERRORISTS THROUGH REVERSE STING OPERATIONS

Reverse sting operations are another method of disruption, though many cases are designed to manufacture terrorists rather than interdict them, so it is unclear what is being disrupted. I worked sting operations as an FBI undercover agent, and I believe they are a justifiable tool when a serious crime is involved, the operation is narrowly tailored to target predicated subjects, and less intrusive methods are unlikely to be successful. A "reverse" sting is a technique that had mostly been used in drug investigations before 9/11. A typical sting involves an undercover agent attempting to buy drugs from a suspected dealer. In a reverse sting, the undercover agents portray drug dealers who sell illegal products to the target of the investigation.

In my sting operations, I bought explosives and illegal firearms from neo-Nazis and militiamen who manufactured them, and I captured evidence of their planned terrorist attacks and other criminal activity. Under the guidelines in place at the time, I needed evidence providing a reasonable indication that a subject was involved in criminal activity before targeting them. I met many people in these groups who expressed an interest in doing harm but lacked the skills or gumption to do much of anything on their own. Setting these people up would have been easy, but that wasn't our goal. We were investigating a crime problem, not seeking to invent one. I found the discipline of documenting the evidence on each subject to build reasonable suspicion helped point my investigations in the right direction, and I credit the success of these operations to that process.

The reverse terrorism stings of today, which commonly but not exclusively target Muslims, involve undercover agents or informants portraying members of designated foreign terrorist groups recruiting subjects who are not part of any terrorist group into a terrorist plot of the government's making. Often in these cases, the informant or undercover agent provides all the weapons and resources and even identifies the target for the attack.

In many reverse stings, the target of the investigation provides very little support to the manufactured plot. The FBI investigated Nicholas

Young, a Washington, D.C., Metropolitan Transit Authority police officer, for more than five years using multiple informants to entice him into committing a crime. One befriended Young over a two-year period, then pretended to have joined ISIL in Syria. Young eventually succumbed to his requests for assistance and sent $245 in Google Play gifts cards.[36] The FBI charged him in 2016 with providing material support to ISIL. Unexplained was how Young remained working as a police officer during the entirety of the FBI investigation if the investigating agents really considered him a terrorist. ISIL received no benefit from the $245 gift cards, which went to an FBI informant who never went to Syria, but the investigation-generated publicity certainly helped promote ISIL's reputation as a menace with a global reach. Meanwhile, arms procured through a billion-dollar CIA program to assist rebel forces fighting the Syrian government ended up in the hands of the al Qaeda–affiliated al Nusra Front.[37] A 2017 study by Conflict Armament Research revealed that a significant portion of ISIL's weapons and ammunition captured from its defeated forces in Iraq had been diverted from U.S. and Saudi arms shipments into Syria.[38] Young was sentenced to fifteen years in prison for an imaginary crime, yet no criminal charges were laid when ill-conceived intelligence operations armed real terrorists.

The FBI has also used reverse sting operations against subjects it knew had serious mental health problems. In Arizona, an FBI informant recruited Mahin Khan, an underage homebound teenager with severe developmental disabilities, into an ISIS plot. Khan's mother asked the informant to leave her son alone and when he didn't, she reported him to the FBI. When Khan's mother took his cellphone away, FBI undercover agents smuggled him another to keep the plot going. The FBI arrested Khan when he turned eighteen, but the U.S. attorney apparently declined to prosecute. The Arizona Attorney General's office charged Khan under an Arizona anti-terrorism statute and obtained a guilty plea.[39]

The informants the FBI employs in these operations are often more serious criminals than those they target. The aforementioned Shahed Hussain began working for the bureau after pleading guilty in a scheme to fraudulently manipulate drivers' license tests while working as a translator. While testifying about his role in an earlier FBI operation in Newburgh, New York, in 2009, Hussain admitted he had fled Pakistan after being arrested for murder, which he says he did not commit, and entered the United States using a fake passport. In addition to the fraud for which he was charged, the trial judge found Hussain made false statements on his asylum application as well as to a U.S. bankruptcy court, his probation officers, the IRS, a local liquor board and school district, and to his FBI handlers during the Newburgh operation. She also found he committed perjury on the witness stand when he testified for the government.[40]

Hussain worked two separate sting operations in New York that resulted in terrorism convictions against six individuals, none of whom had histories of violence or previous associations with terrorist groups. In Albany, the FBI convicted an Iraqi refugee and beloved imam, Yassin Aref, for agreeing to witness a financial transaction that was part of an elaborately concocted money-laundering scheme involving a stinger missile. It remains unclear whether Aref understood the nature of the transaction because Hussain claimed they used a code word for the missile, agreed upon in an earlier, unrecorded conversation.[41] In Newburgh, Hussain induced a bumbling and impoverished petty criminal named James Cromitie to help him bomb a synagogue and a military airport by promising him $250,000, cars, vacations, and a barbershop. Hussain did not record the conversations in which he made these inducements, and he did not tell his handling agents about them.[42] Hussain claimed on the stand that the $250,000 offer was a code for $5,000 but admitted he never had a conversation with Cromitie about the code. The FBI provided a fake stinger missile and made fake bombs for the plot. The trial judge acknowledged that "the government invented all of the details of the scheme."[43]

One of the more troubling aspects of this case was that the FBI allowed the informant to identify a Bronx synagogue as the target for the fake bombing, creating unnecessary alarm and fear in the Jewish community that a Muslim terrorist group had tried to kill them.

In a similarly problematic FBI-manufactured plot in Portland, Oregon, informants and FBI undercover agents coaxed a troubled young Muslim man into attacking a Christmas tree lighting ceremony with a government-manufactured car bomb. Again, the FBI provided all the weapons, and while the young man in that case chose the location, there was no need for the bureau to follow the plot to its dramatic, but fraudulent, completion. Carrying out this theatrical performance did nothing but increase public fear and tension between Christians and Muslims. A man who described himself as a "Christian warrior" firebombed a nearby mosque in retaliation, demonstrating how the FBI's manufactured terrorism attacks can inspire real ones.[44]

A MODEL OF RESISTANCE: THE YOUNG MUSLIM COLLECTIVE

To better understand how the FBI is using disruption strategy tools to suppress and stigmatize communities and intimidate political activists, it is helpful to review its approach to Minneapolis, Minnesota's Somali community through the eyes of resident Burhan Mohumed.

Mohumed is an American success story. His family fled Mogadishu, Somalia, when the civil war broke out in 1991 and ended up in a Kenyan refugee camp when Mohumed was two years old. When he was six, an uncle living in the United States sponsored them, and they moved to Detroit, Michigan. About a year later, they moved to the Cedar-Riverside neighborhood of Minneapolis, Minnesota, where Mohumed did most of his growing up and became a U.S. citizen. Cedar-Riverside is a diverse, poor and working-class, mostly immigrant community. It is home to such a high concentration of Somali Americans that it earned the moniker Little Mogadishu.

Mohumed graduated from high school and college and is finishing a master's degree in counseling and psychology from St. Mary's University of Minnesota. During his studies he has remained active in Cedar-Riverside, interning at a local community center to work with neighborhood youth. He was drawn to this work after witnessing police violence and harassment of young men of color in the area.[45] "They would literally whup us like they were our fathers, you know," Mohumed told me, "just disrupting whatever our activities we had in the neighborhood, flashing lights at us, and just demeaning and really just talking reckless to us as far as our identities were concerned. . . . These guys are the protectors? It was a weird conflict."[46]

Mohumed was still in high school in 2006 when Ethiopia, a predominantly Christian nation, invaded Somalia with U.S. backing and overthrew the Islamic Courts Union, which had only recently wrested control of Mogadishu from a coalition of CIA-funded warlords.[47] Somalia descended into civil war. As with any diaspora community, conflict in the mother country was felt in Little Mogadishu as well. About twenty-three young men from Minneapolis and St. Paul went to fight in the war, out of approximately seventy thousand to eighty thousand living in the Twin Cities at the time.[48] Some of these "travelers" went to defend their ancestral homeland from Ethiopian invaders, others out of a sense of religious obligation, to protect or avenge their families or clans, others simply out a desire for adventure.[49] Americans have participated in foreign wars throughout the country's entire existence, but because Somalia was a Muslim country, the U.S. government designated certain combatants terrorists, even though all factions committed their share of atrocities. Several Minnesota youths died in the fighting, including two as al-Shabab suicide bombers. Others were indicted or arrested by the FBI, prosecuted for material support of foreign terrorist organizations like al-Shabab.[50]

The government's counterterrorism narrative was simple. Al-Shabab terrorist recruiters were brainwashing Minnesota's Somali youth. These radicalized young American citizens posed a threat to the United States and that threat would become more serious if they went to Somalia and participated in the conflict, so they had to be neutralized. Studies show that Westerners who travel to foreign conflicts most often do not commit acts of violence when they return home, but the U.S. counterterrorism discourse lacks such nuance.[51] The FBI saw Somali American youth in Minneapolis as an at-risk population that needed monitoring and censoring.

Agents descended on a local mosque several of the travelers had attended, the largest in Minneapolis, and put the imam and youth coordinator on the no-fly list.[52] FBI agents went to people's homes and pulled students out of classrooms for interviews, in what many saw as harassment and intimidation rather than a genuine attempt to understand the impact that the wars—the war in Somalia, the drug war, the war on gangs, and the war on terror—were having on the black, Muslim, immigrant community in Minneapolis.[53]

It appeared for a time that the FBI was trying to adjust its approach. In 2009, the FBI established a Specialized Community Outreach Team (SCOT) in Minneapolis to attempt to address concerns about its enforcement actions and build positive relationships with the community members and leaders.[54] The SCOT program was actually a collaborative intelligence collection operation designed at FBI headquarters by the Office of Public Affairs and the Counterterrorism Division to target Somali populations in Minneapolis, Columbus, Seattle, San Diego, Denver, and Washington, D.C., for counterterrorism intelligence purposes. The project involved using FBI outreach coordinators to identify key community leaders who would provide information and promote bureau-approved messaging with a more credible voice. It tasked the Directorate of Intelligence to conduct "domain management" demographic analyses in the five targeted cities and the Behavioral Analysis Unit to establish a "baseline profile of Somali individuals that are vulnerable to being radicalized." The goal of this team effort was to increase the "ability for FBI outreach to support operational programs throughout the Bureau."[55] After the Brennan Center for Justice published this document, an FBI spokesman in Minneapolis claimed it had not implemented the intelligence gathering aspects of the SCOT program. In December 2010, the Office of Public Affairs issued a new policy separating community outreach activities from direct involvement with operational components of the FBI, though there were loopholes that allowed outreach programs to "open doors" for other agents and analysts.[56] The policy was amended again in 2013, reiterating the purpose of community outreach programming is to support "priority investigative programs," and simply cautioning coordinators to maintain "appropriate" separation between operational and outreach efforts.[57]

Despite these outreach programs, the FBI seemed to have a warped view of Minnesota's Somali American community. Though many still suffer high unemployment, economic hardship, and crime, the community is in many ways a model of successful assimilation that other cities around the world study to better assist their own immigration programs.[58] Mohumed felt the FBI's heavy-handed efforts were extremely counterproductive. Rather than try to engage with the community to understand the conflict in Somalia and the true motivations of the Minnesota men who traveled there, agents treated youth interest in the conflict as an indicator of radicalization. Mohumed saw the FBI pressure imams and community leaders to stifle debates about the war in Somalia and criticisms of U.S. foreign policy, kicking people out of mosques and forcing these discussions underground. The consequences of this suppression were realized a few years later, when the Syrian civil war began. Mosques and community groups couldn't risk talking to youth about the conflict, the Syrian government's brutality, or ISIL's illegitimacy, so people turned to the internet for information. A relative few made poor choices that cost them their lives or decades in prison. Knowing some of these young men, Mohumed believes open and candid community discussions regarding the wars in Syria and Iraq, unencumbered by government suspicion and monitoring, would have dissuaded some of them from attempting to participate.

In 2014, Attorney General Eric Holder announced Minneapolis would be one of the locations for a new CVE pilot program led by federal prosecutors.[59] The Minneapolis CVE program was another community outreach effort targeting the Somali community led by the U.S. attorney, with the participation of DHS and the FBI.[60] CVE programs were modeled on a controversial and divisive British program called Prevent, which a parliamentary committee called "unhelpful," "stigmatizing," and "potentially alienating" due to its exclusive focus on Muslim communities.[61] The Justice Department's CVE programs relied on the same debunked theory of terrorist radicalization that drove previous surveillance programs, but these were designed to recruit community members who would be trained to spot at-risk individuals and recommend them for intervention. The local U.S. attorney pledged the Minneapolis program, which he named Building Community Resilience, would not be used for intelligence gathering, but DHS and FBI continued their involvement in local CVE activities.

Mohumed worked with other activists to organize public forums to educate the community about the history and perils of participating in

CVE programs. They formed under the umbrella of the Young Muslim Collective (YMC) and established a youth-led program called C-Me, Not CVE.[62] DHS lured community groups to participate in CVE programs by offering grants to fund local programs, so YMC approached these organizations to alert them to the concerns of the impacted youth. As Mohumed told *The Guardian*, CVE programs fuel "divisions, mistrust and the sense that we are being scapegoated."[63] When a CVE-funded mentorship program started in Minneapolis schools, YMC developed its own mentoring program that gave students an alternative to participating in a program funded as a counterterrorism initiative.

Ironically, Mohumed and the YMC are building an effective form of community resilience that is truly community led. If the goal of CVE was really to strengthen and unify communities and increase positive civic participation, Mohumed and the YMC would be its poster children. Instead, in August 2016, a few days before the last C-Me, Not CVE forum, FBI agents unexpectedly visited Mohumed's home. As first reported by freelance journalist Joseph Sabroski, Mohumed refused to open his door without a warrant and told the agents he wasn't comfortable speaking without an attorney present. He recorded the interaction through the door.[64] The agents would not give Mohumed their last names or provide a business card but asked him to come to the FBI office to talk with them about "radicalism in the community." An attorney from the Council on American-Islamic Relations called the FBI on Mohumed's behalf and left a message to contact her if they wanted to talk with him. She never received a call, but a few days later FBI agents arrived at Mohumed's workplace asking for him. This approach was clearly meant to jeopardize Mohumed's employment. He later found out the FBI also subpoenaed Google for his subscriber and billing information.[65]

If these visits and inquiries were intended to intimidate and frighten Mohumed, they worked. If they were intended to stop his efforts to educate people about the harmful effects CVE and other counterterrorism tactics are inflicting on his community, they did not. The Trump administration expanded the DHS CVE grant program and directed more resources to law enforcement rather than community organizations. When President Trump was elected, many of the Muslim groups that had accepted Obama-era CVE funding returned it, realizing at last how dangerous these programs could be to the community when led by an administration that expressed open hostility toward Muslims.

New CVE grants went out to two dozen organizations around the country in 2018. Mohumed and the YMC volunteered to meet with activists in these locations to provide lessons learned through their experience in Minneapolis to ensure they would be equipped to educate and protect their own communities.

THE RADICALIZATION BLIND SPOT

The aggressive attempts by anti-Muslim advocates and policymakers to frame terrorism as a problem of "radical Islam" reminded me of the anti-Semitic conspiracy theories I had to listen to while I was undercover. Both focus on what I characterize as a "magical enemy." The neo-Nazis I investigated saw Jews as backward and subhuman but at the same time cunning and almost omnipotent in their ability to secretly manipulate the levers of power. Likewise, the Islamophobia network's fear of shadowy Muslims spreading Sharia law throughout the U.S. heartland to force the "Islamization of America" struck me as just as fantastical. Claims that President Barack Obama and CIA director John Brennan were secret Muslims who represented a Muslim Brotherhood takeover of the U.S. government sounded just like the "Zionist-occupied government" that white supremacists had warned me about. Understanding how anti-Semitic conspiracy theories drove racist violence made me more concerned when Islamophobia began gaining traction throughout the United States, and particularly within the FBI.

Wittingly or not, the FBI's aggressive counterterrorism actions and rhetoric regarding Muslim terrorists tended to reinforce and validate messages promoted by the Islamophobia network. If law enforcement and intelligence officials presented more sober and objective analyses that explained terrorist attacks in the United States were quite rare, significantly reduced since the 1970s, and more likely to come from domestic far-right extremists than foreigners, it would have been much harder for the anti-Muslim bigotry to gain traction.

The failure to pay heed to how the FBI's counterterrorism tactics were feeding anti-Muslim sentiment is demonstrated most significantly in the persistent increases in anti-Muslim hate crimes since 2002. The sharp rise in post-9/11 attacks dropped in 2002, according to FBI hate crime data, arguably a result of the Bush administration's condemnation of these crimes and the FBI's aggressive investigations and prosecutions. Anti-Muslim hate crimes have crept steadily upward since 2004, however, far exceeding the 2001 toll by 2016.[66] But the FBI doesn't treat violence against Muslim Americans with the same urgency as potential threats from the Muslim community.

Arun Kundnani, scholar-in-residence at the New York Public Library's Schomburg Center for Research in Black Culture, studied how European governments' Muslim-focused counterterrorism efforts influence far-right organizing. He argued that official security narratives treating terrorism as primarily a Muslim acculturation problem created an "enabling environment" for a new generation of far-right anti-Muslim extremists.[67] He called these governments' failure to see far-right violence as equally threatening to European society a "blind spot" that distorts counterterrorism policy in ways that may inadvertently encourage anti-Muslim violence.

When white nationalist Christian supremacist Anders Breivik killed seventy-seven of his fellow Norwegians in a multifaceted attack that included a car bomb and mass shooting in 2011, it put the proponents of the radicalization model in a bind. Before the attack, Breivik published an anti-Muslim manifesto that positively cited many of the American polemicists who make up the Islamophobia network.[68] According to the radicalization theory, and the guilt-by-association logic these anti-Muslim activists promote, they would have to bear some responsibility for this attack themselves. I don't believe that's true because I know the radicalization theory isn't valid. But as Kundnani suggests, it is different when the government promotes security narratives that mirror and reinforce extremist positions. Giving far-right extremists the impression they have government sanction increases the risk of reactionary violence against communities that law enforcement counterterrorists identify as threatening "others."

Unfortunately, the FBI has refused to treat far-right violence with the same urgency as violence from Muslim terrorist groups and continues to promote radicalization theories and CVE programs that stigmatize disenfranchised communities as security threats. This isn't just a problem for American Muslims but for any group of people that challenge government policy. Because once an agency starts using a discredited and racist model to identify suspects for one type of crime, it is more likely to use that same model for others.

8

CRIMINALIZING BLACK IDENTITY

"There is no doubt it was terrorism."[1] That's what FBI director James Comey said when a troubled recluse named Zale Thompson attacked four New York Police Department officers with a hatchet in October 2014, after immersing himself in a toxic mix of al Qaeda, ISIL, black separatist, and anti-government propaganda.[2] Less than a year later, when another angry misfit named Dylann Roof murdered nine people at the Mother Emanuel African Methodist Episcopal Church in Charleston, South Carolina, Comey refused to call it terrorism. "I don't see it as a political act," he said.[3]

That Thompson was a black Muslim convert while Roof was a white racist appears to be the determining factor in applying the terrorist label. Roof's attack was more deliberate and deadly, and more obviously an act of terrorism as defined by federal law.[4] Roof told one victim he would let her live so she could tell others what he did, indicating his intention to intimidate a broader civilian audience.[5] Roof also specifically targeted a state legislator, the Reverend Clementa Pinckney. Yet even the discovery of Roof's manifesto declaring his intention to start a race war failed to convince Comey the attack was sufficiently "political" to be considered terrorism.[6]

Thompson, on the other hand, published no manifesto, leaving his intentions unclear. He had been kicked out of the Navy for drug use, had a history of arrests for assault and domestic violence, and was unemployed and depressed, according to relatives.[7] But his alleged searches of a hodgepodge of anti-government websites were enough to convince Comey that he sought "inspiration from foreign sources like ISIL," and that its "slick" propaganda "played a role."[8] The NYPD, like Comey, mentioned Thompson's interest in black separatist and anti-police websites but emphasized his searches for "jihadist" materials.[9] Neither ISIL nor al Qaeda assisted in Thompson's attack, and neither group could have claimed political advantage from it, absent the FBI's and NYPD's eagerness to publicly credit them.[10]

The ax attack fit the profile of an ISIL-inspired "homegrown violent extremist" (HVE) that the FBI had been promoting for weeks, though. An FBI/DHS joint intelligence bulletin issued on October 11, 2014, warned that ISIL supporters were using social media to urge HVEs to attack police officers in retaliation for the U.S. bombing campaign in Iraq and Syria that had started a few months earlier.[11]

So it was strange to see Thompson's name resurface in 2017 when *Foreign Policy* published an FBI intelligence assessment warning about the threat from "Black Identity Extremists" (BIE).[12] The BIE assessment described Thompson's attack without mention of ISIL or "jihadist" websites and instead focused on tattoos and "pocket litter" that indicated his affiliation with "black separatist extremist" groups. Like the FBI's 2014 warning about ISIL-sympathizing HVEs, the 2017 BIE assessment focused on the threat this new movement posed to law enforcement rather than to the general public.[13]

THE MALLEABILITY OF RADICALIZATION THEORY

That the FBI could so casually reclassify Thompson's motivation exemplifies how the national security establishment uses terrorism as a tool of political manipulation. ISIL and black separatists do not share similar political, ideological, or strategic goals, so it would be hard to be both at the same time. Yet despite weak evidence demonstrating which, if any, extremist ideology motivated Thompson to attack the NYPD officers, the FBI determined unequivocally that he's a terrorist—one of "them" that it is charged with protecting "us" from.

The willingness to quickly label bad acts by people of color as terrorism, but not similar violence committed by white racists, may be influenced by unconscious racial stereotyping. A number of studies have documented that white Americans tend to perceive black men as bigger, more threatening, and less innocent than white men.[14] Some blame this implicit bias for the persistent racial disparities throughout the U.S.

criminal justice system, though others argue such discrimination is more conscious and deliberate than we like to acknowledge.[15] In either event, the lack of diversity within the FBI increases the likelihood that such biases, conscious or not, will result in harsher outcomes for black men who come under scrutiny, particularly where agents are authorized to take action without objective evidence of wrongdoing. Such discrimination can be expected to increase where agents believe national security is at stake, and particularly where, as with the FBI's ISIL and BIE reports, law enforcement officials are the purported targets.

The terrorism label inserts political bias into this mix, as Comey's commentary about Thompson and Roof suggests. Government officials naturally tend to view threats against establishment figures differently than reactionary violence against disenfranchised groups that reinforces the sociopolitical status quo.[16] The first is called "terrorism" and treated as a national security priority, while the second is treated as a crime problem at best and ignored at worst. Unaccountable police violence terrorizes communities of color, but it is rarely called terrorism. A spontaneous ax attack by a lone individual is considered "terrorism" when the perpetrator comes from a suspect class, however, even if his precise motivation is unknown.

When the government needed examples of the ISIL threat to shore up public support for its renewed bombing campaign in Iraq and Syria in the summer of 2014, it made sense to hold Thompson up as an example of the dangerous fanaticism it was protecting us from. By 2017, when a burgeoning black activist movement rose to contest unaccountable police brutality, Thompson's case became more useful to smear black activism as dangerous.

MANUFACTURING A BLACK SEPARATIST THREAT

Robert Mueller's FBI began targeting black "extremist" groups years earlier. One of the bureau's first terrorism reverse sting operations after 9/11, in which government informants portrayed deep-pocketed al Qaeda recruiters willing to pay Americans to commit terrorist acts, targeted not Muslims but an eccentric black religious cult operating in the Liberty City section of Miami, Florida. In June 2006, Attorney General

Alberto Gonzales announced the arrests of seven black men calling themselves the Seas of David, who he alleged were planning to engage in a "full ground war" against the United States.[17]

In a speech that day in Ohio, Director Mueller said the case demonstrated how the FBI's understanding of the radicalization process helped it operationalize its intelligence to detect a new threat: self-radicalizing terrorists who had no connections to al Qaeda. Knowing "the risk factors and the potential targets," he argued, allowed the FBI to "find and stop homegrown terrorists before they strike."[18] In fact, the Liberty City 7, as they became known, never acquired weapons and did little to further the informant's imaginary terrorist plot except try to take his money. Yet their marginalized status as poor, black, and mostly immigrant, with unfamiliar, vaguely anti-establishment religious beliefs, made them the perfect patsies for the FBI to test a provocative new counterterrorism tactic. The first two trials ended with hung juries and one acquittal, which appeared to signal a public rejection of the FBI's new methods. Undaunted, the government tried a third time, finally convicting five of the six remaining defendants.

Mueller described how the FBI's concept of radicalization formed the basis for a new generation of counterterrorism policies targeting communities with no connections to foreign terrorist organizations. He argued, "Whether we are talking about al Qaeda's operations overseas, sleeper operatives who have been in place for years, or the emergence of homegrown terrorists, our greatest challenge is in mapping these underground networks. This can be tedious, intricate work, but it is absolutely essential to the safety of this country. We need to see how certain individuals fit into the big picture. We need to know where to set the trip wires to identify the lines between the extremist and the operational. . . . We call it 'knowing your domain.'"[19]

Few realized at the time that the director wasn't speaking in metaphors. The FBI was creating maps, not of underground terrorist networks but of racial and ethnic groups throughout the United States. In 2005, the FBI started a pilot project called "domain management" which began using census data to map American neighborhoods by race and ethnicity in the hope this exercise would somehow uncover hidden terrorists and spies. If there was any question about how the maps would be used, the program's creator answered them in a 2006 interview with the *New York Times.* Philip Mudd, a former CIA analyst Mueller brought in to run the FBI's intelligence programs, showed off a map of San Francisco with marks indicating where Iranian immigrants lived. Mudd said this was where his agents were "hunting."[20]

The article indicated that many agents resisted this new strategy, finding it operationally suspect and legally dubious. Attorney General John Ashcroft's purported "ban" on racial profiling—the Justice Department's 2003 *Guidance Regarding the Use of Force by Federal Law Enforcement Agencies*—included broad loopholes for national security and border integrity investigations and did not limit profiling based on national origin. Bureau leaders were clearly relying on these loopholes to authorize the racial mapping project. So dissenting FBI officials pushed back the only way they could, by leaking embarrassing details to the press. In 2007, anonymous FBI sources told *Congressional Quarterly*'s Jeff Stein that FBI agents were data mining San Francisco grocery store records for sales of Middle Eastern foods—characterized as tracking falafel purchases—in an attempt to locate Iranian terrorists.[21] The FBI issued a terse denial, calling it "too ridiculous to be true."[22]

In the waning months of the Bush administration, FBI general counsel Valerie Caproni invited privacy and civil liberties organizations to preview the FBI's Domestic Investigations and Operations Guide (DIOG), a four-hundred-page document implementing Michael Mukasey's 2008 Attorney General's Guidelines. Buried within it is an authorization for a racial and ethnic mapping program that sounded as "ridiculous" as the falafel tracking Stein had reported a year earlier. In addition to using census data to map racial and ethnic populations, the new DIOG authorized the FBI to locate "ethnic-oriented businesses and . . . facilities" and track "ethnic behaviors" and "life style characteristics."[23] The DIOG identified "domain management" as an assessment, meaning FBI agents needed no factual predication to conduct this racial and ethnic mapping.

Removing the requirement for factual predication in assessments, the Mukasey guidelines empowered the FBI to conduct investigations and gather intelligence against any suspect population it chooses. No terrorist attacks or evidence of criminal activity are necessary to justify massive surveillance, mapping, investigations, and infiltration of any community that agents believe might become a threat in the future.

In 2009, the FBI's Atlanta Division issued an "Intelligence Note from Domain Management" that tracked the growth of the black population in Georgia from 2000 to 2015 to estimate "the black separatist threat."[24] It identified the New Black Panther Party (NBPP) and the Nation of Islam as examples of black separatist groups and described their participation in protests of police violence and political rallies. The document is heavily redacted, but the only visible allegation of black separatist violence it describes involves an alleged assault by NBPP members on reporters covering a press event for Congresswoman Cynthia McKinney. Contemporaneous media reports indicate the sixty-seven-year-old NBPP member involved in the scuffle claimed a cameraman jostling for position struck him with his camera first. Police made no arrests.[25] At the time it was written, there had been no documented violent attacks by any black separatist group in Georgia, or anywhere else in the United States, for more than twenty-five years. An FBI report listing terrorist attacks in the United States from 1980 through 2005 documented zero attacks by any group identified as black separatist.[26]

Undated Domestic Terrorism Operations Unit training presentations on "black separatist extremists" obtained by the ACLU in 2011 identify no acts of violence attributable to any black separatist groups since the Black Liberation Army attacks in the 1970s, yet present them as a current terrorist threat.[27] Confusingly, the FBI documents state that many of the groups it categorizes as black separatists do not share the same goals or seek physical separation from the United States. What they share, according to the documents, are "racial grievances with the U.S. Government," making them indistinguishable from hundreds of other nonviolent groups that protest racism and police violence.[28] Indeed, one FBI presentation on black separatist extremists notes that "most are non-violent."[29]

The FBI created another new domestic terrorism classification in March 2009: "American Islamic Extremists." Training presentations claimed these groups did not take direction from foreign terrorist groups but "mixed Islamic theology with some levels of black separatism, anarchism, and racial rhetoric."[30] This category was clearly designed to cover black Muslim groups in the United States. Black Muslims make up about one-fifth to one-third of the Muslim American population, and they are often caught in a perfect storm of racism, Islamophobia, and xenophobia.[31] It wouldn't take long for the FBI to organize a splashy arrest to substantiate their new taxonomy.

In October 2009, agents with the FBI's Hostage Rescue Team shot and killed Detroit imam Luqman Abdullah while attempting to arrest him after an informant sold him purportedly stolen property during an FBI sting operation. The arrest warrant affidavit detailed Abdullah's religious and political views over several pages, describing him as a "highly placed leader of a nationwide radical fundamentalist Sunni group consisting primarily of African-Americans." It alleged that Abdullah preached "an offensive *jihad*, rather than a defensive *jihad*," called his followers "soldiers," and used "anti-government and anti-law enforcement rhetoric," even though these statements had nothing to do with the crimes the FBI charged him with: receiving stolen property and illegal possession of a firearm.[32] His previous felony conviction for assault and possession of a concealed weapon had occurred in 1981, almost thirty years prior. He converted to Islam in prison and was well regarded in the community for feeding the poor and homeless.[33] The affidavit was clearly written to portray Abdullah as a violent terrorist, though the crimes charged were relatively minor. The arrest plan included sixty-six FBI agents, a helicopter, and a bureau-trained attack dog.[34]

The Justice Department's review of the shooting determined that Abdullah refused to submit to the arresting agents, who had lured Abdullah and three alleged co-conspirators to an FBI-controlled warehouse to help unload "stolen" TV sets. After flash-bang diversionary devices exploded near them and the heavily armed agents announced their presence, Abdullah retreated into a tractor-trailer while his co-conspirators surrendered. Agents said he refused commands to show his hands, so they ordered the FBI canine to attack him. Abdullah allegedly shot the dog, and four agents returned fire, hitting him with twenty rounds from their .223-caliber rifles. The Justice Department determined the FBI agents were justified in the shooting, but it is hard to square how the minor charges involved warranted such an aggressive arrest plan.[35] Local police had evicted Abdullah from the building housing his mosque only a few months earlier for failing to pay property taxes, apparently without violence or arrests.[36]

These cases highlight how, even in the absence of terrorist acts, the FBI relentlessly pursued African American groups that harbored unusual beliefs or expressed hostility to government policies. The FBI's August 2017 intelligence assessment establishing a "Black Identity Extremist" threat appears to have been an attempt to reorganize its domestic terrorism bureaucracy to focus once again on an emerging black activist movement, even as neo-Nazis and Ku Klux Klansmen were inciting violent confrontations at rallies across the country.

MANUFACTURING A BLACK IDENTITY EXTREMIST MOVEMENT

The FBI's 2017 "Black Identity Extremist" assessment is striking in its poor analytic quality. It identifies just five incidents from 2014 to 2016 in which lone black men attacked police officers, in five different localities, then adds one reverse sting operation in which FBI agents sold fake pipe bombs to a man associated with a black separatist group in St. Louis. The individuals involved in these incidents do not appear to have known one another, belonged to the same organization, or held the same beliefs. Instead, the assessment cherry-picked facts from each case to imagine them as part of a growing "BIE movement" that had inspired retaliatory violence against police officers since the August 2014 police shooting of Michael Brown in Ferguson, Missouri.[37]

The assessment alleges that the BIE movement isn't a unified belief system; rather, it is driven by "perceptions" of police brutality and "influenced by a mix of anti-authoritarian, Moorish sovereign citizen, and BIE ideology." Muddying the water further, the assessment describes both "Moorish sovereign citizen" and "BIE ideologies" as amalgams of different belief systems. "Moorish sovereign citizens," according to the assessment, combine Moorish Science Temple beliefs—a distinctive African American form of Islam—with anti-government attitudes of sovereign citizens, normally considered an extreme far-right ideology. Basically, it appears a "Moorish" sovereign is essentially just a black sovereign citizen.

The FBI's description of BIE ideology was even less intelligible:

> The FBI defines black identity extremists as individuals who seek, wholly or in part, through unlawful acts of force or violence, in response to perceived racism and injustice in American society and some do so in furtherance of establishing a separate black homeland or autonomous black social institutions, communities, or governing organizations within the United States [sic]. This desire for physical or psychological separation is typically based on either a religious or political belief system, which is sometimes formed around or includes a belief in racial superiority or supremacy.[38]

So the BIE movement, according to the FBI, is a mixture of mixed ideologies, beliefs, and desires. The document then claims that violent black nationalist groups from the civil rights era are part of this imagined BIE movement, perhaps to augment its perceived lethality. Its discussion of assassinations, kidnappings, and bombings committed by the Black Liberation Army (BLA), which the writer acknowledges has been inactive since 1984, appear gratuitous. None of the individuals involved in the handful of violent acts committed four decades later are alleged to have any connection to the BLA.

Taken seriously, this assessment could only be expected to increase a police officer's fear of being targeted by a black identity extremist. It provides little information about how police officers can identify a violent BIE. The only necessary qualifications for being considered a "black identity extremist" appear to be identifying as black and expressing concern about racism and police violence, which covers most of the African American population. The Congressional Black Caucus criticized the FBI's assessment as a thinly veiled justification for increased law enforcement action against black political activists.[39] It didn't take long for their fears to be realized.

Armed FBI agents raided the Dallas home of Rakem Balogun on December 12, 2017, seized a handgun and a rifle, and arrested him for illegally possessing firearms. Balogun was a prominent member of Guerrilla Mainframe and the Huey P. Newton Gun Club, armed self-defense groups that patrolled black neighborhoods to bring attention to police violence and racism. News stations had interviewed Balogun carrying firearms during protests, and he was active on social media.

The charge was based on Balogun's 2007 misdemeanor conviction for domestic assault in Tennessee, which in some cases would prohibit a person from possessing a firearm under federal law.[40]

It turned out the FBI had been investigating Balogun since 2015, after viewing a video of one of his protests on the far-right conspiracy website Infowars. Prosecutors argued that Balogun was too dangerous to be released on bond pending trial, citing his social media rhetoric and armed protests against police. It was hard to square how the FBI agents could have let Balogun be on the street with firearms for two years but once they took his guns away he became too dangerous to be released. Balogun remained in jail for five months, until the judge determined the conduct involved in his 2007 misdemeanor conviction did not trigger the federal statute's firearms prohibition. The charges were dropped and Balogun released, but he lost his job and home in the meantime. Absent his activism, it is unlikely he would have been charged at all, much less denied bond before trial. But his case could be considered an effective use of the FBI's disruption strategy, and a warning to like-minded activists.

WEAKENING RESTRAINTS ON RACIAL PROFILING

Though the 2017 BIE assessment scrupulously avoids mentioning Black Lives Matter (BLM), its timing and description of the purported BIE movement clearly establishes black political protests against police violence as a potential threat to law enforcement officers' safety. The BIE assessment references previous FBI intelligence reports on black separatist extremists, but this document seems to be the first use of this revised terminology. The FBI's rules for targeting racial groups might help explain why it chose to establish "Black Identity Extremism" as a domestic terrorism classification.

The Justice Department's 2003 *Guidance Regarding the Use of Race by Federal Law Enforcement Agencies* declares that racial profiling is not just wrong as a legal matter but ineffective. "Race-based assumptions in law enforcement perpetuate negative racial stereotypes that are harmful to our rich and diverse democracy," it argues, "and materially impair our efforts to maintain a fair and just society."[41] I couldn't agree more that racial profiling is counterproductive to effective law enforcement. Unfortunately, the guidance goes on to declare that "given the high stakes involved" in national security and border integrity investigations, law enforcement must be permitted to "use every legitimate tool to prevent future attacks, protect our nation's borders, and deter those who would cause devastating harm to our nation." It does not explain how using an ineffective and counterproductive tool like racial profiling in our most important cases could possibly be helpful.

The Justice Department argued the Constitution authorized law enforcement to use race and ethnicity so long as these characteristics were not the *sole* reason for targeting a particular individual or group. Documents the ACLU obtained from the FBI racial mapping program show how this lax standard permits investigative and intelligence activities that most people would describe as racial and ethnic profiling. In addition to the Atlanta Division's "Intelligence Note from Domain Management" tracking Georgia's black population based on an imagined black separatist threat, a San Francisco FBI document justified mapping the city's Chinese American population because Chinese people historically had been involved in organized crime.[42] A Newark field office memo tracked New Jersey's Latino population by county because many MS-13 gang members were Latino.[43] These negative racial stereotypes guide the FBI's investigative programs despite the harm the Justice Department acknowledged profiling inflicts on our democracy.

After the election of President Barack Obama in 2008, many civil rights groups lobbied Attorney General Eric Holder to reform the racial profiling guidance. The FBI strongly resisted these efforts.[44] When Holder finally issued revised guidance in 2014, it expanded the protected characteristics, prohibiting profiling based on religion, sexual orientation, gender, gender identity, and national origin, but it retained broad national security exemptions and for the first time explicitly authorized the FBI's racial mapping program. A day after Holder issued the new guidance, Director Comey dismissed its relevance to the FBI, declaring its implementation required no changes to bureau policy or procedures.[45]

So the new racial profiling guidance would pose little obstacle to targeting black protest groups so long as an additional "factor" other than race could be identified. The FBI and its law enforcement partners began spying on the BLM movement from the group's inception, demonstrating the weakness of these restraints. A December 2014 email from an FBI Joint Terrorism Task Force (JTTF) officer in Minneapolis to his bureau supervisor reported an informant tip about the date of an upcoming BLM protest at the Mall of America. Lee Fang, a reporter for *The Intercept*, obtained the email and spoke to an FBI spokesman who said the informant tip was properly disseminated through the JTTF because it alleged vandalism might occur at the protest. The email makes no mention of vandalism, however.[46]

In April 2015, the FBI's Washington, D.C., field office disseminated an intelligence bulletin advising that "a review of social media" indicated a protest against police violence would occur in D.C.'s Chinatown that evening.[47] It acknowledged there was no information to suggest violence might occur but passed the information to other law enforcement agencies out of concern the event "may be exploited by individuals seeking to justify criminal or terrorist activity." It said there was "no formal connection to the Baltimore riots."[48] A few days later, the FBI flew surveillance planes outfitted with infrared night-vision cameras over Baltimore to monitor protests after the police killing of Freddie Gray.[49] When these flights were discovered, Director Comey acknowledged the bureau had conducted similar aerial surveillance missions during protests of the shooting of Michael Brown in Ferguson, Missouri.[50]

Emails exchanged between San Francisco agents in July 2016 prepared language for a legal disclaimer to be added to intelligence reports acknowledging that BLM protests were First Amendment–protected activities. It added, however, that violence "against participants, bystanders or law enforcement" could occur. The proposed language disavowed any intention to connect the protests to criminal activity but then stated that "the activity could be used as a means to target law enforcement."[51]

The FBI's most aggressive actions against BLM preceded the 2016 Democratic and Republican National Conventions. The Center for Constitutional Rights obtained two July 8, 2016, emails describing an FBI briefing regarding Micah Xavier Johnson's murder of five Dallas police officers. Johnson was one of the six individuals the FBI later identified as "Black Identity Extremists" in its 2017 intelligence bulletin, but the emails make clear he acted alone. The emails warn about possible copycat attacks, however, and report that several "black supremacist extremist movements" exist in the Dallas area, naming only the New Black Panther Party and its "offshoots." Most alarming, the email alleges a "threat of black supremacist extremists attempting to violently co-opt the upcoming DNC/RNC," without further elaboration.[52] Dozens of prominent BLM activists reported FBI agents contacted them or their families seeking interviews prior to the RNC, and in some cases, warned them not to attend.[53]

These records indicate that the FBI maintained an interest in tracking BLM activists but recognized it often had insufficient justification. BLM is not a separatist movement, nor a supremacist movement. By establishing the existence of an umbrella terrorist movement broad enough to incorporate all forms of black dissent, violent or not, the BIE assessment helps FBI agents elude the sole factor test.

PROMOTING A FALSE NARRATIVE

The 2017 BIE assessment also reinforces a false and divisive "war on cops" narrative heavily promoted in right-wing media. The assessment repeatedly refers to "*perceptions* of police brutality against African Americans" and "*perceived* racism and injustice in American society," as if such views are unjustified or extreme (italics added). This editorial commentary in the assessment echoes a 2016 speech that Director Comey gave to the International Association of Chiefs of Police (IACP), in which he complained the government lacked data on police violence. He ignored that his agency, which has jurisdiction over civil rights violations committed by police officers, should logically be collecting this data as part of its routine law enforcement activities. The FBI knows how many bank robberies there are, after all. Rather, Comey seemed to be criticizing those protesting police violence, who he said "have no idea" whether law enforcement used lethal force disproportionately against black people. He complained they were instead letting "a small group of videos serve as proof of an epidemic."[54]

Comey had reason to believe the protesters were right, though. A year before his IACP speech, *Vox* reporter Dara Lind analyzed 2012 data on "felons killed by police" that law enforcement agencies voluntarily submitted to the FBI through the Uniform Crime Reporting (UCR) system. While UCR data is known to be incomplete, Lind's analysis demonstrated that police killed black people at disproportionately higher rates than white people, and significantly more often when they were not attacking.[55] Several later studies using more complete data verified these findings. Drexel University research published in February 2017 showed that African Americans are almost three times more likely to be killed by police than white people.[56] *The Guardian*'s analysis of data it independently collected showed that black males between the ages of fifteen and thirty-four were four times more likely to be killed by police officers than their white counterparts.[57] A third 2017 study found police killed unarmed black people who were not attacking anyone at significantly higher rates than unarmed, nonattacking white people.[58] Looking at data regarding non-fatal police shootings from 2010 through 2016, Vice News determined that police shot black people two and a half times as often as white people.[59] But Lind's work with 2012 data showed that Comey's FBI had all the data it needed to recognize this disparity existed, if it had cared to do the research.

On the other side of the equation, the FBI's 2017 assessment also claims BIE ideology "spurred an increase in premeditated, retaliatory lethal violence against law enforcement," but it attributes only seven police fatalities to BIE, out of 155 officers feloniously killed during the three-year period the report covered.[60] Intentional homicides of police officers did increase from 2014 to 2016, but these followed a historic low in 2013.[61] The year 2017 recorded the second-lowest number of police officers killed in the line of duty in more than fifty years.[62] While all violence against police officers is unacceptable, data shows that white people kill law enforcement officers more often than black people do, and that far-right extremists murder police officers at greater rates than black extremists do.[63] The FBI should inform police officers of any and all potential threats to their safety, but such information is only helpful when it includes all the facts and the necessary context. The BIE assessment only served to sharpen the divide between law enforcement and black communities, which, regrettably, has been long-standing and persistent.

RACIAL PROFILING IN CRIMINAL INVESTIGATIONS

J. Edgar Hoover viewed African American political activism as a threat to national security and used every tool at his disposal to suppress black leaders from Marcus Garvey to Martin Luther King Jr. The Attorney General's Guidelines issued by Edward Levi in 1976 were designed to curb these extralegal activities by requiring a reasonable indication of criminal activity before the FBI could unleash its most intrusive investigative powers. But black people remained a disproportionate target for law enforcement in everything from routine police stops to complex FBI public corruption operations.

In his book *Rumor, Repression, and Racial Politics*, George Derek Musgrove documented how the Justice Department and FBI replaced COINTELPRO-style disruptions of black radical groups with selective law enforcement operations to suppress black voting and intimidate black politicians in the 1980s. As the Voting Rights Act of 1965 began realizing its intended effect of increasing black voting and electing black public officials, Attorney General William French Smith in 1984 declared election fraud "a crime of the first magnitude." He issued a pamphlet explaining federal election laws and sent it to U.S. attorneys and "every FBI agent assigned to a white collar or public corruption squad."[64]

Then-U.S. attorney for the Southern District of Alabama Jeff Sessions targeted voting rights activists in a predominately black, rural part of the state known as the Black Belt for its rich soil. With little public transportation, many poor and elderly black voters had no means to get to the polls, which were often located miles away in majority-white areas. Community organizers began an absentee ballot drive where activists would go to residents' homes, notarize their ballots, and bring them to the post office to be mailed. FBI agents staked out one of the post offices and seized the ballots. In an enormous operation conducted in the weeks before the November 1984 election, FBI agents "fanned out across the Black Belt to interview between 1,000 and 1,500 voters, *all* of them African Americans," to verify their ballots.[65] Agents took handwriting samples, photographs and fingerprints from these absentee voters and bused more than two dozen of them to testify before grand juries.[66] Sessions indicted three local black activists who participated in the absentee voter drive—Albert Turner, the former director of the Alabama Southern Christian Leadership Council; his wife, Evelyn; and Spencer Hogue Jr.—for mail fraud, alleging they tampered with ballots. "This whole FBI investigation of absentee voting and the scheduled trials were set up to stop the political progress of black people in the Alabama Black Belt," Turner argued at trial.[67] A jury acquitted all three defendants.

The Justice Department unleased another new tactic during this time period, according to Musgrove's research: political corruption investigations as a tool of political warfare. During the Ronald Reagan and George H. W. Bush administrations, the number of Justice Department public corruption investigations doubled, from 727 in 1980 to 1,452 in 1991, disproportionately targeting Democrats and African American public officials. Investigations of federal government officials increased at an even higher rate, from 123 in 1980 to 624 in 1992. Of course, many of those investigated by the FBI were corrupt, as the trials proved. But Musgrove argues that the FBI's development of the public corruption sting operation beginning in the 1980s gave the bureau more latitude to selectively target black politicians and use more deceitful tactics to entice criminal behavior. The FBI seemed comfortable using informants with clear racial or political biases to further these investigations. Musgrove's research showed the vast majority of public corruption investigations during this period were sting operations.[68]

In 1988, the *Washington Post*'s Gwen Ifill examined 465 Justice Department corruption probes and found that 14 percent targeted black politicians, who made up just 3 percent of elected officials at that time.[69] Musgrove noted that two of the five federal judges the Justice Department indicted during this period were African American, even though black judges made up only 0.5 percent of the federal judiciary. Also telling was the failure rate. The Justice Department investigated ten of the thirty-six members of the Congressional Black Caucus in office between 1981 and 1992, but only two were indicted and none were convicted.[70] Corruption investigations targeting prominent black officials during this period were also beset with press leaks, Musgrove reports, which damaged political careers even where no charges were ultimately laid.

The Justice Department continued prosecuting Democrats at a greater rate during the Clinton administration, but the difference was not as pronounced. Of course, while U.S. attorneys often turn over when a new administration is elected, FBI leadership does not. The disparity increased once again under President George W. Bush, however. Studies show the Justice Department prosecuted Democrats up to six times as often as Republicans during his administration.[71] The Justice Department does not regularly publish the race of defendants in its public corruption cases, which makes it difficult to see whether disparities concerning African American public officials persist.

There is evidence the FBI has continued to target black public officials with its most contentious tactics, however. On a Saturday evening, May 20, 2006, for the first time in the history of the republic, FBI agents armed with a judicially authorized search warrant raided the congressional office of a sitting member of Congress. A bipartisan outcry from Congress led the FBI to release the eighty-three-page search warrant affidavit, revealing the fruits of a year-long bribery investigation targeting Representative William Jefferson, a Louisiana Democrat. The affidavit revealed the FBI had already videotaped Representative Jefferson accepting a $100,000 cash payment from an FBI informant, $90,000 of which it recovered from his freezer during an earlier search of his home.[72]

The Bush White House bent to congressional pressure and ordered the FBI to return documents seized from Jefferson's office during the search. Director Mueller reportedly threatened to resign rather than give up the documents.[73] The White House compromised by asking the Justice Department to seal the materials while Representative Jefferson sued for their return. The D.C. Circuit Court of Appeals ultimately found the search unconstitutional, but the Justice Department had indicted Jefferson in the interim, without using the documents, raising the question of why the FBI thought it necessary to spark a constitutional crisis in the first place.[74] Though if the real purpose of the raid was simply to shatter customary limits on FBI powers, having a slam-dunk case would be a prerequisite. And targeting a congressman who could be more easily marginalized couldn't hurt, either.

Public corruption investigations are among the most important cases the FBI works. When public officials betray their oaths it undermines public confidence in government institutions and the rule of law, and the FBI is often the only agency that can do anything about it. This makes it more important for the FBI to pursue these cases in a transparent manner untainted by political or racial bias.

Special Agent Mike McKinney was one of the bureau's most accomplished undercover agents specializing in political corruption cases. He worked more than twenty undercover operations during his career, served as a supervisor in the Economic Crimes Unit and the Undercover and Sensitive Operations Unit, and led a public corruption squad in the Atlanta field office. In 2008, he received the Director's Award for his role supervising a major public corruption undercover operation, the highest honor an agent can achieve.[75]

When McKinney arrived for his first assignment in Buffalo, New York, back in 1991, he was the only black agent in the entire office. He remembers it as a positive experience overall, in particular the wonderful guidance he received from most of his fellow agents. He was encouraged to try out for the SWAT team and become a firearms instructor, invitations that didn't go out to every new agent, and he got his first taste of undercover work. The black agents' class action discrimination lawsuit was still going on, and he thinks office managers may have been eager to appear accommodating to their only black agent. But McKinney told me he saw discrimination everywhere in the FBI. One white agent asked him in a room full of others whether he had ever seen a cow, apparently believing black people were confined to inner cities their whole lives. Another agent, who McKinney joked "didn't know he was prejudiced," offhandedly called him "colored." McKinney knew what he wanted to accomplish in the FBI, however, and that he wouldn't get there if he punched all the bigots he came across in the mouth. He found he could often diffuse a situation with a snappy comeback, but he basically just resigned himself to working through these episodes without letting them get in his way. He let his work speak for itself.

Toward the end of his career, McKinney was tapped to lead a national program that placed undercover agents in public corruption cases all over the country. These are extraordinarily complex investigations that require a substantial investment in establishing and maintaining undercover identities that can withstand the kind of scrutiny public officials can bring to bear. The skinheads and militia members I worked against didn't know my last name, so there was very little checking they could do to examine my background, even if they had the resources and skills necessary to conduct such research. I was portraying myself as a hoodlum, anyway, so gaps in my resume weren't going to be a problem. Portraying yourself as a legitimate—if corrupt—businessperson as McKinney and his undercover crew did requires much more preparation and skill. Suffice to say, McKinney knew what he was doing, and his FBI colleagues knew it too.

So in 2011 when he was asked to assist an undercover operation that he felt targeted black public officials without sufficient evidence suggesting they were corrupt, he refused. When I heard about this a few years later, I wasn't surprised. Most experienced undercover agents I knew recognized that our techniques were extraordinarily intrusive and could easily be misused to entrap the innocent. We weren't shy about acknowledging the deceitful nature of the work. One undercover school instructor liked to start each class by saying, "Our job is to establish deep, trusting relationships and then betray them, and if that makes you uncomfortable, leave now." But we knew that justice depended on the ethical use of these skills. McKinney's pride, integrity, and respect for the law wouldn't allow him to trick innocent people into breaking it.

In selecting an undercover agent for an operation, case agents try to find someone the target will likely feel comfortable with, and people generally feel most comfortable with people similar to them. So most of the cases McKinney had worked as an undercover agent targeted black officials, and that didn't bother him. He never worked an operation where he felt the subject was not properly predicated with evidence of their corrupt intentions, and he is certain all the people he put in jail deserved to be there. But this new assignment gave him a national perspective on FBI corruption operations, and he could see the bureau was disproportionately targeting black politicians with sting operations. The disparity was so stark that white undercover agents on his team began griping about the lack of assignments. When he complained about the 2011 investigation it caused significant rancor among the field office staff and, just like in my case, they falsified the records to cover their misconduct. McKinney reported this file tampering to FBI inspectors, but they refused to investigate. Then, the FBI's Office of Professional Responsibility notified McKinney that it had opened a misconduct investigation against him.

McKinney was able to get the 2011 operation improperly targeting black public officials stopped, but he discovered it was part of a broader headquarters-led program scrutinizing the potential misuse of economic stimulus funding in urban areas. McKinney believed the program encouraged inappropriately aggressive public corruption stings selectively targeting African Americans and other minorities in cases all around the country. His supervisors were asking McKinney to provide the undercover agents for these operations, but his colleagues agreed that many of the cases lacked evidence that the targeted public officials were predisposed to commit corrupt acts. Even when the investigations were properly predicated with evidence of corruption, they disproportionally directed undercover operatives to target minorities rather than their equally unscrupulous white counterparts. He knew that utilizing aggressive undercover operations disproportionately against minority elected officials could potentially dissuade people of color from seeking public office and distort public perceptions about corruption in minority-led governments. McKinney complained to FBI headquarters and stopped the investigations he knew about, but he remained concerned that the FBI was profiling minority elected officials on a larger scale. He asked for an internal audit to document the disparity so it could be corrected. When headquarters didn't respond, he reported it to the Justice Department inspector general.

In August 2014, Director Comey visited the Atlanta FBI office where McKinney was based. McKinney managed to corner Comey and reported his concerns about these cases. As instructed, McKinney then followed up with an email saying, "I believe the conduct of my colleagues at FBI [headquarters] and the aggressiveness with which they have targeted minority politicians is a very serious problem."[76] Comey responded with thanks for his service to the FBI but advised that since McKinney had reported the matter to the inspector general, the FBI would take no action to address the matter, a response McKinney found feeble and absurd.[77] It wasn't clear the inspector general's office would open an investigation, and the FBI was in a better position to address the problem anyway. Given Comey's rhetoric on racial profiling, McKinney had hoped for a stronger response. Comey never contacted McKinney or his colleagues again, and neither did the inspector general's office.

The FBI's retaliatory investigation against McKinney lasted two years but resulted in no disciplinary action. He retired in early 2015 after doing all he could to document the problem of racial and ethnic profiling in FBI corruption investigations and to notify all the responsible authorities. At the very least, his efforts prevented the abuses he witnessed. As the FBI becomes less diverse, there will be fewer agents like Mike McKinney who are sensitive to improper racial targeting and willing to stand against it, and more like his Buffalo colleague who didn't even realize he was prejudiced. McKinney renewed his complaint with the inspector general again in 2018, but the office declined to initiate an investigation.

9

TARGETING INNOCENT "OTHERS"

The FBI's "preventative" approach to addressing national security threats requires identifying the suspect communities from which they believe these threats emerge and employing its disruption strategies against them. The lowered evidentiary thresholds in the FBI's investigative guidelines allow this targeting of innocents. As bureau officials articulated throughout its post-9/11 transition, the bureau's efforts are no longer designed to enforce federal law but to disrupt potential threats. Often, the threatening "other" is not a foreign enemy but a fellow American.

THE PERPETUAL FOREIGNERS

Americans in the past took pride in characterizing the United States as a melting pot, a country where immigrants can come from anywhere in world with nothing, work hard, prosper, and become American citizens equal to those native born. Out of many, one. Jeffrey Wang and Denise Woo are both products of this American dream. Woo is a fourth-generation Californian of mixed Chinese and Japanese ancestry who joined the FBI at thirty-five, walking away from her more lucrative engineering career at IBM to serve her community as a federal agent.[1] She worked white collar crime cases in the Long Beach resident agency for a few years, then transferred to a child pornography squad in Los Angeles in 1999.

Jeffrey Wang's father came to the United States from China in the 1920s on a scholarship, became a radiologist in Hawaii, and married a Chinese American woman from New York whose family had lived here for generations. Wang was born in Honolulu, earned a master's degree in electrical engineering from the University of California, Los

Angeles, and got a job in Raytheon's airborne radar division, where he worked on classified technical projects involving U.S. fighter jets and the stealth bomber.[2]

Wang joined Woo's extended family when he married a Japanese American woman named Diane Misumi. The Woo and Misumi families were not blood relatives but bonded through a shared history when fear and bigotry overruled reason. Misumi's father and Woo's mother went to high school together in Los Angeles after spending World War II in Japanese internment camps. They ended up raising their families in the same neighborhood and going to the same church. Woo babysat Misumi as a child and they remained close through adulthood, continuing to see each other at holidays and family functions after Misumi and Wang married.[3]

Scholars have identified a "perpetual foreigner" stereotype that stigmatizes racial minorities in the United States, particularly Asian Americans, by more closely associating them with their ethnicity and national origin than their nationality, no matter how long they've been Americans. Asians are often regarded as the "model minority" for the relative success many Asian immigrants achieve, particularly in math, science, and engineering. Since the atomic age, these fields have been closely associated with national security, however, which creates a dissonance in intelligence agencies that tend to view Asian Americans as not fully assimilable. "They want us to be Americans and work in their defense labs," one Taiwanese-born scientist said during the Wen Ho Lee scandal, "but they never treat us as Americans."[4]

Robert Vrooman, who led the Los Alamos National Laboratory's counterintelligence investigation of Lee, condemned the notion, popular among intelligence officials, that Chinese spies selectively target Chinese Americans for recruitment. "It was our experience that Chinese intelligence officials contacted everyone from the laboratories with a nuclear weapons background who visited China," he declared in an affidavit. He said he was unaware of any empirical evidence supporting the idea that foreign-born Chinese Americans are not as loyal as other citizens.[5]

However, FBI counterintelligence training materials on "the Chinese" obtained by the ACLU in 2011 rejuvenated these biased perceptions of Asians as treacherous and potentially threatening. One FBI training presentation warns agents against giving too many compliments to a Chinese woman as it might suggest a romantic relationship is desired, another says to never stare at or attempt to shake hands with an Asian.[6] Given this training, it is not surprising that FBI counterintelligence investigators might profile Asian Americans as potential threats. This predisposition would have dire consequences for Wang and Woo.

As David Wise detailed in his book *Tiger Trap*, in 1998 an FBI Chinese counterintelligence informant who had provided reliable information in the past claimed to have seen Wang passing information to a Chinese intelligence officer in exchange for an envelope of money. Wang was an unlikely Chinese spy, however. He had never been to China, had no relationship with Chinese government officials, and didn't speak Mandarin or Cantonese.[7] Nonetheless, the FBI initiated an investigation and put a FISA (Foreign Intelligence Surveillance Act) wiretap on Wang's phones.[8] The investigating agents soon learned of Woo's relationship with Wang and, ignoring conflict of interest rules and the undercover guidelines, the squad supervisor, J.J. Smith, pressured Woo into surreptitiously exploiting their friendship to gather intelligence for the FBI. As discussed in chapter 3, Smith had become accustomed to breaking FBI rules. Unfortunately, Woo did not receive the good advice and support from her office leadership that Gamal Abdel-Hafiz did, and she acquiesced to working undercover in her own name against a close family friend.

The case heated up in 1999, after FBI agents polygraphed Wang, accused him of failing on the question of unreported foreign contacts, and asked to search his home. Now Wang knew the FBI thought he was a spy, but he couldn't fathom why. Though the search turned up nothing incriminating, Wang lost his security clearance and, therefore, his job. The FBI asked Woo to lend a sympathetic ear and pry out information about Wang's spying activities. But the more she heard, the more Woo believed Wang was innocent. Woo raised her concerns with the case agents and FBI management, but no one intervened. The FBI did not send her to undercover training to prepare her to navigate the fraught conversations she would have with Wang as he tried to figure out who had made the false allegations against him. Of course, the Wangs assumed that the FBI was tapping their phones, which Woo surely knew too and could not credibly deny. Wang began to wonder aloud whether an ongoing family dispute over his recently deceased father's will might have been the source of his trouble, which made Woo curious about the informant who originally reported Wang as a spy. It turned out the informant was married to Wang's cousin, something he had not told the FBI when he accused Wang of spying. Wang appears to have figured out his cousin-in-law had some kind of relationship with the FBI.

The FBI believed Woo tipped Wang to these conclusions, however, and despite her denials, suspended her in November 1999. The bureau would later claim tapes of their conversations proved Woo said too much, but she had to have known the FBI tapped the phones, so it is hard to believe she said something she knew to be inappropriate, much less illegal. The FBI's case against Wang ended, finding no evidence that he ever spied for China or any other country. The informant, likely trying to prove his worth after getting caught setting up his cousin-in-law on a false charge, came forward a few months later with an accusation against fellow informant Katrina Leung. He alleged Leung had provided information about the Wang case to Chinese intelligence agents, raising questions about how she would even know about the Wang investigation. Smith, who was Leung's handling agent and secret paramour, was informed of the allegation, but an internal investigation would not start for another year.[9] The FBI finally arrested Smith and Leung in April 2003 for mishandling classified information, which should have brought the Wang investigation into a totally different light. Instead, the FBI fired Woo, and in December 2004 charged her with five felonies relating to her conversations with Wang. After years of wrangling over Woo's access to the classified information necessary to defend herself, in October 2006 the government dismissed the felony charges in exchange for Woo's guilty plea to a misdemeanor. Jeffrey Wang castigated the FBI in comments outside the courtroom after Woo's sentencing: "The government should be ashamed for its reprehensible treatment of me in their unwarranted investigation and for prosecuting and ruining the life of Denise Woo, a person of great integrity, who stood up for an innocent man. Tragically, justice was not served in either of our cases."[10]

It's hard to understand why the FBI would treat Smith, who had compromised twenty years of FBI Chinese counterintelligence operations by sleeping with a Chinese double agent and thwarting efforts to expose her treachery, so leniently while simultaneously persecuting innocents like Denise Woo, along with fellow LA agent Rita Chiang and headquarters analyst Logan, who were falsely accused of disloyalty based on anti-Asian bias rather than evidence of wrongdoing. Unfortunately, this episode and Smith's conviction would not be the end to the FBI's faulty, bias-driven Chinese espionage cases.

From 2013 to 2015, the FBI would upend the lives of four Chinese American scientists by charging them with transferring restricted technology or trade secrets to China, only to dismiss the cases before trial. In 2013, two Chinese American scientists, Guoqing Cao and Shuyu Li, were charged with stealing Eli Lilly trade secrets and providing them to a Chinese drug manufacturer.[11] In 2014, Sherry Chen, a Chinese American hydrologist working for the National Weather Service in Ohio, was charged with using a colleague's computer password to download information about U.S. dams that she passed to Chinese officials.[12] In 2015, Xiaoxing Xi, the interim chair of Temple University's physics department, was charged with transferring superconductor technology that could be used in weapons development to China.[13]

The Justice Department proclaimed each of these cases as major economic espionage investigations in dramatic public statements. In the Eli Lilly case, the federal prosecutors called Cao and Li "traitors" and argued they should be detained pretrial as flight risks. The FBI arrested Sherry Chen at her office. She was humiliated, fired from her job, and, as an accused spy, cut off from friends and professional colleagues. A team of armed FBI agents raided Dr. Xi's home early one morning as if he ran a dangerous drug cartel.

Joyce Xi, then a junior at Yale University majoring in chemistry, had just returned home to Philadelphia for the summer break. Joyce was born in Maryland but grew up in Pennsylvania, where both her parents served as physics professors at Penn State University before her father took over the physics department at Temple. A few days into her vacation, FBI agents woke the family up early on the morning of May 21,

2015, by pounding on their front door. Dr. Xi ran downstairs and opened the door as agents started to swing a battering ram to bring it down. By the time Joyce got to the top of the stairs, the agents had her father pressed up against the wall in handcuffs. It was still quite dark and the agents pointed what she described as "big guns" and flashlights up at her, screaming for her to put her hands up. Her mother and twelve-year-old sister were already downstairs with weapons pointed at them too. "They were asking us if we had firearms and treating us as if we were really dangerous," she told me. Why such an aggressive raid was necessary to arrest a college physics professor has never been explained. The agents took her father away and brought her mother into another room for interrogation. A social worker, or at least a woman who said she was a social worker, introduced herself to Joyce and her sister and chatted with them while they sat on the couch "guarded by agents who were telling us what we could and couldn't do in our own house."[14] Joyce and her sister had to ask permission to go to the bathroom or get a glass of water.

Not realizing the peril they were in, Joyce and her parents all provided lengthy statements to the FBI, answering their questions to prove they had nothing to hide. It wasn't until Dr. Xi's arraignment later that day that the family realized he was charged with offenses that could land him in prison for eighty years. When the family returned to the house, another team of FBI agents was waiting with a search warrant. They took boxes of documents and the family's computers and cell phones. Reporters staked out the house for days on end. Temple suspended Dr. Xi and barred him from the campus.

In its arrest warrant and indictment, the FBI claimed Dr. Xi improperly shared blueprints for a proprietary "pocket heater" technology used in superconductor production with Chinese scientists.[15] This was untrue. The information Dr. Xi shared with his Chinese colleagues was a different technology he had invented, which he had described in published academic papers. Dr. Xi believes the FBI had this exculpating evidence at the time of his indictment but chose to ignore it in pursuit of a highly publicized arrest of a Chinese American scientist for spying.[16] Once the charges were made public, several scientists came forward to challenge the FBI's characterization of the technology Xi shared, including the inventor of the pocket heater. The Justice Department abruptly dismissed the charges without apology, as it did in the Eli Lilly and Sherry Chen cases. But the damage was done. The case cost the Xi family over $200,000 in legal fees. Dr. Xi was reinstated at Temple but lost the opportunity to serve as permanent chair of the physics department.

For Joyce and the entire Xi family, the idea that FBI agents could so dangerously misinterpret innocuous activity and willfully ignore disconfirming facts leaves them fearful that new charges could be manufactured against them at any time. The Xi family remains frightened by the knowledge that the FBI held their computers and cell phones for almost a year, giving agents a wealth of personal information that could be similarly misconstrued to cause them harm. The government's hostility toward China only makes their situation seem more volatile. Once you realize that your innocence doesn't protect you from defamatory government charges and invasions of liberty it is hard to go back to normal.

Dr. Xi is suing the FBI agents and prosecutors involved in his arrest, alleging they recklessly disregarded available evidence that the allegations against him were false and pursued his arrest and prosecution due to bias against his Chinese heritage.[17] After finishing up a tough final year at Yale, Joyce Xi graduated with a chemistry degree and went to work with the civil rights group Asian Americans Advancing Justice in San Francisco. "After the case ended," she told me, "one of the very quick connections we've made was to Arab, Middle Eastern, South Asian, and Muslim communities who have been affected" by unjust law enforcement targeting based on misperceived national security threats. "I think at this moment, something needs to be done about this, she said. "There's just a sense that it's going to keep happening."[18]

Chances are, Joyce Xi is right. It will keep happening. In February 2018, FBI director Christopher Wray testified at a Senate Intelligence Committee hearing on worldwide threats. Senator Marco Rubio (R-FL) asked about the counterintelligence risk posed by Chinese students in advanced science and technology programs. Director Wray said, "They're exploiting the very open research and development environment that we have, which we all revere. But they're taking advantage of it. One of the things we're trying to do is to view the Chinese threat as not just a whole of government threat, but a whole-of-society threat, on their end. And I think it's going to take a whole-of-society response by us."[19]

During his testimony, Wray broke Justice Department protocol by acknowledging the FBI investigation of Confucius Institutes, Chinese language and cultural promotion organizations funded by the Chinese education ministry and embedded at universities around the world, including in the United States.[20] Confucius Institutes have been the target of fear-mongering by conservative outlets like the National Association of Scholars, who accuse them of being tools of Chinese propaganda on U.S. campuses.[21] Even assuming this is true, it is hard to see how what is being taught at U.S. colleges is an appropriate concern for the FBI. Where the FBI has evidence a particular scholar, student, or administrator has broken the law or presents a national security threat, obviously it should bring charges or refer them to the U.S. Citizenship and Immigration Services for deportation. Contributing to a public smear campaign only suppresses academic inquiry and free expression.

Representatives Judy Chu (D-CA), Ted Lieu (D-CA), and Grace Meng (D-NY) of the Congressional Asian Pacific American Caucus castigated Wray for his remarks about Chinese academics. "Our nation's highest law enforcement officials should not condone profiling that encourages individuals to view all Chinese and Chinese Americans with more suspicion," Chu said. "There is no room for this sort of prejudice in our country's laws or practices."[22] That Wray would broadly paint Chinese academics as security risks so quickly after being rebuked for the FBI's racist "Black Identity Extremist" assessment shows how deeply these biased attitudes have been engrained into the security psyche.

It is impossible to know whether treating agents like Denise Woo and Rita Chiang and analysts like Logan as trusted colleagues rather than potential threats could have helped the bureau avoid these bias-driven investigations. But chilling the full participation of Asian Americans in government and academic endeavors doesn't strengthen security, it only makes us more fearful, divided, and ignorant.

STRANGERS IN THEIR OWN LAND

On May 25, 2016, FBI director James Comey spoke at the 16th Street Baptist Church in Birmingham, Alabama, at the Birmingham Civil Rights Institute's annual conference. Comey reiterated the four "hard truths" from his speech at Georgetown University the year before, praising the "great progress" the country has made since the civil rights era but acknowledging there was more work to do. He described the Birmingham of the 1960s: "People may have forgotten what it was like for men and women of color—for Black people—in this city fifty years ago. But so many of you here today remember it because many of you lived it or your relatives lived it. Separate schools, separate neighborhoods, separate lives. Billy clubs, dogs, tear gas, fire hoses. Unless you fought against it, it's hard to know it. I can't possibly know it well enough."[23] Comey emphasized the continuing need to resist what W.E.B. Du Bois called the "peculiar indifference" of good people who ignore racial and economic injustices rather than confront them.

Comey was silent, however, when unlicensed private security guards working for Energy Transfer Partners sicced dogs on Native Americans protesting the construction of an oil pipeline across sacred tribal lands near the Standing Rock Indian Reservation just three months later.[24] He remained quiet that winter when state and local law enforcement officers in military gear fired water cannons at those same protesters in subfreezing temperature and assaulted them with nightsticks, concussion grenades, rubber bullets, and pepper spray.[25] Though his agency is responsible for enforcing civil rights laws, he did not speak out when police arrested hundreds of protesters, including several journalists covering the events. During the eleven months of demonstrations at Standing Rock, police arrested 838 people.[26] When the United Nations special rapporteur on the rights of freedom of peaceful assembly and of association condemned the disproportionate police violence inflicted on the Standing Rock protesters and their "inhuman and degrading conditions of detention," Comey did not respond.[27] Indeed, throughout the protest his FBI treated the police as the victims and the protesters as terrorists.

The FBI had long portrayed "eco-terrorism" as the number one domestic terror threat, despite the fact that not a single death is attributable to the U.S. environmental rights movement.[28] The FBI has pursued investigations of environmental rights activists with a zeal almost as intense as its scrutiny of Muslim American communities, and the tactics it has used are even harder to justify as efforts to address terrorism rather than suppress dissent. This animus toward environmental activism falls hard upon Native Americans, whose reverence for nature is born of religious belief as well as tradition and who already suffer from a high rate of discrimination and violence. Uniform Crime Reporting data collected by the FBI in 2016 shows that 3.8 percent of hate crimes in the United States target Native Americans, even though they represent only 1 percent of the population.[29] Native Americans are also more likely to be killed by law enforcement than any other racial or ethnic group, according to data collected by the Centers for Disease Control and Prevention from 1999 to 2016.[30]

Though too often ignored as crime victims, Native Americans draw unwarranted law enforcement attention when they protest government policies that negatively impact their communities. In 1973, approximately two hundred American Indian Movement (AIM) activists initiated an armed occupation of the town of Wounded Knee, South Dakota, on the Pine Ridge Indian Reservation, to protest corrupt tribal leadership and the U.S. government's failure to live up to its treaty obligations. FBI agents and U.S. marshals engaged them in active gun battles, assisted by National Guard troops and military equipment. Two AIM activists were killed, and a deputy marshal was paralyzed.[31] The activists surrendered after ten weeks, but political violence between tribal authorities, AIM supporters, and federal agents would continue for years, taking the lives of two FBI agents killed on the Pine Ridge reservation in 1975 and dozens of Native Americans.[32] At least forty-five of these homicides remain unsolved. In apparent recognition of the loss of faith the community had in the FBI's willingness to pursue these cases, the South Dakota U.S. attorney hired a private investigator in 2012 in a renewed effort to resolve these killings.[33]

The FBI's alleged failure to pursue justice for Native American homicide victims is also the subject of a groundbreaking equal protection lawsuit brought by the family of Steven Bearcrane-Cole, a Native American shot by a non-Native man on Montana's Crow Indian Reservation in 2005. The shooter claimed self-defense, and there were no witnesses. But the family rejected the FBI's determination to classify the homicide as a non-crime, denying them access to federal and state victim compensation benefits as part of a well-documented pattern of federal complacency toward Native American crime victims.[34]

Yet the FBI seems to find investigative resources when Native Americans complain about government policies. In 2012, the wildlife commission in Reno, Nevada, held a hearing to discuss opening the Lake Tahoe area to bear hunting. Nevada AIM activists spoke at the hearing in opposition to the proposal, citing their religious belief that bears are sacred animals. Afterward, an officer with the FBI Joint Terrorism Task Force (JTTF) visited the AIM activists at their homes and workplaces seeking interviews, purportedly as part of an FBI assessment authorized under the 2008 Mukasey guidelines.[35] The agents claimed that Nevada wildlife officials requested the investigation because people at the hearing felt threatened by the AIM activists, but Nevada officials told reporters they had made no such request. This political intimidation by JTTF officers demonstrated the risks created by loosening the FBI's investigative guidelines, giving local agents power to threaten and intimidate innocent Americans who challenge government policy. But this case was just a precursor to the much more organized law enforcement effort to monitor and suppress Native American protests against construction of the Dakota Access Pipeline (DAPL) at Standing Rock in 2016. The tactics they chose looked a lot like those Comey described the Birmingham police using in the 1960s.

Records obtained by *The Intercept* demonstrate that FBI and Justice Department officials were part of law enforcement intelligence operations monitoring the Standing Rock protests from their beginning in the summer of 2016. The documents show the FBI and other law enforcement agencies formed an "intel group" that worked closely with TigerSwan, a private security contractor hired by Energy Transfer Partners that was not licensed to operate in North Dakota.[36] Their methods included aerial videography, physical surveillance, social media monitoring, and infiltration of the protest groups by both company and law enforcement informants.[37] The intelligence they produced and distributed was sensationalized and highly questionable. Two documents reference "the presence of additional Palestinians" and "Islamic individuals" among the Native American protesters and suggest "terrorist type tactics . . . cannot be ruled out."[38] Another links the Native American protesters to Black Lives Matter and Anonymous in a six-degrees-of-Kevin-Bacon-style link analysis.[39]

The FBI's participation in and apparent sanction of a private company's intelligence operations against protesters is troublingly reminiscent of the Bureau of Investigation's cooperation with the American Protective League in the early 1900s. Just as in the past, treating protesters as terrorists is more about public relations than security. The documents indicate TigerSwan also employed propaganda efforts to "delegitimize the anti-DAPL movement" and produced Facebook pages and online videos purporting to present the views of local citizens criticizing the protests.[40]

The FBI also had at least one informant embedded among the Standing Rock protesters. On October 27, 2016, police initiated an operation to clear a protester encampment on land the Lakota Sioux claimed under the terms of an 1868 treaty. As the militarized police force with armored personnel carriers descended on the protesters, two sheriff's deputies tackled one of the protesters, Red Fawn Fallis. As they struggled to handcuff her, two shots rang out before the deputies were able to wrest a .38-caliber revolver from Fallis's grip. No one was injured, but Fallis was arrested and charged with attempted murder. According to *The Intercept*, an FBI informant named Heath Harmon called his handling agent and advised the gun Fallis used was his, but then he called local police and reported it had been stolen two weeks earlier.[41] He eventually came clean to Bureau of Alcohol, Tobacco, Firearms and Explosives (ATF) agents investigating the incident. The story he told raises serious questions about the FBI's methods and oversight of its informants.

The FBI reportedly hired Harmon to infiltrate the camp and report on the activities of the protesters a few months before the shooting. The Intel group reports had identified Fallis as a key leader among the protesters. Over several weeks Harmon met and initiated a sexual relationship with Fallis. He brought the weapon into the camp and kept it in the trailer he shared with her. He told the ATF that Fallis knew where he kept the gun and that the last time he had seen it was a few days before the shooting. Oddly, Harmon maintained his relationship with Fallis and had several phone conversations with her in jail before she learned he was an informant. The attempted murder charge against Fallis was dropped shortly after her arrest, but the Justice Department filed federal charges of civil disorder, discharging a firearm during a felony crime of violence, and illegal possession of a weapon by a felon, which exposed her to a potential life sentence. Her attorneys sought discovery of information regarding the FBI's handling of its informant, Harmon, and the intelligence that led to Fallis's arrest. Instead, the government offered to drop the discharging a firearm charge and recommend a seven-year sentence in exchange for a guilty plea.[42]

This agreement relieved Fallis of the burden of trial and the potentially longer sentence, but it left many questions unanswered. Why did the deputies suddenly tackle Fallis at the protest site, as opposed to any of the other protesters standing near her? Did they know she was armed, and if so, how? Did the FBI instruct the informant, Harmon, to bring a weapon into the camp? Did the FBI instruct Harmon to seduce Fallis and provide her with access to a weapon? If the FBI did not authorize Harmon to provide the weapon to Fallis, why didn't agents arrest him for providing a convicted felon with a firearm? Why was Harmon not prosecuted for filing a false police report that his weapon had been stolen? These questions are important because the FBI and other law enforcement agencies have used the Fallis shooting as evidence that anti-pipeline protests are violent, justifying further surveillance and disruption activities against environmental activists across the country.

In February 2017, after the Standing Rock demonstrations had ended, FBI JTTF agents began visiting the protesters' homes seeking interviews.[43] They went to a hospital to interview Sophia Wilansky, a protester whose arm was nearly blown off during the intense clash at the Backwater Bridge, where police fired water cannons and tear gas grenades at protesters.[44] The police claimed the injury was caused by a protester's improvised explosive device, but Wilansky and other witnesses allege it was a tear gas or concussion grenade fired by police that did the damage.[45] The FBI has leveled no charges against Wilansky or any other protester regarding this incident, suggesting that it found no evidence of an improvised device. Likewise, there is no evidence that the FBI has investigated any law enforcement officers for potential civil rights violations as a result of their indiscriminate and excessive use of force during these demonstrations. Senator Al Franken (D-MN) wrote Comey in March 2017 seeking information about the JTTF's continuing interest in the Standing Rock protesters, warning that such tactics could chill lawful political activism.[46] President Trump fired Comey before the FBI released any public response to Franken's letter, and Senator Franken resigned in the midst of a sexual harassment scandal the following year. Meanwhile, criminal cases against the protesters continue to work their way through the courts as legislatures in thirty states have introduced anti-protest legislation that would empower police and increase penalties for civil disobedience.[47]

FBI SPYING ON ANTI-ESTABLISHMENT PROTESTERS

The FBI has targeted other antiestablishment protest groups with disruption actions as well, including anarchists, anti-globalists, anti-war protesters, and "anti-fascists."[48] In 2004, FBI agents contacted more than sixty political activists who were planning to demonstrate at the Democratic and Republican National Conventions for voluntary interviews. Some were served grand jury subpoenas that would have required their testimony over the days the conventions took place.[49] When civil rights organizations and members of Congress protested these interviews as an effort to chill oppositional political activity at the convention, the FBI claimed it was investigating a bomb threat against media vans. Justice Department inspector general Glenn Fine later determined this claim was "not correct," but concluded that the interviews were conducted for legitimate law enforcement purposes as authorized by the 2002 Attorney General's Guidelines.[50]

Also in 2004, the ACLU filed Privacy Act requests on behalf of approximately 150 civil rights, peace, labor, and environmental advocacy organizations and individuals seeking records regarding JTTF surveillance of their activities. In 2006, the FBI released documents revealing it had conducted surveillance and investigations against many of these groups, including Greenpeace, People for the Ethical Treatment of Animals (PETA), and the Thomas Merton Center, among others. Harkening back to the days of Hoover's concerns over Bolshevism, one FBI document from May 2001 described the Catholic Worker Movement as a Christian organization that advocated peace with a "semi-communistic ideology."[51]

The FBI utilized its most aggressive tactics in investigations targeting environmental activists. In 2004, the FBI recruited a seventeen-year-old female informant to collect information on environmental rights groups and, ultimately, to lure green anarchist Eric McDavid and two of his friends into a nebulous plan to manufacture an explosive for an ill-defined bomb plot. The informant provided the financing, transportation, and a cabin to stay in, then acted as the leader in prodding the group to action. She even gave them bomb recipes authored by FBI chemists. Their attempt to mix the chemicals failed when their only Pyrex bowl broke. When the informant drove them to a store to buy another, the FBI swooped in and arrested them.

At trial, McDavid's attorney argued that the informant seduced McDavid with promises of a romantic relationship if he went through with the plot. The prosecution scoffed at this suggestion and said there was no evidence of such seduction.[52] McDavid was convicted and sentenced to nineteen years in prison. Through post-trial Freedom of Information Act (FOIA) requests, McDavid's lawyers discovered 2,499 documents the FBI withheld from the defense, including love letters exchanged between the informant and McDavid that the prosecution did not produce at trial.[53] In a negotiated settlement reached in 2015, McDavid pled guilty to conspiracy in exchange for his release.[54] The court denied McDavid's request for an investigation of the FBI's misconduct in failing to turn over the exculpating evidence.

During Seattle's annual May Day demonstration in 2012, a small group of protesters smashed windows and threw paint balloons, reportedly causing tens of thousands of dollars in damage. A police officer was allegedly hit with a bottle of urine and a news cameraman was struck in the face with a stick. Police arrested eight protesters that day.[55] The protesters also broke windows at the federal courthouse in downtown Seattle, establishing federal jurisdiction the FBI used to justify a lengthy and astonishingly aggressive investigation. Two months later, FBI SWAT teams and JTTF agents conducted synchronized raids on activists' homes in Seattle and Olympia, Washington, and Portland, Oregon.

The search warrants didn't seek guns or bombs but paint, sticks, flags, computers, cellphones, address books, "anarchist literature," diaries, and journals.[56] The FBI served four activists with grand jury subpoenas seeking testimony and then jailed them when they refused to answer questions about other activists and their political beliefs. Three of them, Leah-Lynn Plante, Matthew Duran, and Katherine Olejnik, were not even in Seattle for the May Day protests.[57] Duran and Olejnik spent almost six months in jail, much of it in solitary confinement, before a judge determined further incarceration would not secure their testimony and ordered their release.[58]

Olejnik told *The Stranger*'s Brendan Kiley that she answered the prosecutor's questions about her own whereabouts that day but refused to identify photographs of other activists or discuss their political or associational activity. "I truly believe that people have the right to believe whatever they want politically," Olejnik told Kiley. "And it's none of the government's business."[59] The FBI disagreed. Documents showed these activists were under FBI surveillance *before* the May Day protest and remained so long afterward.[60] In April 2013, FBI agents fanned out across Seattle seeking interviews with activists at their homes, schools, and workplaces about the 2012 demonstration. Kiley wrote that "the FBI agents' conspicuous arrival—indiscreetly showing up where people work, sleep, and exercise—just before May Day 2013 does not feel entirely coincidental."[61]

It turned out the FBI had already solved the case of the 2012 courthouse vandalism before it jailed Duran and Olejnik. Cody Ingram, a twenty-three-year-old man from Vermont with a history of mental illness who claimed no association with anarchist groups, pled guilty to a misdemeanor charge of destruction of federal property for damaging the courthouse door. He was sentenced to the two months he had already served in jail after his May Day arrest and $500 in restitution.[62]

INVESTIGATIONS BASED SOLELY ON FIRST AMENDMENT ACTIVITY

The thin reed of protection FBI policy provides to political dissidents is its prohibition against targeting individuals or organizations based *solely* on the exercise of their First Amendment rights.[63] In reality, the FBI has often investigated individuals and groups when agents or analysts dislike the content of their speech or political activism. FBI domestic terrorism training materials identify First Amendment activities as methods used by anarchists and environmental extremists. One presentation describes "anarchist extremists" as "criminals seeking an ideology to justify their activities." It lists "passive civil disobedience" as an extremist tactic and claims activists' activities are "staged to create the image of 'aggressive' law enforcement." Ironically, it calls them "paranoid."[64] Another suggests FOIA requests are an environmental extremist tactic.[65]

Eric Garris is a longtime political activist who went on his first civil rights march in the 1960s, when he was nine years old. He worked on his first political campaign at thirteen and ran a local candidate's office at fifteen.[66] In 1995, Garris established a libertarian website, Antiwar.com, which he built into a daily online magazine publishing news and commentary opposing the Clinton administration's bombing campaign in Iraq. Early on, Antiwar.com was an aggregator. Garris would find interesting articles online and repost them with his own commentary. Justin Raimondo, another libertarian political activist and co-founder of Antiwar.com, became a full-time columnist in 1999.[67] Eventually, Garris received funding and was able to hire a reporting staff to write original articles from their own viewpoints. In early 2001, managing the website became Garris's full-time job.

Of course, the 9/11 attacks and the march to war in Afghanistan and Iraq polarized Americans, and running an anti-war website drew passionate responses. On September 12, 2001, Garris received an angry email threatening to shut Antiwar.com down over an article he published. Garris had received threatening messages before, but this one seemed more serious. He called the FBI and the agent answering the line asked him to forward the email so he could take a look, with no promises that the FBI would take any action. When Garris heard nothing back he just forgot about it.

I met Garris in 2012 after a set of FBI documents released through a FOIA request was posted online. The requester appears to have sought FBI records about the 9/11 "dancing Israelis." Years later, during the 2016 presidential campaign, Donald Trump would famously claim to have seen news coverage of Muslims in New Jersey celebrating the 9/11 attacks, but it was actually Israelis.[68] This was the rare example of an anti-Muslim conspiracy theory colliding with an anti-Israeli conspiracy theory, and Trump misdirecting his bigotry. But there really was a case of dancing Israelis. Five twenty-something Israeli citizens in the United States on tourist visas and working illegally for an Israeli-owned moving company happened to park their truck on the New Jersey side of the Hudson River to take a rest on the morning of 9/11.[69] An old undercover saying that there are no normal reactions to abnormal events rings true: people sometimes act oddly when they see something horrible take place. Witnesses reported that the Israelis on the roof of a parking garage were videotaping the attacks and giving each other high fives, suggesting they had prior knowledge that the attacks were going to occur and were celebrating them. Local police stopped the Israelis, arrested them on immigration violations, and then turned them over to the FBI. The FBI investigation determined the Israelis went to the roof after the attacks to take photographs, not before. Agents remained suspicious that the "high fivers" were linked to Israeli intelligence somehow and interrogated them for two months but ultimately found no evidence they were conducting covert activity in the United States. The agents turned them over to the Immigration and Naturalization Service for deportation.[70] The episode has since become part of the "9/11 truther" conspiracy and the subject of FOIA requests.

Among the documents released in the dancing Israelis FOIA was an April 2004 memorandum describing a Newark FBI analyst's examination of Antiwar.com. The website had run an article about the dancing Israelis, which is how it ended up as part of the investigation. The Newark analyst apparently reviewed several other articles posted to Antiwar.com and didn't like them one bit. One article the analyst focused on linked to a copy of the no-fly list, which had been given out to the airlines. The analyst noted that this document wasn't classified but found it suspicious enough to conduct a threat assessment of Antiwar.com, Garris, and Raimondo. The assessment included searches through FBI indices, identifying several cases in which Antiwar.com, Garris, or Raimondo were mentioned, including FISA records, which wouldn't be unusual for a news website since FISA targets might coincidentally visit the site while a wiretap was up. The analyst also checked commercial databases and reviewed a number of the articles posted on the website. Several articles were printed and placed in the FBI file.[71]

The analyst affirmed that Garris and Raimondo had the right to post articles and express their opinions online but argued that "some material that is circulated on the internet can compromise FBI investigations." The threat assessment concluded with a recommendation that the FBI Counterterrorism Division monitor future postings to Antiwar.com. It asked the San Francisco Division to open preliminary investigations against Garris and Raimondo to determine if they were engaging in "activities which constitute a threat to National Security on behalf of a foreign power."[72] The ACLU of Northern California represented both Garris and Raimondo in FOIA lawsuits to find out whether the FBI was investigating them and if so, why.

The first set of documents we received from Garris's FBI file were enlightening. Colleagues and journalists often ask me to decipher FOIA documents they receive from the FBI based on my sixteen years as an agent. The first thing I look for is whether there is a criminal predicate to justify the investigation. The April 2004 memorandum from Newark that Garris received from the FBI was less redacted than the version posted online, exposing a sentence that said Garris had threatened "to disrupt FBI operations by hacking the FBI website."[73] That seemed like sufficient cause to justify a preliminary investigation. Looking further in the documents, however, I found the intake form that recorded the purported threat from Garris. The analyst who received Garris's September 12, 2001, crime report about the email threatening to shut Antiwar.com down misinterpreted it as a threat *by Garris* to shut down the *FBI*'s website. The intake form included the original email threatening Antiwar.com that Garris forwarded to the FBI, so the mistake would be obvious to anyone who read it. But the other documents in the file made clear that too many FBI analysts either didn't bother to read it or chose to falsely characterize it to justify further investigation. The April 2004 threat assessment appeared to suggest the latter, as it described the intake report in a manner to make it literally true but misleading: "The event was documented as a threat by Garris to hack the FBI website."[74] It was indeed documented as a threat, but it clearly was not one. The Newark analyst used this mischaracterization of Garris's email to justify an investigation anyway.

Garris's FBI file contained records going back to 1972, tracking his political career. But most of the investigations were after 9/11 and seem to start like the April 2004 threat assessment, with an article on Antiwar.com that the analyst or agent didn't like. Luckily, San Francisco FBI supervisors refused Newark's April 2004 request that they open a preliminary investigation against Garris and Raimondo because they determined that Antiwar.com was a news website. But in January 2005, the FBI Counterterrorism Division responded to Newark with the results of database searches it had conducted on Antiwar.com at Newark's request. Then again in September 2005, an analyst in Springfield, Illinois, somehow stumbled across Antiwar.com, found its content suspicious, and again suggested a deeper investigation. The Counterterrorism Division took another look at Antiwar.com in 2006, and again in 2008, each time referencing posted articles and the misleading Newark threat assessment.

Of course, Garris didn't know the FBI considered him a national security threat during this time. He once had a harrowing experience with Homeland Security agents at San Francisco International Airport when he returned from speaking at the Perdana Global Peace Forum in Malaysia in late 2005. He views that event through different eyes now that he has seen these FBI documents.[75] TSA agents pulled Garris out of line as he waited to process through Customs and handed him off to Homeland Security agents for interview. They meticulously went through his luggage but rather than going through his clothes looking for hidden drugs or other contraband, they were reading all his documents and questioning him about them. They asked about the different speakers at the conference he had attended and whether he had met with any Muslims. He explained that Malaysia is a Muslim-majority country but that other speakers at the event were prime ministers, members of the British parliament, and United Nations officials, so it was unlikely any terrorists were there. They raised concerns about a book anti-nuclear activist Helen Caldicott had given Garris, because it had a photograph of a mushroom cloud on the cover. The agents let Garris go after about an hour. At the time he thought this episode was odd, but after learned about the FBI investigations he began to wonder whether he was intentionally targeted. It frightened him to think a mistake could so quickly escalate into a search and interrogation.[76]

Telling these stories, it is easy to forget that these are real people and their awareness that their government views them as enemies has debilitating effects. For Garris, the impact of learning that the FBI considered him a national security threat was both personal and professional. When he first learned of the FBI's investigation of Antiwar .com, he thought publicizing it would be the best response. He figured both supporters and opponents of the website would rally to protect free speech and condemn the FBI for its overreach. That's not what happened. He lost three major sponsors and about $75,000 in annual contributions because the sponsors were worried that being associated with Antiwar.com could draw FBI scrutiny to them.[77] He noticed the website received fewer news tips, and leaked materials from sources dropped to almost nothing, which he attributes to concerns the FBI might be monitoring his communications. "I don't blame them for that," he said.[78]

Garris said he became paranoid and depressed. He always felt that his political views might draw scrutiny from the government but figured he could manage the consequences by ensuring his behavior was always above reproach. Learning that a misinterpreted email had made him the subject of repeated FBI inquiries fractured his sense of security. "I think twice about what I want to report, the positions that I take," he told me, "I no longer do appearances on foreign media because I don't want to be associated [with foreign governments]." He and his partner of more than a dozen years separated, which he attributes to stress over the FBI investigations.

He also knows he was lucky that he could get top-notch legal representation from the ACLU of Northern California and a front-page article in *The Guardian*, which compelled the FBI to acknowledge its error and correct its records.[79] He carries in his phone a copy of a statement from the FBI clearing the error in his file, for whatever protection that can give him if government agents ever pull him into another interrogation.

The 2008 amendments to the Attorney General's Guidelines significantly loosened the FBI's investigative authorities and increased the likelihood that these types of unfounded investigations would happen. The FBI's nationwide harassment of activists associated with Deep Green Resistance is but one example.

Deep Green Resistance (DGR) is an "aboveground" environmental advocacy organization that promotes a strategy of resistance to civilizational forces that damage the planet. It advocates for what it calls "decisive ecological warfare," which consists of four phases beginning with networking, then progressing to sabotage, systems disruption, and dismantling of infrastructure.[80] While DGR maintains that violent tactics like sabotage are likely going to be necessary to accomplish the social and economic changes it desires, its website makes clear that DGR is "strictly an aboveground organization."

"Aboveground" refers to those parts of a resistance movement that work in the open and operate more or less within the boundaries of the law, and certainly involving nonviolent forms of protest. According to their website, "DGR is an aboveground organization; we are public and don't try to hide who we are or what we desire, because openness and broad membership is what makes aboveground organizations effective. . . . We will not answer questions regarding anyone's personal desire to be in or form an underground. We do not want to be involved in or aware of any underground organizing. We do this for the security of everyone involved with Deep Green Resistance."[81]

Reporter Adam Federman, who writes for *The Guardian* and the *Earth Island Journal*, among other publications, obtained hundreds of pages of documents from FBI investigations of DGR through a FOIA request. Though highly redacted, the documents indicate that the Indianapolis field office opened an investigation of DGR in January 2013 after receiving approval as required from the office's chief division counsel (CDC). The investigation involved several other field offices. The

Seattle office, for example, documented trespassing charges against twelve activists for lying down on railroad tracks in Bellingham, Washington, to block a coal train in March 2013.[82] Another document references a May 2013 protest by DGR and AIM activists in Nebraska against alcohol sales near the Pine Ridge Indian Reservation, during which protesters broke beer bottles, vandalized a beer truck, and allegedly threatened a driver.[83] In June 2013, the FBI's Indianapolis office transferred the case to Seattle since DGR is based in Washington State. The investigation lasted for another year and a half.

In November 2013, the Seattle agents became alarmed that Western Washington University (WWU) professors had invited DGR representatives to speak on campus. They apparently learned this from an informant and from a poster on a WWU bulletin board. An FBI supervisor and a JTTF officer went to brief the university's police chief about the DGR's "presence on WWU campus." They asked the chief to be on the lookout for more DGR posters while they investigated "to determine the level of participation of the WWU professors in the DGR movement."[84] They took photographs of the poster and the bulletin board as evidence. In January 2014, the University of Washington (UW) reported that someone had written "deepgreenresistance.com" or "Deep Green Resistance" in Sharpie marker on stall doors in campus bathrooms on twelve occasions.[85] Agents marked this as the first evidence of DGR activity at UW. A custodian was able to remove the scribblings with alcohol.

In September 2014, the investigation escalated. The Seattle FBI sent out leads to interview DGR activists across the country, though the communication noted that "to date no information has been obtained to indicate DGR members are in violation of . . . federal laws."[86] Field offices in Tampa, Atlanta, Philadelphia, Milwaukee, Chicago, Springfield (Illinois), Denver, Sacramento, Portland (Oregon), and San Diego were all tasked to go out and interview local activists. They knocked on doors at the activists' homes and workplaces, interviewed their landlords, neighbors, co-workers, and family members. Washington civil rights attorney Larry Hildes started getting calls. He reached out to the FBI agents and asked them to leave his clients alone. Then Hildes himself started getting harassed. As Federman reported in *The Guardian*,

Homeland Security officials stopped Hildes at Miami International Airport in May 2015 as he returned from an overseas trip and held him for three hours, questioning him about one of his DGR clients.[87] DHS officials twice stopped and questioned him about the same client again while returning home from brief trips to Canada.

The Seattle FBI closed its DGR investigation in December 2014, citing the failure to identify any criminal violation or threat to national security. The investigation was properly designated a "sensitive investigative matter" (SIM), as it involved the investigation of a domestic political organization. SIM cases are supposed to require more stringent legal scrutiny by FBI management to ensure protection of civil rights.[88] Yet here, two FBI CDCs from different field offices authorized a two-year investigation that took place with no indication that anyone in the group intended to break any federal laws or threaten national security, as the documents candidly acknowledge. While the agents cited scary phrases from the DGR mission statement, they ignored the many statements that clearly indicated DGR members would not engage in violence. If CDCs would approve this investigation, it would be hard to imagine what they would prohibit. Even putting aside the civil rights concerns, the investigation wasted law enforcement time, effort, and resources that should have been used to address real public safety threats. The FBI may have reopened the investigation since then, because in September 2015 DGR activists attempting to enter Canada for an event were detained at the border, interrogated about their political activities, and denied entry.[89]

The FBI's disruption strategy holds that this sort of intimidation of these potentially dangerous "others"—activists, lawyers, and journalists—is justifiable because it might inhibit them from moving further down the path of radicalization to committing acts of violence. The FBI claims it disrupts hundreds of acts of terrorism each year, though it pursues far fewer terrorism prosecutions.[90] For all we know, the FBI claimed statistical accomplishments for disrupting terrorism in the cases mentioned throughout this chapter. But actual crime, violence, and credible threats to national security go unaddressed while FBI agents chase phantoms of potential future terrorists. Indeed, crimes and violence committed by individuals the FBI sees as part of the protected establishment receive little of its investigative attention.

Part Three

DISRUPTING DEMOCRATIC CONTROLS

10

THE WATCHDOG THAT DIDN'T BARK—IGNORING EXECUTIVE ABUSE

On July 3, 2016, Republican presidential candidate Donald Trump tweeted, "THE SYSTEM IS RIGGED!"[1] Too many Americans agreed with him. A Gallup poll taken a few weeks earlier showed Americans' confidence in U.S. institutions hovering at record lows.[2] Pew Research Center polling over the last two decades found that trust in government spiked after 9/11 but then started a rapid descent through 2017, when only 20 percent of Americans counted on government to do the right thing all or most of the time.[3]

This cynicism likely had many drivers, including sixteen years of war against terrorism with no clear goal and no end in sight; the partisan bickering, gridlock, and lawful corruption of public officials who seem more interested in serving their donors than their constituents; the slow recovery from the 2008 financial crisis and stagnation of middle-class wages while the Wall Street bankers who caused the crisis only got richer, to name just a few. Many sensed that there was one set of rules for the rich and powerful and a different set for the rest of us. A June 2016 Gallup poll showed only 23 percent of Americans had high confidence in the fairness of the criminal justice system.[4]

I believe the FBI contributed to this breakdown of public trust in government institutions, not just by who it chose to target for disruption but, just as important, who it didn't. Where the FBI poured tremendous time, effort, and resources into monitoring, investigating, and even manufacturing cases against individuals and groups that challenge establishment policies, it chose not to pursue lawbreaking by the politically powerful with equal vigor. By prioritizing its national security and domestic intelligence functions over criminal law enforcement, the FBI widened the divide between us and them—the protected versus the suspected. When members of the public internalized that government institutions could not or would not protect their rights and privileges, they had to decide which side they were on. Many embraced the institutions and symbols that projected strength—the military, police, guns, and God—along with strongman politicians who pledged to dismantle the legal and social restraints they believed allowed their enemies to prosper. As this societal breach expanded, the Justice Department and FBI began to view reactionary violence against out-groups with less concern, and even tacit sanction.

IGNORING EXECUTIVE ABUSE

In *The CIA and the Cult of Intelligence*, Victor Marchetti and John Marks described a "secret fraternity of the American political aristocracy" that included the clandestine service, its "patrons and protectors" in government, and "friends" in industry, finance, and academia.[5] The FBI was once seen as a competitor and potential prosecutor of CIA officials, which was good in so far as it kept CIA lawbreaking in check. This rivalry also created obstacles to cooperation, however, and certainly played a role in the 9/11 intelligence failures. The FBI's post-9/11 transformation into a domestic intelligence agency was intended to remove these barriers and improve information sharing, but I don't think the public understood how this shift in mission would compromise government accountability and the rule of law. As the intelligence agencies went over to Vice President Cheney's "dark side," they took the nation's premier law enforcement agency with them and made it complicit. The "us" the FBI would protect during the war on terror would now literally become "us"—the intelligence establishment that Marchetti and Marks described, which the FBI now joined. Protecting the intelligence community's secrets would become more important than upholding the law.

One reason governments cling to the radicalization theory of terrorism and promote it as the "cause" of political violence is that it absolves the state of responsibility for past and future conduct. Framing terrorism as a product of fanaticism or ideological infection obviates the need to examine whether government action or inaction inflamed oppositional elements in society or influenced their tactics. This modeling of the terrorism problem likewise justifies extraordinary government measures to counter the threat moving forward. What I learned working undercover with people planning terrorist attacks is that this reaction is exactly what they aim to provoke with their atrocities. They hope the government they attack will reveal its unjust nature by responding with extralegal and discriminatory measures.

Unfortunately, the Bush administration fell into this terrorist trap and chose to employ methods that were clearly outside the law. Keeping these activities secret became paramount. The highest-ranking executive branch officials went before Congress, the courts, and the American people and lied about these programs, first to hide them, then to cover up their ineffectiveness. A law enforcement agency that was properly shielded from political influence, which the Church Committee attempted to establish with its reform recommendations in 1976, could have prevented the damage these ill-considered decisions inflicted on public faith in government simply by doing its job.

Once exposed, Bush administration officials talked about "enhanced" interrogations and mass surveillance as get-tough measures against terrorism. But nothing demonstrates a government's weakness more than mistreating helpless prisoners and spying on its own citizens.

TORTURE

Nowhere is the breakdown of the rule of law and the Justice Department's institutional obligations more evident than in the CIA and U.S. military torture scandals. The Bush administration's decision to authorize the cruel, inhuman, and degrading treatment of detainees captured during the global war on terror represents a profound moral, legal, policy, and intelligence failure that continues to roil and divide our nation almost two decades later.

The FBI had some of the best-trained and most-experienced interrogators who were both knowledgeable about al Qaeda's operations and skilled in eliciting cooperation from its adherents using methods that could withstand judicial scrutiny. They also knew that mistreatment and coercion produced unreliable information.[6] FBI director Robert

Mueller should have made sure these agents were leading the government's interrogation program, establishing its parameters, and training the CIA agents and military personnel who were going into conflict zones. Instead, he stood aside as the CIA paid a pair of hack psychologists who had never conducted a real interrogation $81 million to reverse engineer a military training program designed to prepare U.S. soldiers to survive communist torture methods.[7] The military saved $81 million by taking their torture tactics straight from the Fox television series *24*.[8]

If Mueller truly aspired to transform the bureau into a proper intelligence agency, its first mission should have been to leverage its deep experience in interrogations to help the government avoid the entirely predictable—and in fact, predicted—consequences.[9] Failing to throw the brakes on the torture program aided our enemies, alienated our allies, put American captives at greater risk, and forfeited U.S. credibility in promoting human rights and the rule of law abroad.[10] When *Wall Street Journal* reporter Daniel Pearl's captors had him express sympathy for Guantanamo Bay detainees in a statement they taped before cutting his throat, and when Abu Musab al-Zarqawi dressed Nick Berg in an orange jumpsuit like those worn by Abu Ghraib prisoners in Iraq to film his beheading, they sent clear messages that brutality would be met with greater brutality.[11]

Compounding the tragedy, for all that was lost nothing was gained. The Senate Intelligence Committee's six-year examination of CIA records regarding its torture program found that the enhanced interrogation techniques were "not an effective means of obtaining accurate information or gaining detainee cooperation."[12] This conclusion would have surprised few experienced FBI agents. Hoover's FBI began advising custodial suspects of their rights to remain silent and consult counsel in the mid-1940s, in recognition that coerced statements were unreliable and protecting civil liberties was essential to preserving public trust in law enforcement.[13]

The Supreme Court cited the FBI's use of such warnings in *Miranda v. Arizona* in 1966.[14] While the CIA and Defense Department imagined their "enhanced" interrogations tactics were new and experimental, cops had been giving suspects the third degree for decades. As a result, long before the Guantanamo Bay prison opened, a wealth of academic and professional research had shown that torture, coercion, and sleep deprivation commonly produce false confessions.[15] Torture is never really about getting accurate information, it is designed to extract convenient confessions and assert social control.[16]

As the federal government's predominant law enforcement agency, the FBI was best situated to stop the torture programs. Mueller is often credited for protecting the FBI's honor by directing his agents not to participate in military or CIA interrogations that deviated from bureau policies prohibiting the use of coercive tactics. But Congress gave the FBI jurisdiction over crimes committed by U.S. government personnel overseas, and it is apparent the bureau could have done more to stop the abuse than simply turning a blind eye to potential violations of U.S. and international law. Some agents certainly thought so.

New York FBI agent Ali Soufan threatened to put handcuffs on a CIA contractor who first began using what he called "borderline torture" techniques on detainee Abu Zubaydah, who had been providing useful intelligence to Soufan and his FBI partner in noncoercive interviews.[17] Instead, headquarters told him to leave the site. FBI agents in Guantanamo Bay began keeping a "war crimes" file and submitted a legal analysis to headquarters describing the military interrogation tactics as violations of the torture statute and international law. They recognized, as law enforcement officers, the necessity to properly document what was happening to ensure an official record existed for future proceedings. FBI officials at headquarters rebuffed these efforts. They ignored the legal memo and instructed agents not to maintain a war crimes file, arguing that "investigating detainee allegations of abuse was not the FBI's mission."[18] Some agents reported being told not to document allegations of abuse in their reports.[19]

Representative Robert Wexler (D-FL) questioned Mueller during an April 2008 House Judiciary Committee hearing on FBI oversight about why bureau agents did not respond more aggressively to the apparent violations of law they observed during CIA or military interrogations. Mueller said his hands were tied by the Justice Department's "interpretations of law," which effectively authorized these practices through "torture memos" drafted by Office of Legal Counsel attorneys John Yoo and Jay Bybee in 2002.[20] But the FBI's position on abusive interrogations was more flexible than Mueller admitted.

In fact, the FBI provided agents working in Iraq, Afghanistan, and Guantanamo Bay no formal instructions regarding their participation in abusive interrogations until May 2004, after the Abu Ghraib prison abuse scandal broke. In the meantime, some FBI agents participated in "enhanced" CIA and military interrogations, including Soufan's partner, who stayed several more weeks at the black site while CIA agents interrogated Zubaydah. In a handful of cases, FBI agents abused detainees themselves.[21]

A 370-page inspector general report issued by Glenn Fine in May 2008 revealed these episodes and criticized bureau leaders for failing to respond to a multitude of requests for guidance coming in from the field.[22] Even the FBI's May 2004 policy guidance to "not participate" and report "abuse" left the agents questioning what standard they were expected to apply to non-FBI interrogations and how long after suspected abuse they were permitted to reengage. The FBI's Office of the General Counsel drafted clarifications, but none were finalized or disseminated. One supervisor working in Afghanistan who complained about the lack of guidance told the inspector general that it appeared headquarters officials favored a less restrictive interrogations policy. He said, "These guys did not want rules because they might have to follow [them]."[23] The supervisor was recalled from Afghanistan "because of concerns about whether he was emotionally suited to the Afghanistan assignment."[24] Contrary to the policy directive, the FBI dissuaded reports of abuse from the field by retaliating against whistleblowers. The inspector general report documented two additional FBI agents who suffered reprisals for reporting detainee abuse in Guantanamo and Iraq.

Mueller apparently felt less bound by Justice Department policy after Barack Obama was elected. Attorney General Eric Holder attempted to fulfill Obama's campaign promise of closing the military detention center in Guantanamo Bay by bringing the detainees to the United States to stand trial in federal court. Under questioning by House Republicans in a May 2009 Judiciary Committee hearing, Mueller said he was concerned that former Guantanamo detainees brought to the United States for trial could "radicalize" other federal prisoners, assist in financing terrorism, and instigate domestic attacks.[25] He dismissed the suggestion that maximum security federal prisons were equipped to mitigate such threats. Congress voted later that day to deny funding for the Obama administration's plan to finally bring these terrorists to justice in U.S. courts.

Even after President Obama banned enhanced interrogations by U.S. personnel in January 2009, some in the FBI seemed comfortable with its agents' proximity to torture, so long as they weren't inflicting the abuse themselves. In 2012, the ACLU obtained an FBI interrogation manual called *Cross Cultural, Rapport-Based Interrogations* that appeared to confirm the practice of proxy detention.[26] Proxy detentions occur when the FBI provides information foreign governments use to arrest people and hold them for agents to interview.[27] In a number of documented cases, mostly in the Middle East and Africa, foreign governments have arrested and detained Americans, compelling them to submit to interviews with FBI agents who profess the authority to secure their release if they agree to become informants.[28] Some have been held without charge, abused by their captors, and in one case, moved from one country to another at the request of the FBI.[29]

Two future FBI directors were implicated in the torture scandal as well. When James Comey became deputy attorney general in 2003, he withdrew the Justice Department's 2002 torture memos as legally insufficient and replaced them with new ones that amended the legal reasoning but concurred in their conclusion that tactics like waterboarding, sleep deprivation, stress positions, and "walling" were lawful.[30] Christopher Wray was also touched by the torture scandal while serving as assistant attorney general over the Justice Department's Criminal Division. The CIA Office of Inspector General notified Wray in February 2004 of a possible criminal violation regarding the death of an Iraqi detainee during an interrogation at Abu Ghraib prison.[31] During a Senate Judiciary Committee hearing in May 2004, after the Abu Ghraib torture photos became public, Wray claimed he learned of the abuse through media reports. He denied receiving any criminal referrals from the Defense Department.[32] Upon learning about the CIA inspector general's referral, Senator Patrick Leahy, the committee chairman, called Wray's testimony "less than a complete and truthful answer."[33] No one was charged for this homicide, which wasn't unusual. Despite approximately one hundred deaths resulting from U.S. interrogations and detainee abuse, the Justice Department charged and convicted just one CIA contractor with assault.[34]

The excessive secrecy surrounding the torture program created space for proponents of the interrogation policy to portray the tactics as less abusive and more effective than they actually were, according to an internal CIA review conducted under Director Leon Panetta in 2009 and a six-year Senate Intelligence Committee investigation concluded in December 2014.[35] According to these reports, CIA officials intentionally misled congressional overseers and both Bush and Obama White House officials, as well as the public. CIA officials also destroyed videotapes of the interrogations despite court orders and congressional requests to retain this evidence. The Justice Department's investigations into the homicides, false statements, and evidence destruction were opportunities for accountability, but they resulted in no charges, and the Obama administration opposed public records requests for information regarding the investigations.[36] It's not hard to imagine why a Justice Department complicit in authorizing torture would want to keep the manner of its implementation and all downstream effects under wraps.

The lack of accountability allowed the issue of torture to become highly politicized. Even after the shock of the 9/11 attacks, a 2004 Pew Research Center poll showed that 53 percent of Americans said torture could rarely or never be justified to obtain information from suspected terrorists, while 43 percent said it could sometimes be justified. By 2011, the numbers were almost exactly reversed.[37] And like most issues today, torture approval or disapproval breaks across party lines. In 2017, 67 percent of Democrats said there were no circumstances in which torture is acceptable, while 71 percent of Republicans said there sometimes were circumstances justifying torture.[38] President Trump's first CIA director, former congressman Mike Pompeo, was a torture program supporter, and his second, career CIA officer Gina Haspel, ran a black site where waterboarding and other abuses took place. Haspel disseminated the order to destroy videotapes depicting the abuse.[39] Without accountability, the likelihood of torture again becoming official U.S. policy increased.

WIRETAPPING AND WHISTLEBLOWERS

The secret expansion of warrantless domestic wiretapping in the aftermath of 9/11 created a similar dilemma for Mueller, Comey, and Wray. They couldn't protect these new electronic surveillance programs they knew might be found unconstitutional, if not criminal violations of the Foreign Intelligence Surveillance Act, and be fully forthcoming with their overseers in Congress and the courts.[40] When Comey became deputy attorney general in 2003, he and his staff determined the Justice Department's November 2001 legal opinion supporting the NSA's warrantless wiretapping program was deficient and that one part of it, the bulk collection of domestic internet metadata, was illegal. His refusal to reauthorize the program led to a mythic March 2004 confrontation in Attorney General John Ashcroft's hospital room, where White House counsel Alberto Gonzales and chief of staff Andrew Card tried to convince the ailing attorney general to override his deputy's decision. Though Mueller had not previously complained about the legal underpinnings of the warrantless surveillance program, he joined Comey in threatening to resign in March 2004 if it wasn't modified. The Bush administration altered the program only slightly, by convincing a FISA judge to authorize the mass surveillance program that the Justice Department wouldn't.[41]

Several provisions of the Patriot Act were due to expire at the end of 2005. In April of that year, Director Mueller testified before the Senate Intelligence Committee in favor of reauthorizing those provisions. He said he was "unaware of any substantiated allegation that the government has abused its authority under the Patriot Act."[42] In June 2005 testimony before the House Judiciary Committee, Deputy Attorney General Comey said, "Under the Patriot Act, I'm very confident in saying there have been no abuses found; none documented."[43] Neither mentioned their determination that the mass collection of internet metadata had been illegal, the dramatic confrontation in Attorney General Ashcroft's hospital room, their threats to resign if it wasn't modified, or that the program continued with just a veneer of additional oversight. They also failed to mention that the FBI self-reported at least thirteen Patriot Act violations to the Intelligence Oversight

Board, an independent executive branch entity established to notify the president of violations of intelligence laws and directives.[44] But these were the least of the Patriot Act violations the FBI could have found if it had only looked.

Congress reauthorized the expiring provisions of the Patriot Act in 2006, but it ordered the inspector general to audit the FBI's use of these authorities. In a series of reports beginning in 2007, the inspector general documented hundreds of violations of the FBI's statutory obligations, particularly involving misuse of a secret type of administrative subpoena called a "national security letter," and the broad use of illegal "exigent letters," which faked emergencies to obtain Americans' telecommunications data without legal process.[45] The FBI promised reform, but subsequent inspector general reviews found these efforts lacking.[46]

In the meantime, the Justice Department had secretly adopted a new interpretation of the Patriot Act's business records provision, Section 215, to justify another part of the warrantless wiretapping program: the bulk collection of virtually all Americans' telephone metadata. The inspector general reports on Section 215 did not reveal this new interpretation of the law, so many of the members of Congress who reauthorized the provision in 2010 and again in 2011 did not know that the handful of Section 215 requests reported swept up millions of Americans' calling records.

When Senator Ron Wyden (D-OR) asked Director of National Intelligence James Clapper if the intelligence community collected "any type of data" about millions of Americans in a 2013 Senate Intelligence Committee hearing, Clapper replied falsely, "No, sir, not wittingly."[47] Around the same time, Major League Baseball Hall of Fame pitcher Roger Clemens denied taking steroids before a congressional committee, and the FBI and Justice Department charged him with perjury to "ensure the integrity of the investigative process."[48] Clapper admitted his statement was untruthful, but he was not charged. Apparently ensuring integrity in intelligence oversight was not as important as protecting the integrity of America's Pastime.[49] After a first trial resulted in a mistrial, a jury acquitted Clemens after a second trial.[50]

The FBI and Justice Department also kept the courts in the dark about the nature and scope of their intelligence activities. They did this primarily through a technique known as parallel construction. It had long been used as a way to mask the name or nature of a confidential source. Rather than identifying the source, the FBI or federal prosecutors would refer in court documents to a "source of known reliability." That source could be a person or an intercepted communication by a spy satellite. A defendant could petition to unmask the source and the court could review the matter in camera to balance the government's secrecy demands against the defendant's right to confront the witnesses against him. In this newer version of parallel construction, the government first gathers evidence through a secret intelligence technique. Once evidence is located, agents utilize a more traditional legal process, like a grand jury subpoena or a search warrant, to collect the same evidence. When the evidence is submitted in court, the government claims the second legal process was the source of the evidence and never mentions the first collection. This way, no defendant or judge will know a secret intelligence method was used and therefore cannot challenge it to evaluate its legality.

For instance, the Drug Enforcement Administration (DEA) had a program called Hemisphere that allowed law enforcement agencies, including the FBI, to secretly search through and analyze millions of AT&T communications records.[51] The DEA instructed agents to never mention the Hemisphere program in court records and to instead use grand jury subpoenas to gather the same data if they wanted to use the evidence in any proceedings. "Walling off" the Hemisphere program this way was intended to protect it from constitutional scrutiny.[52] Similarly, the FBI actually entered into formal nondisclosure contracts with law enforcement agencies using "StingRay" devices that mimic cell phone towers to capture the signal and locate all cell phones in a particular area.[53] The contracts directed law enforcement agencies to use the StingRay for "lead purposes" but to then use a secondary legal process to obtain the same evidence for court.[54] The bureau went so far as to instruct local prosecutors to drop or reduce the charges against criminal defendants rather than expose the device to legal challenges in court.[55]

Because the FBI and Justice Department subvert the constitutional checks on their power by withholding information from Congress and the courts on secrecy grounds, the only way the public can learn about these intelligence programs is through conscientious government whistleblowers and the journalists who tell their stories. So the FBI targets them as spies. During the Bush administration, the FBI used illegal exigent letters to obtain the telephone records of *New York Times* and *Washington Post* reporters.[56] It secretly seized a FedEx package an Associated Press reporter in the Philippines sent to a U.S. colleague, without a warrant or notification.[57] The FBI maintained a national security investigation against documentary filmmaker Laura Poitras for six years, which led Customs and Border Protection officers at airports to detain her over fifty times from 2006 to 2012, subjecting her to repeated interrogations and often searching her notes and electronic equipment.[58] This was all *before* she met Edward Snowden and made an Oscar-winning documentary about him.

The Obama Justice Department subpoenaed the records from twenty Associated Press telephone lines used by more than one hundred reporters in one leak investigation, referred to Fox News reporter James Rosen as a co-conspirator in a search warrant affidavit in an espionage investigation, and threatened to force *New York Times* reporter James Risen to choose between betraying his source or jail.[59] In response to criticism over these actions, Attorney General Holder stiffened protections for journalists in the Justice Department's media guidelines in 2015.[60] As internal department guidance, these rules have no external enforcement mechanism and can be changed at any time.

The Obama administration also prosecuted more U.S. government whistleblowers than all previous administrations combined, often charging them aggressively under the Espionage Act, a World War I–era statute designed to target wartime spies. Not only are most whistleblower leaks not damaging to the national security, they improve it by exposing waste, fraud, abuse, or illegality that undermine the effectiveness of intelligence community programs. Moreover, the government selectively prosecutes whistleblowers rather than leakers who expose secrets for other purposes. The intelligence community leaks classified information regularly, often to promote government programs or policies, or to self-aggrandize. Harsh prosecutions and punishment only occur when the leak embarrasses the government or exposes error or abuse.[61]

Even more problematic are cases in which the FBI investigates its overseers. Diane Roark had decades of experience in the national security establishment, working for the Departments of Energy and Defense, the National Security Council, and finally as staff to the House Intelligence Committee, where she served for seventeen years. She held the highest security clearances available and in 1997 was assigned to oversee the NSA. She discovered the warrantless wiretapping program in 2001 and had serious concerns about its legality. She also knew that the NSA had developed another methodology that collected the same information but was much less expensive and automatically encrypted U.S. person information, so the privacy of Americans inadvertently caught in the dragnet would be protected. She brought her concerns to the Intelligence Committee chairman and ranking member but was rebuffed. She went to the NSA director, the White House, a FISA Court judge, and even a Supreme Court justice, but none would listen to her concerns. She retired in 2002 but continued collaborating with current and former NSA officials Tom Drake, J. Kirk Wiebe, and Bill Binney to press for an investigation by the Defense Department inspector general.[62]

In 2005, when James Risen and Eric Lichtblau exposed the NSA's warrantless wiretapping program on the front page of the *New York Times*, Roark felt there would finally be an opportunity to publicly challenge the program.[63] She didn't know the FBI was already investigating her as the possible leaker. A few months after the article came out, FBI agents requested an interview that turned into an interrogation. Then, in 2007, FBI agents conducted coordinated raids at the homes of Roark, Drake, Wiebe, and Binney early one morning, pulling Binney out of the shower at gunpoint.[64] Agents seized their computers and notebooks, and Roark learned that the Intelligence Committee had allowed the FBI to search her old work computer, agenda books, and telephone logs, potentially exposing all the sources she used to conduct committee oversight and forfeiting important separation of powers prerogatives.

The investigation dragged on for more than two years before the Justice Department charged Tom Drake with Espionage Act violations that could have put him in jail for decades. The prosecution collapsed, however, when a former government classification expert challenged whether the evidence Drake was accused of mishandling was properly classified. Drake ultimately pled guilty to a misdemeanor count of "exceeding authorized use of a government computer."[65] The government let the possibility of charges hang over Roark's head for years, and she had to sue the FBI to get her computer back.[66]

During the Senate Intelligence Committee's investigation of the CIA torture program, agency personnel scanned a committee staffer's computer, reconstructed his emails, and removed documents, violating agreements with committee members, long-standing limitations against CIA spying on Americans, and potentially the same criminal law Drake pled guilty to.[67] The Justice Department declined to bring charges against the CIA officials involved in the matter.

AMBIVALENCE TO POLICE VIOLENCE

Law enforcement makes up another element of the protected classes who can use force with near impunity, particularly against communities of color. Police violence is rarely mentioned in discussions regarding national security threats, though many American communities certainly have their security threatened by it.

After President Trump fired Director Comey, Howard University recruited Comey for a lecture series as the Gwendolyn S. and Colbert I. King Endowed Chair in Public Policy.[68] He donated his $100,000 salary to a Howard University scholarship fund to benefit students coming from foster homes. Some Howard students protested his selection, citing the FBI's historical mistreatment of black leaders, its monitoring of Black Lives Matter protesters, and Comey's apparent endorsement of the "Ferguson effect," which suggests spikes in crime result from a chilling effect protests against police violence have on law enforcement.[69] They attempted to shout down his keynote speech at Howard's September 2017 convocation with chants of, "James Comey, you're not our homie!"

Comey took the dissension with good humor, chiding them that a conversation requires talking but then being quiet and listening to the other side. As it became clear the protesters were not going to stop, he just read his speech over their chanting. When he returned to Howard the following month to give his first official King Chair lecture on law enforcement and race, he essentially repeated the speeches that he had given at Georgetown in 2015 and Birmingham in 2016, making it clear it was he who was not listening to his critics.[70] In each lecture he attributed increased homicide rates in cities like Chicago and Baltimore to a growing distrust between law enforcement and communities of color. He argued that community members need to imagine what police officers on patrol "see through their windshields" and feel what they feel when they walk up to a door "not knowing what is on the other side." He said once they do they will find, as he has, that law enforcement officials devote their lives to helping "communities that a whole lot of America decides to drive around" and are "overwhelmingly doing the right thing for the right reasons."[71]

As a lifelong prosecutor, FBI director, and grandson of a police chief, it isn't surprising that Comey holds a positive view of law enforcement. But hearing such praise coming from the director of the agency responsible for enforcing civil rights laws must have been a bitter pill for people who've seen their families, friends, and neighbors humiliated by racial profiling, stopped and frisked without cause, and victimized by unaccountable police violence. Comey's myopic perception of law enforcement misconduct as good intentions gone awry rather than intentional abuse reflects an unwillingness to acknowledge relevant facts that challenge his worldview.

Comey again complained about a lack of data, but between his Georgetown speech and the Howard lecture, many researchers had stepped in to fill that void. According to Police-Public Contact Survey data collected by the Bureau of Justice Statistics from 2002 to 2011 and published in November 2015, police officers used or threatened to use force against people in the United States an average of 715,500 times a year. About three-fourths of those on the receiving end of this violence described the level of force used as "excessive." The data showed police threatened or used force against African Americans at more than twice the rate used against white people.[72] The Center for Policing Equity studied police-use-of-force records submitted by twelve participating departments and documented an even greater disparity, finding police used force against African Americans at 3.6 times the rate used against white people.[73] Data collected by *The Guardian* showed police killed 1,093 people in the United States in 2016, down slightly from 1,146 in 2015.[74] Young black men were five times more likely to be killed by police than their white counterparts in 2015.[75]

The FBI has responsibility for enforcing civil rights violations by law enforcement officers under a Reconstruction-era statute prohibiting the "deprivation of rights under color of law," but prosecutions are relatively rare.[76] The *Pittsburgh Tribune-Review* examined Justice Department data from 1995 to 2015 that showed the FBI and other federal agencies referred 13,233 complaints involving 21,364 law enforcement officers for prosecution. U.S. attorneys' offices declined to prosecute 96 percent of these complaints, and ultimately convicted only 631 law enforcement officers over that 21-year period.[77] The high declination rate is a product of an FBI policy to refer all color of law complaints to prosecutors, even if the investigation found no inculpating evidence, removing all discretion from agents investigating their fellow law enforcement colleagues. The low conviction rate is partly due to the 1945 Supreme Court decision in *Screws v. United States*, which requires prosecutors to prove law enforcement officers charged in color of law violations acted with a specific intent to deprive the victim of a particular constitutional right, a high standard to meet.[78] There is no doubt that these are difficult cases to make, but FBI directors never hesitate to go to Congress to demand stronger anti-terrorism laws when they think they need better tools.

The FBI simply doesn't prioritize these cases. When New Orleans flooded after Hurricane Katrina hit the Gulf coast in 2005, the FBI sent almost five hundred agents in to assist local police with violent crime and prevent fraud against federal programs responsible for helping residents recover from the disaster.[79] FBI SWAT teams patrolled the streets with New Orleans police officers, and bureau agents staffed the Hurricane Katrina Fraud Task Force to prevent people from plundering the billions of federal disaster dollars flowing into the region. By October 2008, the FBI had charged more than nine hundred people with procurement fraud, embezzlement, and bribery involving disaster-related projects.[80]

On December 19, 2008, ProPublica reporter A.C. Thompson published a bombshell of a story about the unexamined police murder of Henry Glover, whose charred body was found in a burned vehicle just down the street from a New Orleans Police Department station house after the flood.[81] He also wrote about white vigilantes in the Algiers Point neighborhood who shot at least eleven African American refugees trying to get to an evacuation point set up by the Department of Homeland Security. None had been investigated, much less charged.[82]

Thompson wasn't a local reporter with a deep network of informants who would never cooperate with out-of-town FBI agents. He had flown in from California eighteen months earlier because he'd heard stories—"myths" he called them—that he wanted to dig into. He discovered everyone was interested in talking about it: the victims and their families, and even the vigilantes themselves. Timely complaints had been filed that supported these stories, and plenty of witnesses were just waiting for someone to listen. It's hard to imagine that all those FBI agents in New Orleans didn't hear some of the same stories over the three years before Thompson's articles started running. Belated federal prosecutions that followed were burdened by the passage of time and prosecutorial misconduct, leading to some acquittals and adverse appellate decisions, but the Justice Department finally managed to obtain guilty pleas from a number of officers involved in the killings or the cover-ups.[83]

In Chicago, one of the cities Comey often references in his "hard truths" speeches, police officers shot 702 people over fifteen years, according to the *Chicago Tribune*. The Justice Department didn't file a single civil rights charge against any of the officers.[84] But unaccountable police violence is only half the story. Even as African Americans are overpoliced as crime suspects, they are underserved as crime victims. The Chicago Police Department's (CPD) homicide clearance rate started dropping more than a decade ago. The CPD cleared less than 20 percent of Chicago's homicides in 2017, according to the *Chicago Sun-Times*, a historic low.[85] It isn't hard to figure out why the homicide rate isn't dropping if murderers are running free.

It isn't hard to figure why community member would be reluctant to trust the police, either. *The Intercept* published the harrowing story of two Chicago police officers who went to the FBI in 2007 to report that CPD sergeant Ronald Watts was running a crew of police officers who robbed drug dealers and filed false criminal charges against housing project residents who wouldn't cooperate with his criminal schemes. The

FBI struggled with the investigation for years, before finally snaring Watts and one of his officers stealing purported drug money in a sting operation in 2012.[86] More than half a dozen other officers from Watts's crew have been placed on desk duty as the FBI investigation continues.[87] A separate CPD gang squad led by a sergeant who had been the subject of twenty-three citizen complaints and four federal lawsuits over twenty-one years is also under FBI investigation for similar conduct.[88] Yet the two whistleblowers in the Watts case were ostracized by CPD leadership rather than rewarded for breaking the blue wall of silence.

Baltimore, another city Comey focuses on during his race and law enforcement talks, has been suffering under a similar police corruption scandal. The FBI recently won convictions against eight officers from the Baltimore Police Department's Gun Trace Task Force after a fourteen-month investigation that uncovered police robberies, drug dealing, and fraud against the city.[89] These clearly aren't the type of officers that patrol Comey's neighborhood, and they certainly aren't the norm. But they are a big part of the problem that too often isn't acknowledged in policy debates about violent crime.

The odd thing is these are FBI investigations that Comey should have been bragging about. But these success stories don't fit the narrative that pathologizes urban violence, excuses police bias as an understandable product of working in dangerous communities, and urges public support for tough-on-crime policing.

This again is where the lack of diversity within the FBI and U.S. attorneys' offices undermines the federal government's ability to fully understand and properly serve the needs of all communities. As of May 2018, only 8 percent of President Trump's U.S. attorney nominees were people of color.[90]

11

WHITE NATIONALISTS AND WHITE COLLARS

Another blind spot for the FBI was failing to view white nationalist violence and white collar crime as national security threats. Minimizing the impact of these crimes undermines the rule of law by creating classes of criminals exempt from government scrutiny, and classes of victims that fail to receive the equal protection of the law.

MINIMIZING HATE CRIMES AND WHITE SUPREMACIST VIOLENCE

In October 2006, the FBI produced an intelligence assessment warning about "White Supremacist Infiltration of Law Enforcement."[1] It documents efforts by white supremacist groups to encourage members to join law enforcement agencies or recruit police officers into their ranks. Sections discussing FBI investigations are redacted from the document, but the "key judgments" are mostly legible.

The assessment states that the "primary threat" from white supremacist police officers is that they could steal intelligence, compromise investigations, and "jeopardize the safety of law enforcement sources and personnel." The other security concerns it lists relate to these racist officers' access to secure spaces and protected persons, such as elected officials, and the potential that they would distribute purloined intelligence among affiliated white supremacist groups. Though the published report contains significant redactions, it does not appear to even mention the threat white supremacist law enforcement officers pose to the communities of color they police on a daily basis.

A three-sentence paragraph in the watch-listing section of the FBI's 2015 counterterrorism policy guide notes that "domestic terrorism investigations focused on militia extremists, white supremacist extremists, and sovereign citizen extremists often have identified active links to law enforcement officers and those in a position to check [national criminal databases] for warrants."[2] To address this concern, it again advises agents to take measures to protect FBI intelligence rather than protect the public from racist police officers. It suggests using the "silent hit" feature of the terrorist watch lists for subjects of investigations involving far-right groups so corrupt police officers searching the lists won't discover they or their associates are under investigation. While protecting the integrity of FBI investigations is important, it is hard to imagine such a blithe response if the bureau discovered any other type of terrorist group had infiltrated police agencies, underscoring how differently law enforcement views far-right violence than other forms of terrorism.

Broadly speaking, the "extremists" researchers label as "far-right" kill more people in the United States in an average year than any other terrorist groups, though it is important to acknowledge that all terrorism fatalities make up a tiny proportion of the roughly fifteen thousand murders committed each year. The government doesn't keep accurate statistics on far-right violence, however, and a small minority of police agencies report hate crimes, so private entities and academic institutions attempt to fill the void. The Combating Terrorism Center (CTC) at the U.S. Military Academy at West Point documented 10 to 52 fatalities from far-right attacks each year from 2000 to 2011, totaling 306 deaths over that period.[3] Other academic and advocacy organizations employ different criteria to determine what counts as an act of far-right violence, leading to data sets that vary significantly.

One issue undermining confidence in the data produced by terrorism researchers is the reliance on news reports to identify and categorize terror attacks. A 2017 media study showed that an act of terrorism committed by a Muslim receives 449 percent more news coverage than a similar attack committed by any other perpetrator.[4] Since terrorism databases are heavily, if not entirely, dependent on news reports to track events, the disparity in coverage likely obscures the scope of non-Muslim violence. Several organizations keep terrorism scorecards comparing the lethality of one type of terrorism over others. This has become a contentious part of the counterterrorism debate as these figures can be very misleading.

Counting plots and attacks by different Muslim terrorist groups such as Hezbollah, ISIL, and al Qaeda as "jihadist" or "Islamist" terrorism obscures the fact that these groups have different beliefs and political agendas and are actively fighting one another in Syria and elsewhere. Most terrorism databases also include attacks by Muslim Americans with no real connection to any foreign terrorist group under the same banner, essentially treating any violence by Muslim Americans as a form of international terrorism. Treating anti-abortion homicides and anti-tax violence in the same "far-right" category as white supremacist murders, as most far-right terrorism researchers do, makes little more sense.[5] The white supremacist movement is fractured into competing ideological factions as well. Combining them into one basket also masks that much of the violence extremists perpetrate takes place within their ideological groups and movements. But the number of attacks and killings resulting from the organized activities of white supremacists, anti-government militias, and so-called sovereign citizens certainly calls for a commensurate investment of law enforcement resources as those devoted to international terrorism, and major incidents like the Oklahoma City bombing make clear the scale of violence these groups are capable of if ignored.

For several years, though, the FBI called "eco-terrorists" the number one domestic threat and inflated their activities by labeling acts of vandalism as terrorism.[6] Including minor property crimes and civil disobedience committed by environmental activists as terrorism is misleading, however, as the FBI categorizes similar vandalism by white supremacist groups as hate crimes rather than terrorism.

After 9/11, I noticed the FBI officially de-emphasizing white supremacist violence. In 2005, the FBI published a report, *Terrorism 2002–2005*, which indicated that except for a 2004 synagogue firebombing by a neo-Nazi skinhead, all the acts of domestic terrorism over that four-year period had been conducted by extremists associated with environmental and animal rights movements.[7] It is important to remember that there are no U.S. deaths associated with environmental or animal rights terrorism, and just a few injuries.[8] The CTC documented several hundred far-right extremist attacks over the same four years, resulting in 380 injuries and 81 deaths.[9] The National Consortium for the Study of Terrorism and Responses to Terrorism maintains the Extremist Crime Database, which documented 272 homicides from far-right violence between 1990 and 2017, not counting the 168 killed in the Oklahoma City bombing.[10] And given the enormous disparity in hate crimes statistics between those collected by the FBI Uniform Crime Reports, which document around 5,000 to 7,000 hate crimes a year, and those collected in Justice Department victim surveys, which report more than 250,000 victimizations a year, it is likely that racist violence is severely undercounted.[11]

Traditional far-right groups were in flux in the beginning of the new century due to effective, proactive law enforcement operations through the 1990s and civil suits brought by victims of attacks that took their properties, but they didn't go away. Many migrated online to interact on over two thousand different hate websites or joined heavily armed vigilante militias patrolling the border for undocumented immigrants. Terrorizing migrants wasn't considered terrorism. There was a propensity for violence, and law enforcement uncovered caches of illegal weapons and explosives from time to time, but these were mostly treated as local matters. In 2009, three members of the Minutemen American Defense militia conducted a "false flag" home invasion robbery of a Mexican American family, murdering a nine-year-old girl and her father and wounding her mother. They were hoping migrants would be blamed.[12] While these far-right murderers were caught, migrants are often victims of unsolved violence in border areas, which police can write off as drug-related or victims of human traffickers. Shooting incidents in 2007 and 2012 that left four migrants dead also left witnesses who described four camouflage-wearing gunmen who opened fire on them and then fled, without attempting to rob them.[13]

In 2010, the FBI produced an intelligence assessment analyzing data from 2007 to 2009 to argue that white supremacist violence was decreasing. Most analysts during this time were clocking a sharp rise in white supremacist activity as candidate Barack Obama became the first black president.[14] The FBI report cited 23 "incidents" including 4 homicides in 2007, 19 incidents including 1 homicide in 2008, and 10 incidents including 2 homicides in 2009.[15] In contrast, the CTC documented an upward trend in far-right violence beginning in 2005. While its data set included anti-abortion and militia violence, most of the attacks it documented were committed by white supremacist groups. The CTC registered over 400 attacks resulting in 43 fatalities in 2007, more than 500 attacks resulting in 33 fatalities in 2008, and more than 400 attacks resulting in 32 fatalities in 2009.[16]

In 2017, the FBI published a report calling white supremacist violence "persistent," but again it included a woefully undercounted data set. The 2017 report claimed no white supremacist homicides in 2010 and 2011, where CTC counted 47 far-right fatalities in those two years. As perplexing was the FBI's report of only one fatality in 2016. The CTC report only included data through 2011, but since I follow this issue, I knew of an FBI investigation in Vancouver, Washington, involving a triple-homicide. Agents had advised neo-Nazi skinhead Brent Luyster he was going to be indicted for possessing a firearm as a convicted felon, a charge arising from an earlier assault. The agents did not arrest him, however, and he went to a friend's house and shot four skinhead associates, killing three.[17] This FBI-related incident alone would have quadrupled the report's 2016 white supremacist fatality count, and it is inexplicable how a bureau analyst could have missed it.

Beginning in 2016, I also began noticing a troubling change in the way law enforcement reacted to far-right violence in the streets. A KKK rally in Anaheim in February 2016 was stormed by anti-fascist counterprotesters and a Klansman stabbed three protesters. Using public rallies to provoke violence is a common tactic for far-right groups. They know they can attract angry counterprotesters when they hold public events, so they come armed and ready to use a higher degree of violence than their opponents expect. Usually, the police understand this strategy and keep the two sides separated. In Anaheim they didn't. Police arrested five Klansmen but later released them, saying all had acted in self-defense, including the one who stabbed three people. Police instead charged seven counterprotesters with a variety of crimes.[18]

In June 2016, the white nationalist Traditionalist Worker Party and the Golden State Skinheads held a much larger rally in Sacramento that drew counterprotesters. Police allowed them to brawl, leaving six counterprotesters and one skinhead stabbed. After a year-long investigation, police arrested one skinhead and three counterprotesters.[19] The arrested skinhead was a thirty-four-year-old, twice-convicted violent felon. He had fled to Colorado after the rally, where he was arrested for defacing a synagogue, and was then brought back to California to face an assault with a deadly weapon charge.[20] One of the arrested counterprotesters was a forty-seven-year-old middle school teacher.

The Anaheim and Sacramento rallies were precursors of even larger and more violent rallies in 2017: a Seattle event in January saw a counterprotester shot; Berkeley, California, rallies in March and April devolved into running street battles; and in Charlottesville, Virginia, a neo-Nazi rammed his car into counterprotesters, killing one and injuring nineteen others. I assumed the racist events in Anaheim and Sacramento just caught the police off guard. But I followed the planning for these later protests with alarm at how openly white nationalists, many I knew had serious criminal records, were preparing for violence. With the ubiquity of streaming video, I was able to watch these violent episodes in my living room.

Having seen the militarized police responses to nonviolent protests in Ferguson and Standing Rock, the mass arrests during the Occupy and J20 protests, and the aggressive grand jury investigations from the Seattle May Day window breaking, it was perplexing to watch convicted felons engaging in unpoliced violence at these white nationalist rallies and, rather than being arrested, becoming featured speakers at the next rally. Police actions and statements at these events gave many the impression that they sympathized with the white nationalists and regarded the counterprotesters as the problem. I found this odd since it is well known in law enforcement that far-right extremists often target police, killing fifty officers since 1991, according to the Anti-Defamation League.[21] But it proved to be true.

The most overt example was a June 4, 2017, far-right rally in Portland, Oregon, timed just ten days after a local white nationalist murdered two men who came to the aid of two teenaged Muslim girls he attacked. During the rally Portland police detained a group of 389 counterprotesters, journalists, and bystanders without legal justification, and photographed them with their identification, which led to complaints of police bias and intimidation. Videos later surfaced showing militia members assisting DHS officers in arresting a counterprotester by tackling him and helping the officers handcuff him.[22] One of the militiamen confirmed that the DHS officers had requested their assistance. A report by Portland's Independent Police Review indicated that police planning documents labeled antifascist groups as "more confrontational" and "volatile."[23] A draft of the report quoted a Portland police lieutenant describing the far-right extremists as "much more mainstream" than the counterprotesters who came out to oppose them.[24]

Law enforcement's tacit sanctioning of far-right violence during these protests encouraged an escalation. It appeared that years of demonizing anarchists and other left-wing protesters in law enforcement intelligence reports had led the police to believe black-clad anti-fascist fighters were somehow as bad or worse than the far-right extremists who were organizing these disruptive events. A March 2017 Trump rally in Huntington Beach, California, took place in a more open area, so it was easier to see this dynamic in action. The *Los Angeles Times* reported the day of the event that violence "erupted" at the rally after a counterprotester pepper-sprayed Trump supporters.[25] But that's not what happened. The entire attack was recorded, so there should be few facts in dispute. The first people attacked were *OC Weekly* journalists specifically targeted by individuals aligned with the pro-Trump marchers.[26] The police stood too far away to see who started the brawl but arrested a woman that one of these attackers dragged over to them and accused of pepper-spraying the Trump supporters. In all, police arrested five counterprotesters, but not the attackers or any other Trump supporters who can be seen assaulting counterprotesters on the videos. The female counterprotester who was dragged to the police was charged with battery.[27]

The *OC Weekly* reporters, armed with videos of the skirmish, identified their attackers and appealed to the California State Parks Police to arrest them.[28] They used the video to defend the female counterprotester, who had come to their aid by pepper-spraying their attackers, ending the assault. The police ultimately dropped the charges against her and other counterprotesters, but they did not arrest the men who attacked the reporters.

ProPublica reporters A.C. Thompson, Ali Winston, and Darwin BondGraham identified some of the Huntington Beach attackers as members of a white supremacist fight club called the Rise Above Movement (RAM), based in Southern California.[29] RAM posted stylized videos online showing its members engaged in martial arts training, dropping racist banners over highway overpasses, and brawling at protests. The videos made subtle use of white supremacist symbols, but they were easy to spot if you knew what to look for. They tended to be less guarded in expressing their racism in other social media activities. ProPublica identified several RAM members with serious criminal records, including one who was on probation when he was captured on video attacking the *OC Weekly* journalists.[30] A California Parks Police spokesman said it didn't have the resources to conduct an investigation. ProPublica also identified RAM members at the April 2017 protest in Berkeley working in combination with other white supremacist groups to attack counterprotesters and a *Mother Jones* journalist. One RAM member, who had previously spent time in a New York state prison for stabbing a Latino man in a gang assault, was arrested for battering a police officer and resisting arrest at the Berkeley rally, but prosecutors later dropped the charges.[31] RAM members also attacked counterprotesters at an anti-Muslim rally in San Bernardino in June 2017.[32]

Several RAM members, at least two with previous arrests on firearms charges, traveled across the country and joined fellow white supremacists in attacking students and counterprotesters in Charlottesville the following August. They weren't the only former convicts leading white supremacist groups who should have been on law enforcement's radar for the Unite the Right rally, including: a former Klansman and Green Beret who spent almost five years in prison for robbing a cache of weapons and explosives from a U.S. military base;[33] a former U.S. Marine previously convicted of armed robbery who sucker punched a female counterprotester at an earlier Berkeley protest;[34] a Traditionalist Worker Party member who pled guilty to disorderly conduct for assaulting a black woman at a 2016 Trump rally;[35] and a Texas white supremacist with previous convictions for kidnapping and weapons violations who would later be arrested with two colleagues who shot at counterprotesters at an alt-right rally in Gainesville, Florida.[36] Of these, only the sucker-punching former Marine was initially charged, receiving a $200 fine for failing to disperse.[37]

The FBI, Justice Department, and DHS had spent sixteen years building a national infrastructure for sharing terrorism-related information. The bureau expanded its Joint Terrorism Task Forces and participated in a national network of state and local law enforcement intelligence fusion centers. I struggled to understand how law enforcement didn't recognize this far-right violence as organized criminal activity and how the FBI didn't treat racists who broadcast their intention to travel interstate to commit violence as domestic terrorists. Independent journalist Will Parrish obtained a DHS intelligence report disseminated in advance of the Charlottesville rally that assessed that "anarchist extremists" would likely initiate violence at future white supremacist rallies and that racist groups would "counterattack."[38] It referenced none of the known violent criminals from the far-right groups who had been attending these rallies and attacking counterprotesters without regard to whether they were "anarchist extremists," journalists, or just people expressing opposition to Nazis marching in their streets. *Politico* reported that joint FBI/DHS intelligence assessments in 2016 indicated anarchist extremists were the "primary instigators of violence at public rallies."[39]

An after-action report chartered by the Charlottesville City Council said the FBI's Richmond office had provided intelligence predicting that Unite the Right supporters would bring weapons such as bats, firearms, and knives, and that "left-wing counterprotesters, such as Antifa, would attempt to disrupt the event" with cement-filled cans and water bottles with caustic substances. The report also recounted a conversation between a Charlottesville police officer and an FBI agent in Kentucky, where the Traditionalist Worker Party had previously held a rally. The FBI agent reportedly said the neo-Nazi group wouldn't cause problems, but their opponents might.[40] The agent apparently didn't mention that the Traditionalist Worker Party had been involved in the Sacramento riot that left counterprotesters stabbed, or that its leader had just pled guilty to disorderly conduct in a Kentucky court and was serving a suspended sentence that could land him in jail for ninety days if he was arrested for another offense. FBI director Christopher Wray told Congress in December 2017 that the bureau had active domestic terrorism investigations targeting individuals motivated to commit violent crimes based on "Antifa ideology."[41]

The failure to recognize that these events weren't a matter of two violently opposed protest groups getting together and brawling reflects a significant intelligence breakdown that mimics President Trump's divisive "both sides" rhetoric. While some anarchists and anti-fascists do engage in property destruction, street fighting, and even rioting, comparing that behavior to a 150-year campaign of racist and anti-government murders, bombings, and intimidation is dangerously naïve. I'm not aware of a single death attributed to Antifa actions in the United States. They certainly can pose a public safety issue at these protests, and it is important for law enforcement to understand and mitigate their tactics, but suggesting they are the instigators and the white supremacists the victims at these events will only empower far-right groups whose antipathy for law enforcement is too often fatal. The white supremacists have certainly interpreted the lack of enforcement as sympathy among the police for their viewpoint, as reflected in their online communications.[42] Minority and left-wing protest groups have received this message as well, deepening the rift with law enforcement at all levels. Lawyers defending the counterprotesters arrested in Sacramento filed court documents accusing the police of collaborating with the neo-Nazis to identify anti-racist activists.[43]

The FBI and Justice Department have contributed to the perception of a double standard of justice with regard to these white supremacist protests. After neo-Nazi enthusiast James Fields killed Heather Heyer at the Unite the Right protest in Charlottesville, the FBI's Richmond office announced it "opened a civil rights investigation into the circumstances of the deadly vehicular incident."[44] Treating the matter as a civil rights investigation rather than a domestic terrorism investigation has important implications.

First, terrorism is the FBI's highest priority, so treating the incident as a civil rights violation reduces its import. Perhaps more crucially, the FBI's Civil Rights Program Policy Implementation Guide distinguishes between hate crimes that are civil rights violations versus those that should be classified as domestic terrorism in a way that suggests the bureau may have predetermined the scope of its investigation. The policy guide says a hate crime incident must be dual-captioned as civil rights and domestic terrorism if "the subject has a nexus to any type of white supremacy extremist group." A hate crime incident can be opened as a civil rights investigation only "if the subject has no nexus to any type of white supremacy extremist group."[45]

Apparently, the FBI believes Fields traveled interstate to participate in a white supremacist rally, dressed in the uniform of a white supremacist group, carried a shield with a white supremacist logo, and committed murder in a manner proscribed in white supremacist message boards, but did not have a nexus to any type of white supremacist group.[46] The FBI treated the attack as a simple hate crime rather than as part of a broader white supremacist conspiracy to commit terroristic violence that day.

To make matters worse, the FBI and U.S. attorney's office have alienated the victims of Fields's attack by serving them with grand jury subpoenas.[47] It is unusual for the government to demand grand jury testimony from victims and prosecution-friendly witnesses whose statements are trusted by the prosecution. Law enforcement agents are allowed to provide summary testimony to a grand jury that would describe witness statements.[48] Prosecutors usually prefer this route because it avoids creating multiple witness statements that a defense attorney could later pick apart for inconsistencies. The victims believe the government is using the grand jury as a fishing expedition to gather information about counterprotesters rather than to collect evidence regarding the vehicle attack. Several witnesses resisted the grand jury subpoena and refused to cooperate.[49]

That the FBI has so politicized its counterterrorism enforcement over the last seventeen years that terrorism victims are not willing to cooperate with its investigations should be a wake-up call for anyone concerned about national security. On June 27, 2018, the Justice Department charged Fields with a thirty-count indictment charging hate crimes and civil rights violations.[50]

Almost a year after the Charlottesville rally, PBS's *Frontline* aired a documentary highlighting the ProPublica reporting about the Rise

Above Movement's participation in the violence. Three months later, and a year after the original ProPublica reporting, the FBI arrested eight RAM members highlighted in the film, charging them under federal anti-riot and conspiracy statutes.[51] Once again, A.C. Thompson's reporting prodded the FBI into action.

WHITE COLLAR CRIME AND INTELLIGENCE

When Robert Mueller's FBI sought to transform itself into a domestic intelligence agency, it reached into its ignoble past for a model and a lexicon. Like J. Edgar Hoover's bureau, the new FBI saw protecting the establishment as its mission and disrupting the political mobilization of dissident and disenfranchised communities as its most potent weapon. In doing so, the FBI compromised its ability to accomplish an intelligence agency's most important job: predicting emerging threats and convincing policymakers of the need to address them. As previously described, many FBI agents saw critical pieces of the 9/11 attacks as they were coming together, but a sclerotic bureaucracy ignored their warnings. After the predicted tragedy, the FBI received a bigger budget and expanded authorities, just as Senator Chuck Grassley said it would. But its leadership did not reform the bureaucracy, so continuing failures were inevitable.

In 2004, FBI assistant director Chris Swecker warned that mortgage fraud was becoming an "epidemic" that could cause a financial crisis as significant as the savings and loan crisis.[52] Mueller had transferred about five hundred agents from white collar crime squads to terrorism, leaving a skeleton crew of approximately one hundred agents to address the growing mortgage fraud crisis.[53] Congress denied the FBI's requests for more agents following Swecker's warning, and Mueller refused to reprioritize his national security assets. But the resources the FBI did apply to address mortgage fraud were also focusing on the wrong end of the problem, targeting thousands of "small-fry" borrowers who inflated their incomes and the corrupt brokers who assisted them rather than the elite financial institutions who committed the accounting control frauds that encouraged this criminal behavior in the first place and more seriously undermined the economy.[54] A true intelligence agency is charged with identifying and interdicting emerging threats, and the FBI failed to recognize that this elite fraud posed a growing risk to national security. In February 2009, after the U.S. mortgage market collapsed, Director of National Intelligence Dennis Blair testified at the Senate's annual threat assessment that the "primary near-term security concern of the United States is the global economic crisis."[55]

It was bad enough that the FBI didn't adequately react to a crisis it saw on the horizon. After the predicted collapse materialized, the FBI and Justice Department failed to marshal the assets necessary to hold the top corporate beneficiaries of these frauds, which cost U.S. homeowners over $9 trillion, criminally liable.[56] "Too big to jail" became the motto for a class of plutocrats beyond the reach of the criminal justice system, as the Justice Department pursued a strategy of foregoing criminal prosecutions in favor of civil settlements that came from bank shareholders rather than CEO pockets. These policy developments were beyond the FBI's control, but even where major banks and corporations had provided material support to designated terrorist organizations and other banned entities—and therefore fell squarely within the FBI's priority mandate—no criminal penalties were levied against the responsible corporate officers.[57] Chiquita Brands International had given $1.7 million to a right-wing paramilitary group in Colombia that the State Department had previously designated a foreign terrorist organization. Chiquita paid a $25 million fine and the Justice Department declined criminal charges.[58] The British bank HSBC paid a much bigger fine, almost $2 billion, for laundering money for drug cartels, rogue nations like North Korea and Iran, and entities linked to terrorist groups, including providing $1 billion to a Saudi bank that had ties to al Qaeda, but no one went to jail.[59] Former D.C. policeman Nicholas Young, by contrast, got fifteen years for sending $245 in gift cards to a friend he thought had joined ISIL in Syria.[60]

UNDERMINING INSTITUTIONS

In 2014, the FBI quietly removed "law enforcement" from its mission statement. The FBI mission is now "to protect the American people and uphold the Constitution of the United States."[61] It is a symbolic recognition of the way the FBI has changed as the measures it uses to accomplish its mission become untethered from the law. Protecting some Americans' security has too often justified depriving other Americans of theirs. Law enforcement has always included elements of both crime control and social control. Removing "law enforcement" from the mission statement now makes clear which is the priority for the FBI.

When people lose respect for government institutions and confidence in the rule of law, they tend to look for stability in authoritarian leadership, placing their faith in a strong individual who they hope can "drain the swamp" and restore a period of lost privilege.[62]

Donald Trump's determined appeal to racial, ethnic, and religious bigotry and nativism during the campaign and in his first two years in office comes straight from the right-wing populist playbook. Enough voters who were simply sick of the political establishment voted to send a hand grenade to Washington, D.C., and they continue to cheer as Trump dismantles regulations and destroys norms of presidential behavior.

James Comey's public explanation for his actions regarding the FBI's investigations of Hillary Clinton during the election and Trump both during and after reveal a similar pattern of thinking. Comey said he decided to ignore long-standing Justice Department rules by publicly commenting on the Clinton investigation because he felt Attorney General Loretta Lynch was fatally compromised after meeting privately with former president Bill Clinton at the Phoenix airport on June 27, 2016.[63] The logic is that because one rule was broken, the rulebook was no longer operative, and he could, as a self-described ethical public leader, decide what the new rules were.

Comey's announcement on July 5, 2016, that the FBI would not recommend criminal charges against Hillary Clinton for using a private email server probably would have been within the rules, given the public nature of the investigation, and would have accomplished his purported goal of reinforcing the integrity of the Justice Department's final decision. But he didn't stop there. His decision to rebuke Clinton for being "extremely careless" in handling "very sensitive, highly classified information" broke a cardinal rule prohibiting derogatory public comments about an investigative subject's uncharged behavior. Federal investigations are not designed to measure a person's character but to determine whether there is sufficient evidence to prove they committed a crime beyond a reasonable doubt. Using information gathered during an investigation to smear a person or organization without giving them a forum to defend themselves is wholly inappropriate whether it is a presidential candidate or a Muslim civil rights group.[64]

Comey's acceptance of an invitation to testify about the Clinton investigation before the House Judiciary Committee on September 28, 2016, was even more difficult to understand. Another time-honored Justice Department policy demands that investigators and prosecutors take no action during an election that might influence the outcome. With the Clinton investigation closed, Comey clearly could have delayed his testimony until after the election.

Then, on October 28, 2016, just eleven days before the election, Comey wrote a letter to sixteen members of Congress announcing he was reopening the Clinton investigation. He claimed a contrived "duty to correct" compelled this response.[65] The problem is there is no such obligation, at least not in the way Comey conceptualizes it. There simply is no duty to correct accurate testimony, much less one that would override other fundamental obligations designed to protect the integrity of FBI investigations and the privacy of innocent persons falling under its powerful gaze. Comey testified accurately in September 2016 that the FBI had closed its investigation of Hillary Clinton. Regardless of whether new facts that later came to light justified reopening the inquiry, they would certainly not demand a correction, as there was nothing to correct. Comey's concept would better be described as a "duty to update." Of course, no such obligation exists. Yet Comey used this imaginary duty to override the genuine obligations of existing policy, to the detriment of our democratic process and the FBI's reputation for objectivity.

Comey's actions arguably tipped the tightest presidential election in history and cast a cloud of illegitimacy over the Trump government even before it took office, a possibility only made worse if the then–FBI director also inadvertently assisted a hostile foreign nation in accomplishing the same goal. Though he claims this possibility mildly sickens him, he vowed he would do it all again, even knowing the outcome.[66]

Those now convinced the FBI director was somehow planning to sink the administration he helped bring to power have to gloss over some troubling facts. The available evidence suggests Comey's FBI did not pursue allegations that Russia was illicitly supporting the Trump campaign with the necessary urgency, at least if you believe that a hostile foreign nation's effort to influence a U.S. presidential election presents a national security threat of the highest dimension. And his postelection behavior with President Trump was as norm breaking as his pre-election actions regarding Clinton.

The Guardian reported that British intelligence services warned the United States in late 2015 that Russian intelligence operatives were engaged in suspicious "interactions" with Trump associates.[67] Similar warnings from other nations followed over the next six months.

Yet the FBI did not open a counterintelligence investigation on the allegations until late July 2016. The delayed initiation of the Trump/Russia counterintelligence investigation is mirrored by the FBI's nonchalant response to evidence that Russians were hacking Democratic National Committee (DNC) computers. The bureau learned of the cyberattacks in September 2015, but its agents gave the DNC "help desk" only a tepid warning to check its servers.[68] DNC officials claim the FBI did not advise them that Russian intelligence was behind the hacking, and they did not begin to recognize the severity of the threat until late April 2016, after the damage was done.[69] Contrary to his public discussions of the Clinton investigation, Comey refused to sign the FBI onto a joint intelligence statement issued by DHS and the Office of the Director of National Intelligence (DNI) that declared the Russian government's hacking operations targeting Democratic campaign officials were meant to interfere with the election.[70] He cited the same Justice Department policy prohibiting preelection activities that might influence an election that he ignored with the Clinton investigation. Only after the election did Comey acknowledge that the Russian government was trying to get Trump elected.

But his meeting with president-elect Trump at Trump Tower in New York City on January 6, 2017, is even more perplexing. It was the first intelligence briefing Trump received, attended by CIA director John Brennan, DNI James Clapper, and Comey.[71] After the briefing, and according to a plan Comey worked out with the other intelligence heads, Comey met alone with Trump to show him an oppositional research dossier written by a former British intelligence officer that contained explosive allegations against Trump and his campaign. No FBI agent or federal prosecutor would ever show a potential subject of an investigation a key piece of evidence except to elicit an inculpating response. An FBI agent is also trained to never meet a subject or even an important witness alone because it creates a "he said, she said" situation that can easily be avoided. There is also a Justice Department policy designed to protect the FBI from political influence that requires communications related to active investigations to go through the attorney general or deputy attorney general. Comey has said Trump was not a subject of the investigation at the time of the Trump Tower meeting, but he was certainly the subject of the dossier's allegations. The idea that Comey wanted to meet alone because he didn't want to embarrass Trump is laughable, as the dossier was already being shared among journalists all across D.C.[72]

Then the story gets stranger. Comey said he was troubled by Trump's reaction so he wrote a memo, which he sent to an old law school buddy rather than to the investigative files, or even to his personal files at the bureau. Comey claims Trump then asked for a series of one-on-one meetings that made him uncomfortable, but it makes perfect sense why Trump would feel such arrangements were fine, since Comey set up their first meeting this way. Comey continued writing memos regarding his personal interactions with President Trump, which he continued to send to his friend rather than to official files. Trump finally fired him in the most humiliating manner possible, which was unfortunate, as it fueled further politicization of the bureau.

In the end, there are only two possibilities: that the Russian government successfully conspired with representatives of the Trump campaign to undermine the legitimacy of our most important election, or it did not. If it did, the FBI's and its partner agencies' inability to interdict the plot before a corrupted election elevated an illegitimate president to power is an intelligence failure of a magnitude rivaled only by the failure to quickly bring the conspirators to justice afterward. If not, the FBI and other intelligence agencies have used their covert intelligence powers to undermine a duly elected U.S. president and his administration in ways that would make J. Edgar Hoover blush. Either possibility suggests a significant part of our government has forfeited its legitimacy and is no longer serving in the public interest.

Special Counsel Robert Mueller has indicted twelve Russian intelligence agents for hacking the computers of Democratic Party and Clinton campaign officials, and another thirteen for interfering in the election. Four Trump aides have pled guilty to fraud and false statements, and a fifth, Paul Manafort, was convicted at trial. Manafort, who worked as a political consultant in Ukraine before volunteering to serve as Trump's campaign manager, was convicted of bank fraud and tax violations, then pled guilty to conspiracy charges and agreed to cooperate.[73] Court records indicate that Manafort shared Trump campaign polling data with a former business partner with ties to Russian intelligence agencies before the election.[74] Manafort's crimes, including $30 million funneled through offshore accounts into the United States without paying necessary taxes, stretch back to 2008, raising questions about how Mueller's FBI didn't notice an American political consultant hobnobbing with foreign kleptocrats and returning home with tens of millions in unexplained wealth.[75]

The same needs to be asked about the FBI's relationship with Donald Trump, who ran a fraudulent charity, a fraudulent university, and a casino that the Treasury Department fined $10 million for failing to establish money-laundering controls for the ten years he owned it.[76] Trump went through six corporate bankruptcies; was sued hundreds of times by employees, customers, clients, and business partners; and paid fines to settle securities and antitrust complaints. How did the FBI not see criminal liability in any of these legal violations as Trump accumulated his fortune?

The practical immunity Trump and his retinue enjoyed as they amassed wealth and power also gives lie to his supporters' contention that Mueller, Comey, and the FBI somehow had it in for Trump and manufactured a case against him. The failure to prioritize the economic crimes of the politically powerful left the nation vulnerable to a hostile foreign nation's effort to delegitimize U.S. elections. This is exactly the sort of threat a domestic intelligence agency is supposed to protect against.

The long-awaited release of a heavily redacted "Mueller report" detailing the results of the special counsel's investigation into whether the Trump campaign conspired with Russians to tilt the election did not resolve the matter, it only fueled more partisan rancor. Trump's opponents read in it grounds for impeachment, while his supporters claimed it was a complete exoneration. The only thing that is clear in this sordid mess is that the American public deserves better. We deserve to know that FBI investigations are based entirely on objective evidence establishing a reasonable suspicion of criminal activity and free from political influence of any kind. The stain of the FBI's J. Edgar Hoover–era abuses should have served as a strong warning that public trust can be lost much more easily than it can be recovered.

CONCLUSION: WHAT THEN MUST WE DO?

The measures necessary to reform the FBI to reduce discriminatory surveillance and investigations are not mysterious. They are the same as those Attorney General Harlan Fiske Stone took in 1924 to rein in the Bureau of Investigation's anti-radical work at the beginning of J. Edgar Hoover's career, and those Attorney General Edward Levi put in place in 1976 to end COINTELPRO after Hoover died. They both required the FBI to focus its investigative powers on its law enforcement mission, where constitutional protections designed to ensure public oversight and accountability are strongest. Terrorism and espionage are crimes, so there is no need for separate authorities to manage these threats. The unfettered collection of foreign and domestic intelligence has not made us safer; it has undermined democratic controls and weakened our collective security. Time and again the flood of data has overwhelmed and distracted investigators, while evidence of real threats, like the Russian government's interference in an election to determine the leader of our republic, is all but ignored.

Requiring agents to document the reasonable factual basis to believe a violation of law is taking place before intruding on individual privacy and civil liberties shouldn't be seen as a trade-off against security but as the proper management of security resources. Monitoring and bullying innocents does not make anyone safer, particularly when the exercise of their First Amendment rights is seen as the justification for scrutiny. As with any human endeavor, clear standards and independent oversight will improve effectiveness and efficiency. The Justice Department must reform the Attorney General's Guidelines governing the FBI's investigative authorities to reestablish more rigorous standards. Congress should codify them to make them more resilient to immediate crises.

Likewise, law enforcement leaders from both political parties and every level of government denounced racial and ethnic profiling as ineffective and counterproductive decades ago. Yet the Justice Department guidelines issued by Republican and Democratic administrations alike authorize the FBI and Department of Homeland Security to rely on profiling in carrying out their most important functions, even in its crudest form of racial and ethnic mapping. These loopholes swallow the rule and send an unmistakable but untrue message to law enforcement officers across the land that despite the rhetoric, profiling really works and should be used. Targeting someone because of the color of their skin, what neighborhood they live in, or who they pray to tears at the fabric of society. Congress should ban profiling based on race, ethnicity, gender, religion, national origin, sexual orientation, or gender identity once and for all, not just for federal law enforcement agencies but for state, local, and tribal law enforcement agencies that receive federal funding or participate in federal task forces.

These will be big lifts. Recent history has shown that no matter which party is in the White House or controls Congress, the intelligence agencies effectively resist attempts to impose oversight or restrictions. Even killing programs the agencies acknowledge are ineffective is almost impossible. When Edward Snowden's revelations about the astonishing scope of NSA spying sparked public outrage and forced the government's admission that the wholesale collection of Americans' domestic communications data didn't stop a single terrorist plot, the ensuing reforms were largely symbolic and completely ineffective.

Interim steps to these goals should focus on compelling the Justice Department to release data about how the FBI uses its intelligence and investigative powers. Accurate and objective data on serious crimes, particularly crimes against women and racial, ethnic, and religious minorities, can help make the case for a redistribution of security resources toward actual threats rather than manufactured ones. The FBI has ready access to who it investigates, how, and why, and the public has a right to know if the bureau disproportionately targets minority communities for assessment, investigation, and prosecution, and what tools it uses when it does so. We also need better data on how state and local law enforcement use federal resources, particularly when these funds purchase surveillance products, weapons, or military equipment. The FBI should collect and publish this information, along with data regarding police violence, as a normal part of its civil rights mandate, just as it does with data relating to its counterterrorism mission.

INCREASING DIVERSITY

The last five FBI directors have all identified the bureau's lack of diversity as a critical problem that undermines its effectiveness. But the slow progress made by William Sessions and Louis Freeh was lost under Robert Mueller and James Comey. This fact does not mean Mueller and Comey made no effort to increase diversity, but rather the efforts they pursued for fifteen years were not effective. They both attempted to solve the problem almost entirely through new recruitment efforts, rather than by reforming the FBI's application and security clearance processes to ensure they are fair and equitable. The FBI could do more to attract and, more important, retain onboard employees of diverse backgrounds by overhauling its unjust and arbitrary personnel policies and disciplinary system.

In a Q&A session following his 2015 "Hard Truths" speech at Georgetown University, Comey suggested that a significant part of the problem was that qualified minority candidates were lured away by corporate recruiters who could "throw all kinds of dough" at them.[1] This seemed to blame the victim too much. As the country's most storied law enforcement agency, the FBI is fortunate to be able to attract incredibly talented people who all can go out and make more money in a corporate environment. Why Comey would believe white agents were more willing to make this trade-off than minority applicants is difficult to understand. Malik Aziz, the national chairman of the National Black Police Association, dismissed this argument. Aziz said the bureau was wrong to recruit at colleges rather than among the 110,000 black police officers around the country who have already shown their commitment to law enforcement. "The pool of qualified candidates of color is there," he told the *Washington Post*.[2]

There are plenty of qualified minority candidates at colleges, too, according to former FBI agent Erroll Southers, director of the Safe Communities Institute at the University of Southern California. "Every time they recruit here, that line is long, and I would imagine it's the same on most campuses," he told me. "I know my fair share of African Americans with degrees who decided to go into local law enforcement."[3] Southers was a police officer in Santa Monica, California, when he was recruited into the FBI in 1984. He was the only black agent in the FBI's San Diego field office, but he was treated well personally and professionally. He worked counterintelligence, joined the SWAT team, and worked two undercover cases.

If qualified minority candidates are applying, as Southers suggests, the problem may instead lie in the bureau's application process and its personnel practices. Applicant screening is an inherently subjective process where the types of implicit biases Comey highlighted during his "Hard Truths" speech can be expected to influence decisions. I don't think it is a coincidence that diversity in the FBI went down as polygraphs became more widely used in employment and security screenings. Here again, the bureau has the data necessary to evaluate whether its hiring protocols disproportionately reject qualified minority and female applicants but doesn't publish it for researchers or provide it to Congress, so it is impossible to identify problems and find solutions. We know scientific research doesn't support the use of polygraph testing for employment or security screenings, and if the FBI cannot produce peer-reviewed studies to demonstrate its fairness and effectiveness, it should be abandoned.

If the data shows no disparities in the application process, the problem may lie in other personnel practices that could then be modified to retain more FBI employees. Though Southers enjoyed his work with the bureau, he left after just four years because the FBI was going to move him across the country. The bureau has traditional practices that date back to the Hoover era that often seem designed solely to make everyone miserable. The bureau's transfer policy during Southers's time assigned new agents to small offices for a few years after training at the FBI Academy, then transferred them to one of the twelve largest cities, where they would spend the bulk of their careers. Southers was divorced with a young son in Southern California, so when he got word he was going to be transferred to the East Coast, he decided to resign and go back to the Santa Monica Police Department so he could remain involved in his son's life.

Southers's experience is a perfect example of the FBI letting hidebound traditional practices override common sense. The FBI's Los Angeles Division, where I worked, was one of the most difficult offices to staff at that time because of the high cost of living. With an office that size, I guarantee that Southers could have found an agent of similar seniority who wanted to transfer to the East Coast city where the bureau planned to dispatch him. They could simply switch assignments, at no cost to the FBI, making everyone happy. But the FBI does not allow such innovation. It is a counterproductive mentality, and if the bureau considers increasing diversity a priority, cost-free solutions like this should be embraced. Southers went on to hold a number of leadership roles in law enforcement and academia, so his career wasn't harmed by leaving the bureau. But it would have been better for the FBI to have figured out a way to keep him.

The FBI also doesn't let agents choose the types of cases they work, which is necessary to a certain degree to ensure it can staff all assignments according to its needs. I was hired during the savings and loan crisis, when the FBI was heavily recruiting accountants and giving them preferences in hiring and assignment. If the lack of diversity in the FBI is truly a crisis, as the last five directors have acknowledged, similar allowances should be made. Given the rising number of hate crimes, perhaps the FBI could recruit agents with the guarantee they would work civil rights enforcement for the first five years of their career. This might motivate people of color who would otherwise be reluctant to consider a law enforcement career because of the disparate impact criminal justice measures have in their communities to join the FBI.

The FBI also needs to reform personnel practices that weed out ideological diversity within the bureau. The lack of effective whistleblower protections combined with an arbitrary and unfair disciplinary system can make standing up against abusive FBI practices dangerous, stifling innovation. Independent audits and surveys have confirmed the widely held perception that senior managers receive more lenient treatment than lower-level employees.[4] Any disciplinary system that produces different outcomes based on internal politics can also mete out unfair punishments based on racial and ethnic bias or other improper considerations. The Justice Department should consider taking over the FBI's disciplinary process to remove the taint of internal politics and provide more independent and accountable oversight.

In March 2015, I testified before the Senate Judiciary Committee in favor of a bill that would have given FBI whistleblowers protections equal to those of other federal employees.[5] Only one small, but important, provision protecting chain-of-command reports passed, leaving much work to be done. Congress should revisit the remaining portions of the bill to ensure FBI whistleblowers are properly protected and have access to federal courts to vindicate their rights when these protections fail.

Of course, given the politics of the day, there is little chance of either the White House, Justice Department, or Congress reining in the FBI in the short term.

POPULAR RESISTANCE TO COMPEL FBI REFORM

When I speak about the challenges to intelligence reform around the country, the key question people ask is what they can do when their congressional representatives aren't willing to rein in the FBI. My response is to continue supporting national organizations like the Brennan Center for Justice, ACLU, Electronic Frontier Foundation, Council on American-Islamic Relations, and others that are filing legal challenges and lobbying in Washington, D.C., to bring transparency and accountability to all intelligence activities. But it is also important to work locally, organizing communities and working with local government officials to protect civil rights where the federal government has failed. Crucially, many of those targeted by disruption measures refuse to be silenced, and their resistance can serve as a model for civic activism to reassert democratic controls over the FBI.

Committee to Stop FBI Repression

On Friday, September 24, 2010, FBI agents simultaneously raided seven homes in Minneapolis and Chicago, executing search warrants and serving grand jury subpoenas on eleven anti-war and solidarity activists living there and in Grand Rapids, Michigan. The FBI made no arrests but would continue serving additional subpoenas on a total of twenty-three activists from North Carolina to California over the following days, weeks, and months. An FBI spokesman told the news media that the Joint Terrorism Task Force conducted the raids as part of an investigation "concerning the material support of terrorism."[6] Publicly declaring political activists terrorism supporters was a tactic designed to neutralize, discredit, and vilify them in order to isolate them from their political and social support. It didn't work.

Jess Sundin had been an activist in Minneapolis for more than a decade, primarily associated with the Committee in Solidarity with the People of El Salvador (CISPES). In 2008, Sundin was asked to help organize an anti-war march for the first day of the 2008 Republican National Convention in St. Paul. Sundin reached out to longtime colleagues who had worked together on social justice and solidarity issues under the banner of the Freedom Road Socialist Organization (FRSO). These included Linden Gawboy and her husband, Mick Kelly, the editor of FRSO's publication *Fight Back! News*, and Chicagoans Joe Iosbaker, a civil service employee at the University of Illinois at Chicago and chief steward of the Service Employees International Union Local 73, and his wife, Stephanie Weiner, an artist who ran a small company called the Revolutionary Lemonade Stand.[7]

While there were protest groups planning unpermitted actions at the convention, Sundin's Anti-War Committee obtained permits for their march and held planning meetings well in advance of the event.[8] The FBI and St. Paul Police Department took an aggressive approach to policing the protests. Even before the convention began, they raided the work space of some of the unpermitted protest organizers as well as an apartment rented by I-Witness Video journalists whose videography during the 2004 RNC had led to the dismissal of charges against four hundred protesters arrested on what they revealed to be false NYPD testimony. The authorities later said they were in "disruption mode."[9] Once the 2008 RNC protests got under way, St. Paul police used tear gas and smoke grenades and arrested hundreds of protesters and approximately four dozen journalists.[10] About thirty thousand people participated in the anti-war march, which Iosbaker said was the largest peace protest in the Midwest.[11] The Anti-War Committee considered it a huge success, though police shot Mick Kelly in the stomach with a plastic bullet on the last day of the convention. He later received a settlement from the police department.[12]

What the Anti-War Committee members didn't realize, however, was that the FBI had tasked an undercover agent, "Karen Sullivan," with infiltrating its permitted march. Sullivan befriended Sundin, joined the FRSO, and spent the next two and a half years planning protests, fact-finding trips, and events, sharing meals and drinks, and even staying in group members' homes. She found no explosives or illegal firearms and uncovered no terrorist plots. She recorded lots of fiery talk about the need for a revolution in the United States, even a violent one if necessary, but such statements were typically caveated with acknowledgments that neither the FRSO nor the country would be ready for that kind of action anytime soon. What kept the investigation going, apparently, was the FRSO's solidarity work with Colombian and Palestinian leftist groups.

The FBI affidavit for the 2010 search warrants used fragments from surreptitiously recorded conversations to allege FRSO members had held meetings with individuals associated with the Revolutionary Armed Forces of Colombia (FARC) and plotted to provide a $2,000 donation to people associated with the Popular Front for the Liberation of Palestine (PFLP).[13] Several snippets from these conversations were likely taken out of context. In planning for a meeting with Palestinian activists, for instance, someone asks if there is anything they should not say during the meeting. The affidavit ominously quotes an unidentified FRSO member replying, "Don't say we need money for lawyers, guns, and money or anything like that."[14] Apparently the agents weren't Warren Zevon fans and didn't get the reference to his song "Lawyers, Guns, and Money," from the 1978 album *Excitable Boy*.

With the nationwide raids, the FBI treated the FRSO members and associates like violent organized crime figures rather than middle-aged political activists with families and deep ties to their communities. Yet the search warrants sought only political literature, photographs, journals, and associational materials like address books, correspondence, and electronic records. Kelly, a cook by profession, was working that Friday morning when FBI agents banged on the door of his Minneapolis apartment, waking Gawboy. When she asked to see the warrant, the

FBI took the door down with a battering ram.[15] Sundin and her partner, Stephanie Yorek, were still in bed when the FBI demanded entry. Yorek got to the door and opened it just as agents were preparing to knock it down. The agents at Iosbaker's house just waited for him to open the door. All of the FRSO members began reaching out to lawyers and to each other, confused and terrified at seeing the material support for terrorism charge listed on the warrant. Sundin tried to stay calm for the sake of her six-year-old daughter.

But these were experienced organizers and activists, and the networking worked. They were relieved when their friends and neighbors began showing up to check on them. A fellow activist who worked as a child-care provider showed up at Sundin's house while the search was ongoing, despite felony charges still pending against him from the RNC protests. He told the agents he was Sundin's daughter's babysitter and he was there to take care of her. He stayed with her in the front yard for the rest of the morning. News reporters, who had become friendly with Sundin during the preparations for the RNC anti-war march, came to her home, and she gave them interviews even as the FBI was searching inside. Sundin told me there was a natural instinct to run and hide but that the lessons of history had shown her that "there is no safety in that. . . . Especially if someone had been working [undercover] with us for two and a half years, we couldn't unthink things, we couldn't unsay things, all we could do was stand by them. So, I think that it was extremely meaningful to be able to have people believe us, and I think even local media believed us."[16]

Another activist came by and told Sundin that friends were setting up a meeting at a nearby coffee shop, where they wrote up a press release to put out her side of the story. They called a press conference on her front lawn and one hundred people came. A meeting that evening at a local church drew five hundred.

Reporters in Chicago who knew Iosbaker also showed up at his home. One asked if he thought the search was about his labor activism. "No, this has to do with my anti-war activity," he replied.[17] A neighbor came by and asked what he could do to help. Iosbaker said, "Just believe me, we didn't do anything wrong." Watching the news coverage that night was rough. He wondered what all his neighbors and the people he worked with and negotiated against would think. "It was one thing to be a militant, big-mouth trade union activist," he told me. "Now I am a communist engaged in terrorism. It was devastating."

Iosbaker and Weiner also held a press conference and eighty supporters attended. They called for a protest in front of the FBI office the following Monday and five hundred showed up, including faith-based and African American community leaders. Iosbaker and Weiner talked to an attorney the following day and learned how expansive the material support statute was, and how grand juries worked. The subpoenaed activists decided they would not appear at the grand jury, which raised the stakes considerably as they risked being jailed for this refusal, even if there was nothing to the terrorism allegations. Iosbaker and Weiner's son was seventeen, so they had to prepare papers to arrange for his care, as did Sundin and Yorek for their six-year-old.

They knew the first fourteen activists the FBI served within days of the raids pretty well, but then when a second round of subpoenas went out to a wider group, those personal ties weren't as strong. Yet all remained committed to the no-cooperation strategy. Sundin said it wasn't a onetime decision not to cooperate with the grand jury. It was a choice she had to make anew every day. They never knew whether today would be their last day of freedom. Iosbaker gained twenty pounds from the stress, and Weiner lost twenty.

Unions and other labor organizations stood behind them and put out statements condemning the FBI's actions. The subpoenaed activists formed a new organization, the Committee to Stop FBI Repression (CSFR), and organized rallies in front of FBI offices and federal buildings all over the country. The CSFR went to Washington, D.C., to talk with their members of Congress. Iosbaker had once lived in the same building as Representative Luis Gutiérrez and had campaigned for him when he ran for city council. When Iosbaker arrived at Gutiérrez's office at the Capitol, the congressman embraced him. Iosbaker thought maybe he wasn't going to prison after all. Several members of Congress wrote letters to Attorney General Eric Holder asking for information about the investigation.[18]

Iosbaker and Sundin were now spending most of their time with the CSFR, rather than doing the union and solidarity work they had been doing, but they had little choice because the bureau's investigation was unrelenting. On May 17, 2011, the FBI and a Los Angeles Sheriff's Department SWAT team raided the home of legendary Chicano activist and FRSO supporter Carlos Montes and arrested him for possessing firearms despite a 1969 felony conviction for throwing a can of soda at a police officer during a protest.[19] The police knew about the guns because Montes had registered them years before. The apparent reason for this belated interest in his weapons was revealed when FBI agents questioned him about his involvement with the FRSO. Though the original charges could have imprisoned him for decades, he ultimately pled no contest to one perjury charge and was sentenced to probation and community service.[20]

The government also came after sixty-nine-year-old Palestinian activist Rasmea Odeh, who had worked closely with FRSO members on Palestinian solidarity issues. Odeh had been living in the United States for more than twenty-three years. The Justice Department charged her in 2013 with failing to disclose a 1970 terrorism conviction by an Israeli military court when she immigrated to the United States in 1988, obtained a green card in 1994, and filed to become a citizen in 2004. But the government had to have known about Odeh's case when it authorized her entry into the country and upgraded her status. She was one of the first women to testify before a United Nations special committee in Geneva about the torture and sexual abuse she suffered during her interrogation in an Israeli prison, parts of which her father was forced to watch, before she signed the confession that justified her conviction.[21] After her 1979 release in a prisoner exchange, she testified before the UN and later earned a law degree in Jordan before immigrating to the United States.[22]

Iosbaker believes the government targeted Odeh because her organization, the Arab American Action Network (AAAN) of Chicago, had worked closely with the FRSO. Hatem Abudayyeh, the executive director of AAAN, was part of the Anti-War Committee for the 2008 RNC, and though he was not a member of the FRSO, he had helped organize one of their trips to the Palestinian territories. The FBI searched his house at the same time as the FRSO raids. Iosbaker explained to me what he thinks is going on within the Justice Department and FBI JTTF: "We believe there is a group of people, a faction, a caucus, whatever, who think alike and they look out at the world and they see enemies everywhere, and they see people in the U.S. who are acting in concert with their enemies as domestic enemies. We fit their profile. They're not done with us. Maybe they won't get to put us on trial, but it's not because they don't want to. It's because we didn't give them anyone to their grand jury and we have tremendous political support. They can't move on us, but they come after our friends."

On the one hand, the FBI seems to have successfully disrupted the work Iosbaker, Sundin, and the FRSO did before the bureau initiated its undercover operation. But it also created a resistance movement and undermined its own credibility with the public and with many members of Congress who did not receive satisfactory answers to their questions about its raids against political activists. The FRSO developed a model for resisting FBI abuses, but they came from a position of strength in their experience and their access to levers of power. The FRSO members and supporters I spoke with recognize the importance of supporting other activists who, because of their race, ethnicity, religion, national origin, or immigration status, rarely get the benefit of the doubt when the government identifies them as enemies. FRSO members spoke up in defense of other targeted groups, like Minnesota's Young Muslim Collective.[23] Supporting local resistance organizations like the Committee to Stop FBI Repression and the Young Muslim Collective builds community resilience to the divisive rhetoric and policies coming from Washington.

Leaving Joint Terrorism Task Forces

Another form of protest against FBI abuses that has increasingly shown success is appealing to local government officials to remove law enforcement officers from FBI Joint Terrorism Task Forces. The city of Portland, Oregon, was the first to pull out of a JTTF, in 2005. The Portland Police Bureau (PPB) was one of the local law enforcement agencies that refused to assist the FBI's 2001 effort to conduct thousands of "voluntary" interviews of Middle Eastern immigrants around the country, but two PPB officers remained on the JTTF despite the disagreement.[24] In

2004, activists and city officials began raising questions about the lack of local government oversight over PPB activities, as required under Oregon state law, while these officers were working with the FBI. Portland mayor Tom Potter, a former chief of the PPB, requested top secret clearance so he could perform proper oversight. When the FBI refused, the Portland City Council voted 4 to 1 to pull its officers out of the JTTF.

In November 2010, the FBI ensnared Mohamed Mohamud, an eighteen-year-old Somali American student at Oregon State University in Corvallis, in a reverse sting operation. The FBI said it targeted Mohamud after discovering through NSA electronic surveillance that he had communicated with a suspected terrorist in Pakistan. FBI undercover agents convinced him they were recruiters for a global terrorist organization. Mohamud agreed to join them and said he wanted to be "operational." Mohamud accompanied the agents to a remote location in Lincoln County, Oregon, to detonate a small test bomb. The agents helped Mohamud tape a martyrdom video in his Corvallis apartment and then showed him a large bomb they had in a van. A few weeks later, Mohamud accompanied the agents to Portland, where they parked the van near a downtown Christmas tree lighting ceremony and gave him a cell phone with which to detonate the explosive. When Mohamud dialed the prearranged number, the FBI arrested him and announced the interdiction of a major terrorist attack in Portland.[25] The Portland City Council scheduled a hearing to determine whether to have the PPB go back into the JTTF, at which I testified on behalf of the ACLU.

It was Mohamud who picked the target for his attack, which from his "terrorist" perspective was intended to terrorize Portland Christians. But there was no need for the FBI to actually scare anyone, as it did by providing Mohamud with a mocked-up weapon of mass destruction and placing it in the middle of a crowded Pioneer Square. Not surprisingly, the staged attack succeeded in spreading fear and anti-Muslim hostility as if it had been genuine. Sadly, the FBI's fake terrorist plot provoked a real one, as self-proclaimed "Christian warrior" Cody Crawford firebombed a Corvallis mosque in retaliation two days later.[26] The FBI could have arrested Mohamud with little fanfare after he tested the explosive in the woods of Lincoln County weeks earlier. There was no need to go through the theatrics of the fake bombing except to aggrandize the accomplishments of the FBI and scare Portland citizens and officials into having the PPB rejoin the JTTF.[27] Now it might seem the FBI wouldn't care about a small liberal-minded city opting out of a JTTF, but when I arrived at the city council hearing, I was surprised to see FBI general counsel Valerie Caproni and Deputy Assistant Attorney General Todd Hinnen had both flown in from Washington, D.C., to testify as well.[28] In April 2011, the Portland City Council voted to have the PPB reengage with the JTTF on a limited basis.[29] The FBI's cynical ploy had worked.

But resistance to JTTF spying was only beginning. In San Francisco, eighty activist groups came together in 2010 to form the Coalition for a Safe San Francisco (CSSF) to protest racial, ethnic, and religious profiling and harassment by the FBI and local police. Due to past spying scandals, the San Francisco Police Department had strong regulations against conducting investigations without "articulable and reasonable suspicion" of criminal activity. This rule prevented SFPD from enlisting with the JTTF when the FBI first asked it to in 1998. But SFPD joined the JTTF in the wake of 9/11, with a stipulation written into the memorandum of understanding (MOU) that SFPD officers on the task force would follow local rules. A CSSF public records act request discovered in 2011 that the FBI and SFPD had secretly negotiated a new MOU in 2007, which, like the JTTF MOUs in other localities, required the SFPD officers on the task force to follow FBI rules, even though the Attorney General's Guidelines authorized investigative activities at significantly lower evidentiary thresholds that did local regulations. The issuance of the Mukasey guidelines in 2008 only exacerbated this problem.[30]

The CSSF activists lobbied the San Francisco Board of Supervisors to pass an ordinance requiring SFPD officers on the JTTF to follow state and local laws and regulations, which they did in 2012. The ordinance also included a public transparency provision requiring SFPD to file annual reports describing the SFPD officers' activities while engaged with the JTTF. The widely anticipated first report was only one page in length and simply averred that the three SFPD inspectors assigned to the JTTF were complying with local laws and regulations.[31]

The controversy heated up again in 2015 when an FBI agent and SFPD inspector assigned to the JTTF arrived unannounced at Google headquarters to interview a Muslim American software engineer about his FOIA request regarding security delays during a recent overseas trips.[32] After the election of President Trump in November 2016, activists renewed their demands for information about SFPD activities on the JTTF as required by the ordinance.[33] Rather than produce the overdue reports, the SFPD suspended its participation in the JTTF in February 2017.[34] Later that year, the FBI initiated an undercover operation against a Modesto, California, man who had "liked" online materials regarding ISIL and terrorism. The FBI alleged he had planned a Christmas attack on Pier 39 in San Francisco. The man apparently backed out of the plot when he became suspicious of the undercover agent, but the FBI arrested him for material support of a foreign terrorist organization anyway.[35] The SFPD remains out of the JTTF at the time of this writing.

Across the bay in Oakland, the Trump election similarly inspired a rethinking of local participation in the JTTF. In October 2017, the Oakland City Council voted to impose greater oversight of Oakland Police Department activities on federal task forces, including the JTTF.[36] The Portland City Council revisited its decision to participate in the JTTF with hearings in 2018 and again in 2019, and voted 3–2 to withdraw the Portland police officers from the FBI's task force on February 13, 2019.[37] These actions demonstrate that local government officials and activists can effectively limit FBI authorities.

With only about eight thousand agents working in field offices around the country, the FBI depends on the cooperation of local police and the American people to accomplish its law enforcement and national security missions. If enough police departments pull out of JTTFs based on the laxness of the Attorney General's Guidelines, it might compel the next attorney general to strengthen them in a way that improves both our security and our liberty so that no one but actual criminals needs to fear a knock on the door by an FBI agent.

The FBI has many challenges ahead. The American public is so polarized that when Special Counsel Robert Mueller completes his investigation a significant segment of the population will believe the results were rigged, no matter the outcome. The reverse sting operations have taken a toll, so that announcements of interdicted terrorist plots are met with immediate skepticism. When agents take the stand in courtrooms across the country, and when bureau leaders testify before Congress, it has become more difficult to know whether they are telling the whole truth. The FBI cannot remain effective without public confidence in its work, and regaining this faith should be its top priority. As United State Supreme Court Justice Louis Brandeis said, sunlight is the best disinfectant.

Congress should conduct, or at least order, a comprehensive review of FBI policies and practices designed to ensure its methods are effective, comply with the law, and do not infringe on the individual rights and liberties enshrined in our Constitution. As the Church Committee investigation demonstrated more than forty years ago, uncovering past abuses won't harm the FBI. It is the necessary first step toward reform.

ACKNOWLEDGMENTS

I would like to thank those at the New Press who encouraged the development of this book and shepherded it to completion, particularly Diane Wachtell, Carl Bromley, Emily Albarillo, and Michael O'Connor. I deeply appreciate my colleagues at the Brennan Center for Justice at New York University Law School for their support before, during, and since the completion of this book, under the leadership of Michael Waldman, John Kowal, Faiza Patel, and Liza Goitein. The support of Liberty and National Security program interns and staff, especially the incomparable Emily Hockett, was particularly helpful. I would also like to thank those that took a chance and helped me develop a second career after I left the FBI, especially Tom Blau of the National Defense University; John Pike at GlobalSecurity.org; my attorney Lynn Bernabei; Senator Chuck Grassley and his senior investigator Jason Foster; Anthony Romero, Caroline Fredrickson, Laura Murphy, Greg Nojeim, and all of my former colleagues at the American Civil Liberties Union. Finally, I am indebted to all of the FBI agents who trusted me with their cases as an undercover agent, and those agents, analysts, and victims of FBI abuses that trusted me with their stories, on the record and off, in the hopes that the telling would drive reform. Thank you all.

NOTES

Introduction: A Lawless Law Enforcer

1. FBI, Domestic Investigations and Operations Guide (DIOG), December 16, 2008, 32–33.

2. John Hudson, "FBI Drops Law Enforcement as 'Primary' Mission," *Foreign Policy*, January 5, 2014.

3. Dep't of Justice Inspector Gen., *A Review of Various Actions by the Federal Bureau of Investigation and Department of Justice in Advance of the 2016 Election* (June 2018); Statement by Dir. Comey on the investigation of Sec. Hillary Clinton's use of a personal e-mail system, July 5, 2016.

4. Memo from Attorney General Eric Holder to all Justice Department employees, "Re: Election Year Sensitivities," March 9, 2012.

5. James Comey, *A Higher Loyalty: Truth, Lies, and Leadership* (Flatiron Books, 2018), 198.

6. Sean McElwee et al., "4 Pieces of Evidence Showing FBI Director James Comey Cost Clinton the Election," *Vox*, January 11, 2017.

7. Eric Lipton et al., "The Perfect Weapon: How Russian Cyberpower Invaded the U.S.," *New York Times*, December 13, 2016.

8. Luke Harding et al., "British Spies Were First to Spot Trump Team's Links with Russia," *The Guardian*, April 13, 2017.

9. Eamon Javers, "FBI's Comey Opposed Naming Russians, Citing Election Timing: Source," CNBC, October 31, 2016.

10. Ali Vitali and Corky Siemaszko, "Trump Interview with Lester Holt: President Asked Comey If He Was Under Investigation," NBC News, May 11, 2017.

11. Reuters, "U.S. Hate Crimes Up 20 Percent in 2016, Fueled by Election Campaign: Report," NBC News, March 14, 2017; Abigail Hauslohner, "Hate Crimes Jump for Fourth Straight Year in Largest U.S. Cities, Study Shows," *Washington Post*, May 11, 2018.

12. Theodore Roosevelt, "Special Message to the House of Representatives," January 4, 1909.

13. FBI records on "COINTELPRO Black Extremist," vault.fbi.gov/cointel-pro/cointel-pro-black-extremists/cointelpro-black-extremists-part-01-of.

14. S. Select Comm. to Study Governmental Operations with Respect to Intelligence Activities, *Supplementary Detailed Staff Reports on Intelligence Activities and the Rights of Americans*, Book III, S. Rep. No. 94-755 at 27 (1976).

15. James Risen and Michael S. Schmidt, "2004 Showdown Shaped Reputation of Pick for F.B.I.," *New York Times*, June 21, 2013.

16. *Confirmation on the Nomination of James B. Comey Jr., of New York, to be Deputy Attorney General, Department of Justice: Hearing Before S. Comm. on the Judiciary*, 108th Cong. (2003).

17. Kevin Johnson, "New FBI Agents to Visit MLK Memorial," *USA Today*, April 28, 2014.

18. Dir. Comey, "Hard Truths: Law Enforcement and Race," speech at Georgetown University, February 12, 2015.

19. See Juliette Gatto et al., "Prejudice in the Police: On the Processes Underlying the Effects of Selection and Group Socialisation," *European Journal of Social Psychology* 40, no. 2 (March 2010): 252–69; Alison V. Hall et al., "Black and Blue: Exploring Racial Bias and Law Enforcement in the Killings of Unarmed Black Male Civilians," *American Psychologist* 71, no. 3 (April 2016): 175–86; Joshua Correll et al., "The Police Officer's Dilemma: Using Ethnicity to Disambiguate Potentially Threatening Individuals," *Journal of Personality and Social Psychology* 83, no. 6 (January 2002): 1314–29.

20. Joe Domanick, "Daryl Gates' Downfall," *Los Angeles Times*, April 18, 2010.

21. Jesse Eisinger, "Why Only One Top Banker Went to Jail for the Financial Crisis," *New York Times Magazine*, April 30, 2014; "Two Financial Crises Compared: The Savings and Loan Debacle and the Mortgage Mess," *New York Times*, April 13, 2011.

22. Tom Furlong, "The Keating Indictment: Targets of Bond Sellers: The 'Weak, Meek, Ignorant,'" *Los Angeles Times*, September 19, 1990.

23. "Coast Police Chief Accused of Racism," *New York Times*, May 13, 1982.

24. "Deaths During the L.A. Riots," *Los Angeles Times*, April 25, 2012

25. Michael Newton, *The FBI Encyclopedia* (Jefferson, NC: McFarland, 2003), 36; "Integrating the FBI: An Interview with Retired Special Agent Wayne Davis," *Common Reader*, October 30, 2015.

26. United Press International, "Job Practices: FBI Guilty of Bias Against Latino Agents," *Los Angeles Times*, October 2, 1988; "FBI, Black Agents Reach Agreement in Bias Case," *Chicago Tribune*, April 22, 1992; Seth Mydans, "Female Agents Sue F.B.I., Alleging Discrimination," *New York Times*, March 13, 1994.

27. Athan Theoharis, ed., *The FBI: A Comprehensive Reference Guide* (Oryx Press, 1999), 197.

28. Michael Decourcy Hinds, "White F.B.I. Agents Dispute Bureau Accord with Blacks," *New York Times*, June 13, 1992.

29. Michael Isikoff, "Questions of Diversity," *Washington Post*, June 10, 1993.

30. See Tyrone Powers, *Eyes to My Soul: The Rise or Decline of a Black FBI Agent* (Dover, MA: The Majority Press, 1996), 318–20.

31. Colbert I. King, "The Sessions Record: A Different View," *Washington Post*, January 25, 1993.

32. *Nomination of Louis J. Freeh to Be Director of the Federal Bureau of Investigation: Hearing Before S. Comm. on the Judiciary*, 103rd Cong. (1993).

33. Brian A. Reaves and Timothy C. Hart, "Federal Law Enforcement Officers, 2000," *U.S. Dep't of Justice Bureau of Justice Statistics Bulletin*, July 2001; U.S. Census Bureau, "Profile of General Demographic Characteristics: 2000," table DP-1.

34. Josh Gerstein, "The FBI Looks like Trump's America," *Politico*, November 4, 2016.

35. U.S. Census Bureau, "Facts for Features: Hispanic Heritage Month 2016," October 12, 2016.

36. Adam Goldman, "Where Are Women in F.B.I.'s Top Ranks?" *New York Times*, October 22, 2016.

37. Edward Orehek et al., "Need for Closure and the Social Response to Terrorism," *Basic and Applied Social Psychology* 32, no. 4 (November 2010): 280.

38. Karen Stenner, *The Authoritarian Dynamic* (Cambridge University Press, 2005), 13.

39. Clem Brooks and Jeff Manza, *Whose Rights?: Counterterrorism and the Dark Side of American Public Opinion* (Russell Sage Foundation, 2013), 51, 101.

40. Eric Black, "We're Polarized as a Nation (but It Could Be Worse)," *MinnPost*, February 4, 2016.

41. See Christopher Webber et al., "How Authoritarianism Is Shaping American Politics (and It's Not Just About Trump)," *Washington Post*, May 10, 2017.

42. John Mueller and Mark G. Stewart, "American Public Opinion on Terrorism Since 9/11: Trends and Puzzles," (presented at the National Convention of the International Studies Association, Atlanta, GA, March 17, 2016), politicalscience.osu.edu/faculty/jmueller/tpoISA16.pdf; Dave Mosher and Skye Gould, "How Likely Are Foreign Terrorists to Kill Americans? The Odds May Surprise You," *Business Insider*, January 31, 2017; Peter Bergen and Courtney Schuster, "The Golden Age of Terrorism," CNN.com, August 21, 2015.

43. Mueller and Stewart, "American Public Opinion on Terrorism," 5.

44. John Gramlich, "Voters' Perceptions of Crime Continue to Conflict with Reality," Pew Research Center, November 16, 2016.

45. Robert P. Jones et al., *How Immigration and Concerns About Cultural Change Are Shaping the 2016 Election*, PRRI/Brookings Survey, June 23, 2016, 28.

46. "Terrorism," Gallup, gallup.com/poll/4909/Terrorism-United-States.aspx.

47. Christopher A. Bail, "The Fringe Effect: Civil Society Organizations and the Evolution of Media Discourse About Islam Since the September 11th Attacks," *American Sociological Review* 77, no. 6 (December 2012): 855–79.

48. Spencer Ackerman, "New Evidence of Anti-Islam Bias Underscores Deep Challenges for FBI's Reform Pledge," *Wired*, September 23, 2011.

49. Arie Perliger, *Challengers from the Sidelines: Understanding America's Violent Far-Right*, Combating Terrorism Center, November 2012.

50. Meagan Meuchel Wilson, "Hate Crime Victimization, 2004–2012," U.S. Dep't of Justice, Bureau of Justice Statistics, February 2014.

51. Matthew Yglesias, "What Really Happened in 2016, in 7 Charts," *Vox*, September 18, 2017.

52. Patrick O'Neill, "Report: FBI Infiltrated Nonviolent Protest Outside Georgia Army Base," *National Catholic Reporter*, November 12, 2015.

53. Comey, "Hard Truths."

54. Cora Currier, "Despite Anti-profiling Rules, the FBI Uses Race and Religion When Deciding Who to Target," *The Intercept*, January 31, 2017.

55. Spencer Ackerman, "FBI Taught Its Agents They Could 'Bend or Suspend the Law,'" *Wired*, March 28, 2012.

1. A "Culture of Arrogance"

1. *Oversight of the FBI: Hearings Before the S. Comm. on the Judiciary*, 107th Cong. (2001), 1.

2. *Oversight of the FBI* (2001), 7–8.

3. *Oversight of the FBI* (2001), 10–12.

4. Patrick Radden Keefe, "Whitey Bulger, Inside Man," *New Yorker*, September 21, 2015; H. Comm. on Government Reform, *Everything Secret Degenerates: The FBI's Use of Murderers as Informants*, H.R. Rep. No. 108-414 (2004).

5. U.S. Dep't of Justice Inspector Gen., *A Review of the FBI's Performance in Deterring, Detecting, and Investigating the Espionage Activities of Robert Philip Hanssen* (2003).

6. James Risen, "Jailed Agent Says He Voiced Suspicion About Spy Suspect," *New York Times*, May 28, 2001.

7. U.S. Dep't of Justice Inspector Gen., *A Review of the FBI's Performance*, 17.

8. David Johnston, "F.B.I. Paid $7 Million for File on American Spying for Russia," *New York Times*, October 18, 2002.

9. Affidavit of Michael Lowe, U.S. v. Wen Ho Lee, 79 F. Supp. 2d 1280 (D.N.M. 1999).

10. "Wen Ho Lee's Problematic Polygraph," CBS News, February 4, 2000.

11. "Racial Bias in the Wen Ho Lee Case?" *PBS NewsHour*, December 14, 1999.

12. Matthew Purdy, "The Making of a Suspect: The Case of Wen Ho Lee," *New York Times*, February 4, 2001; Patrick Martin, "Report Confirms US Government Misconduct in Wen Ho Lee Spy Case," World Socialist Web Site, August 21, 2001, www.wsws.org/en/articles/2001/08/lee-a21.html; Defendant Motion for Discovery, *Lee*, 79 D.N.M. 1280; "Statement by Judge in Los Alamos Case, with Apology for Abuse of Power," *New York Times*, September 14, 2000.

13. U.S. Dep't of Justice, *Report of the Ruby Ridge Task Force to the Office of Professional Responsibility of Investigation of Allegations of Improper Governmental Conduct in the Investigation, Apprehension and Prosecution of Randall C. Weaver and Kevin L. Harris* (1994), 4.

14. Associated Press, "FBI Agent Gets Prison Term for Destroying Ruby Ridge Report," *Los Angeles Times*, October 11, 1997.

15. U.S. Dep't of Justice, *Report to the Deputy Attorney General on the Events at Waco, Texas* (October 8, 1993); Office of Special Counsel John C. Danforth, *Final Report to the Deputy Attorney General Concerning the 1993 Confrontation at the Mt. Carmel Complex, Waco, Texas* (Oct. 8, 1993); U.S. Dep't of Treasury, *Report of the Department of the Treasury on the Bureau of Alcohol, Tobacco, and Firearms Investigation of Vernon Wayne Howell also known as David Koresh* (September 1993).

16. Office of Special Counsel Danforth, *Final Report to the Deputy Attorney General Concerning the 1993 Confrontation at the Mt. Carmel Complex, Waco, Texas* (Oct. 8, 1993).

17. "Oklahoma City Bombing," FBI, fbi.gov/history/famous-cases/oklahoma-city-bombing.

18. Nolan Clay, "FBI Discovered Bomb Truck Key at Getaway Car Site, Jury Told," *Oklahoman*, May 14, 1997.

19. *Oversight of the FBI* (2001), 6–7.

20. *Oversight of the FBI* (2001), 10.

21. *Oversight of the FBI* (2001), 3.

22. *Oversight of the FBI* (2001), 10–11.

23. *Oversight of the FBI* (2001), 32.

24. *Oversight of the FBI* (2001), 29.

25. *Oversight of the FBI* (2001), 56–57.

26. *Oversight of the FBI* (2001), 29, 55; "FBI Whistle-Blower Leaves, Gets $1.16 Million," CNN.com, February 27, 1998.

27. Peter Slevin and Dan Eggen, "FBI Nominee Lauded for Tenacity," *Washington Post*, July 30, 2001.

28. *Oversight of the FBI* (2001), 139.

29. *Confirmation Hearing on the Nomination of Robert S. Mueller, III to Be Director of the Federal Bureau of Investigation Before S. Comm. on the Judiciary*, 107th Cong. (2001), 71 (statement of Robert Mueller, FBI director nominee).

30. William Safire, "Essay; B.C.C.I.: Justice Delayed," *New York Times*, July 25, 1991; William Safire, "Essay; Crimes of Iraqgate, II," *New York Times*, May 25, 1992; William Safire, "Essay; 1st Global Political Scandal," *New York Times*, November 12, 1992.

31. Sens. John Kerry and Hank Brown, *The BCCI Affair: A Report to* the S. Comm. on Foreign Relations, 102nd Cong., S. Prt. 102-140 (1992), 188.

32. Kerry and Brown, *The BCCI Affair*, 278, 306, 579; S. Select Comm. on Intelligence, *Report on the Intelligence Community's Involvement in the Banca Nazionale del Lavoro (BNL) Affair*, S. Prt. 103-12 (1993); Richard Lacayo, "Iran-Contra: The Cover-Up Begins to Crack," *Time Magazine*, June 24, 2001.

33. "Questions for Mr. Mueller," *Wall Street Journal*, June 26, 2001.

34. Fox Butterfield, "Trial Ending for Boston F.B.I. Agent Accused of Mob Ties," *New York Times*, May 24, 2002; Rikki Klieman, "Whitey Bulger's Secret Deal with FBI Infuriates Cops," *Daily Beast*, October 21, 2011.

35. *Investigation of Allegations of Law Enforcement Conduct in New England—Volume 3, Hearings Before the H. Comm. on Government Reform*, 107th Congress, Serial No. 107-56 (2002), 289–335.

36. H. Comm. on Gov. Reform, *Everything Secret Degenerates*; Fox Butterfield, "Ex-prosecutor Tells of Ties Between F.B.I. and Mob," *New York Times*, December 6, 2002.

37. *Confirmation Hearing on the Nomination of Robert S. Mueller, III*, 122–23.

38. *Confirmation Hearing on the Nomination of Robert S. Mueller, III*, 67–68.

39. The FBI received more than 96,000 tips in the first week after the attacks. U.S. Dep't of Justice Inspector Gen., *The September 11 Detainees: A Review of the Treatment of Aliens Held on Immigration Charges in Connection with the Investigation of the September 11 Attacks* (2003), 12.

40. Eric Lichtblau, *Bush's Law: The Remaking of American Justice* (Pantheon Books, 2008), 5 (quoting an FBI investigation status report).

41. U.S. Dep't of Justice Inspector Gen., *The September 11 Detainees*, 4n8.

42. Richard A. Serrano, "FBI Monitors for Radiation at Some Mosques," *Los Angeles Times*, December 24, 2005.

43. Att'y Gen. John Ashcroft, prepared remarks for the U.S. Mayors Conference, October 25, 2001.

44. U.S. Dep't of Justice Inspector Gen., *The September 11 Detainees*, 1n2, 13.

45. *September 11 Detainees*, 144–50.

46. *September 11 Detainees*, 16.

47. *September 11 Detainees*, 13 (quoting Alice Fisher's recollection of Chertoff's statement).

48. *September 11 Detainees*, 51–52.

49. Human Rights Watch, "Witness to Abuse," June 26, 2005, hrw.org/report/2005/06/26/witness-abuse/human-rights-abuses-under-material-witness-law-september-11.

50. Lichtblau, *Bush's Law*, 27.

51. Garrett M. Graff, *The Threat Matrix: The FBI at War in the Age of Global Terror* (Little, Brown and Co., 2011), 322.

52. *Frontline* interview with Arthur Cummings, posted October 10, 2006, pbs.org/wgbh/pages/frontline/enemywithin/interviews/cummings.html.

53. U.S. Dep't of Justice, "Strategic Plan 2001–2006," goal 1, subheading 1.1 (2001), justice.gov/archive/mps/strategic2001-2006/goal1.htm.

54. Lichtblau, *Bush's Law*, 84.

55. Frederick A.O. Schwarz Jr., *Democracy in the Dark: The Seduction of Government Secrecy* (The New Press, 2015), 173.

56. John Prados and Arturo Jimenez-Bacardi, eds., "White House Efforts to Blunt 1975 Church Committee Investigation into CIA Abuses Foreshadowed Executive-Congressional Battles After 9/11," National Security Archive at George Washington University, July 20, 2015.

57. Att'y Gen. Ashcroft and Dir. Mueller, press conference, September 17, 2001.

58. H.R.3162, 107th Congress (2001–2002): Uniting and Strengthening America by Providing Appropriate Tools Required to Intercept and Obstruct Terrorism (USA PATRIOT ACT) Act of 2001, webpage, October 26, 2001, congress.gov/bill/107th-congress/house-bill/3162; "ACLU Releases Comprehensive Report on Patriot Act Abuses," news release, March 11, 2009.

59. Marvin J. Johnson, "Interested Persons Memo: Analysis of Changes to Attorney General Guidelines," ACLU, June 5, 2002.

60. Ronald Kessler, *The Secrets of the FBI* (Crown Forum, 2011), 200.

61. Graff, *Threat Matrix*, 398.

62. Att'y Gen. Ashcroft and Dir. Mueller, press conference, September 17, 2001.

63. "Selected Suspicious Activity Reports from the Central California Intelligence Center and Joint Regional Intelligence Center," ACLU California, June 2012; Jeremy Scahill and Ryan Devereaux, "Watch Commander: Barack Obama's Secret Terrorist-Tracking System, by the Numbers," *The Intercept*, August 5, 2014.

64. "Justice Department Issues Policy Guidance to Ban Racial Profiling," U.S. Dep't of Justice news release no. 03-335, June 17, 2003.

65. Interview by Tim Russert with Dick Cheney, vice president of the United States, in Camp David, MD (September 16, 2001), georgewbush-whitehouse.archives.gov/vicepresident/news-speeches/speeches/vp20010916.html.

66. Ali H. Soufan with Daniel Freedman, *The Black Banners: The Inside Story of 9/11 and the War Against al-Qaeda* (W.W. Norton & Company, 2011), 287.

67. Jane Mayer, *The Dark Side: The Inside Story of How the War on Terror Turned into a War on American Ideals* (Anchor Books, 2009), 34.

68. Michael Hayden, *Playing to the Edge: American Intelligence in the Age of Terror* (Penguin: 2016).

69. Graff, *Threat Matrix*, 331.

2. A Lack of Internal Controls

1. Indictment, U.S. v. Moussaoui, No. 01-455-A (E.D. Va. 2001); Ex 330 of Defense, U.S. v. Moussaoui 365 F.3d 292 (4th Cir. 2004).

2. U.S. Dep't of Justice Inspector Gen., *A Review of the FBI's Handling of Intelligence Information Related to the September 11 Attacks* (2004), 102–22.

3. National Commission on Terrorist Attacks in the United States, *The 9/11 Commission Report* (2004), 275.

4. U.S. Dep't of Justice Inspector Gen., *Review of the FBI's Handling of Intel. Information Related to the Sept. 11 Attacks*, 101–222.

5. *Review of the FBI's Handling of Intel. Information Related to the Sept. 11 Attacks*, 178.

6. Greg Gordon, "Suspect's Notebook Held 9/11 Clues," *Columbus Dispatch*, September 11, 2007.

7. Ex. 792 of Defense, *Moussaoui*, 365 F.3d. 292.

8. Philip Shenon, "The Terrible Missed Chance," *Newsweek*, September 4, 2011.

9. Ali Soufan with Daniel Freedman, *The Black Banners: The Inside Story of 9/11 and the War Against al-Qaeda* (W. W. Norton & Company, 2011), 243–50, 288–96.

10. Dir. Mueller and Att'y Gen. Ashcroft, press conference, September 14, 2001.

11. Dir. Mueller and Att'y Gen. Ashcroft, press conference, September 17, 2001.

12. Jeff Zeleny et al., "Bin Laden Associate Is Detained," *Chicago Tribune*, September 18, 2011.

13. Robert Mueller, speaking at Att'y Gen. Ashcroft press conference about Zacarias Moussaoui, December 11, 2001.

14. Coleen Rowley, interview with author (July 11, 2016).

15. Rowley, interview with author.

16. Sens. Patrick Leahy, Charles Grassley, and Arlen Specter, *Interim Report on FBI Oversight in the 107th Congress by the S. Judiciary Comm.: FISA Implementation Failures* (2003), 20.

17. *Reforming the FBI in the 21st Century.*

18. Rowley, memo to Dir. Mueller, May 21, 2002.

19. *Intelligence Activities and the Rights of Americans: Hearings Before the S. Select Comm. to Study Governmental Operations with Respect to Intelligence Activities*, 94th Cong. (1976), Vol. II, 225–52.

20. *Intelligence Activities and the Rights of Americans*, 226.

21. *Reforming the FBI in the 21st Century.*

22. James Risen and Eric Lichtblau, "Bush Lets U.S. Spy on Callers Without Courts," *New York Times*, December 16, 2005.

23. Eric Lichtblau, *Bush's Law: The Remaking of American Justice* (Pantheon Books, 2008), 160. See also Lowell Bergman et al., "Domestic Surveillance: The Program; Spy Agency Data After Sept. 11 Led F.B.I. to Dead Ends," *New York Times*, January 17, 2006.

24. Jane Mayer, *The Dark Side: The Inside Story of How the War on Terror Turned into a War on American Ideals* (Anchor Books, 2009); Jane Mayer, "Outsourcing Torture," *New Yorker*, February 14, 2005.

25. Mayer, *The Dark Side*, 106.

26. Michael Isikoff, "Senate Report's New Findings on Pre-war Deception," *Newsweek*, June 10, 2008.

27. Mayer, *The Dark Side*, 106.

28. Dana Bash and Terry Frieden, "FBI Agent Blows Whistle on Moussaoui Probe," CNN.com, May 23, 2002.

29. *Time*, June 3, 2002.

30. Romesh Ratnesar and Michael Weisskopf, "How the FBI Blew the Case," CNN.com, May 27, 2002.

31. *Oversight Hearing on Counterterrorism Before S. Comm. on the Judiciary*, 107th Cong. (2002), 25.

32. Rowley, interview with author.

33. Don Van Natta Jr., "Traces of Terror: Surveillance; Government Will Ease Limits on Domestic Spying by F.B.I.," *New York Times*, May 30, 2002.

34. "FBI Chief: 9/11 Surveillance Taxing Bureau," *Washington Post*, June 6, 2002.

35. *Oversight Hearing on Counterterrorism*, 62–63.

36. *Oversight Hearing on Counterterrorism*, 17.

37. Richard Lacayo and Amanda Ripley, "Persons of The Year 2002: The Whistleblowers," *Time*, December 30, 2002.

38. S. Select Comm. on Intelligence, H. Permanent Select Comm. on Intelligence, *J. Inquiry into Intelligence Community Activities Before and After the Terrorist Attacks of September 11, 2001*, S. Rep. No. 107-351, H.R. Rep. No. 107-792 at 168–71 (2002).

39. *J. Hearing Before S. Select Comm. on Intelligence and H. Permanent Select Comm. on Intelligence to Examine Activities of the Intelligence Community in Connection with the September 11, 2001 Terrorist Attacks*, 107th Cong., October 17, 2002 (testimony of Dir. Mueller).

40. A 2009 inspector general study showed that 42 percent of FBI agents surveyed said they didn't report all the misconduct they witnessed on the job. Twenty-eight percent of street agents and nonmanager support staff said they never reported

such wrongdoing. Reasons for not reporting included fear of retaliation (16 percent), a belief the misconduct would not be punished (14 percent), and lack of managerial support for reporting misconduct (13 percent). U.S. Dep't of Justice Inspector Gen., General Evaluations and Inspections Division, *Review of the Federal Bureau of Investigation's Disciplinary System* (2009).

41. 28 C.F.R. § 0.29d.

42. U.S. Gov't Accountability Office, GAO-15-112, *Whistleblower Protection: Additional Action Needed to Improve DOJ's Handling of FBI Retaliation Complaints*, January 23, 2015, 22.

43. Lichtblau, *Bush's Law*, 106.

44. 18 U.S.C. §2511.

45. U.S. Dep't of Justice Inspector Gen., *Report of Investigation into Allegations from Michael German* (2006), 12.

46. "Lost in Translation," *60 Minutes*, aired October 25, 2002, on CBS, cbsnews.com/news/lost-in-translation-25-10-2002.

47. U.S. Dep't of Justice Inspector Gen., *A Review of the FBI's Response to John Roberts' Statements on* 60 Minutes (2003); U.S. Dep't of Justice Inspector Gen., *A Review of Allegations of a Continuing Double Standard of Discipline at the FBI* (2003).

48. Inspector Gen., *Review of the FBI's Disciplinary System*, 125–130.

49. *Current and Projected Threats to the United States: Hearing Before S. Select Comm. on Intelligence*, 108th Cong. (2003).

50. Coleen Rowley, memo to Dir. Mueller, February 26, 2003.

51. *Hearing on FBI Oversight Before S. Comm. on the Judiciary*, 110th Cong. (2007) (statement of Sen. Chuck Grassley).

52. "The Obama-Biden Plan: Protect Whistleblowers," Change.gov, Office of the President-Elect, web.archive.org/web/20130425082834/http://change.gov/agenda/ethics_agenda/; See also David K. Colapinto, "President Obama's Whistleblower Legacy (Part Three)," *Whistleblower Blog*, June 27, 2017, web.archive.org/web/20170627195539/www.whistleblowersblog.com/2017/01/president-obamas-whistleblower-legacy-part-three.

53. Nicole Ogrysko, "FBI Whistleblowers See Glimmer of Hope with New Law, but Still Face Uphill Battle," Federal News Radio, December 23, 2016.

3. Fear of Foreignness

1. Todd Bensman, "The Quiet American," *D Magazine*, March 2007.

2. Joseph P. Fried, "The Terror Conspiracy: The Overview; Sheik and 9 Followers Guilty of a Conspiracy of Terrorism," *New York Times*, October 2, 1995.

3. Gamal Abdel-Hafiz, interview with author (January 25–26, 2017). See also Marlena Telvick, "The Story of Gamal Abdel-Hafiz: Former Agent in the FBI's

International Terrorism Squad," *Frontline*, PBS, October 16, 2003, pbs.org/wgbh/pages/frontline/shows/sleeper/fbi/gamal.html.

4. Abdel-Hafiz, interview with author.

5. Youssef v. FBI, 402 U.S. App. D.C. 64, 687 F.3d 397 (2012).

6. Richard Esposito, "Exclusive: Mole Who Met Bin Laden Killed by Al Qaeda in Bosnia," NBC News, February 27, 2014.

7. Guy Taylor and John Solomon, "Exclusive: FBI Had Human Source in Contact with Bin Laden as Far Back as 1993," *Washington Times*, February 25, 2014.

8. Ex. 5 at 6–7, 15, Youssef v. FBI, 2008 U.S. Dist. LEXIS 130340 No. 1:03-cv-01551 (D.D.C. 2008).

9. *Youssef*, D.D.C. No. 1:03-cv-01551 at 6.

10. See Glenn Simpson, "Muslim FBI Agent Is Accused of Not Taping Terror Suspects," *Wall Street Journal*, November 26, 2002.

11. Abdel-Hafiz, interview with author.

12. Bensman, "The Quiet American."

13. As discussed in chapter 6, the Vulgar Betrayal investigation did result in the seizure of $1.4 million from the Quranic Literacy Institute and Muhammad Salah under civil forfeiture laws in 1998, and the FBI later charged and convicted several subjects of the investigation for a variety of criminal activity, some allegedly related to terrorism. See Matt O'Connor and Sarah Downey, "FBI Seizes $1 Million Linked to Terrorism," *Chicago Tribune*, June 10, 1998; Jim Crogan, "A Vulgar Betrayal," *LA Weekly*, August 26, 2004.

14. Ex. 5 at 20, *Youssef*, D.D.C. No. 1:03-cv-01551.

15. Judgment on the Verdict for Plaintiff at 10, Rattigan v. Holder, 982 F. Supp. 2d 69 (D.D.C. 2013).

16. *Rattigan*, 982 F. Supp. 2d 69.

17. Remarks by President George W. Bush at Islamic Center of Washington, D.C., September 17, 2001.

18. President George W. Bush, State of the Union address before a joint session of Congress, September 21, 2001.

19. Pres. George W. Bush, press conference, November 6, 2001.

20. *J. Inquiry into Events of September 11, 2001: Hearings Before S. Select Comm. on Intelligence and H. Permanent Select Comm. on Intelligence*, 107th Cong. (2002) (testimony of Michael E. Rolince, FBI special agent in charge of counterterrorism).

21. FBI, "Ten Years After: The FBI Since 9/11," August 2011, archives.fbi.gov/archives/about-us/ten-years-after-the-fbi-since-9-11/just-the-facts-1/security.

22. FBI, *The FBI's Counterterrorism Program Since September 2001*, 12 (report presented to the National Commission on Terrorist Attacks upon the United States by Dir. Mueller, April 14, 2004).

23. Wajahat Ali et al., *Fear, Inc.: The Roots of the Islamophobia Network in America*, Center for American Progress, August 26, 2011.

24. Spencer Ackerman, "FBI Teaches Agents: 'Mainstream' Muslims Are 'Violent, Radical,'" *Wired*, September 14, 2011.

25. Judgment on the Verdict for the Plaintiff at 26, *Rattigan*, 982 F. Supp. 2d 69.

26. Judgment on the Verdict for the Plaintiff at 28, *Rattigan*, 982 F. Supp. 2d 69.

27. Rattigan v. Holder, 414 U.S. App. D.C. 295, 780 F.3d 413 (2015).

28. Rattigan v. Holder, 395 U.S. App. D.C. 437, 643 F.3d 975 (2011).

29. Gamal Abdel-Hafiz, interview with *PBS Frontline*, October 16, 2003, www.pbs.org/wgbh/pages/frontline/shows/sleeper/interviews/hafiz.html.

30. Simpson, "Muslim FBI Agent Is Accused of Not Taping Terror Suspects."

31. Brian Ross and Vic Walter, "FBI Called Off Terror Investigations," ABC News, December 19, 2002; FOX Entertainment Group, Inc. v. Abdel-Hafiz, S.W.3d 524 (2007).

32. Bill O. Reilly, "Talking Points Memo" transcript: "All Hell Is Breaking Lose Inside the FBI," Fox News, March 6, 2003.

33. Bensman, "The Quiet American"; Telvick, "The Story of Gamal Abdel-Hafiz."

34. Bruce Falconer, "The FBI's Least Wanted," *Mother Jones*, May/June, 2009.

35. U.S. Dep't of Justice, Office of Professional Responsibility, memorandum on investigation of whistleblower allegations by FBI Special Agent Bassem Youssef, July 3, 2006, whistleblowers.org/storage/documents/order_and_opr_report.pdf.

36. Stephen M. Kohn et al., letter to Senate Judiciary Committee members Leahy, Specter, and Grassley on initial disclosures under E.O. 12731 and 42 U.S.C. § 2000e-3(a) and 5 U.S.C. § 7211, June 17, 2005.

37. National Commission on Terrorist Attacks in the United States, "Reforming Law Enforcement, Counterterrorism, and Intelligence Collection in the United States," Staff Statement No. 12, April 13–14, 2004.

38. U.S. Dep't of Justice Inspector Gen., *A Review of the FBI's Handling and Oversight of FBI Asset Katrina Leung* 2006), 1.

39. Order Granting Defendants' Motion to Dismiss, Suei-Te Chiang v. FBI, No. CV-05-03273-MMM (C.D. Cal., 2006).

40. H.G. Reza, "'A Great Agent' Sues FBI in Case Filled with Intrigue," *Los Angeles Times*, September 14, 2007.

41. Randall Thomas, affidavit in support of a complaint and arrest warrant for James J. Smith, April 2003, fas.org/irp/ops/ci/smith.html.

42. Order Granting Defendants' Motion to Dismiss at 4, *Suei-Te Chiang*, C.D. Cal. No. CV-05-03273-MMM.

43. Declaration of Robert S. Mueller III, Chiang v. Ashcroft, EEOC Case No. 100-2004-00352X, March 31, 2004.

44. Reza, "'A Great Agent' Sues FBI in Case Filled with Intrigue."

45. See Carol Gordon and Asher Arian, "Threat and Decision Making," *Journal of Conflict Resolution* 45, no. 2 (April 2001): 196–215; Marc Hetherington and Elizabeth Suhay, "Authoritarianism, Threat, and Americans' Support for the War on Terror," *American Journal of Political Science* 55, no. 3 (July 2011): 546–60.

46. U.S. Dep't of Justice Inspector Gen., *The Federal Bureau of Investigation's Foreign Language Translation Program*, Audit Report 10-02 (2009), 86.

47. Spencer Ackerman, "Muslims Inside FBI Describe Culture of Suspicion and Fear: 'It Is Cancer,'" *The Guardian*, March 22, 2017.

48. U.S. Dep't of Justice Inspector Gen., *The Federal Bureau of Investigation's Foreign Language Translation Program*, Audit Report 04-25 (2004), xvii; U.S. Dep't of Justice Inspector Gen., *Use of Polygraph Examinations in the Dep't of Justice*, I-2006-08 (2006), 66.

49. National Research Council et al., *The Polygraph and Lie Detection* (National Academies Press, 2003), 6.

50. National Research Council et al., 218.

51. *Oversight Hearings to Review the Operations of the FBI Crime Laboratory Before the S. Comm. on the Judiciary, Subcomm. on Administrative Oversight and the Courts*, 105th Cong. (1997) (statement of Dr. Drew C. Richardson, FBI crime lab unit chief).

52. Aldrich H. Ames, letter to Steven Aftergood at the Federation of American Scientists, November 28, 2000.

53. U.S. Dep't of Justice Inspector Gen., *Federal Bureau of Investigation's Foreign Language Translation Program*, 77.

54. *Federal Bureau of Investigation's Foreign Language Translation Program*, viii, xxiv.

55. *Federal Bureau of Investigation's Foreign Language Translation Program*, 86.

56. Eric Schmitt, "F.B.I. Employees with Ties Abroad See Security Bias," *New York Times*, January 3, 2015.

57. Dep't of the Navy v. Egan, 484 U.S. 518, 108 S. Ct. 818 (1988).

58. Schmitt, "F.B.I. Employees with Ties Abroad See Security Bias."

59. FBI Academy, presentation on Islam, slide 36 (obtained through FOIA December 10, 2010, by ACLU, aclu.org/foia-document/racial-mapping-foia-northern-california-aclurm000463).

60. Draft of FBI training materials, October 3, 2003, 14 (obtained through FOIA by ACLU, aclu.org/foia-document/racial-mapping-foia-northern-california-aclurm013039).

61. Spencer Ackerman, "FBI 'Islam 101' Guide Depicted Muslims as 7th-Century Simpletons," *Wired*, July 27, 2011; Spencer Ackerman and Noah Shachtman, "Video: FBI Trainer Says Forget 'Irrelevant' Al-Qaida, Target Islam," *Wired*, September 20, 2011.

62. FBI, "The Chinese: Cross-Cultural Considerations" (obtained through FOIA by ACLU, aclu.org/files/fbimappingfoia/20120518/ACLURM032381.pdf); FBI Academy, Behavioral Science Unit, "Principles of Cultural Awareness in Operations," slide 24 (obtained through FOIA by ACLU, aclu.org/sites/default/files/field_document /aclurm036861.pdf).

63. Said Barodi, interview with author (December 15, 2016).

64. Spencer Ackerman, "FBI Fired Sebastian Gorka for Anti-Muslim Diatribes," *Daily Beast*, June 21, 2017.

65. *Hearing on Domestic Threat Intelligence Before H. Permanent Select Comm. on Intelligence*, 112th Cong., October 6, 2011 (testimony of Robert S. Mueller III, FBI director).

66. Sen. Dick Durbin, letter to Dir. Mueller, March 27, 2012.

67. Shane Harris, "Conservative Pundit Sebastian Gorka Brings 'Global Jihadist Movement' Theory into White House," *Wall Street Journal*, February 21, 2017.

68. Ackerman, "FBI Fired Sebastian Gorka."

69. Jane Eisner, "What *The Forward* Really Said About Gorka—and Why We're Proud We Did," *The Forward*, August 30, 2017.

70. Topher Sanders, "The Curious Case of the Twice-Fired FBI Analyst," *ProPublica*, April 24, 2018.

71. Ackerman, "Muslims Inside FBI."

72. Ackerman, "Muslims Inside FBI."

73. Katherine L. Herbig, *Changes in Espionage by Americans: 1947–2007*, U.S. Dep't of Defense, Defense Personnel Security Research Center, Technical Report 08-05, March 2008, 10.

74. Sanders, "The Curious Case."

4. Targeting Their Own

1. U.S. Dep't of Justice Inspector Gen., *General Evaluations and Inspections Division Review of the Federal Bureau of Investigation's Disciplinary System* (2009), 125–30.

2. U.S. Dep't of Justice Inspector Gen., *Use of Polygraph Examinations in the Dep't of Justice*, I-2006-08 (2006), 37.

3. U.S. Dep't of Justice, *A Review of FBI Security Programs* (March 2002).

4. U.S. Dep't of Justice, *A Review of FBI Security Programs* (March 2002), 70; U.S. Dep't of Justice Inspector Gen., *Use of Polygraph Examinations in the Department of Justice*, 48n15.

5. U.S. Dep't of Justice Inspector Gen., *Public Summary: Review of the Federal Bureau of Investigation's Response to Unresolved Results in Polygraph Examinations* (2018).

6. Jessica Schulberg, "The FBI Insists It Doesn't Fire People over Polygraphs. This Man Says It Happened to Him," *Huffington Post*, October 17, 2016.

7. Logan, interview with author, April 2017.

8. Logan, interview.

9. Schulberg, "The FBI Insists It Doesn't Fire People over Polygraphs."

10. National Research Council et al., *The Polygraph and Lie Detection* (National Academies Press, 2003), 139; John R. Schwartz, "On Eve of Polygraph Trial, Leaked Case Files Contradict CBP Polygraph Chief's Countermeasure Detection Claim," Antipolygraph.org, May 5, 2015.

11. Drew Richardson, declaration on antipolygraph.org, September 7, 2001, antipolygraph.org/cgi-bin/forums/YaBB.pl?num=1442686514/2.

12. National Research Council et al., *The Polygraph and Lie Detection*, 88–89. The National Research Council also pointed to a Department of Defense Polygraph Institute (DODPI) data set from a study involving 1,141 student examinations. It revealed a significantly higher rate of false positives among African American examinees than among white examinees. DODPI did not publish a report regarding this data set, however, and anti-polygraph activists have suggested DOD intentionally suppressed this research. Document available at: antipolygraph.org/documents/dodpi-racial-bias-study.pdf.

13. National Research Council et al., *The Polygraph and Lie Detection*, 3.

14. U.S. Dep't of Justice Inspector Gen., *Use of Polygraph Examinations in the Department of Justice*, 66; Dan Eggen and Shankar Vedantam, "Polygraph Results Often in Question," *Washington Post*, May 1, 2006.

15. U.S. Dep't of Justice Inspector Gen., *A Review of the Department's Tribal Law Enforcement Efforts Pursuant to the Tribal Law and Order Act of 2010* (December 2017); André B. Rosay, *Violence Against American Indian and Alaskan Native Women and Men: 2010 Findings from the National Intimate Partner and Sexual Violence Survey*, National Institute of Justice, May 2016; Mike Males, "Who Are Police Killing?" Center on Juvenile and Criminal Justice, August 26, 2014.

16. Tad Vezner, "The Open Case of Agent Turner," *Pioneer Press* (MN), July 21, 2007.

17. See, for example, Adrian Jawort, "'Just Another Dead Indian': Steven Bearcrane-Cole Case Has One More Chance," *Indian Country Today*, February 7, 2017.

18. Vezner, "The Open Case of Agent Turner."

19. Turner v. Gonzales, 421 F. 3d 688 (8th Cir. 2005).

20. Jane Turner, correspondence with author.

21. Jane Turner, correspondence with author.

22. U.S. Dep't of Justice Inspector Gen., *An Investigation Regarding the Removal of a Tiffany Globe from the Fresh Kills Recovery Site* (December 2003).

23. Vezner, "The Open Case of Agent Turner."

24. Turner v. U.S. Dep't of Justice, 815 F.3d 1108 (8th Cir. 2016) *aff'd*, (D. Minn. Sep. 29, 2014).

25. Appellants' Motion for Leave to File Supplemental Joint Appendix, Cowley et al., v. Loretta Lynch, 4th Cir., No. 15-2122, (E.D.Va. 2016); Opening Brief for Appellants, Cowley v. Lynch, No. 15-2122 (4th Cir. 2015).

26. Laura Phelon, "Westfield State Hosts FBI Agent Julia Cowley," Westfield State University, news release, October 13, 2016, westfield.ma.edu/news/view/westfield-state-hosts-fbi-agent-julia-cowley.

27. U.S. Dep't of Justice Inspector Gen., *Investigation of Alleged Retaliation Against FBI Employee Julia A. Cowley* (February 2016), 7.

28. Sen. Charles Chuck Grassley, "More FBI Whistleblowers Allege Retaliation Through Loss of Effectiveness Orders," news release, October 1, 2014, grassley.senate.gov/news/news-releases/more-fbi-whistleblowers-allege-retaliation-through-loss-effectiveness-orders.

29. U.S. Dep't of Justice Inspector Gen., *Investigation of Alleged Retaliation Against FBI Employee Julia A. Cowley*, 19.

30. *Investigation of Alleged Retaliation Against FBI Employee Julia A. Cowley*, 20.

31. Sen. Charles Grassley, "FBI's Announced Loss of Effectiveness Policy Update Is Small Step Forward," news release, March 5, 2015, grassley.senate.gov/news/news-releases/grassley-fbi%E2%80%99s-announced-loss-effectiveness-policy-update-small-step-forward.

5. The Radicalization Theory

1. See Shearson v. U.S. Dep't of Homeland Sec., 638 F.3d 498 (6th Cir. 2011); Julia Shearson, letter to Sen. George Voinovich, January 9, 2006; Robert L. Smith, "Julia Shearson Tells How a Weekend Trip to Canada Became 5-Year Fight for Rights," *Plain Dealer* (Cleveland), June 4, 2011.

2. Julia Shearson, email to author, July 6, 2012.

3. U.S. Dep't of Homeland Security, SITROOM Incident Report (January 8, 2006)(on file with author).

4. See Shearson v. Holder, 865 F. Supp. 2d 850 (2011).

5. Julia Shearson, presentation on "Privacy in Perspective: Implications of Government Surveillance on Human Rights and Civil Liberties," Plenary Session I: Securing Our Rights in the Information-Sharing Era, A Convening on National Security, Surveillance, and Immigration Enforcement, Rights Working Group (2012) (on file with author).

6. U.S. Dep't of Homeland Security SPOT Report, January 8, 2006.

7. *Trapped in a Black Box: Growing Terrorism Watchlisting in Everyday Policing*, Civil Liberties and National Security Clinic at Yale Law School and ACLU, April 2016, 15–21.

8. U.S. Dep't of Justice Inspector Gen., *Review of the Terrorist Screening Center*, Audit Report 05-27 (2005); U.S. Dep't of Justice Inspector Gen., *Follow-Up Audit of the Terrorist Screening Center*, Audit Report 07-41 (2007); U.S. Dep't of Justice Inspector Gen., *The FBI's Terrorist Watchlist Nomination Practices*, Audit Report 09-25 (2009); *The Progress and Pitfalls of the Terrorist Watch List: Field Hearing of the H. Comm. on Homeland Security*, 110th Cong. (2007); National Counterterrorism Center, fact sheet on Terrorist Identifies Datamart Environment (TIDE), February 10, 2017, dni.gov/files/NCTC/documents/features_documents/TIDEfactsheet10FEB2017.pdf.

9. Declaration of Eric Holder Jr., Att'y Gen. of the U.S., Ibrahim v. Dep't of Homeland Sec., 62 F. Supp. 3d 909 (N.D. Cal. 2014).

10. "The FBI Checked the Wrong Box and a Woman Ended Up on the Terrorism Watch List for Years," ProPublica, December 15, 2015; *Ibrahim*, 62 F. Supp. 3d 909.

11. FBI Counterterrorism Division, "The Radicalization Process: From Conversion to Jihad," intelligence assessment, May 10, 2006. The four-step radicalization process also appeared in an FBI bulletin in 2003. A version of the 2006 intelligence assessment was published in the *FBI Law Enforcement Bulletin* in 2007.

12. Ryan Hunter and Daniel Heinke, "Perspective: Radicalization of Islamist Terrorists in the Western World," *FBI Law Enforcement Bulletin*, September 1, 2011.

13. FBI Counterterrorism Division, "The Radicalization Process," 4.

14. "The Radicalization Process," 7.

15. Cora Currier and Murtaza Hussain, "48 Questions the FBI Uses to Determine if Someone Is a Likely Terrorist," *The Intercept*, February 13, 2017.

16. Faiza Patel and Meghan Koushik, *Countering Violent Extremism*, Brennan Center for Justice, March 16, 2017, 9–11.

17. Jamie Bartlett et al., *The Edge of Violence: A Radical Approach to Extremism*, Demos, January 2010.

18. Randy Borum, "Radicalization into Violent Extremism I: A Review of Social Science Theories," *Journal of Strategic Security* 4, no. 4 (Winter 2011): 9; Clark McCauley and Sophia Moskalenko, "Individual and Group Mechanisms of Radicalization," in *Protecting the Homeland from International and Domestic Security Threats: Current Multi-disciplinary Perspectives on Root Causes, the Role of Ideology, and Programs for Counter-radicalization and Disengagement*, eds. Laurie Fenstermacher et al. (Washington, D.C., 2010), 85.

19. Declaration of Marc Sageman in Opposition to Defendants' Cross-Motion for Summary Judgment at 7–8, Latif v. Lynch, No. 3:10-cv-00750-BR, 2016 U.S. Dist. LEXIS 40177 (D. Or. March 28, 2016).

20. 43 Cong. Rec. 672 (1909). See also Max Lowenthal, *The Federal Bureau of Investigation* (William Sloane Associates, 1950), 3–9.

21. H. Select Comm. on Appropriations, *Report of the Select Comm. on Appropriations for Employees Engaged in the Detection and Prevention of Fraud*, H. R. Rep. No. 2320 at 375 (1909).

22. Aaron J. Stockham, "Lack of Oversight: The Relationship Between the FBI and Congress, 1907–1975," dissertation, Marquette University (2011), 17–70.

23. Athan G. Theoharis et al., eds., *The FBI: A Comprehensive Reference Guide* (Greenwood Publishing Group, 1999), 3–4; Athan G. Theoharis, "A Reassessment of the Wickersham Commission Report: The Evolution of a Security Consensus," *Marquette Law Review* 96 (Summer 2013):1147, 1148.

24. H. Select Comm. on Appropriations, *Report of the Select Comm. on Appropriations*, 84.

25. President Theodore Roosevelt, special message to the House of Representatives, January 4, 1909. See also Rhodri Jeffreys-Jones, *The FBI: A History* (Yale University Press, 2007), 51.

26. Jeffreys-Jones, *The FBI: A History*, 52; "Done for Spite: The President Links Tillman with Land Grab," *Times and Democrat* (Orangeburg, SC), January 12, 1909.

27. H. Select Comm. on Appropriations, *Report of the Select Comm. on Appropriations*, 491.

28. 61 P.L. 277, 36 Stat. 825, 61 Cong. Ch. 395; Jessica Rae Pliley, "Any Other Immoral Purpose: The Mann Act, Policing Women, and the American State: 1900–1941," dissertation, Ohio State University (2010).

29. Richard J. Samuels, ed., *Encyclopedia of United States National Security*, Vol. 1 (Sage Publications, 2006), 252.

30. John Sbardellati and Tony Shaw, "Booting a Tramp: Charlie Chaplin, the FBI, and the Construction of the Subversive Image in Red Scare America," *Pacific Historical Review* 72, no. 4 (November 2003): 495–530.

31. *Brewing and Liquor Interests and German Propaganda: Hearings Before Subcomm. of S. Comm. on the Judiciary Pursuant to S. Res. 307*, 65th Cong. (1919), Vol. II, 1388.

32. *Brewing and Liquor Interests*, 1389.

33. *Brewing and Liquor Interests*, 1388.

34. Lowenthal, *The Federal Bureau of Investigation*, 36–38.

35. *Brewing and Liquor Interests*, 1648–54.

36. *Brewing and Liquor Interests*, 1652–54.

37. *Bolshevik Propaganda: Hearings Before Subcomm. of the S. Comm. on the Judiciary Pursuant to S. Res. 439 and 469*, 65th Cong. (1919), 465.

38. T. Henry Walnut, review of *The Federal Bureau of Investigation*, by Max Lowenthal, *University of Chicago Law Review* 19, no. 3 (Spring 1952): 635.

39. *Brewing and Liquor Interests*, 2690.

40. *Brewing and Liquor Interests*, 2690, 2729.

41. *Brewing and Liquor Interests*, 2695, 2701.

42. *Brewing and Liquor Interests*, 2716–17.

43. *Brewing and Liquor Interests*, 2709–10.

44. *Brewing and Liquor Interests*, 2707–8, 2732–35.

45. Brian Farmer, *American Conservatism: History, Theory and Practice* (Cambridge Scholars Press, 2005).

46. Michael Linfield, *Freedom Under Fire: U.S. Civil Liberties in Times of War* (South End Press, 1990), 37–40.

47. Mark Ellis, "J. Edgar Hoover and the 'Red Summer' of 1919," *Journal of American Studies* 28, no. 1 (April 1994): 56; Patrick S. Washburn, *A Question of Sedition: J. Edgar Hoover and the Black Press in World War II* (Oxford University Press, 1986).

48. *Brewing and Liquor Interests*, 2780.

49. "Filibuster Kills Anti-lynching Bill: Republican Senators in Caucus Agree to Abandon the Dyer Measure," *New York Times*, December 3, 1922.

50. Robert Murray, *Red Scare: A Study in National Hysteria* (Univ. of Minn. Press, 1955), 57–73; Robert L. Friedheim, *The Seattle General Strike of 1919*, Pacific Northwest Quarterly, Vol. 52 no. 3 (July 1961), 81–98.

51. Charles H. McCormick, *Hopeless Cases: The Hunt for the Red Scare Terrorist Bombers* (University Press of America, 2005), 38; Geoffrey R. Stone, *Perilous Times: Free Speech in Wartime—from the Sedition Act of 1798 to the War on Terrorism* (W. W. Norton & Company, 2004).

52. Joseph T. McCann, *Terrorism on American Soil: A Concise History of Plots and Perpetrators from the Famous to the Forgotten* (Sentient Publications, 2006).

53. "1919 Bombings," FBI, fbi.gov/philadelphia/about-us/history/famous-cases/famous-cases-1919-bombings.

54. Fred J. Cook, *The FBI Nobody Knows* (Macmillan, 1964), 94.

55. Lowenthal, *The Federal Bureau of Investigation*, 91.

56. Jeffreys-Jones, *The FBI: A History*, 75.

57. Jeffreys-Jones, 73–74.

58. "For Action on Race Riot Peril: Radical Propaganda Among Negroes Growing, and Increase Violence Set Out in Senate Brief for Federal Inquiry," *New York Times*, October 5, 1919.

59. Ellis, "J. Edgar Hoover and the 'Red Summer' of 1919," 39.

60. Lowenthal, *The Federal Bureau of Investigation*, 129.

61. "Radicalism and Sedition Among the Negroes, as Reflected in Their Publications," *New York Times*, November 23, 1919. The report has often been attributed to J. Edgar Hoover, but it was actually written by Robert Bowen. See Ellis, "J. Edgar Hoover and the 'Red Summer' of 1919," 53.

62. The National Association for the Promotion of Labor Unionism Among Negroes to the Union Club of New York City (included in U.S. Cong. H. Comm. on Rules and Alexander Mitchell Palmer, *Attorney General A. Mitchell Palmer on Charges Made Against Department of Justice by Louis F. Post and Others* [U.S. Government Printing Office, 1920]).

63. Louis Freeland Post, *The Deportations Delirium of Nineteen-Twenty: A Personal Narrative of an Historic Official Experience* (C.H. Kerr, 1923), 93.

64. Post, 93–95.

65. Post, 95.

66. Colyer v. Skeffington, 265 F.17 (D. Mass. 1920).

67. National Popular Government League, *Report Upon the Illegal Practices of the United States Department of Justice* (1920).

68. *Report Upon the Illegal Practices of the United States Dep't of Justice*, 8.

69. Walnut, review of *The Federal Bureau of Investigation*, 634.

70. Beverly Gage, *The Day Wall Street Exploded: A Story of America in its First Age of Terror* (Oxford University Press, 2010).

71. Lowenthal, *The Federal Bureau of Investigation*, 298.

72. 18 U.S.C.S. § 2385; 8 U.S.C.S. § 1227.

73. Hoover supported Sen. Joseph McCarthy's efforts on the U.S. Senate Permanent Subcommittee on Investigations to uncover Communist moles burrowed into the U.S. government and shared information with a former FBI agent who served as a committee staffer. Hoover distanced himself, however, once Sen. McCarthy began threatening the intelligence community by focusing his inquiries on the U.S. Army and the CIA. Tim Weiner, *Enemies: A History of the FBI* (Random House, 2012), 119–28, 182–87.

74. See John F. Fox Jr., "The Birth of the FBI's Technical Laboratory—1924 to 1935," FBI, fbi.gov/history/history-publications-reports/the-birth-of-the-fbis-technical-laboratory1924-to-1935.

75. Stephen M. Underhill, "J. Edgar Hoover's Domestic Propaganda: Narrating the Spectacle of the Karpis Arrest," *Western Journal of Communication* 76, no. 4 (July–September 2012): 438–57.

76. Theoharis et al., *The FBI: A Comprehensive Reference Guide*, 57.

77. Betty Medsger, "Stolen Documents Describe FBI Surveillance Activities," *Washington Post*, March 24, 1971.

78. S. Select Comm. to Study Governmental Operations with Respect to Intelligence Activities, *Final Report on Intelligence Activities and the Rights of Americans*, Book II, S. Rep. No. 94-755 (1976), 212.

79. Select Comm. to Study Governmental Operations, *Final Report on Intelligence Activities*, 3.

80. *Final Report on Intelligence Activities*, 6–7.

81. Deposition of Black Nationalist Division supervisor, October 17, 1975 (quoted in S. Rep. No. 94-755 at 4).

82. Weiner, *Enemies*, 123, 241–248.

83. Select Comm. to Study Governmental Operations, *Final Report on Intelligence Activities*.

84. *FBI Statutory Charter: Hearings Before the S. Comm. on the Judiciary*, 95th Cong. (1978).

85. *FBI Statutory Charter*, 22.

86. S. Select Comm. on Intelligence, *The FBI and CISPES*, S. Rep.101-46 at 20 (1989).

87. *The FBI and CISPES*, 20–21.

88. *The FBI and CISPES*, 31.

89. *The FBI and CISPES*, 2.

90. *The FBI and CISPES*, 14–15, 104.

91. *Break-Ins at Sanctuary Churches and Organizations Opposed to Administration Policy in Central America: Hearings Before H. Comm. on the Judiciary*, 100th Cong. (1987) (statement of Frank Varelli, FBI informant).

92. Hearings Before H. Comm. On the Judiciary, *Break-ins at Sanctuary Churches and Organizations*, 432.

93. S. Select Comm. on Intelligence, *The FBI and CISPES*, 37.

94. *The FBI and CISPES*, 29.

95. *The FBI and CISPES*, 57.

96. *The FBI and CISPES*, 61–62.

97. David Miller et al., *Critical Terrorism Studies Since 11 September 2001: What Has Been Learned?* (Routledge, 2016), 43.

6. Disrupting Muslim Civil Society

1. It is important to note that Shearson doubts that her employment was the source of her troubles. She points out that she was still fairly new to the organization and many more prominent CAIR officials traveled internationally without any hindrance.

2. Christopher A. Bail, "The Fringe Effect: Civil Society Organizations and the Evolution of Media Discourse About Islam Since the September 11th Attacks," *American Sociological Review* 77, no. 6 (December 2012): 855–79; Christopher Bail, *Terrified: How Anti-Muslim Fringe Organizations Became Mainstream* (Princeton University Press, 2014), 28.

3. Engy Abdelkader, "The Origins, Evolution, and Impact of the Term 'Radical Islam,'" University of Pennsylvania Law School *Global Affairs Blog*, October 29, 2016, law.upenn.edu/live/news/6593-the-origins-evolution-and-impact-of-the-term/news/international-blog.php (quoting interview with Sen. Henry M. Jackson (D-WA) in *New York Jewish Weekly*, January 1979).

4. Daniel Pipes, "The Rise of Muslim Fundamentalism," *St. Louis Post Dispatch*, August 22, 1984. See also Daniel Pipes, "The Western Mind of Radical Islam," *First Things*, December 1995.

5. Daniel Pipes, "Islamic Fundamentalists Are the New Big Threat to the West," *Philadelphia Inquirer*, September 16, 1994.

6. Spencer Ackerman, "New Evidence of Anti-Islam Bias Underscores Deep Challenges for FBI's Reform Pledge," *Wired*, September 23, 2011.

7. In fact, by 1992 Emerson had already written two books about terrorism and a third about Saudi petrodollars being used to influence U.S. politics. See Steven Emerson, *The American House of Saud: The Secret Petrodollar Connection* (Franklin Watts, 1985); Steven Emerson and Brian Duffy, *The Fall of Pan Am 103: Inside the Lockerbie Investigation* (Penguin Group, 1990); Steven Emerson and Cristina del Sesto, *Terrorist: The Inside Story of the Highest-Ranking Iraqi Terrorist Ever to Defect to the West* (Villard Books, 1991).

8. Steven Emerson, *American Jihad: The Terrorists Living Among Us* (Simon & Schuster, 2003), 5–8.

9. Emerson, *American Jihad*, 7–8.

10. Todd J. Gillman, "Muslims, Ex-FBI Official Clash on Documentary," *Dallas Morning News*, November 11, 1994.

11. Oliver Revell, "Protecting America," *Middle East Quarterly* 2, no. 1 (Winter 1995).

12. Revell, "Protecting America."

13. "Islamophobia: Understanding Anti-Muslim Sentiment in the West," Gallup, news.gallup.com/poll/157082/islamophobia-understanding-anti-muslim-sentiment-west.aspx; Khaled A. Beydoun, *American Islamophobia: Understanding the Roots and Rise of Fear* (Univ. of California Press, 2018).

14. David Barsamian, "Edward Said Interview," *The Progressive*, November 1, 2001.

15. David Price, "How the FBI Spied on Edward Said," *Counterpunch*, January 13, 2006,; Ivan Greenberg, *The Dangers of Dissent: The FBI and Civil Liberties Since 1965* (Lexington Books, 2010), 138–39.

16. See, for example, David Cole and James Dempsey, *Terrorism and the Constitution: Sacrificing Civil Liberties in the Name of National Security* (The New Press, 2006), 41–55; Henry Weinstein, "Final Two L.A. 8 Defendants Cleared," *Los Angeles Times*, November 1, 2007.

17. John-Thor Dahlburg, "Line Between Ideas, Aid Is at Issue as Terrorism Trial Begins," *Los Angeles Times*, June 7, 2005; Peter Whoriskey, "Ex-professor Won Court Case but Not His Freedom," *Washington Post*, December 14, 2005.

18. Associated Press, "Agent: Small Amount of Evidence from Search Used Against al-Arian," *Sarasota (FL) Herald Tribune*, June 9, 2005.

19. Susan Aschoff, "Al-Najjar Finally Out After 3 Years," *St. Petersburg (FL) Times*, December 16, 2000; "Statement by Tampa Bay Coalition for Justice and Peace," June 25, 2002, academicfreespeech.com/pr_062502.html; American Association of University Professors, "Academic Freedom and Tenure: University of South Florida,"

Academe, May/June 2003, aaup.org/report/academic-freedom-and-tenure-university-south-florida.

20. Nancy Hollander, "The Holy Land Foundation Case: The Collapse of American Justice," *Washington and Lee Journal of Civil Rights and Social Justice* 20, no. 1 (Fall 2013): 45–61.

21. "No Cash for Terror: Convictions Returned in Holy Land Case," FBI, November 25, 2008, fbi.gov/news/stories/2008/november/hlf112508.

22. FBI Chicago Field Office, request to open subfiles of Operation Vulgar Betrayal, February 26, 1999 (obtained through FOIA, archive.org/details/VulgarBetrayal section 10, 98).

23. FBI Chicago Field Office, memo to Dir. Freeh regarding Operation Vulgar Betrayal, April 29, 1998 (obtained through FOIA, archive.org/details/VulgarBetrayal section 9, 59).

24. FBI Chicago Field Office, requests for surveillance of individuals and organizations as a part of Operation Vulgar Betrayal (obtained through FOIA, archive.org/details/VulgarBetrayal section 7).

25. Steven Emerson, "The Other Fundamentalists," *New Republic*, June 12, 1995.

26. Emerson, "The Other Fundamentalists."

27. Michael E. Deutsch and Erica Thompson, "Secrets and Lies: The Persecution of Muhammad Salah (Part I)," *Journal of Palestine Studies* 37, no. 4 (Summer 2008): 38–58; results of polygraph administered to Muhammad Salah, April 13, 1993 (obtained through FOIA by the Investigative Project, investigativeproject.org/documents/case_docs/317.pdf).

28. Judith Miller, "Israel Says That a Prisoner's Tale Links Arabs in U.S. to Terrorism," *New York Times*, February 17, 1993.

29. Exec. Order No. 12947, 60 Fed. Reg. 95–2040, January 25, 1995.

30. U.S. Dep't of Treasury, Office of Foreign Assets Control, Specially Designated Nationals List, treasury.gov/ofac/downloads/sdnlist.pdf (October 2018).

31. Pub. L. No. 104-132, 110 Stat. 1214 (1996).

32. Holder v. Humanitarian Law Project, 561 U.S. 1, 130 S. Ct. 2705 (2010).

33. Sharon Cohen, "Humanitarian or Terrorist—the Mystery of Muhammad Salah," *Los Angeles Times*, August 16, 1998.

34. Hooper83, "The Strange Case of Sami al-Arian," *National Review*, February 21, 2003.

35. Todd Lighty and Laurie Cohen, "Hamas Probe Nearly Fell Apart," *Chicago Tribune*, August 22, 2004.

36. There have been post-9/11 claims of an al Qaeda link to the Vulgar Betrayal investigation. The case did at one point involve a Saudi philanthropist named Yassin Kadi, who provided a 1991 loan to the Quranic Literacy Institute, where Salah

later worked. In October 2001, the Treasury Department designated Kadi an SDT and froze his U.S. assets, based on suspected links to al Qaeda. Kadi successfully fought related U.N. and European Union sanctions, lawsuits by 9/11 victims, and the U.S. designation. In 2014 the Treasury Department removed Kadi from the SDT list. He was never charged with a crime.

37. Charles Doyle, *Terrorist Material Support: An Overview of 18 U.S.C. §2339A and §2339B*, Congressional Research Service, December 8, 2016.

38. U.S. Dep't of Justice, *The Attorney General's Guidelines on General Crimes, Racketeering Enterprise and Terrorism Enterprise Investigations*, May 30, 2002.

39. Marvin Johnson, "Interested Persons Memo: Analysis of Changes to Attorney General Guidelines," ACLU, June 5, 2002.

40. *U.S. Muslim Charities and the War on Terrorism: A Decade in Review*, Charity and Security Network, December 2011.

41. *Anti-Money Laundering: Blocking Terrorist Financing and Its Impact on Lawful Charities: Hearing Before H. Comm. on Financial Services, Subcomm. on Oversight and Investigations*, 111th Cong. (2010) (written statement of Michael German, ACLU policy counsel).

42. *Blocking Faith, Freezing Charity: Chilling Muslim Charitable Giving in the "War on Terrorism Financing,"* ACLU, June 2009, 60.

43. U.S. v. Holy Land Found., No. 3:04-CR-240-G ECF, 2007 U.S. Dist. LEXIS 51184 (N.D. Tex. July 16, 2007).

44. Peter Erlinder, "Despite Acquittal on Terrorism Charges, No Prospect of Release for Dr. Sami Al-Arian," *Washington Report on Middle East Affairs* (April 2007).

45. Dan Eggen, "Justice Dept. Statistics on Terrorism Faulted," *Washington Post*, February 21, 2007.

46. Michael E. Deutsch and Erica Thompson, "Secrets and Lies: The Persecution of Muhammad Salah (Part II)," *Journal of Palestine Studies* 38, no. 1 (Autumn 2008): 48.

47. Associated Press, "Ex-professor Is Sentenced in a Hamas Case," *New York Times*, November 22, 2007.

48. "Anti-terrorism Designations; Anti-terrorism Designations Removal," U.S. Dep't of Treasury, November 5, 2012, treasury.gov/resource-center/sanctions /OFAC-Enforcement/Pages/20121105.aspx.

49. Meg Laughlin, "In His Plea Deal, What Did Sami al-Arian Admit To?" *Tampa Bay Times*, April 23, 2006.

50. Meg Laughlin, "Judge: Al-Arian Plea Deal Matters," *Tampa Bay Times*, March 6, 2009.

51. John F. Sugg, "Steven Emerson's Crusade," FAIR, January 1999, fair.org/extra /steven-emersons-crusade; "Reply to CAIR's Attack on Daniel Pipes," Daniel Pipes, accessed February 25, 2018, danielpipes.org/cair.php.

52. Jim Naureckas, "The Oklahoma Bombing: The Jihad That Wasn't," FAIR, July 1995.

53. Martha Crenshaw, "The Causes of Terrorism Comparative Politics," *Comparative Politics* 13, no. 4 (July 1981): 379–99.

54. Jerrold Post, "Terrorist Psycho-Logic: Terrorist Behavior as a Product of Psychological Forces," in *Origins of Terrorism: Psychologies, Ideologies, Theologies, States of Mind*, ed. Walter Reich (Woodrow Wilson Center Press, 1990), 25–40.

55. Lisa Stampnitzky, "Disciplining an Unruly Field: Terrorism Experts and Theories of Scientific/Intellectual Production," *Qualitative Sociology* 34 (2011): 1–19.

56. Andrew Silke, "Cheshire-Cat Logic: The Recurring Theme of Terrorist Abnormality in Psychological Research," *Psychology, Crime & Law* 4, no. 1 (January 1998): 51–69.

57. See *Hearing Before H. Comm. on Homeland Security: The Rise of Radicalization: Is the U.S. Government Failing to Counter International and Domestic Terrorism?* (2015) (statement of Farah Pandith, adjunct senior fellow, Council on Foreign Relations); "TSG IntelBrief: Countering Violent Extremism: Challenges and Solutions," Soufan Group, February 19, 2015, soufangroup.com/tsg-intelbrief-countering-violent-extremism-challenges-and-solutions.

58. Bill Braniff, director of the National Consortium for the Study of Terrorism and Responses to Terrorism at the University of Maryland, "Introduction to Radicalization," presentation, scribd.com/document/210226787/understandingterror-Module3-Lecture1.

59. "When applied to Islam and Muslims, the term radical is often being used interchangeably and opaquely with terms such as fundamentalist, Islamist, Jihadist and neo-Salafist or Wahhabist with little regard for what these terms actually mean, and instead indicate signals about political Islam that these members of the media and politicians wish to transmit," Jonathan Githens-Mazer, "Causal Processes, Radicalisation and Bad Policy: The Importance of Case Studies of Radical Violent Takfiri Jihadism for Establishing Logical Causality," ASPA 2009 Toronto meeting paper (2009): 9.

60. Hollander, "The Holy Land Foundation Case."

61. U.S. v. El-Mezain, 664 F.3d 467 (5th Cir. 2011).

62. Indictment, *Holy Land Found.*, 2007 U.S. Dist. LEXIS 51184.

63. Government's Trial Brief at 16, *Holy Land Found.*, 2007 U.S. Dist. LEXIS 51184.

64. Stephen Downs and Kathy Manley, "Why All Americans Should Care About the Holy Land Foundation Case," *Washington Report on Middle East Affairs*, January/February 2013.

65. Hollander, "The Holy Land Foundation Case."

66. Amicus Brief of Charities et al. in Support of Defendants and Urging Reversal of Convictions of Counts 2–10, *El-Mezain*, 664 F.3d 467; Kay Guinane et al.,

Collateral Damage: How the War on Terror Hurts Charities, Foundations, and the People They Serve (OMB Watch, 2008), foreffectivegov.org/sites/default/files/npadv/PDF/collateraldamage.pdf.

67. See ACLU, *Blocking Faith, Freezing Charity.*

68. Attachment A, *Holy Land Found.*, 2007 U.S. Dist. LEXIS 51184.

69. U.S. v. Holy Land Found. for Relief & Dev., 624 F.3d 685, at 688, (5th Cir. 2010).

70. U.S. v. Holy Land Found. for Relief & Dev., No. 3:04-CR-0240-P, 2011 U.S. Dist. LEXIS 46155 (N.D. Tex. Apr. 27, 2011).

71. Josh Gerstein, "Holder: DOJ Nixed CAIR Leader's Prosecution," *Politico*, April 26, 2011.

72. Jason Trahan, "U.S. Attorney in Dallas Says Obama's White House Didn't Meddle in Case," *Dallas Morning News*, April 29, 2011.

73. "About Us: CAIR's Anti-terrorism Campaigns," CAIR, cair.com/cair_s_anti_terrorism_campaigns.

74. Asst. Dir Richard Powers, FBI Office of Congressional Affairs, letter to Sen. Jon Kyl, April 28, 2009.

75. *FBI: Hearing Before the H. Comm. on the Judiciary*, 112th Cong. (2011).

76. Associated Press, "Arrested Americans Came to Pakistan for Jihad, Say Police," *The Guardian*, December 10, 2009.

77. *ACLU Challenges Threat by Government to Designate Charity as "Terrorist,"* ACLU, October 9, 2008.

78. KindHearts for Charitable Humanitarian Dev., Inc. v. Geithner, 710 F. Supp. 2d 637 (N.D. Ohio 2010).

79. FBI, "No Cash for Terror."

80. Scott Wilson, "Hamas Sweeps Palestinian Elections, Complicating Peace Efforts in Mideast," *Washington Post*, January 27, 2006.

81. Tamar Pileggi, "Hamas Military Capabilities Said Restored to Pre-2014 War Strength," *Times of Israel*, January 31, 2017.

82. Yaakov Lappin, "Islamic Jihad Gaining Strength in the West Bank," *Jerusalem Post*, March 23, 2015.

83. Zack Beauchamp, "16 Years After 9/11, Al-Qaeda Is Back," *Vox*, September 11, 2017.

84. Karen Greenberg, ed., *The American Exception: Terrorism Prosecutions in the United States: The ISIS Cases, March 2014–August 2017*, Center on National Security, Fordham University School of Law September 2017, 1, 28.

7. Scapegoating Muslim American Communities

1. FBI Counterterrorism Division, electronic communication to all field offices on Baseline Collection Plan, September 24, 2009 (obtained by ACLU through FOIA, aclu.org/files/fbimappingfoia/20111019/ACLURM004887.pdf).

2. Emily Berman, *Domestic Intelligence: New Powers, New Risks*, Brennan Center for Justice, January 18, 2011, 33.

3. Frank Bures, "Why All Aren't Heeding Call to Quiz Arabs," *Christian Science Monitor*, December 4, 2001.

4. Danny Hakim with Nick Madigan, "A Nation at War: Iraqi-Americans; Immigrants Questioned by F.B.I.," *New York Times*, March 22, 2003.

5. "FBI Question Yemeni Americans over Possible Links with Al-Qaeda," *Yemen Observer*, September 5, 2010; Brian Padden, "FBI Interviews Boston Area Chechens About Bombing Suspects," *VOA News* (Voice of America), April 28, 2013.

6. Diala Shamas, "Where's the Outrage When the FBI Targets Muslims?" *The Nation*, October 31, 2013.

7. Shirin Sinnar, "Questioning Law Enforcement: The First Amendment and Counterterrorism Interviews," *Brooklyn Law Review* 77, no. 1 (2011): 41–66.

8. Brig Barker and Molly Amman, "Counterterrorism Interview and Interrogation Strategies: Understanding and Responding to the Domestic Threat," in *Terrorism and Political Islam: Origins, Ideologies, and Methods*, eds. Erich Marquardt and Christopher Heffelfinger (Combating Terrorism Center, 2008), 377–78.

9. Mazin Sidahmed, "FBI's Pre-election Sweep of Muslim Americans Raises Surveillance Fears," *The Guardian*, January 16, 2017.

10. Brogan v. U.S., 522 U.S. 398, at 408, 118 S. Ct. 805 (1998) (J. Ginsburg, concurring).

11. Matthew Barakat, Associated Press, "Paintballer Sentenced in Terror Case," *Washington Post*, July 24, 2007.

12. *Hearing on the Executive Office for the U.S. Att'ys Before H. Comm. on the Judiciary, Subcomm. on Commercial and Administrative Law*, 110th Cong. (2008) (written statement, Jonathan Turley, GW law professor).

13. See Patsy R. Brumfield, "Indicted FBI Agent: Greenlee Was Out to Get Me," *Daily Journal* (Tupelo, MS), January 29, 2010.

14. Curtis Wilkie, *The Fall of the House of Zeus: The Rise and Ruin of America's Most Powerful Trial Lawyer* (Crown/Archetype, 2011), 154.

15. Patsy R. Brumfield, "Ex-FBI Chief Wants Justice After 'Horror,'" *Daily Journal* (Tupelo, MS), October 27, 2013.

16. *Laptop Searches and Other Violations of Privacy Faced by Americans Returning from Overseas: Hearing Before S. Comm. on the Judiciary, Subcomm. on the Constitution*, 110th Cong. (2008) (written statement of Farhana Khera, president and executive director, Muslim Advocates); Shirin Sinnar and Veena Dubal, *Returning Home: How U.S. Government Practices Undermine Civil Rights at Our Nation's Doorstep*, Asian Law Caucus and Stanford Law School Immigrants' Rights Clinic, April 2009.

17. Jennie Pasquarella, *Muslims Need Not Apply: CARRP*, ACLU of Southern California, August 2013.

18. FBI presentation on "Responding to the Yemeni Threat: Scenarios for CHS Development," (obtained through FOIA by *The Intercept*, theintercept.com/document/2016/09/29/responding-to-the-yemeni-threat-scenarios-for-chs-development).

19. Maggie Astor, "Former F.B.I. Agent Admits He Shared Classified Documents," *New York Times*, April 17, 2018.

20. Rachel Weiner and Ellen Nakashima, "Former FBI Agent Gets Four Years in Prison for Leaking Classified Documents," *New York Times*, October 17, 2018.

21. "FBI Chief: No Racial Targeting with Guidelines," TBO.com, July 28, 2010.

22. Kareem Fahim, "Agent Tied to Informant Testifies in Bomb Plot Case," *New York Times*, August 25, 2010 (quoting FBI agent Robert Fuller).

23. Victoria Kim, "Federal Judge Throws Out Lawsuit over Spying on O.C. Muslims," *Los Angeles Times*, August 15, 2012.

24. Declarations of Craig Monteilh Submitted by Plaintiffs in Support of Their Opposition to Motions to Dismiss at 6, Fazaga v. FBI, 884 F. Supp. 2d 1022 (C.D. Cal. 2012); First Amended Complaint, *Fazaga* 884 F. Supp. 2d 1022, at 1031.

25. Paul Harris, "The Ex-FBI Informant with a Change of Heart: 'There Is No Real Hunt. It's Fixed,'" *The Guardian*, March 20, 2012.

26. Berman, *Domestic Intelligence*.

27. The *New York Times* reported that FBI assessments on potential terrorists or spies led to 1,986 preliminary or full investigations, and FBI assessments on ordinary crime led to 1,329 preliminary or full investigations. Together, assessments led to preliminary or full investigations in 3,315 cases from March 25, 2009 to March 31, 2011. See Charlie Savage, "F.B.I. Focusing on Security over Ordinary Crime," *New York Times*, August 23, 2011.

28. Charlie Savage, "F.B.I. Agents Get Leeway to Push Privacy Bounds," *New York Times*, June 12, 2011.

29. *Unleased and Unaccountable: The FBI's Unchecked Abuse of Authority*, ACLU, September 2013, 46–48.

30. ACLU, *Unleased and Unaccountable*, 46–47; Adam Goldman, "U.S. to Inform Americans Whether They Are on 'No-Fly' List, and Possibly Why," *Washington Post*, April 14, 2015.

31. "ACLU Eye on the FBI Alert: Community Outreach as Intelligence Gathering," ACLU, December 1, 2011.

32. "ACLU Eye on the FBI Alert: Mosque Outreach for Intelligence Gathering," ACLU, March 27, 2012.

33. "Don't Be a Puppet: Pull Back the Curtain on Extremism," FBI, cve.fbi.gov; FBI Office of Partner Engagement, "Preventing Violent Extremism in Schools," report, January 2016.

34. Michael German, "Is Your Kid a Threat? The Feds Want to Know," *USA Today*, June 17, 2016.

35. Kristin McCarthy, "Is the FBI's Flawed Terrorist Intervention Program Really Cancelled? There's Reason to Believe 'Shared Responsibility Committees' Are Still Alive," Arab American Institute, November 3, 2016.

36. Eric Lichtblau, "How an American Ended Up Accused of Aiding ISIS with Gift Cards," *New York Times*, January 28, 2017.

37. Adam Goldman et al., "Behind the Sudden Death of a $1 Billion CIA Secret War in Syria," *New York Times*, August 2, 2017.

38. *Weapons of the Islamic State: A Three-Year Investigation in Iraq and Syria*, Conflict Armament Research, December 2017; Bethan McKernan, "US and Saudi Arabia Arms Significantly Enhanced Isis' Military Capabilities, Report Reveals," *The Independent*, December 15, 2017.

39. Beau Hodai, "Arizona's Manufactured Terrorism Threat," *The Progressive*, May 23, 2017.

40. U.S. v. Cromitie, 727 F.3d 194, at 221 (2nd Cir. 2013).

41. Motion to Vacate Sentence/Conviction Pursuant to 28 U.S.C. § 2255, U.S. v. Aref, No. 04-CR-402, U.S. Dist. LEXIS 12228 (N.D.N.Y. 2007); Christopher S. Stewart "'Little Gitmo,'" *New York*, July 10, 2011.

42. Transcript, U.S. v. Cromitie, 781 F. Supp. 2d 211 (S.D.N.Y. 2011).

43. U.S. v. Cromitie, 727 F.3d 194, at 219 (2nd Cir. 2013).

44. Kim Murphy, "Mosque Firebomb Suspect in Oregon Called Self 'Christian Warrior,'" *Los Angeles Times*, August 26, 2011.

45. Burhan Mohumed, interview with author, October 22, 2016.

46. Mohumed, interview with author.

47. Jeremy Scahill, "Blowback in Somalia," *The Nation*, September 7, 2011; Mark Mazzetti, "Efforts by C.I.A. Fail in Somalia, Officials Charge," *New York Times*, June 8, 2006.

48. *Hearing Before H. Comm. on Homeland Security on the American Muslim Response to Hearings on Radicalization Within Their Community*, 112th Cong. (2012) (written statement of CAIR).

49. Laura Yuen and Sasha Aslanian, "Minnesota Pipeline to al-Shabab," *MPR News* (Minnesota Public Radio), September 25, 2013.

50. Yuen and Aslanian, "Minnesota Pipeline to al-Shabab."

51. Jeanine de Roy van Zuijdewijn and Edwin Bakker, *Returning Western Foreign Fighters: The Case of Afghanistan, Bosnia and Somalia*, International Centre for Counter-Terrorism—the Hague, June 2014; Jeanine de Roy van Zuidewijin, "The Foreign Fighters Threat: What History Can (Not) Tell Us," *Perspectives on Terrorism* 8, no. 5 (2018).

52. Sharon Schmickle, "Sudden Notoriety: Mosque in Minneapolis Draws Scrutiny from U.S. Senate, FBI and International Media," *MinnPost*, March 20, 2009; Laura Yuen, "Minneapolis Imam Pleased to Be Off No-Fly List," *MPR News* (Minnesota Public Radio), November 11, 2009.

53. Cawo Abdi, "Disclaimed or Reclaimed? Muslim Refugee Youth and Belonging in the Age of Hyperbolisation," *Journal of Intercultural Studies* 36, no. 5 (September 2015): 564–78.

54. Michael Price, "Community Outreach or Intelligence Gathering? A Closer Look at 'Countering Violent Extremism' Programs," Brennan Center for Justice, January 21, 2015; "FBI Reaching Out to Minneapolis Somali Community," *VOA News* (Voice of America), November 2, 2009.

55. FBI, memo to all field offices on "Implementation of Specialized Community Outreach Team (SCOT)," January 7, 2009 (document obtained by the Brennan Center through FOIA, bit.ly/1yrQGae); Price, "Community Outreach or Intelligence Gathering?"

56. Price, "Community Outreach or Intelligence Gathering?" 7n76.

57. Price, "Community Outreach or Intelligence Gathering?"; FBI, "Community Outreach in Field Offices Corporate Policy Directive and Policy Implementation Guide," March 2013, https://www.brennancenter.org/sites/default/files/blog/FBI%202013%20Community%20Outreach%20Guidelines%20combined%20w.o%20redactions.pdf.

58. Ibrahim Hirsi, "The Complicated Reality Behind the Story of the Somali Community's Success in Minnesota," *MinnPost*, August 14, 2017; Eric Boehm, "The War on Terror Is a War on Minnesota's Peaceful, Entrepreneurial Somali Immigrants," *Reason*, January 3, 2018.

59. U.S. Dep't. of Justice, *Attorney General Holder Announces Pilot Program to Counter Violent Extremists*, September 15, 2014.

60. U.S. Att'y of Minneapolis, *Building Community Resilience, Minneapolis–St. Paul Pilot Program: A Community-Led Framework*, February 2015.

61. U.K. House of Commons, Communities and Local Government Committee, *Preventing Violent Extremism*, Sixth Report of Session 2009–10, March 16, 2010, 3.

62. C-Me, Not CVE Facebook page, facebook.com/C-ME-NOT-CVE-1578109782488738.

63. Jalal Baig et al., "We Live in the Muslim Neighborhoods Cruz Wants to 'Patrol and Secure.' This Is What It's Really Like," *The Guardian*, March 28, 2016.

64. Joseph Sabroski, "Video of FBI Visit of Muslim Activist Highlights Disturbing Nature of Federal Counter-extremism Programs," *AlterNet*, August 28, 2016.

65. Joseph Sabroski, "How Somali Americans Struggle with Warrantless FBI Visits," *TRT World*, May 30, 2018.

66. Katayoun Kishi, "Assaults Against Muslims in U.S. Surpass 2001 Level," Pew Research Center, November 15, 2017.

67. Arun Kundnani, *Blind Spot? Security Narratives and Far-Right Violence in Europe*, International Centre for Counter-Terrorism—the Hague, June 2012.

68. Scott Shane, "Killings in Norway Spotlight Anti-Muslim Thought in U.S.," *New York Times*, July 24, 2011.

8. Criminalizing Black Identity

1. Dir. Comey, news conference at FBI field office in Newark, New Jersey, November 17, 2014 (quoted in Jonathan Dienst, "Hatchet Attack on NYPD Officers Was 'Act of Terror': FBI Director," NBC New York, November 17, 2014).

2. Richard Esposito and Jonathan Dienst, "Hatchet Attack Was Terrorist Act, Say Police," NBC News, October 24, 2014.

3. Andrew Husband, "FBI Director Says Charleston Shooting Not Terrorism," *Mediaite*, June 20, 2015.

4. 18 U.S.C.S. § 2331.

5. CNN Wire, "Survivor Says Charleston Shooter Spared Her to 'Tell Everyone' What Happened," WHNT.com, June 18, 2015.

6. Ryan J. Reilly, "FBI Director Still Unsure If White Supremacist's Charleston Attack Was Terrorism," *Huffington Post*, July 9, 2015.

7. Kevin Fasick et al., "Ax Attacker Wanted 'White People to Pay' for Slavery," *New York Post*, October 25, 2014.

8. Dir. Comey, news conference, November 17, 2014.

9. NYPD, "Preliminary Investigation Findings from 'Lone Wolf' Terror Attack on NYPD Officers as Police Officer Attacked with Ax in Washington, DC," intelligence assessment, June 5, 2015.

10. Jonathan Dienst, "Bratton: Hatchet Attack on Cops Was Lone Wolf 'Act of Terror,'" NBC News New York, October 24, 2014.

11. "ISIL and Its Supporters Encouraging Attacks Against Law Enforcement and Gov't Personnel," FBI and DHS joint intelligence bulletin, IA-0017-15, October 11, 2014.

12. FBI, "Black Identity Extremists Likely Motivated to Target Law Enforcement Officers," intelligence assessment, August 3, 2017 (quoted in Jana Winter and Sharon Weinberger, "The FBI's New U.S. Terrorist Threat: 'Black Identity Extremists,'" *Foreign Policy*, October 6, 2017).

13. FBI, "Black Identity Extremists Likely Motivated to Target Law Enforcement Officers."

14. John Paul Wilson et al., "Racial Bias in Judgments of Physical Size and Formidability: From Size to Threat," *Journal of Personality and Social Psychology* 113, no. 1 (July 2017): 59–80.

15. Jerry Kang et al., "Implicit Bias in the Courtroom," *UCLA Law* Review 59, no. 5 (June 2012): 1124–86; Michael Selmi, "The Paradox of Implicit Bias and a Plea for a New Narrative," GWU Law School Public Law Research Paper No. 2017-63 (2017), scholarship.law.gwu.edu/faculty_publications/1303.

16. H. Jon Rosenbaum and Peter C. Sederberg, "Vigilantism: An Analysis of Establishment Violence," *Comparative Politics* 6, no. 4 (July 1974): 541–70.

17. Att'y Gen. Alberto Gonzalez, press conference, June 23, 2006.

18. Dir. Mueller, speech at the City Club of Cleveland, Cleveland, Ohio, June 23, 2006.

19. Dir. Mueller, speech at the City Club of Cleveland.

20. Scott Shane and Lowell Bergman, "F.B.I. Struggling to Reinvent Itself to Fight Terror," *New York Times*, October 10, 2006.

21. Jeff Stein, "FBI Hoped to Follow Falafel Trail to Iranian Terrorists Here," *Congressional Quarterly*, November 6, 2007.

22. "FBI Response to Congressional Quarterly Article Alleging Willie T. Hulon and Phil Mudd's Involvement in So-Called 'Falafel Investigation,'" FBI news release, November 26, 2007.

23. FBI, Domestic Investigations and Operations Guide (DIOG), December 16, 2008, 33..

24. FBI Atlanta Field Office, "Intelligence Note from Domain Management: Intelligence Related to the Black Separatist Threat," October 7, 2009 (obtained through FOIA by ACLU, aclu.org/files/fbimappingfoia/20111019/ACLURM011454.pdf).

25. Associated Press, "Cameraman, Legislator's Guard Scuffle After Ga. Vote," *Washington Post*, August 11, 2006.

26. FBI, *Terrorism: 2002–2005*, fbi.gov/stats-services/publications/terrorism-2002-2005.

27. FBI training presentation on "Black Separatist Extremists," 6 (obtained through FOIA by ACLU, aclu.org/files/fbimappingfoia/20120518/ACLURM026634.pdf).

28. Second FBI training presentation on "Black Separatist Extremists," 2 (obtained through FOIA by ACLU, aclu.org/files/fbimappingfoia/20120518/ACLURM026655.pdf#page=2).

29. FBI training presentation on "Black Separatist Extremists," 13, 16 (obtained through FOIA by ACLU, aclu.org/files/fbimappingfoia/20120518/ACLURM026634.pdf).

30. FBI training presentation on "American Islamic Extremists" (obtained through FOIA by ACLU, aclu.org/files/fbimappingfoia/20120518/ACLURM026662.pdf).

31. "Demographic Portrait of Muslim Americans," Pew Research Center, July 26, 2017; Emma Green, "Muslim Americans Are United by Trump—and Divided by Race," *The Atlantic*, March 11, 2017.

32. Complaint, U.S. v. Abdullah, No. 2:09-mj-30436 (E.D. Mich. 2009).

33. Hamdan Azhar, "Death of a Detroit Imam Leaves Many Questions Unanswered," *Huffington Post*, March 18, 2010.

34. Mike Cox, Att'y Gen. of Michigan, *Report on the FBI Fatal Shooting of Luqman Ameen Abdullah*, September 30, 2010, 2.

35. "Justice Department Concludes No Federal Criminal Violation in the Death of Imam Abdullah in Dearborn," U.S. Dep't of Justice news release, October 13, 2010.

36. Att'y Gen. Cox, *Report on the FBI Fatal Shooting of Luqman Ameen* Abdullah; Azhar, "Death of a Detroit Imam."

37. FBI, "Black Identity Extremists Likely Motivated to Target Law Enforcement Officers."

38. FBI, "Black Identity Extremists Likely Motivated to Target Law Enforcement Officers," 2.

39. Cong. Black Caucus, letter to Dir. Christopher Wray, FBI, on the "Black Identity Extremists" intelligence assessment, October 13, 2017.

40. Sam Levin, "Black Activist Jailed for His Facebook Posts Speaks Out About Secret FBI Surveillance," *The Guardian*, May 11, 2018.

41. U.S. Dep't of Justice, Civil Rights Division, *Guidance Regarding the Use of Race by Federal Law Enforcement Agencies*, June 2003.

42. FBI, Oakland Resident Agency electronic communication to San Francisco, "Domain Management—Criminal, Eurasian Organized Crime," June 8, 2009 (obtained through FOIA by ACLU, aclu.org/files/fbimappingfoia/20111019/ACLURM011495.pdf).

43. FBI Newark Field Office, "Intelligence Note from Domain Management, Intelligence Related to MS-13 Locations," September 22, 2008 (obtained through FOIA by ACLU, aclu.org/files/fbimappingfoia/20111019/ACLURM008040.pdf).

44. Sari Horwitz and Jerry Markon, "New Ban on Racial Profiling to Exempt TSA, Customs and Border Agents," *Chicago Tribune*, December 6, 2014.

45. Timothy M. Phelps, "Comey Says New Profiling Guidelines Will Have No Effect on the FBI," *Los Angeles Times*, December 9, 2014.

46. Lee Fang, "Why Was an FBI Joint Terrorism Task Force Tracking a Black Lives Matter Protest?" *The Intercept*, March 12, 2015.

47. George Joseph, "Exclusive: Feds Regularly Monitored Black Lives Matter Since Ferguson," *The Intercept*, July 24, 2015.

48. "28 April 2015 Demonstration Could Impact Public Safety in Washington, DC," FBI/Washington Area Threat Analysis Center joint intelligence bulletin, April 28, 2015 (obtained through FOIA by *The Intercept*, documentcloud.org/documents/2178938-6-2015-4-28-pre-dc-protest-justification.html).

49. Dustin Volz, "FBI Spy Planes Flew 10 Times over Freddie Gray Protests: Documents," Reuters, October 30, 2015.

50. *Oversight of the FBI: Hearing Before the H. Comm. on the Judiciary*, 114th Cong. (2015) (statement of Dir. Comey).

51. Emails between FBI intelligence officials on the subject of "Language from the OGC Ref Collecting Info Touching on Protests," July 8, 2016 (obtained through FOIA by *Al Jazeera*, aljazeera.com/mritems/Documents/2017/11/28/81a951f0088c4bda9a34d6f3239e947c_100.pdf).

52. Emails between Dallas Police Department and FBI, July 8, 2016 (obtained through FOIA by *Al Jazeera*, aljazeera.com/mritems/Documents/2017/11/28/69da06c8c3294bddbc71e907db27264e_100.pdf).

53. Feliks Garcia, "Black Lives Matter Activists Say FBI Told Them Not to Protest GOP Convention," *The Independent*, July 14, 2016; Brandon Patterson, "Are Police Targeting Black Lives Matters Activists Ahead of the GOP Convention?" *Mother Jones*, June 30, 2016; Mary Jordan and Wesley Lowery, "Empty Cells and Hotels: Cleveland Takes Stock Before the Convention Comes to Town," *Washington Post*, July 13, 2016.

54. Dir. Comey, speech at the International Association of Chiefs of Police Annual Conference in San Diego, California, October 16, 2016.

55. Dara Lind, "The FBI Is Trying to Get Better Data on Police Killings. Here's What We Know Now," *Vox*, April 10, 2015.

56. James W. Buehler, "Racial/Ethnic Disparities in the Use of Lethal Force by US Police, 2010–2014," *American Journal of Public Health* 107, no. 2 (February 1, 2017): 295–97.

57. Jon Swaine and Ciara McCarthy, "Young Black Men Again Faced Highest Rate of US Police Killings in 2016," *The Guardian*, January 8, 2017.

58. Geoff Alpert et al., "A Bird's Eye View of Civilians Killed by Police in 2015: Further Evidence of Implicit Bias," *Criminology and Public Policy* 16, no. 1 (2017): 309–40..

59. "Shot by Cops and Forgotten," *Vice News*, December 11, 2017.

60. FBI, "Black Identity Extremists Likely Motivated to Target Law Enforcement Officers."

61. "Resources," Law Enforcement Officers Killed and Assaulted Program (LEOKA), FBI Uniform Crime Reporting, ucr.fbi.gov/leoka-resources.

62. Christal Hayes, "Number of Officers Killed Hits 2nd-Lowest in More Than 50 Years," *USA Today*, December 28, 2017.

63. Kate Irby, "White and Far-Right Extremists Kill More Cops, but FBI Tracks Black Extremists More Closely, Many Worry," McClatchy (DC), January 25, 2018.

64. Associated Press, "U.S. to Fight Vote Fraud on Nov. 6," *Arizona Republic*, September 28, 1984.

65. George Derek Musgrove, *Rumor, Repression, and Racial Politics: How the Harassment of Black Elected Officials Shaped Post–Civil Rights America* (University of Georgia Press, 2012), 153–55.

66. Allen Tullos, "Crackdown in the Black Belt," *Southern Changes* 7, no. 1 (March/April 1985): 1–5.

67. Tullos, "Crackdown in the Black Belt."

68. Musgrove, *Rumor, Repression, and Racial Politics*, 112–44.

69. Gwen Ifill, "Black Officials Probes and Prejudice," *Washington Post*, February 28, 1988.

70. Musgrove, *Rumor, Repression, and Racial Politics*, 118, 144.

71. Sanford C. Gordon, "Assessing Partisan Bias in Federal Public Corruption Prosecutions," *American Political Science Review* 103, no. 4 (November 2009): 542.

72. Allan Lengel, "FBI Says Jefferson Was Filmed Taking Cash," *Washington Post*, May 22, 2006.

73. Derek Hawkins, "Twice Robert Mueller Threatened to Resign from the FBI. Twice He Decided Not To," *Washington Post*, May 18, 2017.

74. Allan Lengel, "Rep. Jefferson Wins Ruling Against FBI," *Washington Post*, August 4, 2007.

75. Mike McKinney, interview with author, January 23, 2018.

76. Email from Mike McKinney to James Comey, August 25, 2014.

77. McKinney, interview with author.

9. Targeting Innocent "Others"

1. Alison Frankel, "The Deception of Denise Woo," *American Lawyer*, June 2006.

2. David Wise, *Tiger Trap: America's Secret Spy War with China* (Houghton Mifflin Harcourt, 2011), 121–33.

3. Frankel, "The Deception of Denise Woo."

4. Ron Gluckman, "The Spy of the Century?" *Asiaweek*, April 21, 2000 (quoted in Spencer Turnbull, "Wen Ho Lee and the Consequences of Enduring Asian American Stereotypes," *Asian Pacific American Law Journal* 7 [2001]: 76).

5. Declaration of Robert Vrooman, U.S. v. Wen Ho Lee, No. 00-2002, 2000 U.S. App. LEXIS, 3082 (10th Cir. Feb. 29, 2000).

6. "Interaction with the Opposite Sex" in FBI presentation on "The Chinese: Cross Cultural Considerations," slide 12, (obtained through FOIA by ACLU, aclu.org/files/fbimappingfoia/20120518/ACLURM032381.pdf#page=12); FBI Academy, Behavioral Science Unit "Principles of Cultural Awareness in Operations," slide 24 (obtained through FOIA by ACLU, aclu.org/files/fbimappingfoia/20120518/ACLURM036861.pdf).

7. Matt Krasnowski, "Probation for Former FBI Agent Is 'Bittersweet Ending' to Trial," *San Diego Union Tribune*, November 5, 2006.

8. Wise, *Tiger Trap*, 128.

9. U.S. Dep't of Justice Inspector Gen., *Review of the FBI's Handling and Oversight of FBI Asset Katrina Leung* (2006), 16-18.

10. Greg Krikorian, "Ex-FBI Agent Is Sentenced in Plea Agreement," *Los Angeles Times*, October 31, 2006 (quoting Jeffrey Wang).

11. J.K. Wall and Indianapolis Business Journal Staff, "Feds Drop Case Against Former Eli Lilly Scientists Accused of Stealing Secrets," *Indiana Lawyer*, December 5, 2014.

12. Nicole Perlroth, "Accused of Spying for China, Until She Wasn't," *New York Times*, May 9, 2015.

13. Matt Apuzzo, "U.S. Drops Charges That Professor Shared Technology with China," *New York Times*, September 11, 2015.

14. Joyce Xi, interview with author, December 22, 2016.

15. Indictment, U.S. v. Xi, No. 2:15-cr-00204-RBS-1 (E.D. Pa. May 14, 2015).

16. Second Amended Complaint, Xi v. U.S., No. 17-cv-2132 (E.D. Pa. Oct 14, 2015).

17. Second Amended Complaint, *Xi*, E.D. Pa. No. 17-cv-2132.

18. Xi, interview with author.

19. *Worldwide Threats: Hearing Before S. Select Comm. on Intelligence*, 115th Cong. (2018) (testimony of Dir. Wray); Betsy Woodruff and Julia Arciga, "FBI Director's Shock Claim: Chinese Students Are a Potential Threat," *Daily Beast*, February 13, 2018.

20. *Worldwide Threats* (testimony of Dir. Wray).

21. Rachelle Peterson, *Outsourced to China: Confucius Institutes and Soft Power in American Higher Education*, National Association of Scholars (2017).

22. "CAPAC Members on Rubio and Wray's Remarks Singling Out Chinese Students as National Security Threats," Congressional Asian Pacific American Caucus, news release, February 15, 2018.

23. Dir. Comey, speech at FBI/BCRI Annual Conference on Civil Rights, May 25, 2016.

24. Sam Levin, "Guards for North Dakota Pipeline Could Be Charged for Using Dogs on Activists," *The Guardian*, October 26, 2016.

25. Sam Levin, "Dakota Access Pipeline Protests: UN Group Investigates Human Rights Abuses," *The Guardian*, October 31, 2016; Declaration of Thomas C. Frazier, Dundon v. Kirchmeier, No. 1:16-cv-00406-DLH-CSM (D.N.D. 2017); Alleen Brown, "Arrests of Journalists at Standing Rock Test the Boundaries of the First Amendment," *The Intercept*, November 27, 2016.

26. "ND State Criminal Cases," Water Protector Legal Collective, February 16, 2018, waterprotectorlegal.org/nd-state-criminal-defense.

27. "Native Americans Facing Excessive Force in North Dakota Pipeline Protests—UN Expert," United Nations Human Rights Office of the High Commissioner, news release, November 15, 2016.

28. Associated Press, "FBI Surprise on Top Domestic Terror Threat," NBC News, May 19, 2005. Some consider Theodore Kaczynski, the Unabomber, an environmental anarchist and would credit the three people he killed as victims of eco-terrorism. These would be the only three victims. But five psychiatrists diagnosed Kaczynski with paranoid schizophrenia, and labeling his acts as part of any cognizable domestic terrorism movement is difficult.

29. "Hate Crime Statistics 2016," FBI Uniform Crime Reporting, ucr.fbi.gov/hate-crime/2016/topic-pages/victims.

30. "About Underlying Cause of Death 1999–2016," Centers for Disease Control and Prevention, wonder.cdc.gov/ucd-icd10.html; Elise Hansen, "The Forgotten Minority in Police Shootings," CNN, November 13, 2017.

31. Andrew H. Malcolm, "Occupation of Wounded Knee Is Ended," *New York Times*, May 9, 1973; Martin Waldron, "U.S. Marshal Shot at Wounded Knee," *New York Times*, March 27, 1973.

32. Grace Lichtenstein, "16 Sioux Sought by the F.B.I. in the Slaying of 2 Agents," *New York Times*, June 28, 1975.

33. Richard A. Serrano, "Pine Ridge Indian Homicide Cases Get New Scrutiny," *Los Angeles Times*, August 8, 2012.

34. Adrian Jawort, "'Just Another Dead Indian': Steven Bearcrane-Cole Case Has One More Chance," *Indian Country Today*, February 7, 2017.

35. Jeff DeLong, "American Indians Questioned About Nevada Bear Hunt by FBI," *Reno Gazette-Journal*, April 11, 2012.

36. Alleen Brown et al., "Leaked Documents Reveal Counterterrorism Tactics Used at Standing Rock to 'Defeat Pipeline Insurgencies,'" *The Intercept*, May 27, 2017.

37. Complaint and Request for Injunction, N.D. Private Investigative Security Board v. TigerSwan, No. 08-2017-CV-01873 (D.N.D. 2017).

38. "Internal TigerSwan Situation Report" September 22, 2016, 2-3 (obtained by *The Intercept*), theintercept.com/document/2017/05/27/internal-tigerswan-situation-report-2016-09-22.

39. Will Parrish, "An Activist Stands Accused of Firing a Gun at Standing Rock. It Belonged to Her Lover—an FBI Informant," *The Intercept*, December 11, 2017.

40. Brown et al., "Leaked Documents Reveal Counterterrorism Tactics Used at Standing Rock."

41. Parrish, "An Activist Stands Accused of Firing a Gun at Standing Rock."

42. C.S. Hagen, "Stonewalled by Federal Court, Red Fawn Fallis Changes Plea," *High Plains Reader* (Fargo, ND), January 16, 2018.

43. Sam Levin, "Revealed: FBI Terrorism Taskforce Investigating Standing Rock Activists," *The Guardian*, February 10, 2017; C.S. Hagen, "FBI Joint Terrorism Task Force Targets Standing Rock Activist," *High Plains Reader* (Fargo, ND), March 23, 2017.

44. Stephen Montemayor, "Dakota Access Pipeline Protester Injured in Blast Sues Government for Return of Evidence," *Star Tribune* (Minneapolis), February 5, 2018.

45. Melkorka Licea, "Pipeline Protester Speaks Out for First Time After Nearly Losing Her Arm," *New York Post*, November 18, 2017.

46. Sen. Al Franken, letter to Dir. Comey, March 1, 2017.

47. "Arrestee Updates," Water Protector Legal Collective, waterprotectorlegal.org/arrestee-updates; Zoë Carpenter and Tracie Williams, "PHOTOS: Since Standing Rock, 56 Bills Have Been Introduced in 30 States to Restrict Protests," *Nation*, February 16, 2018.

48. Michael Edison Hayden, "'Antifa' Sympathizers Being Investigated by FBI, Director Tells Lawmakers," *Newsweek*, December 1, 2017.

49. Eric Lichtblau, "FBI Goes Knocking for Political Troublemakers," *New York Times*, August 16, 2004.

50. U.S. Dep't of Justice Inspector Gen., *A Review of the FBI's Investigative Activities Concerning Potential Protesters at the 2004 Democratic and Republican National Political Conventions* (2006).

51. FBI Los Angeles Field Office, summary of National Missile Defense Initiative case, May 22, 2001 (obtained through FOIA by ACLU, aclu.org/sites/default/files/spyfiles/jttf/672_674.pdf); "FBI/JTTF SPYING," ACLU, aclu.org/other/fbi-jttf-spying.

52. United States' Motion in Limine to Preclude an Entrapment Defense, U.S. v. McDavid, No. 2:06-cr-00035-MCE, 2008 WL 850307 (E.D. Cal. March 28, 2008).

53. Defendant's Supplemental Memorandum in Support and Related Motion for Discovery, *McDavid*, E.D. Cal. No. 2:06-cr-00035-MCE.

54. Trevor Aaronson and Katie Galloway, "Manufacturing Terror: An FBI Informant Seduced Eric McDavid into a Bomb Plot. Then the Government Lied About It," *The Intercept*, November 19, 2015.

55. Casey McNerthney, "May Day Protests Turn Violent in Downtown Seattle," *Seattle Post-Intelligencer*, May 2, 2012.

56. Will Potter, "FBI Agents Raid Homes in Search of 'Anarchist Literature,'" Green Is the New Red, July 30, 2012, greenisthenewred.com/blog/fbi-raid-anarchist-literature-portland-seattle/6267.

57. Rose Lichter-Marck, "Leah-Lynn Plante and Portland's Anarchist Grand Jury Resistors," *VICE*, November 3, 2012; Alexa Vaughn, "Pair Jailed over May Day in '12 Steer Clear—Again," *Seattle Times*, May 1, 2013.

58. *In re* Olejnik and Duran, No. 12-GJ-145 and No. 12-GJ-149 (W.D. Wa. Feb. 27, 2013); Motion for Termination of Order, *In re* Duran, 12-GJ-149 W.D. Wa.

59. Brendan Kiley, "Christmas in Prison," *The Stranger*, December 19, 2012.

60. Mike Carter and Maureen O'Hagan, "Affidavit: Feds Trailed Portland Anarchists, Link Them to Seattle's May Day," *Seattle Times*, October 20, 2012.

61. Brendan Kiley, "You Know a May Day Protest Was Successful When . . ." *The Stranger*, May 1, 2013.

62. Levi Pulkkinen, "May Day Vandal Sentenced," *Seattle Post-Intelligencer*, June 13, 2012.

63. DIOG §§ 4.1.2, 4.2 (2013); *Att'y Gen.'s Guidelines*, 13.

64. FBI training presentation on "Anarchist Extremist Tactics," slides 6–7 (obtained through FOIA by ACLU, aclu.org/files/fbimappingfoia/20120518/ACLURM026485.pdf#page=6).

65. FBI training presentation on "Animal Rights/Environmental Extremism," slides 4, 7 (obtained through FOIA by ACLU, aclu.org/files/fbimappingfoia/20120518/ACLURM026701.pdf).

66. Eric Garris, interview with author, January 21, 2017.

67. Justin Raimondo, "Behind the Headlines," Antiwar.com, November 29, 1999, antiwar.com/justin/j112999.html.

68. Glenn Kessler, "Trump's Outrageous Claim That 'Thousands' of New Jersey Muslims Celebrated the 9/11 Attacks," *Washington Post*, November 22, 2015.

69. "Dancing Israelis Police and FBI Reports 9/11/01," Archive.org, archive.org/details/DancingIsraelisFBIReport.

70. "Dancing Israelis Police and FBI Reports 9/11/01," archive.org/stream/DancingIsraelisFBIReport/fbi%20report%20section%206#page/n51/mode/1up, Section 6, 52.

71. FBI records on Antiwar.com, Justin Raimondo, and Eric Garris (obtained through FOIA by ACLU, aclunc.org/sites/default/files/fist_interim_release.pdf), 17–38; Raimondo et al. v. FBI, No. 13-cv-02295-JSC, 2016 U.S. Dist. LEXIS 61958 (N.D. Cal. May 10, 2016).

72. FBI records on Antiwar.com, Justin Raimondo, and Eric Garris, 26.

73. FBI records on Antiwar.com, Justin Raimondo, and Eric Garris, 50.

74. FBI records on Antiwar.com, Justin Raimondo, and Eric Garris, 19.

75. Garris interview with author.

76. Garris interview with author.

77. Helen Christophi, "FBI Agrees to Give Records to Anti-war Reporters," Courthouse News Service, April 17, 2017.

78. Garris interview with author.

79. Spencer Ackerman, "FBI Monitored Anti-war Website in Error for Six Years, Documents Show," *The Guardian*, November 6, 2013.

80. "Decisive Ecological Warfare," Deep Green Resistance, deepgreenresistance.org/en/deep-green-resistance-strategy/decisive-ecological-warfare#four-phases.

81. Deep Green Resistance, "Decisive Ecological Warfare."

82. FBI electronic communication about arrests in Bellingham, Washington, March 22, 2013 (obtained by *The Guardian* through FOIA).

83. Joe Duggan, "Protesters File Complaint over Beer Sales to Native Americans in Whiteclay," *Omaha World-Herald*, May 24, 2013; FBI Seattle Field Office, FD-1057, December 12, 2013; FBI summary of investigative activities relating to Deep Green Resistance: protest/vandalism by Pine Ridge Indian Reservation subjects at Whiteclay, Nebraska, May 6, 2013 (obtained by the *Guardian* through FOIA).

84. FBI Seattle Field Office electronic communication about Deep Green Resistance, November 22, 2013 (obtained by *The Guardian* through FOIA).

85. FBI FD-302 documenting special agent and task force officer meeting with sergeant of University of Washington Police Department, January 16, 2014 (obtained by *The Guardian* through FOIA); FBI FD-1057 on Deep Green Resistance at the University of Washington, Seattle, February 4, 2014 (obtained by *The Guardian* through FOIA).

86. FBI Seattle Field Office electronic communication requesting assistance conducting interviews with members of Deep Green Resistance, September 23, 2014 (obtained by *The Guardian* through FOIA).

87. Adam Federman, "Lawyer for Environmental Group 'Interrogated Repeatedly' at US Border," *The Guardian*, July 6, 2015.

88. FBI, Domestic Investigations and Operations Guide (DIOG), October 15, 2011, 5–32.

89. Adam Federman, "Environmental Activists Continue to Face Interrogations at U.S.-Canada border," *Earth Island Journal*, September 20, 2015.

90. FBI, "FY 2015 Report on Selected Results" (quoted in Jenna McLaughlin, "FBI Won't Explain Its Bizarre New Way of Measuring Its Success Fighting Terror," *The Intercept*, February 18, 2016).

10. The Watchdog That Didn't Bark—Ignoring Executive Abuse

1. Donald J. Trump (@realdonaldtrump), "THE SYSTEM IS RIGGED!" Twitter, July 3, 2016, 2:00 p.m., twitter.com/realdonaldtrump/status/749709462974435329?lang=en.

2. "Americans' Confidence in Institutions Stays Low," Gallup, June 13, 2016.

3. "Public Trust in Government Remains Near Historic Lows as Partisan Attitudes Shift," Pew Research Center, May 3, 2017.

4. Gallup, "Americans' Confidence in Institutions Stays Low."

5. Victor Marchetti and John D. Marks, *The CIA and the Cult of Intelligence* (Knopf, 1974).

6. Richard P. Conti, "The Psychology of False Confessions," *Journal of Credibility Assessment and Witness Psychology* 2, no. 1 (1999): 14–36; Brown v. Mississippi, 297 U.S. 278, 56 S. Ct. 461 (1936).

7. Nathan Vardi, "The Money Behind the CIA's Torture Program," *Forbes*, December 9, 2014.

8. Philippe Sands, "The Green Light," *Vanity Fair*, May 2008.

9. Michael German, "U.S. Torture: A Catastrophic Intelligence Failure on Every Level," *Defense One*, December 11, 2014.

10. S. Select Comm. on Intelligence, *Comm. Study of the Central Intelligence Agency's Detention and Interrogation Program: Findings and Executive Summary* (2012) (released by the Comm. on December 9, 2014).

11. Massoud Ansari, "Daniel Pearl 'Refused to Be Sedated Before His Throat Was Cut,'" *The Telegraph*, May 9, 2004; Brian Whitaker and Luke Harding, "American Beheaded in Revenge for Torture," *The Guardian*, May 12, 2004.

12. S. Select Comm. on Intelligence, *Comm. Study of the CIA's Detention and Interrogation Program.*

13. Richard Willing, "The Right to Remain Silent, Brought You by J. Edgar Hoover and the FBI," *Washington Post*, June 10, 2016.

14. Miranda v. Arizona, 384 U.S. 436, 86 S. Ct. 1602 (1966).

15. Richard A. Leo, "False Confessions: Causes, Consequences, and Implications," *Journal of the American Academy of Psychiatry and the Law* 37, no. 3 (September 2009): 332–43; Mark Blagrove, "Effects of Length of Sleep Deprivation on Interrogative Suggestibility," *Journal of Experimental Psychology: Applied* 2, no. 1 (March 1996): 48–59; Conti, "The Psychology of False Confessions."

16. Ruth Blakeley, "Why Torture?" *Review of International Studies* 33, no. 3 (July 2007): 373–94.

17. Ali H. Soufan with Daniel Freedman, *The Black Banners: The Inside Story of 9/11 and the War Against al-Qaeda* (W.W. Norton & Company, 2011), 421.

18. U.S. Dep't of Justice Inspector Gen., *A Review of the FBI's Involvement in and Observations of Detainee Interrogations in Guantanamo Bay, Afghanistan, and Iraq* (2008), 207.

19. U.S. Dep't of Justice Inspector Gen., *Review of FBI's Involvement in and Observations of Detainee Interrogations*, 208.

20. *Federal Bureau of Investigation (Part II): Hearings Before H. Comm. on the Judiciary*, 110th Cong. (2008). See also "A Guide to the Memos on Torture," *New York Times*, archive.nytimes.com/www.nytimes.com/ref/international/24MEMO-GUIDE.html.

21. U.S. Dep't of Justice Inspector Gen., *Review of FBI's Involvement in and Observations of Detainee Interrogations*, 67-69.

22. *Review of FBI's Involvement in and Observations of Detainee Interrogations.*

23. *Review of FBI's Involvement in and Observations of Detainee Interrogations*, 136.

24. *Review of FBI's Involvement in and Observations of Detainee Interrogations*, 136.

25. Devlin Barrett, "FBI Chief Concerned About Moving Gitmo Prisoners," Associated Press, May 20, 2009.

26. Nick Baumann, "'Extremely Troubling' Documents Show How Obama Administration Embraced Foreign Detention of Terror Suspects," *Mother Jones*, June 9, 2014.

27. FBI response to questions from *Mother Jones* reporter Nick Baumann about foreign detention of Americas, July 8, 2011, documentcloud.org/documents/235035-fbistatementtomotherjones.html.

28. Nick Baumann, "Locked Up Abroad—for the FBI," *Mother Jones*, September/October 2011; Chris McGreal, "Portland Man: I Was Tortured in UAE for Refusing to Become an FBI Informant," *The Guardian*, March 16, 2015.

29. Meshal v. Higgenbotham, 47 F. Supp. 3d 115 (D.D.C. 2014); "Meshal v. Higgenbotham," ACLU, May 31, 2016.

30. Daniel Levin, Acting Assistant Att'y Gen., Mem. for James Comey, Deputy Att'y Gen., Legal Standards Applicable Under 18 U.S.C. §§ 2340-2340A, December 30, 2004; Steven Bradbury, Principal Deputy Assistant Att'y Gen., Mem. for John Rizzo, Senior Deputy General Counsel, CIA, Application of 18 U.S.C. §§ 2340-2340A to the Combined Use of Certain Techniques in the Interrogation of High Value al Qaeda Detainees, May 10, 2005; ACLU et al., letter to Sens. Patrick Leahy and Chuck Grassley regarding confirmation hearing for James B. Comey, July 1, 2013.

31. Mona B. Alderson, Assistant Inspector Gen. for Investigations and redacted signatory from CIA, letter to Christopher Wray, Assistant Att'y Gen., Criminal Division, Possible Violations of Federal Criminal Law, February 20, 2004.

32. *Aiding Terrorists: An Examination of the Material Support Statute: Hearing Before the S. Comm. on the Judiciary*, 108th Cong. (2004), 15 (statement of Asst. Atty. Gen. Wray).

33. Carol Rosenberg, "Trump's Pick for FBI Director Was Alerted Early to Detainee Abuse," *Miami Herald*, June 7, 2017.

34. Clyde Haberman, "A Singular Conviction Amid the Debate on Torture and Terrorism," *New York Times*, April 19, 2015; John Sifton, "The Bush Administration Homicides," *Daily Beast*, May 5, 2009; Hina Shamsi, *Command's Responsibility: Detainee Deaths in U.S. Custody in Iraq and Afghanistan*, ed. Deborah Pearlstein, Human Rights First, February 2006.

35. Mark Mazzetti, "C.I.A. Report Found Value of Brutal Interrogation Was Inflated," *New York Times*, January 20, 2015; S. Select Comm. on Intelligence, *Comm. Study of the CIA's Detention and Interrogation Program*.

36. Charlie Savage, "U.S. Tells Court That Documents from Torture Investigation Should Remain Secret," *New York Times*, December 10, 2014.

37. Bruce Drake, "Americans' Views on Use of Torture in Fighting Terrorism Have Been Mixed," Pew Research Center, December 9, 2014.

38. Alec Tyson, "Americans Divided in Views of Use of Torture in U.S. Anti-terror Efforts," Pew Research Center, January 226, 2017.

39. Annabelle Timsit, "What Happened at the Thailand 'Black Site' Run by Trump's CIA Pick," *The Atlantic*, March 14, 2018.

40. Charlie Savage, "George W. Bush Made Retroactive N.S.A. 'Fix' After Hospital Room Showdown," *New York Times*, September 20, 2015.

41. Marcy Wheeler, "George Bush's False Heroes: The Real Story of a Secret Washington Sham," *Salon*, August 14, 2014; Wells Bennett, "The November NSA Trove II: Judge Kollar-Kotelly's Opinion on Internet Metadata," *Lawfare*, November 20, 2013.

42. *USA PATRIOT Act: Hearing Before the S. Select Comm. on Intelligence*, 109th Cong. (2005) (statement of Dir. Mueller).

43. *Reauthorization of the USA PATRIOT Act: Hearing Before the H. Comm. on the Judiciary*, 110th Cong. (2005).

44. Electronic Privacy Information Center, letter to Sens. Specter and Leahy about FBI use of PATRIOT Act powers, October 24, 2005.

45. U.S. Dep't of Justice Inspector Gen., *A Review of the Federal Bureau of Investigation's Use of National Security Letters* (2007).

46. U.S. Dep't of Justice Inspector Gen., *A Review of the FBI's Use of National Security Letters: Assessment of Corrective Actions and Examination of NSL Usage in 2006* (2008); U.S. Dep't of Justice Inspector Gen., *A Review of the FBI's Use of Section 215 Orders for Business Records in 2006* (2008).

47. Aaron Blake, "Sen. Wyden: Clapper Didn't Give 'Straight Answer' on NSA Programs," *Washington Post*, June 11, 2013; Glenn Kessler, "Clapper's 'Least Untruthful' Statement to the Senate," *Washington Post*, June 12, 2013.

48. "Former Major League Baseball Player Roger Clemens Indicted, Charged with Obstruction of Congress, Making False Statements, and Committing Perjury Before Congressional Committee," FBI news release, August 19, 2010.

49. Rep. Sensenbrenner, "Sensenbrenner Presses Holder on Clapper's Perjury," YouTube video, youtube.com/watch?v=jjXDDsn5blA.

50. Juliet Macur, "Clemens Is Found Not Guilty in Perjury Trial," *New York Times*, June 18, 2012.

51. Scott Shane and Colin Moynihan, "Drug Agents Use Vast Phone Trove, Eclipsing N.S.A.'s," *New York Times*, September 1, 2013.

52. "Synopsis of the Hemisphere Project," *New York Times*, archive.nytimes.com/www.nytimes.com/interactive/2013/09/02/us/hemisphere-project.html.

53. "Non-Disclosure Agreements Between FBI and Local Law Enforcement for StingRay," Center for Human Rights and Privacy, cehrp.org/non-disclosure-agreements-between-fbi-and-local-law-enforcement.

54. Jeremy Seth Davis, "FBI StingRay NDA Instructs Police to Use Parallel Construction," SC Media US, May 10, 2016, scmagazine.com/news/fbi-stingray-nda-instructs-police-to-use-parallel-construction/article/528046.

55. Jose Pagliery, "FBI Lets Suspects Go to Protect 'Stingray' Secrets," CNN.com, March 18, 2015.

56. Carrie Johnson, "FBI Apologizes to *Post*, *Times*," *Washington Post*, August 9, 2008.

57. "FBI Returns Contents of Intercepted Package to AP," Reporters Committee for Freedom of the Press, May 9, 2003.

58. Jamie Williams and Karen Gullo, "Government Documents Show FBI Cleared Filmmaker Laura Poitras After Six-Year Fishing Expedition," Electronic Frontier Foundation, December 6, 2017.

59. "Govt. Obtains Wide AP Phone Records in Probe," Associated Press, May 13, 2013; Ann E. Marimow, "Justice Department's Scrutiny of Fox News Reporter James Rosen in Leak Case Draws Fire," *Washington Post*, May 20, 2013; Alex Park, "A Judge May Soon Send This NYT Reporter to Jail. Here Are the Embarrassing Secrets He Exposed," *Mother Jones*, August 19, 2014.

60. "Attorney General Holder Announces Updates to Justice Department Media Guidelines," U.S. Dep't of Justice news release, January 14, 2015.

61. Spencer Ackerman, "Petraeus Leaks: Obama's Leniency Reveals Profound Double Standard, Lawyer Says," *The Guardian*, March 16, 2015.

62. *Strengthening Intelligence Oversight*, conference report, Brennan Center for Justice, May 28, 2015, 24–40.

63. James Risen and Eric Lichtblau, "Bush Lets U.S. Spy on Callers Without Courts," *New York Times*, December 16, 2005.

64. "Exclusive: National Security Agency Whistleblower William Binney on Growing State Surveillance," *Democracy Now!*, April 20, 2012.

65. Sentencing, U.S. v. Drake, 818 F. Supp. 2d 909 (D. Md. 2011).

66. Josh Gerstein, "Ex-House Intel Aide Sues over Property Seized in Leak Raid," *Politico*, July 28, 2012.

67. Spencer Ackerman, "'A Constitutional Crisis': The CIA Turns on the Senate," *The Guardian*, September 10, 2016.

68. Brittany Bell Surratt, "Howard University Appoints James Comey 2017 Opening Convocation Keynote Speaker and Endowed Chair in Public Policy," Howard University news release, August 23, 2017.

69. Devlin Barrett and Sarah Larimer, "'James Comey, You're Not Our Homie!': Protesters Disrupt Ex–FBI Director's Speech at Howard University," *Washington Post*, September 22, 2017.

70. Max Kutner, "James Comey Blames Donald Trump for Distracting from Police Violence and Uses Howard Talk to Announce Book Tour," *Newsweek*, October 26, 2017.

71. Dir. Comey, "Hard Truths: Law Enforcement and Race," speech at Georgetown University, February 12, 2015; James Comey, speech at Howard University, October 25, 2017; Kutner, "James Comey Blames Donald Trump,"

72. Shelley Hyland et al., "Police Use of Nonfatal Force, 2002–11," U.S. Dep't of Justice, Bureau of Justice Statistics Special Report NCJ 249216, November 2015, table 1.

73. Phillip Atiba Goff et al., "The Science of Justice: Race, Arrests, and Police Use of Force," Center for Policing Equity, July 2016.

74. "The Counted: People Killed by Police in the United States—Interactive," *The Guardian*, theguardian.com/us-news/ng-interactive/2015/jun/01/the-counted-police-killings-us-database.

75. Jon Swain et al., "Young Black Men Killed by US Police at Highest Rate in Year of 1,134 Deaths," *The Guardian*, December 31, 2015.

76. 18 U.S.C. § 242 (1948); See Henry Putzel, Jr., "Federal Civil Rights Enforcement: An Appraisal," *Univ. of Penn. L. Rev.*, Vol. 99 No. 4, (January 1951).

77. Brian Bowling and Andrew Conte, "Trib Investigation: Cops Often Let off Hook for Civil Rights Complaints," TribLIVE.com, March 12, 2016.

78. Mia Teitelbaum, "Willful Intent: *U.S. v. Screws* and the Legal Strategies of the Department of Justice and NAACP," *University of Pennsylvania Journal of Law and Social Change* 20, no. 3 (2017): 185.

79. "Hurricane Katrina Fraud," FBI, fbi.gov/history/famous-cases/hurricane-katrina-fraud.

80. "More Than 900 Defendants Charged with Disaster-Related Fraud by Hurricane Katrina Fraud Task Force During Three Years in Operation," FBI news release, October 1, 2008.

81. A.C. Thompson, "Body of Evidence," ProPublica, December 19, 2008.

82. A.C. Thompson, "Post-Katrina, White Vigilantes Shot African-Americans with Impunity," ProPublica, December 19, 2008.

83. Dan Lawton, "Ex-NOPD Officer, Last Defendant in Danziger Case, Gets 1-Year Probation, $10 Fine," *New Orleans Advocate*, November 4, 2016.

84. Jason Grotto et al., "In 702 Shootings by Chicago Police, Zero Federal Civil Rights Charges Filed," *Chicago Tribune*, August 8, 2016.

85. Andy Grimm, "As Violence Persists, CPD Murder 'Clearance Rate' Continues to Slide," *Chicago Sun-Times*, August 27, 2017; Frank Main, "Murder 'Clearance' Rate in Chicago Hit New Low in 2017," *Chicago Sun-Times*, February 9, 2018.

86. Jamie Kalven, "Operation Smoke and Mirrors: In the Chicago Police Department, If the Bosses Say It Didn't Happen, It Didn't Happen," *The Intercept*, October 6, 2016; "Chicago Police Sergeant and Officer Charged with Stealing $5,200 from Individual They Believed Was Transporting Drug Proceeds," FBI news release, February 13, 2012.

87. Megan Crepeau et al., "7 Officers on Desk Duty as Charges Dropped Against 15, Cases Linked to Corrupt Ex-cop Reviewed," *Chicago Tribune*, November 17, 2017.

88. Jeremy Gorner et al., "Chicago Cops Stripped of Powers as FBI Probes Rip-offs of Drug Dealers, Sources Say," *Chicago Tribune*, February 1, 2018.

89. Rachel Weiner, "Baltimore Detectives Convicted in Shocking Corruption Trial," *Washington Post*, February 12, 2018.

90. S. Judiciary Comm. Minority Members, *Review of Republican Efforts to Stack Federal Courts*, 115th Cong. (May 10, 2018).

11. White Nationalists and White Collars

1. FBI, "White Supremacist Infiltration of Law Enforcement," intelligence assessment, October 17, 2006.

2. Alice Speri, "The FBI Has Quietly Investigated White Supremacist Infiltration of Law Enforcement," *The Intercept*, January 31, 2017; FBI, *Counterterrorism Policy Directive and Policy Guide*, April 1, 2015, 89.

3. Arie Perliger, *Challengers from the Sidelines: Understanding America's Violent Far-Right*, Combating Terrorism Center, November 2012, 100.

4. Erin Kearns et al., "Why Do Some Terrorist Attacks Receive More Media Attention than Others?" *Justice Quarterly* (forthcoming), ssrn.com/abstract=2928138.

5. See, for example, U.S. Gov't Accountability Office, GAO-17-300, *Countering Violent Extremism: Actions Needed to Define Strategy and Assess Progress of Federal Efforts*, April 2017 (describing criteria used by the National Consortium for the Study of Terrorism and Responses to Terrorism's Extremist Crime Database); and Arie Perliger, *Challengers from the Sidelines.*

6. *Hearing on Eco-Terrorism Specifically Examining the Earth Liberation Front and the Animal Liberation Front Before S. Comm. on Environment and Public Works*, 119th Cong. (2005).

7. FBI, *Terrorism 2002–2005*, fbi.gov/stats-services/publications/terrorism-2002-2005.

8. Some consider Theodore Kaczynski, the Unabomber, an environmental anarchist and would credit the three people he killed as victims of eco-terrorism. But five different psychiatrists diagnosed Kaczynski with paranoid schizophrenia, which raises questions whether his writings truly reflect a political goal. See Sally Johnson, psychological evaluation of Theodore Kaczynski, January 16, 1998, unazod.com/psych.pdf.

9. Perliger, *Challengers from the Sidelines*, 87, 100.

10. William Parkin, et. al, "Analysis: Deadly Threat from Far Right Violence Is Overshadowed by Fear of Islamist Terrorism," *PBS NewsHour*, February 24, 2017.

11. Lynn Langton and Madeline Masucci, "Hate Crime Victimization, 2004–2015," Bureau of Justice Statistics, June 2017; Sheela Nimishakavi, "FBI Data Doesn't Show the True Picture of the Rise in Hate Crimes," *Nonprofit Quarterly*, December 22, 2017.

12. Dean Schabner, "Border Vigilante Shawna Forde Sentenced to Death for Home Invasion," ABC News, February 22, 2011.

13. Ryan Lenz, "Investigating Deaths of Undocumented Immigrants on the Border," *Intelligence Report* (Southern Poverty Law Center), August 26, 2012.

14. Joseph Williams, "Obama Election Spurs Wave of Hate Group Violence," *Boston Globe*, May 11, 2009.

15. "White Supremacist Extremist Violence Possibly Decreases but Racist Skinheads Remain the Most Violent," FBI intelligence bulletin, January 28, 2010.

16. Perliger, *Challengers from the Sidelines*, 87, 100.

17. Motion and Declaration for Order Authorizing Issuance of Warrant of Arrest, Washington v. Luyster, No. 16-1-01503-4 (Wash. Super. 2016); Shuly Wasserstrom, "Brent Luyster Found Guilty in 2016 Triple Murder," KOIN (Portland, OR), November 17, 2017.

18. Liam Stack, "Seven Face Charges After Melee at Klan Rally in Anaheim," *New York Times*, February 28, 2016.

19. Darrell Smith, "Trial Date Set for White Nationalist in Capitol Riot Case," *Sacramento Bee*, July 19, 2018.

20. Associated Press, "White Nationalist Ordered to Stand Trial in Capitol Melee Assault," *Mercury News* (San Jose, CA), January 27, 2018.

21. *Murder and Extremism in the United States in 2017*, Anti-Defamation League, January 17, 2018.

22. Bryan M. Vance, "Man Confirms Officers Asked for Help Arresting Portland Protester," Oregon Public Broadcasting, June 8, 2017.

23. Portland City Auditor Independent Police Review, "Policy Review: Portland Police Bureau Can Improve Its Approach to Crowd Control During Street Protests" (May 2018).

24. Katie Shepherd, "Portland Police Saw Right-Wing Protesters as 'Much More Mainstream' than Leftist Ones," *Willamette Week*, June 27, 2018.

25. Cindy Carcamo et al., "Violence Erupts at Pro-Trump Rally in Huntington Beach," *Los Angeles Times*, March 26, 2017.

26. Frank John Tristan, "Huntington Beach Pro-Trump March Turns into Attack on Anti-Trump Protesters," *OC Weekly* (Orange County, CA), March 26, 2017.

27. Gustavo Arellano, "OCDA Prosecutes #MAGAmarch Antifa on Charges Made Up by Neo-Nazis, Unreliable 'Victims,'" *OC Weekly* (Orange County, CA), October 5, 2017.

28. Gustavo Arellano, "California State Parks Police Don't Care That *OC Weekly* Reporters Got Assaulted on Their Watch," *OC Weekly* (Orange County, CA), September 6, 2017.

29. A.C. Thompson et al., "Racist, Violent, Unpunished: A White Hate Group's Campaign of Menace," ProPublica, October 19, 2017.

30. ProPublica (@ProPublica), tweet thread, October 20, 2017, twitter.com/propublica/status/921446200057958401?lang=en.

31. Emilie Raguso, "Despite Dozens of Arrests, No Charges Yet Filed After Berkeley Protest," *Berkeleyside*, April 26, 2017.

32. Deepa Bharath, "Rise Above Movement: What Extremism Experts Are Saying About These White Supremacists in Orange County," *Orange County Register*, October 4, 2018.

33. Derek Gannon, "Disavowed: White Nationalist and Ex-Green Beret Part of Charlottesville Violence," *NEWSREP*, August 15, 2017.

34. Shane Bauer, "I Met the White Nationalist Who 'Falcon Punched' a 95-Pound Female Protester," *Mother Jones*, May 9, 2017.

35. Lois Beckett, "Neo-Nazi Pleads Guilty After Shoving Black Protester at Trump Rally," *The Guardian*, July 19, 2017.

36. John Bogna, "Even Before His Involvement with a Florida Shooting, Records Show William Fears Was a Wanted Man in Houston," Rare Houston, January 24, 2018, rare.us/local/houston/even-before-his-involvement-with-a-florida-shooting-records-show-william-fears-was-a-wanted-man-in-houston.

37. Samantha Baars, "Alt-Righters Found Guilty of Failing to Disperse," *C-VILLE Weekly*, October 13, 2017.

38. Will Parrish, "Police Targeted Anti-racists in Charlottesville Ahead of the 'Unite the Right' Rally, Documents Show," *Shadowproof*, March 7, 2018, shadowproof.com/2018/03/07/documents-reveal-police-targeting-anti-racists-charlottesville.

39. Josh Meyer, "FBI, Homeland Security Warn of More 'Antifa' Attacks," *Politico*, September 1, 2017.

40. Hunton & Williams LLP, *Independent Review of the 2017 Protest Events in Charlottesville, Virginia*, November 24, 2017, 70.

41. Michael Edison Hayden, "'Antifa' Sympathizers Being Investigated by FBI, Director Tells Lawmakers," *Newsweek*, December 1, 2017.

42. Jackson Landers, "A Leaked Message Board Shows What White Supremacists Think of the Police," *Rewire.News*, March 9, 2018.

43. Sam Levin, "California Police Worked with Neo-Nazis to Pursue 'Anti-racist' Activists, Documents Show," *The Guardian*, February 9, 2018.

44. FBI Richmond and United States Attorney's Office, Western District of Virginia, "Joint Press Release Regarding Charlottesville Incident," August 12, 2017.

45. FBI, Civil Rights Program Policy Implementation Guide, October 18, 2010, 15 (obtained through FOIA by ACLU, aclu.org/sites/default/files/field_document/ACLURM003541.pdf).

46. See Henry Grabar, "In January, Fox News Posted a Video of Cars Mowing Down Protesters That Urged Viewers to 'Study the Technique,'" *Slate*, August 15, 2017.

47. Samantha Baars, "Activist Group Encourages Resistance—to Grand Juries," *C-VILLE Weekly* (Charlottesville, VA), December 14, 2017.

48. Costello v. United States, 350 U.S. 359, 76 S. Ct. 406 (1956); Beverly A. Patterson, "The Prosecutor's Unnecessary Use of Hearsay Evidence Before the Grand Jury," *Washington University Law Quarterly* 61, no. 1 (January 1983): 191–218.

49. Chris Suarez, "Activists Urge Unite the Right Counterprotesters to Resist Grand Jury Summons," *Roanoke (VA) Times*, December 13, 2017.

50. Sadie Gurman, "Charlottesville Subject Charged Indicted on Federal Hate Crimes Charges," *Wall Street Journal*, June 27, 2018.

51. Rahima Nasa, "Four Men Arrested Over Unrest During 2017 'Unite the Right' Rally," ProPublica, October 2, 2018; Ali Winston, "F.B.I. Arrests White Nationalist Who Fled the Country," *New York Times*, October 24, 2018. Four RAM members and associates indicted in Virginia, and a fifth charged in California, entered guilty pleas in 2018 and 2019. As this book went to print, a U.S. district judge in California dismissed the charges against the three remaining defendants, finding the fifty-year-old federal Anti-Riot Act was unconstitutionally over-broad. See, A.C. Thompson, "Federal Judge Dismisses Charges Against Three White Supremacists," ProPublica, June 4, 2019.

52. Terry Frieden, "FBI Warns of Mortgage Fraud 'Epidemic,'" CNN, September 17, 2004.

53. Richard B. Schmitt, "FBI Saw Threat of Loan Crisis," *Los Angeles Times*, August 25, 2008.

54. *Examining Lending Discrimination Practices and Foreclosure Abuses: Hearing Before S. Comm. on the Judiciary*, 112th Cong. (2012) (written testimony of William K. Black, professor at Univ. of Missouri–Kansas City).

55. Dennis Blair, *Annual Threat Assessment of the Intelligence Community for the S. Select Comm. on Intelligence*, February 12, 2009, 2.

56. U.S. Gov't Accountability Office, GAO-13-180, *Financial Regulatory Reform: Financial Crisis Losses and Potential Impacts of the Dodd-Frank Act*, January 2013, 21.

57. See Jesse Eisinger, "Why Only One Top Banker Went to Jail for the Financial Crisis," *New York Times Magazine*, April 30, 2014; Patrick Radden Keefe, "Why Corrupt Bankers Avoid Jail," *New Yorker*, July 31, 2017.

58. Associated Press, "Chiquita Admits to Paying Colombia Terrorists," NBC News, March 15, 2007.

59. S. Comm. on Homeland Security and Gov't Affairs, Permanent Subcomm. on Investigations, Majority and Minority Staff Report, *U.S. Vulnerabilities to Money Laundering, Drugs, and Terrorist Financing: HSBC Case History*, 112th Cong. (2012).

60. Rachel Weiner, "Former Metro Police Officer Sentenced to 15 Years in Prison for Supporting ISIS," *Washington Post*, February 23, 2018.

61. Tom McKay, "The FBI Just Edited Its Mission Statement . . . and Took Out One Big Thing," Mic, January 6, 2014, mic.com/articles/78229/the-fbi-just-edited-its-mission-statement-and-took-out-one-big-thing.

62. Roberto Stefan Foa and Yascha Mounk, "The Danger of Deconsolidation: The Democratic Disconnect," *Journal of Democracy* 27, no. 3 (July 2016): 11–14.

63. *Oversight of the Federal Bureau of Investigation: Hearing Before S. Comm. on the Judiciary*, 115th Cong. (2017) (statement of Dir. Comey).

64. Letters from the White House and Att'y Gen. Jeff Sessions regarding the termination of Dir. Comey, May 9, 2017.

65. Yoni Appelbaum, "Comey's Duty to Correct," *The Atlantic*, June 7, 2017.

66. James Comey, *A Higher Loyalty: Truth, Lies, and Leadership* (Flatiron Books, 2018); James Comey, "Opinion: This Report Says I Was Wrong. But That's Good for the F.B.I.," *New York Times*, June 14, 2018.

67. Luke Harding et al., "British Spies Were First to Spot Trump Team's Links with Russia," *The Guardian*, April 13, 2017.

68. Eric Lipton et al., "The Perfect Weapon: How Russian Cyberpower Invaded the U.S.," *New York Times*, December 13, 2016.

69. John Podesta, "Something Is Deeply Broken at the FBI," *Washington Post*, December 15, 2016.

70. Eamon Javers, "FBI's Comey Opposed Naming Russians, Citing Election Timing: Source," CNBC, October 31, 2016.

71. Spencer Ackerman et al., "Trump Meets with Intelligence Leaders After Calling Russia Case 'Witch-Hunt,'" *The Guardian*, January 6, 2017.

72. Mary Katharine Ham, "Comey Was the First to Call a Private, One-on-One Meeting with Trump," *The Federalist*, June 8, 2017.

73. Sharon LaFraniere, "Manafort Agrees to Cooperate with Special Counsel; Pleads Guilty to Reduced Charges, *New York Times*, September 14, 2018.

74. Sharon LaFraniere, Kenneth P. Vogel, and Maggie Haberman, "Manafort Accused of Sharing Trump Polling Data with Russian Associate," *New York Times*, January 8, 2019.

75. Mike Levine, "Special Counsel Files 32-Count Indictment Against Former Trump Campaign Officials," ABC News, February 22, 2018.

76. See Matthew Yglesias, "There's So Much More About Trump to Investigate than Russia," *Vox*, January 8, 2017; Johnathan Stempel, "Trump Taj Mahal Casino Settles U.S. Money Laundering Claims," *Reuters*, February 11, 2015.

Conclusion: What Then Must We Do?

1. Dir. Comey, "Hard Truths: Law Enforcement and Race," speech at Georgetown University, February 12, 2015 (quoted in Sari Horwitz, "As U.S. Pushes Police to Diversify, FBI Struggles to Get Minorities in the Door," *Washington Post*, March 12, 2015).

2. Horwitz, "As U.S. Pushes Police to Diversify."

3. Erroll Southers, interview with author, March 2017.

4. U.S. Dep't of Justice Inspector Gen., *A Review of the Federal Bureau of Investigation's Disciplinary System* (2009).

5. *Hearing Before the S. Judiciary Comm. on Whistleblower Retaliation at the FBI: Improving Protections and Oversight,* 114th Cong. (2015).

6. Andy Grimm and Cynthia Dizikes, "FBI Raids Anti-war Activists' Homes," *Chicago Tribune,* September 24, 2010.

7. Jess Sundin, interview with author, July 11, 2016.

8. Mick Kelly, "Organizers Announce Route of Anti-War Protest," Fight Back! News, June 8, 2007, www.fightbacknews.org/2007/06/rncprotestroute.htm.

9. G. W. Schulz, "Looking Back at GOP Convention: Police Kicked into 'Disruption Mode,'" *MinnPost*, September 2, 2009; "I-Witness Video Collective Forced Out of Living Space After Second Raid by St. Paul Police in Five Days," *Democracy Now!*, September 4, 2008; "NY Law Enforcement Caught Doctoring Video of RNC Arrests," *Democracy Now!*, April 14, 2005.

10. *Report of the Republican National Convention: Safety Planning and Implementation Review,* January 14, 2009, 57 (commissioned by the St. Paul City Council).

11. Joe Iosbaker, interview with author, July 7, 2016; "30,000 March against War at the RNC," *Fight Back! News*, September 4, 2008, fightbacknews.org/2008/09/30000-march-against-war-at-rnc.htm.

12. Sheila Regan, "RNC Settlements Rolling In," *Twin Cities (MN) Daily Planet*, June 6, 2011.

13. Search and Seizure Warrant, No. 0:10-mj-00389-SER (D. Minn. 2010) (published by *VICE* s3.amazonaws.com/vice_asset_uploader/files/1396281030Search_Warrant_Files_Part_I_r.pdf).

14. Search and Seizure Warrant, 19 (page 80 of the PDF).

15. "Secret FBI Documents Reveal Attack on Democratic Rights of Anti-war and International Solidarity Activists," Committee to Stop FBI Repression, May 18, 2011, stopfbi.net/2011/5/18/secret-fbi-documents-reveal-attack-democratic-rights-anti-war-and-international-solidarity; Peter Wallsten, "Activists Cry Foul over FBI Probe," *Washington Post*, June 13, 2011.

16. Sundin, interview with author.

17. Iosbaker, interview with author.

18. See for example, "Congresswoman Jan Schakowsky Writes Letter to Attorney General Eric Holder Regarding FBI Raids on Activists," Committee to Stop FBI

Repression, April 26, 2011, stopfbi.net/2011/4/26/congresswoman-jan-schakowsky-writes-letter-attorney-general-eric-holder-regarding-fbi-raid.

19. Paul Harris, "Carlos Montes: Political Activist Faces 22 Years in Jail over Thrown Soda Can," *The Guardian*, May 30, 2012.

20. Terelle Jerricks, "Activist, Carlos Montes, Pleads No Contest to Gun Charge," *Random Lengths News*, June 5, 2012, randomlengthsnews.com/2012/06/montes-pleads-no-contest-to-gun-charge.

21. Ruhan Nagra and Thomas Power, "Taking Trauma Seriously: Torture Orgs File Amicus Brief in Support of Rasmea Odeh," *Daily Outrage* (Center for Constitutional Rights blog), July 2, 2015; Rasmea Odeh, testimony before the U.N. Gen. Assembly (quoted in *Report of the Special Committee to Investigate Israeli Practices Affecting the Human Rights of the Population of the Occupied Territories*, November 13, 1979).

22. Charlotte Silver, "Will Rasmea Odeh Go to Prison Because of a Confession Obtained Through Torture?," *The Nation*, November 4, 2014; Maureen Clare Murphy, "Palestinian Arrested in Chicago Because of Her Community Activism, Groups Say," *Electronic Intifada*, October 26, 2013, electronicintifada.net/blogs/maureen-clare-murphy/palestinian-arrested-chicago-because-her-community-activism-groups-say.

23. Sue Udry, "Young Muslim Collective Hosts Forum on CVE," *Defending Rights and Dissent*, October 14, 2017.

24. Frank Bures, "Why All Aren't Heeding Call to Quiz Arabs," *Christian Science Monitor*, December 4, 2001.

25. Affidavit of Ryan Dwyer, FBI special agent, United States v. Mohamed Osman Mohamud, No. 3:10-CR-00475-KI, 2012 U.S. Dist. LEXIS 197623 (D. Or. July 23, 2012).

26. Maxine Bernstein, "Man Accused of Hate Crime in Corvallis Mosque Arson," *The Oregonian*, August 25, 2011.

27. Hal Bernton, "Was FBI Grooming Portland Suspect for Terror?" *Seattle Times*, November 29, 2010; Nicolás Medina Mora and Mike Hayes, "Did The FBI Transform This Teenager into a Terrorist After Reading His Emails?" *BuzzFeed*, November 15, 2015.

28. Denis C. Theriault, "At Today's JTTF Throwdown at City Hall," *Portland Mercury*, February 15, 2011.

29. Brad Schmidt, "JTTF Agreement Tiptoes Gray Line with Portland City Council Vote Looming," *The Oregonian*, April 27, 2011.

30. Veena Dubal, "The Demise of Community Policing?: The Impact of Post-9/11 Federal Surveillance Programs on Local Law Enforcement," *Asian American Law Journal* 19 (2012): 35–59.

31. Neel Lalchandani, "To Protect and Spy: The San Francisco Police Department & the Civil Rights Ordinance," *Stanford Law & Policy Review* 26 (2015): 701–8.

32. Jonah Owen Lamb, "SF Police Could Be Violating City Law in Work with FBI's Joint Terrorism Task Force," *San Francisco Examiner,* March 3, 2015.

33. ACLU et al., letter to San Francisco Police Commission, "Update on SFPD's Participation in FBI's Joint Terrorism Task Force," January 5, 2017.

34. Ellen Nakashima, "San Francisco Police Department Pulls Out of FBI Anti-terrorism Task Force," *Washington Post*, March 10, 2017.

35. Ralph Ellis, "Terror Attack at San Francisco's Pier 39 Thwarted, Federal Authorities Say," CNN.com, December 23, 2017.

36. Darwin BondGraham, "Town Business: Oakland Police Agreements with Federal Law Enforcement Will Be Subjected to Greater Oversight," *East Bay Express*, October 2, 2017.

37. Kelly Kenoyer, "Former FBI Investigator Testifies Against Portland's Joint Terrorism Task Force," *Portland Mercury*, April 18, 2018; Katie Shepherd, "Portland Leaves Joint Terrorism Task Force Again, Becoming Second U.S. City to Cut Ties," *Willamette Week*, February 13, 2019.

INDEX

ABOUT THE AUTHOR

Mike German is a fellow with the Liberty and National Security program at the Brennan Center for Justice at NYU Law School. He has worked at the ACLU and served sixteen years as an FBI special agent. He is the author of *Thinking Like a Terrorist*.

PUBLISHING IN THE PUBLIC INTEREST

Thank you for reading this book published by The New Press. The New Press is a nonprofit, public interest publisher. New Press books and authors play a crucial role in sparking conversations about the key political and social issues of our day.

We hope you enjoyed this book and that you will stay in touch with The New Press. Here are a few ways to stay up to date with our books, events, and the issues we cover:

- Sign up at www.thenewpress.com/subscribe to receive updates on New Press authors and issues and to be notified about local events
- Like us on Facebook: www.facebook.com/newpressbooks
- Follow us on Twitter: www.twitter.com/thenewpress

Please consider buying New Press books for yourself; for friends and family; or to donate to schools, libraries, community centers, prison libraries, and other organizations involved with the issues our authors write about.

The New Press is a 501(c)(3) nonprofit organization. You can also support our work with a tax-deductible gift by visiting www.thenewpress.com/donate.